SAS® Programming 1: Essentials

Course Notes

SAS® Programming 1: Essentials Course Notes was developed by Michele Ensor and Susan Farmer. Additional contributions were made by by Michelle Buchecker, Christine Dillon, Marty Hultgren, Marya Ilgen-Lieth, Mike Kalt, Natalie McGowan, Linda Mitterling, Georg Morsing, Dr. Sue Rakes, Warren Repole, and Larry Stewart. Editing and production support was provided by the Curriculum Development and Support Department.

SAS® Programming 1: Essentials Course Notes

Book code E1218, course code LWPRG1/PRG1, prepared date 01Jun2008.   LWPRG1_001

ISBN 978-1-59994-733-4

Table of Contents

Course Description

This course is for users who want to learn how to write SAS programs. It is the entry point to learning SAS programming and is a prerequisite to many other SAS courses. If you do not plan to write SAS programs and you prefer a point-and-click interface, you should attend the *SAS® Enterprise Guide® 1: Querying and Reporting* course.

To learn more...

A full curriculum of general and statistical instructor-based training is available at any of the Institute's training facilities. Institute instructors can also provide on-site training.

For information on other courses in the curriculum, contact the SAS Education Division at 1-800-333-7660, or send e-mail to training@sas.com. You can also find this information on the Web at support.sas.com/training/ as well as in the Training Course Catalog.

For a list of other SAS books that relate to the topics covered in this Course Notes, USA customers can contact our SAS Publishing Department at 1-800-727-3228 or send e-mail to sasbook@sas.com. Customers outside the USA, please contact your local SAS office.

Also, see the Publications Catalog on the Web at support.sas.com/pubs for a complete list of books and a convenient order form.

Prerequisites

Before attending this course, you should have experience using computer software. Specifically, you should be able to

- understand file structures and system commands on your operating systems

- access data files on your operating systems

No prior SAS experience is needed. If you do not feel comfortable with the prerequisites or are new to programming and think that the pace of this course might be too demanding, you can take the *Introduction to Programming Concepts Using SAS Software* course before attending this course. *Introduction to Programming Concepts Using SAS Software* is designed to introduce you to computer programming and presents a portion of the *SAS Programming 1: Essentials* material at a slower pace.

Chapter 1 Introduction

1.1   Course Logistics

Objectives

- Explain the naming convention that is used for the course files.
- Compare the three levels of exercises that are used in the course.
- Describe at a high level how data is used and stored at Orion Star Sports & Outdoors.
- Navigate to the Help facility.

3

Filename Conventions

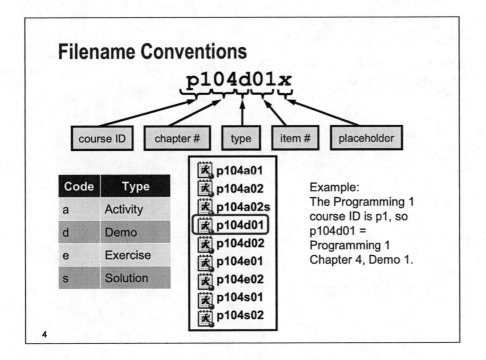

p104d01*x*

course ID	chapter #	type	item #	placeholder

Code	Type
a	Activity
d	Demo
e	Exercise
s	Solution

p104a01
p104a02
p104a02s
p104d01
p104d02
p104e01
p104e02
p104s01
p104s02

Example:
The Programming 1
course ID is p1, so
p104d01 =
Programming 1
Chapter 4, Demo 1.

4

Three Levels of Exercises

Level 1	The exercise mimics an example presented in the section.
Level 2	Less information and guidance are provided in the exercise instructions.
Level 3	Only the task you are to perform or the results to be obtained are provided. Typically, you will need to use the Help facility.

✎ You are not expected to complete all of the exercises in the time allotted. Choose the exercise or exercises that are at the level you are most comfortable with.

5

Orion Star Sports & Outdoors

Orion Star Sports & Outdoors is a fictitious global sports and outdoors retailer with traditional stores, an online store, and a large catalog business.

The corporate headquarters is located in the United States with offices and stores in many countries throughout the world.

Orion Star has about 1,000 employees and 90,000 customers, processes approximately 150,000 orders annually, and purchases products from 64 suppliers.

6

Orion Star Data

As is the case with most organizations, Orion Star has a large amount of data about its customers, suppliers, products, and employees. Much of this information is stored in transactional systems in various formats.

Using applications and processes such as SAS Data Integration Studio, this transactional information was extracted, transformed, and loaded into a data warehouse.

Data marts were created to meet the needs of specific departments such as Marketing.

7

The SAS Help Facility

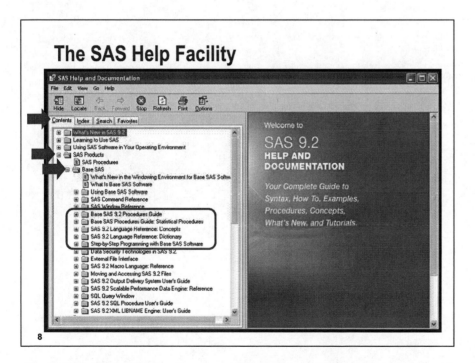

8

The Help facility can also be accessed from a Web browser at the following link:

http://support.sas.com/documentation/index.html

Setup for the Poll

- Start your SAS session.
- Open the Help facility.

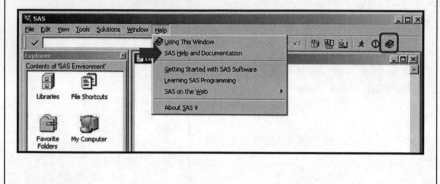

10

1.01 Poll

Were you able to open the Help facility in your
SAS session?

O Yes

O No

11

1.2   An Overview of Foundation SAS

Objectives

- Describe the structure and design of Foundation SAS.
- Describe the functionality of Foundation SAS.

14

What Is Foundation SAS?

Foundation SAS is a highly flexible and integrated software environment that can be used in virtually any setting to access, manipulate, manage, store, analyze, and report on data.

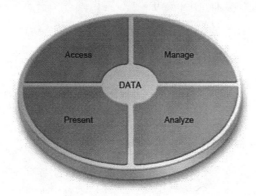

15

What Is Foundation SAS?

Foundation SAS provides the following:

- a graphical user interface for administering SAS tasks
- a highly flexible and extensible programming language
- a rich library of prewritten, ready-to-use SAS procedures
- the flexibility to run on all major operating environments such as Windows, UNIX, and z/OS (OS/390)
- the access to virtually any data source such as DB2, Oracle, SYBASE, Teradata, SAP, and Microsoft Excel
- the support for most widely used character encodings for globalization

16

What Is Foundation SAS?

At the core of Foundation SAS is Base SAS software.

Components of Foundation SAS		
Reporting and Graphics	Data Access and Management	User Interfaces
Analytics	Base SAS	Application Development
Visualization and Discovery	Business Solutions	Web Enablement

Base SAS capabilities can be extended with additional components.

17

1.02 Poll

Are you currently using SAS?

O Yes

O No

19

Chapter 2   Getting Started with SAS

2.1 Introduction to SAS Programs

Objectives

- List the components of a SAS program.
- State the modes in which you can run a SAS program.

3

SAS Programs

A SAS program is a sequence of steps that the user
submits for execution.

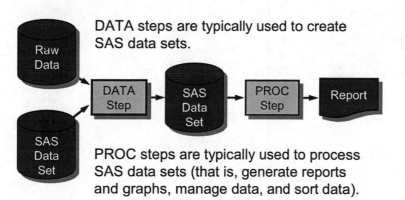

DATA steps are typically used to create
SAS data sets.

PROC steps are typically used to process
SAS data sets (that is, generate reports
and graphs, manage data, and sort data).

4

2.01 Quiz

How many steps are in this program?

```
data work.NewSalesEmps;
   length First_Name $ 12
          Last_Name $ 18 Job_Title $ 25;
   infile 'newemps.csv' dlm=',';
   input First_Name $ Last_Name $
         Job_Title $ Salary;
run;

proc print data=work.NewSalesEmps;
run;

proc means data=work.NewSalesEmps;
   class Job_Title;
   var Salary;
run;
```

6   p102d01

SAS Program Example

This DATA step creates a temporary SAS data set named
work.NewSalesEmps by reading four fields from a
raw data file.

```
data work.NewSalesEmps;
   length First_Name $ 12
          Last_Name $ 18 Job_Title $ 25;
   infile 'newemps.csv' dlm=',';
   input First_Name $ Last_Name $
         Job_Title $ Salary;
run;

proc print data=work.NewSalesEmps;
run;

proc means data=work.NewSalesEmps;
   class Job_Title;
   var Salary;
run;
```

8

The raw data filename specified in the INFILE statement needs to be specific to your operating environment.

Examples of raw data filenames:

Windows	`s:\workshop\newemps.csv`
UNIX	`/users/userid/newemps.csv`
z/OS (OS/390)	`userid.workshop.rawdata(newemps)`

SAS Program Example

This PROC PRINT step creates a listing report
of the **work.NewSalesEmps** data set.

```
data work.NewSalesEmps;
   length First_Name $ 12
          Last_Name $ 18 Job_Title $ 25;
   infile 'newemps.csv' dlm=',';
   input First_Name $ Last_Name $
         Job_Title $ Salary;
run;

proc print data=work.NewSalesEmps;
run;

proc means data=work.NewSalesEmps;
   class Job_Title;
   var Salary;
run;
```

9

SAS Program Example

This PROC MEANS step creates a summary report of the
work.NewSalesEmps data set with statistics for the
variable **Salary** for each value of **Job_Title**.

```
data work.NewSalesEmps;
   length First_Name $ 12
          Last_Name $ 18 Job_Title $ 25;
   infile 'newemps.csv' dlm=',';
   input First_Name $ Last_Name $
         Job_Title $ Salary;
run;

proc print data=work.NewSalesEmps;
run;

proc means data=work.NewSalesEmps;
   class Job_Title;
   var Salary;
run;
```

10

Step Boundaries

SAS steps begin with either of the following:

- DATA statement
- PROC statement

SAS detects the end of a step when it encounters
one of the following:

- a RUN statement (for most steps)
- a QUIT statement (for some procedures)
- the beginning of another step (DATA statement
  or PROC statement)

11

 A SAS program executed in batch or noninteractive mode can contain RUN statements, but does not require any RUN statements to execute successfully because the entire program is executed by default. The presence of the RUN statement depends on the programmer's preference.

Step Boundaries

SAS detects the end of the DATA step when it encounters
the RUN statement.

```
data work.NewSalesEmps;
    length First_Name $ 12
           Last_Name $ 18 Job_Title $ 25;
    infile 'newemps.csv' dlm=',';
    input First_Name $ Last_Name $
          Job_Title $ Salary;
run;

proc print data=work.NewSalesEmps;

proc means data=work.NewSalesEmps;
    class Job_Title;
    var Salary;
```

SAS detects the end of the PROC PRINT step when it
encounters the beginning of the PROC MEANS step.

12

2.02 Quiz

How does SAS detect the end of the PROC MEANS step?

```
data work.NewSalesEmps;
    length First_Name $ 12
           Last_Name $ 18 Job_Title $ 25;
    infile 'newemps.csv' dlm=',';
    input First_Name $ Last_Name $
          Job_Title $ Salary;
run;

proc print data=work.NewSalesEmps;

proc means data=work.NewSalesEmps;
    class Job_Title;
    var Salary;
```

14

Step Boundaries

SAS detects the end of the PROC MEANS step when it encounters the RUN statement.

```
data work.NewSalesEmps;
    length First_Name $ 12
           Last_Name $ 18 Job_Title $ 25;
    infile 'newemps.csv' dlm=',';
    input First_Name $ Last_Name $
          Job_Title $ Salary;
run;

proc print data=work.NewSalesEmps;

proc means data=work.NewSalesEmps;
    class Job_Title;
    var Salary;
run;
```

16

Running a SAS Program

You can invoke SAS in the following ways:

- interactive mode (for example, SAS windowing environment and SAS Enterprise Guide)
- batch mode
- noninteractive mode

17

SAS Windowing Environment

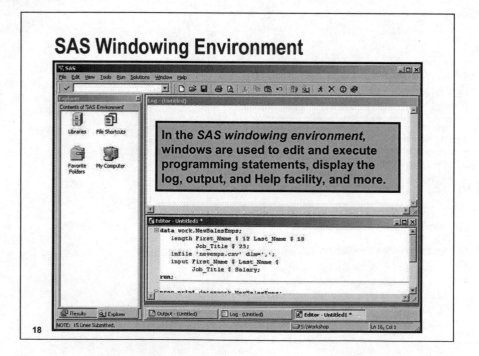

In the *SAS windowing environment*, windows are used to edit and execute programming statements, display the log, output, and Help facility, and more.

18

SAS Enterprise Guide

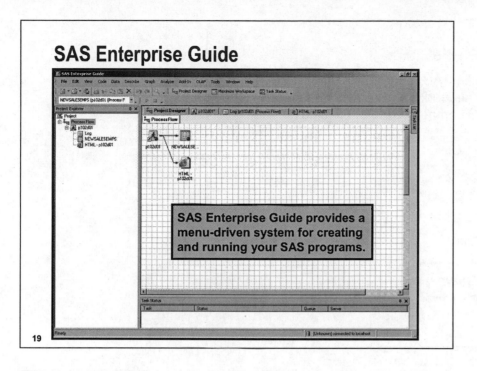

SAS Enterprise Guide provides a menu-driven system for creating and running your SAS programs.

19

Batch Mode

Batch mode is a method of running SAS programs in which you prepare a file that contains SAS statements plus any necessary operating system control statements and submit the file to the operating system.

Partial z/OS (OS/390) Example:

```
//jobname JOB accounting info,name ...
// EXEC SAS
//SYSIN DD *

data work.NewSalesEmps;
   length First_Name $ 12
          Last_Name $ 18 Job_Title $ 25;
   infile '.workshop.rawdata(newemps)' dlm=',';
   input First_Name $ Last_Name $
         Job_Title $ Salary;
run;
```

appropriate JCL is placed before SAS statements

20

Noninteractive Mode

In *noninteractive mode*, SAS program statements are stored in an external file and are executed immediately after you issue a SAS command referencing the file.

Directory-based Example:

SAS *filename*

z/OS (OS/390) Example:

SAS INPUT(*filename***)**

21

  The command for invoking SAS at your site might be different from the default shown above. Ask your SAS administrator for the command to invoke SAS at your site.

2.03 Multiple Answer Poll

Which mode(s) will you use for running SAS programs?

a. SAS windowing environment
b. SAS Enterprise Guide
c. batch mode
d. noninteractive mode
e. other
f. unknown

23

2.2 Submitting a SAS Program

Objectives

- Include a SAS program in your session.
- Submit a program and browse the results.
- Navigate the SAS windowing environment.

26

Three Primary Windows

You submit and view the results of a SAS program in the SAS windowing environment using three primary windows.

Editor - Untitled1 Program Editor - (Untitled)	contains the SAS program to submit.
Log - (Untitled)	contains information about the processing of the SAS program, including any warning and error messages.
Output - (Untitled)	contains reports generated by the SAS program.

27

Editor Windows

Enhanced Editor	Program Editor
[Editor - Untitled1]	[Program Editor - (Untitled)]
Only available in the Windows operating environment	Available in all operating environments
Default editor for Windows operating environment	Default editor for all operating environments except Windows
Multiple instances of the editor can be open at one time	Only one instance of the editor can be open at one time
Code does not disappear after it is submitted	Code disappears after it is submitted
Incorporates color-coding as you type	Incorporates color-coding after you press ENTER

28

Editor Windows

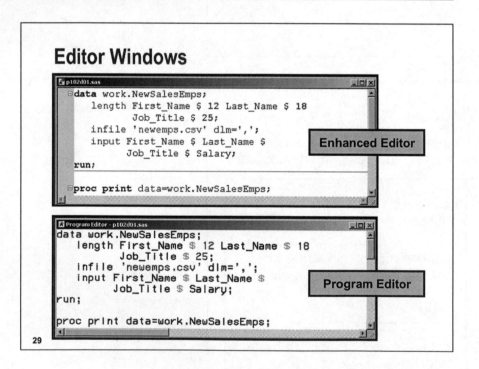

29

Log Window

Partial SAS Log

```
33    data work.NewSalesEmps;
34       length First_Name $ 12 Last_Name $ 18
35             Job_Title $ 25;
36       infile 'newemps.csv' dlm=',';
37       input First_Name $ Last_Name $
38             Job_Title $ Salary;
39    run;

NOTE: The infile 'newemps.csv' is:
      File Name=S:\Workshop\newemps.csv,
      RECFM=V,LRECL=256

NOTE: 71 records were read from the infile 'newemps.csv'.
      The minimum record length was 28.
      The maximum record length was 47.
NOTE: The data set WORK.NEWSALESEMPS has 71 observations and 4 variables.

40
41    proc print data=work.NewSalesEmps;
42    run;

NOTE: There were 71 observations read from the data set WORK.NEWSALESEMPS.
```

30

Output Window

Partial PROC PRINT Output

Obs	First_Name	Last_Name	Job_Title	Salary
1	Satyakam	Denny	Sales Rep. II	26780
2	Monica	Kletschkus	Sales Rep. IV	30890
3	Kevin	Lyon	Sales Rep. I	26955
4	Petrea	Soltau	Sales Rep. II	27440
5	Marina	Iyengar	Sales Rep. III	29715
6	Shani	Duckett	Sales Rep. I	25795
7	Fang	Wilson	Sales Rep. II	26810
8	Michael	Minas	Sales Rep. I	26970
9	Amanda	Liebman	Sales Rep. II	27465
10	Vincent	Eastley	Sales Rep. III	29695
11	Viney	Barbis	Sales Rep. III	30265
12	Skev	Rusli	Sales Rep. II	26580
13	Narelle	James	Sales Rep. III	29990
14	Gerry	Snellings	Sales Rep. I	26445
15	Leonid	Karavdic	Sales Rep. II	27860

31

Output Window

PROC MEANS Output

```
                        The MEANS Procedure

                      Analysis Variable : Salary

                   N
Job_Title        Obs    N         Mean       Std Dev       Minimum       Maximum

Sales Rep. I      21   21     26418.81    713.1898498     25275.00      27475.00

Sales Rep. II      9    9     26902.22    592.9487283     26080.00      27860.00

Sales Rep. III    11   11     29345.91    989.4311956     28025.00      30785.00

Sales Rep. IV      6    6     31215.00    545.4997709     30305.00      31865.00

Temp. Sales Rep.  24   24     26265.83    732.6480659     25020.00      27480.00
```

32

2.04 Multiple Answer Poll

Which operating environment(s) will you use with SAS?

a. Windows
b. UNIX
c. z/OS (OS/390)
d. other
e. unknown

34

Submitting a SAS Program – Windows

p102d01

- Start a SAS session.
- Include and submit a SAS program.
- Examine the results.
- Use the Help facility.

Starting a SAS Session

1. Double-click the SAS icon to start your SAS session.

    ✎   The method that you use to invoke SAS varies by your operating environment and any customizations in effect at your site.

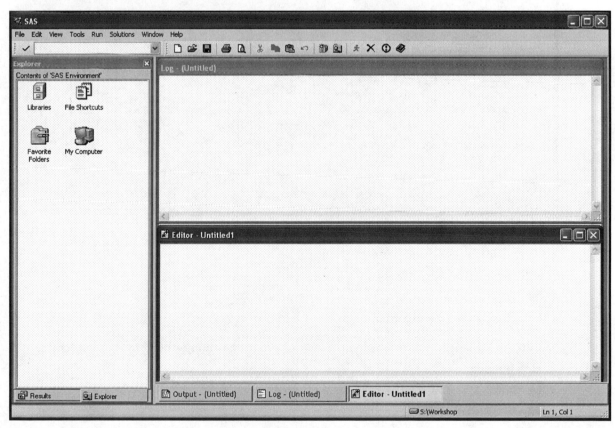

Including and Submitting a SAS Program

1. To open a SAS program into your SAS session, select **File** ⇨ **Open Program** or click  and then select the file that you want to include. To open a program, your Enhanced Editor must be active.

    You can also issue the INCLUDE command to open (include) a program into your SAS session.

    a. With the Enhanced Editor active, on the command bar type `include` and the name of the file containing the program.

    b. Press **ENTER**.

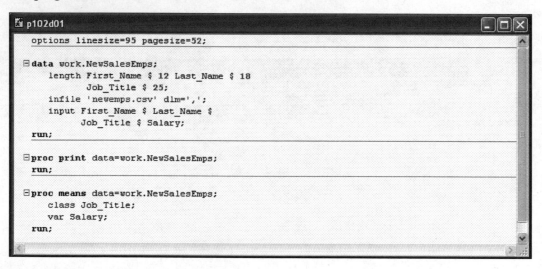

    The program is included in the Enhanced Editor window.

```
options linesize=95 pagesize=52;

data work.NewSalesEmps;
    length First_Name $ 12 Last_Name $ 18
           Job_Title $ 25;
    infile 'newemps.csv' dlm=',';
    input First_Name $ Last_Name $
          Job_Title $ Salary;
run;

proc print data=work.NewSalesEmps;
run;

proc means data=work.NewSalesEmps;
    class Job_Title;
    var Salary;
run;
```

    You can use the Enhanced Editor window to do the following:
    *   access and edit existing SAS programs
    *   write new SAS programs
    *   submit SAS programs
    *   save SAS programs to a file

    Within the Enhanced Editor, the syntax in your program is color-coded to show these items:
    *   step boundaries
    *   keywords
    *   variable and data set names

2. To submit the program for execution, issue the SUBMIT command or click 🏃 or select **Run** ⇨ **Submit**. The output from the program is displayed in the Output window.

Examining the Results

The Output window

- is one of the primary windows and is open by default.

- becomes the active window each time that it receives output.

- automatically accumulates output in the order in which it is generated. You can issue the CLEAR command or select **Edit** ⇨ **Clear All** to clear the contents of the window, or you can click on the NEW icon ⬜.

To scroll horizontally within the Output window, use the horizontal scroll bar or issue the RIGHT and LEFT commands.

In the Windows environment, the Output window displays the last page of output generated by the program submitted.

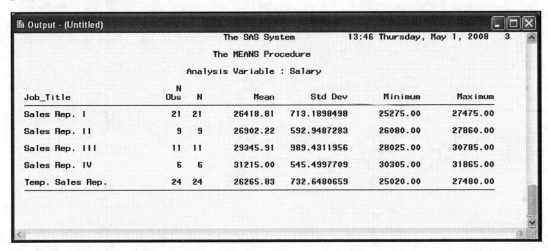

To scroll vertically within the Output window, use the vertical scroll bar or issue the FORWARD and BACKWARD commands or use the PAGE UP or PAGE DOWN keys on the keyboard.

✎   You also can use the TOP and BOTTOM commands to scroll vertically within the Output window.

1.   Scroll to the top to view the output from the PRINT procedure.

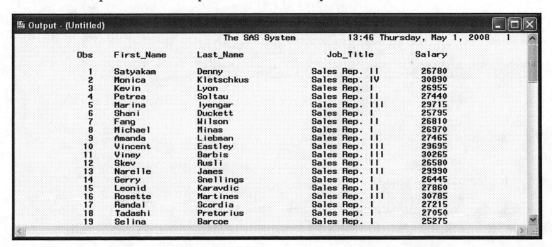

2. To open the Log window and browse the messages that the program generated, issue the
    LOG command or select **Window** ⇨ **Log** or click on the log.

    The Log window

    - is one of the primary windows and is open by default

    - acts as an audit trail of your SAS session; messages are written to the log in the order in which
      they are generated by the program.

3. To clear the contents of the window, issue the CLEAR command or select **Edit** ⇨ **Clear All**, or
    you can click on the NEW icon 🗋 .

```
Log - (Untitled)                                                    [_][□][X]
69    options linesize=95 pagesize=52;
70
71    data work.NewSalesEmps;
72       length First_Name $ 12 Last_Name $ 18
73             Job_Title $ 25;
74       infile 'newemps.csv' dlm=',';
75       input First_Name $ Last_Name $
76             Job_Title $ Salary;
77    run;

NOTE: The infile 'newemps.csv' is:
      Filename=S:\Workshop\newemps.csv,
      RECFM=V,LRECL=256,File Size (bytes)=2604,
      Last Modified=02Apr2008:09:10:12,
      Create Time=01May2008:13:52:50

NOTE: 71 records were read from the infile 'newemps.csv'.
      The minimum record length was 28.
      The maximum record length was 47.
NOTE: The data set WORK.NEWSALESEMPS has 71 observations and 4 variables.
NOTE: DATA statement used (Total process time):
      real time           0.00 seconds
      cpu time            0.00 seconds


78
79    proc print data=work.NewSalesEmps;
80    run;

NOTE: There were 71 observations read from the data set WORK.NEWSALESEMPS.
NOTE: PROCEDURE PRINT used (Total process time):
      real time           0.00 seconds
      cpu time            0.00 seconds


81
82    proc means data=work.NewSalesEmps;
83       class Job_Title;
84       var Salary;
85    run;

NOTE: There were 71 observations read from the data set WORK.NEWSALESEMPS.
NOTE: PROCEDURE MEANS used (Total process time):
      real time           0.01 seconds
      cpu time            0.01 seconds
```

The Log window contains the programming statements that are submitted, as well as notes about the
following:

- any files that were read

- the records that were read

- the program execution and results

In this example, the Log window contains no warning or error messages. If the program contains
errors, relevant warning and error messages are also written to the SAS log.

Using the Help Facility

1. To open the Help facility, select **Help** ⇨ **SAS Help and Documentation** or click .

2. Select the **Contents** tab.

3. From the Contents tab, select **SAS Products** ⇨ **Base SAS**.

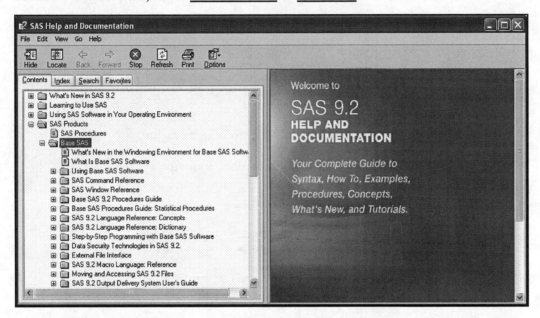

The primary Base SAS syntax books are the *Base SAS 9.2 Procedures Guide* and *SAS 9.2 Language Reference: Dictionary*. The *SAS 9.2 Language Reference: Concepts* and *Step-by-Step Programming with Base SAS Software* are good books to learn SAS concepts.

4. For example, select **Base SAS 9.2 Procedures Guide** ⇨ **Procedures** ⇨ **The PRINT Procedure** to find the documentation for the PRINT procedure.

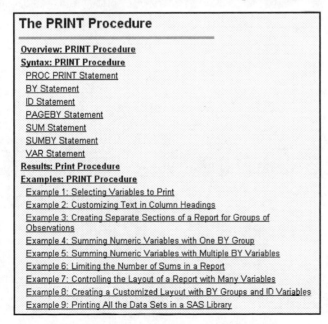

Submitting a SAS Program – UNIX

p102d01

- Start a SAS session.
- Include and submit a SAS program.
- Examine the results.
- Use the Help facility.

Starting a SAS Session

1. In your UNIX session, type the appropriate command to start a SAS session.

      The method that you use to invoke SAS varies by your operating environment and any
      customizations in effect at your site.

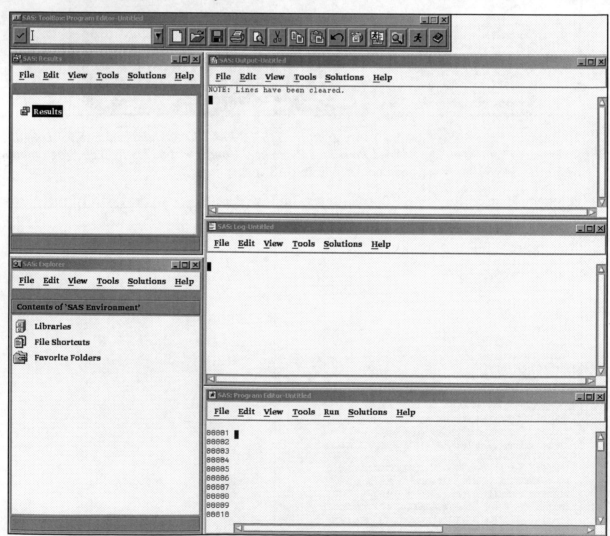

Including and Submitting a SAS Program

1. To open a SAS program into your SAS session, select **File** ⇨ **Open** or click [icon] and then select the file that you want to include. To open a program, your Program Editor must be active.

    You can also issue the INCLUDE command to open (include) a SAS program into your SAS session.

    a. With the Program Editor active, on the command bar type **include** and the name of the file containing the program.

    b. Press **ENTER**.

    The program is included in the Program Editor window.

```
SAS: Program Editor-p102d01.sas                          _ □ ×

 File  Edit  View  Tools  Run  Solutions  Help

00001 options linesize=95 pagesize=52;
00002
00003 data work.NewSalesEmps;
00004     length First_Name $ 12 Last_Name $ 18
00005          Job_Title $ 25;
00006     infile 'newemps.csv' dlm=',';
00007     input First_Name $ Last_Name $
00008          Job_Title $ Salary;
00009 run;
00010
00011 proc print data=work.NewSalesEmps;
00012 run;
00013
00014 proc means data=work.NewSalesEmps;
00015    class Job_Title;
00016    var Salary;
00017 run;
```

    You can use the Program Editor window to do the following:
    - access and edit existing SAS programs
    - write new SAS programs
    - submit SAS programs
    - save SAS programs to a file

    Within the Program Editor, the syntax in your program is color-coded to show these items:
    - step boundaries
    - keywords
    - variable and data set names

2. To submit the program for execution, issue the SUBMIT command or click [icon] or select **Run** ⇨ **Submit**. The output from the program is displayed in the Output window.

Examining the Results

The Output window

- is one of the primary windows and is open by default.
- becomes the active window each time it receives output.
- automatically accumulates output in the order in which it is generated. To clear the contents of the window, issue the CLEAR command or select **Edit** ⇨ **Clear All** or click .

To scroll horizontally within the Output window, use the horizontal scroll bar or issue the RIGHT and LEFT commands.

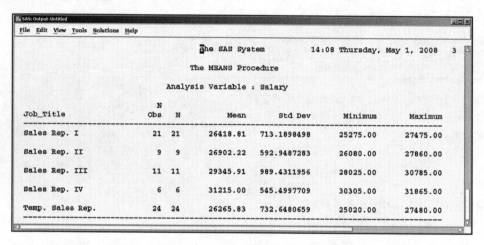

To scroll vertically within the Output window, use the vertical scroll bar or issue the FORWARD and BACKWARD commands.

> You also can use the TOP and BOTTOM commands to scroll vertically within the Output window.

1. Scroll to the top to view the output from the PRINT procedure.

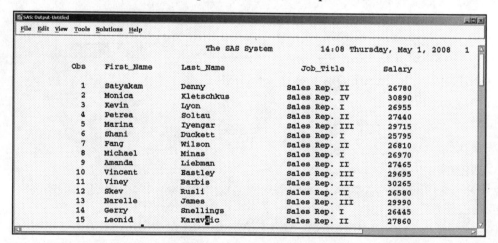

2. To open the Log window and browse the messages that the program generated, issue the LOG command or select **View** ⇨ **Log**.

    The Log window

    - is one of the primary windows and is open by default
    - acts as a record of your SAS session; messages are written to the log in the order in which they are generated by the program.

3. To clear the contents of the window, issue the CLEAR command or select **Edit** ⇨ **Clear All** or click .

    The Log window contains the programming statements that were most recently submitted, as well as notes about the following:

    - any files that were read
    - the records that were read
    - the program execution and results

    In this example, the Log window contains no warning or error messages. If your program contains errors, relevant warning and error messages are also written to the SAS log.

4. Issue the END command or select **View** ⇨ **Program Editor** to return to the Program Editor window

Using the Help Facility

1. To open the Help facility, select **<u>Help</u>** ⇨ **<u>SAS Help and Documentation</u>** or click .

2. Select the **<u>Contents</u>** tab.

3. From the Contents tab, select **<u>SAS Products</u>** ⇨ **<u>Base SAS</u>**.

   The primary Base SAS syntax books are the *Base SAS 9.2 Procedures Guide* and *SAS 9.2 Language Reference: Dictionary*. The *SAS 9.2 Language Reference: Concepts* and *Step-by-Step Programming with Base SAS Software* are good books to learn SAS concepts.

4. For example, select **<u>Base SAS 9.2 Procedures Guide</u>** ⇨ **<u>Procedures</u>** ⇨ **<u>The PRINT Procedure</u>** to find the documentation for the PRINT procedure.

    The Help facility can also be accessed from a Web browser at the following link:

   http://support.sas.com/documentation/index.html

   From this Web page, **<u>Base SAS</u>** can be selected. The SAS syntax books are available in HTML or PDF version.

Submitting a SAS Program – z/OS (OS/390)

.workshop.sascode(p102d01)

- Start a SAS session.
- Include and submit a SAS program.
- Examine the results.
- Use the Help facility.

Starting a SAS Session

1. Type the appropriate command to start your SAS session.

    ✎   The method that you use to invoke SAS varies by your operating environment and any
          customizations in effect at your site.

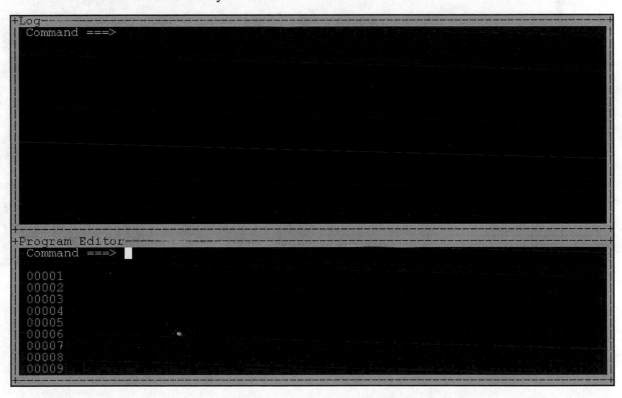

Including and Submitting a SAS Program

1. To include (copy) a SAS program into your SAS session, issue the INCLUDE command.

   a. Type **include** and the name of the file that contain your program on the command line of the Program Editor.

   b. Press **ENTER**.

```
+Program Editor──────────────────────────────────────────────────────────────
  Command ===> inc '.workshop.sascode(p102d01)'

  00001
  00002
  00003
  00004
  00005
  00006
  00007
  00008
  00009
```

The program is included in the Program Editor window.

```
+Program Editor──────────────────────────────────────────────────────────────
  Command ===>

  00001 options linesize=95 pagesize=52;
  00002
  00003 data work.NewSalesEmps;
  00004    length First_Name $ 12 Last_Name $ 18
  00005           Job_Title $ 25;
  00006    infile '.workshop.rawdata(newemps)' dlm=',';
  00007    input First_Name $ Last_Name $
  00008          Job_Title $ Salary;
  00009 run;
  00010
  00011 proc print data=work.NewSalesEmps;
  00012 run;
  00013
  00014 proc means data=work.NewSalesEmps;
  00015    class Job_Title;
  00016    var Salary;
  00017 run;
  00018
  00019
```

You can use the Program Editor window to do the following:

- access and edit existing SAS programs
- write new SAS programs
- submit SAS programs
- save programming statements in a file

The program contains three steps: a DATA step and two PROC steps.

Issue the SUBMIT command to execute your program.

2. The first page of the output from your program is displayed in the Output window.

Examining the Results

The Output window

- is one of the primary windows and is open by default.
- becomes the active window each time that it receives output.
- automatically accumulates output in the order in which it is generated. You can issue the CLEAR command or select **Edit** ⇨ **Clear All** to clear the contents of the window.

To scroll horizontally within the Output window, issue the RIGHT and LEFT commands.

To scroll vertically within the Output window, issue the FORWARD and BACKWARD commands.

✐ You also can use the TOP and BOTTOM commands to scroll vertically within the Output window.

1. Issue the END command. If the PRINT procedure produces more than one page of output, you are taken to the last page of output. If the PRINT procedure produces only one page of output, the END command enables the MEANS procedure to execute and produce its output.

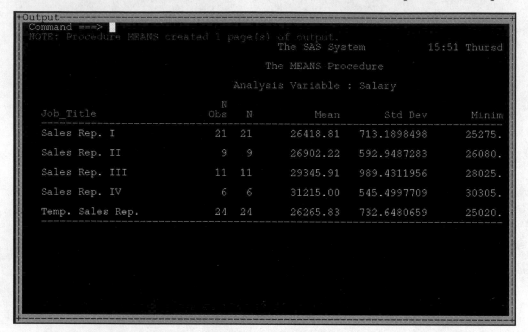

 You can issue an AUTOSCROLL 0 command on the command line of the Output window to have all of your SAS output from one submission placed in the Output window at one time. This eliminates the need to issue an END command to run each step separately.

The AUTOSCROLL command is in effect for the duration of your SAS session. If you want this every time that you invoke SAS, you can save this setting by typing **autoscroll 0; wsave** on the command line of the Output window.

2. Issue the END command to return to the Program Editor window.

After the program executes, you can view messages in the Log window.

The Log window

- is one of the primary windows and is open by default.
- acts as a record of your SAS session; messages are written to the log in the order in which they are generated by the program. You can issue the CLEAR command to clear the contents of the window.

The Log window contains the programming statements that were recently submitted, as well as notes about the following:

- any files that were read
- the records that were read
- the program execution and results

In this example, the Log window contains no warning or error messages. If your program contains errors, relevant warning and error messages are also written to the SAS log.

Issue the END command to return to the Program Editor window.

Using the Help Facility

1. To open the Help facility, select **Help** ⇨ **SAS Help and Documentation** or click .

2. Select the **Contents** tab.

3. From the Contents tab, select **SAS Products** ⇨ **Base SAS**.

   The primary Base SAS syntax books are the *Base SAS 9.2 Procedures Guide* and *SAS 9.2 Language Reference: Dictionary*. The *SAS 9.2 Language Reference: Concepts* and *Step-by-Step Programming with Base SAS Software* are good books to learn SAS concepts.

4. For example, select **Base SAS 9.2 Procedures Guide** ⇨ **Procedures** ⇨ **The PRINT Procedure** to find the documentation for the PRINT procedure.

    The Help facility can also be accessed from a Web browser at the following link:

   http://support.sas.com/documentation/index.html

   From this Web page, **Base SAS** can be selected. The SAS syntax books are available in HTML or PDF version.

 **Exercises**

Level 1

1. Submitting a Program and Using the Help Facility

   a. With the appropriate Editor window active, include a SAS program.

Windows	Select **File** ⇨ **Open Program** and select the **p102e01.sas** program.
UNIX	Select **File** ⇨ **Open** and select the **p102e01.sas** program.
z/OS (OS/390)	Issue the command: `include '.workshop.sascode(p102e01)`.

   b. Submit the program for execution. Based on the report in the Output window, how many rows and columns are in the report?

     rows: _____   columns: _____

   c. Examine the Log window. Based on the log notes, how many observations and variables are in the `work.country` data set?

     observations: _____   variables: _____

   d. Clear the Log and Output windows.

   e. Use the Help facility to find documentation on the LINESIZE= option.

     Go to the CONTENTS tab in the SAS Help and Documentation, select **SAS Products** ⇨ **Base SAS** ⇨ **SAS 9.2 Language Reference: Dictionary** ⇨ **Dictionary of Language Elements** ⇨ **SAS System Options** ⇨ **LINESIZE= System Option**.

     What is an alias for the LINESIZE= system option? _____

Level 2

2. Identifying SAS Components

   a. With the appropriate Editor window active, type the following SAS program:

```
proc setinit;
run;
```

   b. Submit the program for execution, and then look at the results in the Log window.

     ✏️   The SETINIT procedure produces a list of the SAS components licensed at a given site.

c. If you see SAS/GRAPH in the list of components in the log, include a SAS program.

Windows	Select **File** ⇨ **Open Program** and select the **p102e02.sas** program.
UNIX	Select **File** ⇨ **Open** and select the **p102e02.sas** program.
z/OS (OS/390)	Issue the command: `include '.workshop.sascode(p102e02).`

d. Submit the program for execution. View the results in the GRAPH window.

e. Close the GRAPH window.

3. Setting Up Function Keys

a. Issue the KEYS command or select **Tools** ⇨ **Options** ⇨ **Keys** to open the KEYS window.

> The KEYS window is a secondary window used to browse or change function key definitions.

b. Add the following commands to the F12 key:

```
clear log; clear output
```

c. Close the KEYS window.

d. Press the F12 key and confirm that the Log and Output windows are cleared.

Level 3

4. Exploring Your SAS Environment – Windows

a. Customize the appearance and functionality of the Enhanced Editor by selecting **Tools** ⇨ **Options** ⇨ **Enhanced Editor**. For example, select the Appearance tab to modify the font size.

b. In the Help facility, look up the documentation for the Enhanced Editor.

From the Contents tab, select **Using SAS Software in Your Operating Environment** ⇨ **SAS 9.2 Companion for Windows** ⇨ **Running SAS under Windows** ⇨ **Using the SAS Editors** ⇨ **Using the Enhanced Editor**

5. Exploring Your SAS Environment – UNIX and z/OS (OS/390)

a. From a Web browser, access the following link: http://support.sas.com/documentation/

b. Select **Base SAS**.

c. Select the HTML version of **Step-by-Step Programming with Base SAS Software**.

d. On the Contents tab, select **Understanding Your SAS Environment** ⇨ **Using the SAS Windowing Environment** ⇨ **Working with SAS Programs**.

e. Refer to **Command Line Commands and the Editor** and **Line Commands and the Editor**.

2.3 Solutions

Solutions to Exercises

1. **Submitting a Program and Using the Help Facility**

   a. Include a SAS program.

```
options linesize=95 pagesize=52;

data work.country;
   length Country_Code $ 2 Country_Name $ 48;
   infile 'country.dat' dlm='!';
   input Country_Code $ Country_Name $;
run;

proc print data=work.country;
run;
```

   b. Submit the program.

   rows: **238**   columns: **3**

   c. Examine the Log window.

   observations: **238**   variables: **2**

   d. Clear the Log and Output windows.

   e. Use the Help facility.

   What is an alias for the LINESIZE= system option? **LS=**

2. **Identifying SAS Components**

   a. Type the following SAS program:

```
proc setinit;
run;
```

   b. Submit the program.

Partial SAS Log

Product expiration dates:	
---Base Product	31DEC2008
---SAS/STAT	31DEC2008
---SAS/GRAPH	31DEC2008
---SAS/ETS	31DEC2008

c. Include a SAS program.

```
data work.SalesEmps;
   length Job_Title $ 25;
   infile 'sales.csv' dlm=',';
   input Employee_ID First_Name $ Last_Name $
         Gender $ Salary Job_Title $ Country $;
run;

goptions reset=all;
proc gchart data=work.SalesEmps;
   vbar3d Job_Title / sumvar=Salary type=mean;
   hbar Job_Title / group=Gender sumvar=Salary
                    patternid=midpoint;
   pie3d Job_Title / noheading;
   where Job_Title contains 'Sales Rep';
   label Job_Title='Job Title';
   format Salary dollar12.;
   title 'Orion Star Sales Employees';
run;
quit;
```

d. Submit the program.

e. Close the GRAPH window.

3. **Setting Up Function Keys**

   a. Issue the KEYS command.

   b. Add a command to the F12 key.

   Keys Window (Windows):

```
KEYS <DMKEYS>                              _ □ ×
Key         Definition

F1          help
F2          reshow
F3          end; /*gsubmit buffer=default*/
F4          recall
F5          wpgm
F6          log
F7          output
F8          zoom off;submit
F9          keys
F11         command focus
F12         clear log; clear out
SHF F1      subtop
SHF F2
```

   c. Close the KEYS window.

   d. Press the F12 key.

4. Exploring Your SAS Environment – Windows

   a. Customize the appearance and functionality of the Enhanced Editor.

   b. Use the Help facility.

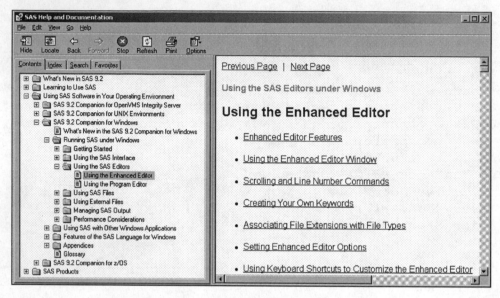

5. Exploring Your SAS Environment – UNIX and z/OS (OS/390)

   a. From a Web browser, access the following link: http://support.sas.com/documentation/

   b. Select **Base SAS**.

   c. Select the HTML version of **Step-by-Step Programming with Base SAS Software**.

   d. On the Contents tab, select **Understanding Your SAS Environment** ⇨
        Using the SAS Windowing Environment ⇨ **Working with SAS Programs**.

   e. Refer to **Command Line Commands and the Editor** and **Line Commands and the Editor**.

   Partial Documentation

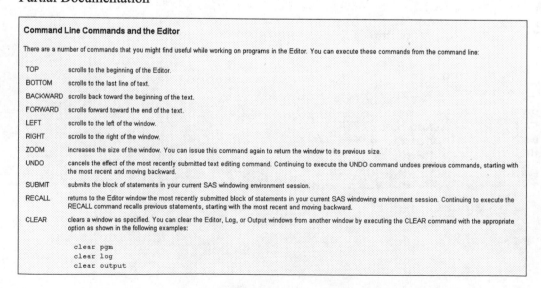

Solutions to Student Activities (Polls/Quizzes)

2.01 Quiz – Correct Answer

How many steps are in this program?

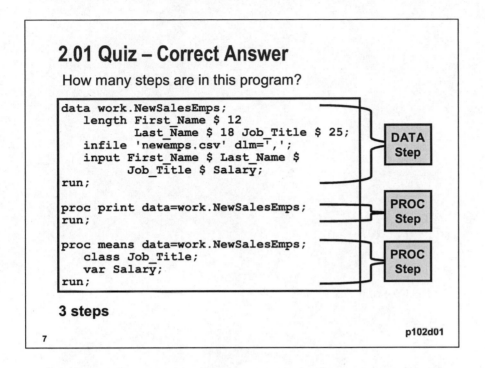

```
data work.NewSalesEmps;
    length First_Name $ 12
           Last_Name $ 18 Job_Title $ 25;
    infile 'newemps.csv' dlm=',';
    input First_Name $ Last_Name $
          Job_Title $ Salary;
run;

proc print data=work.NewSalesEmps;
run;

proc means data=work.NewSalesEmps;
    class Job_Title;
    var Salary;
run;
```

DATA Step

PROC Step

PROC Step

3 steps

7   p102d01

2.02 Quiz – Correct Answer

How does SAS detect the end of the PROC MEANS step?

```
data work.NewSalesEmps;
    length First_Name $ 12
           Last_Name $ 18 Job_Title $ 25;
    infile 'newemps.csv' dlm=',';
    input First_Name $ Last_Name $
          Job_Title $ Salary;
run;

proc print data=work.NewSalesEmps;

proc means data=work.NewSalesEmps;
    class Job_Title;
    var Salary;
```

SAS does not detect the end of the PROC MEANS step.
SAS needs a RUN statement to detect the end.

15

Chapter 3 Working with SAS Syntax

3.1 Mastering Fundamental Concepts

Objectives

- Identify the characteristics of SAS statements.
- Explain SAS syntax rules.
- Insert SAS comments using two methods.

3

SAS Programs

A SAS program is a sequence of steps.

```
data work.NewSalesEmps;
   length First_Name $ 12
          Last_Name $ 18 Job_Title $ 25;
   infile 'newemps.csv' dlm=',';
   input First_Name $ Last_Name $
         Job_Title $ Salary;
run;

proc print data=work.NewSalesEmps;
run;

proc means data=work.NewSalesEmps;
   class Job_Title;
   var Salary;
run;
```

DATA
Step

PROC
Step

PROC
Step

A step is a sequence of SAS statements.

4

Statements

SAS statements have these characteristics:

- usually begin with an **identifying keyword**
- always end with a **semicolon**

```
data work.NewSalesEmps;
   length First_Name $ 12
          Last_Name $ 18 Job_Title $ 25;
   infile 'newemps.csv' dlm=',';
   input First_Name $ Last_Name $
         Job_Title $ Salary;
run;

proc print data=work.NewSalesEmps;
run;

proc means data=work.NewSalesEmps;
   class Job_Title;
   var Salary;
run;
```

5   p103d01

3.01 Quiz

How many statements are in the DATA step?

a. 1

b. 3

c. 5

d. 7

```
data work.NewSalesEmps;
   length First_Name $ 12
          Last_Name $ 18 Job_Title $ 25;
   infile 'newemps.csv' dlm=',';
   input First_Name $ Last_Name $
         Job_Title $ Salary;
run;
```

7

SAS Syntax Rules

Structured, consistent spacing makes a SAS program easier to read.

```
data work.NewSalesEmps;          Conventional Formatting
    length First_Name $ 12
           Last_Name $ 18 Job_Title $ 25;
    infile 'newemps.csv' dlm=',';
    input First_Name $ Last_Name $
          Job_Title $ Salary;
run;

proc print data=work.NewSalesEmps;
run;

proc means data=work.NewSalesEmps;
    class Job_Title;
    var Salary;
run;
```

9

SAS programming statements are easier to read if you begin DATA, PROC, and RUN statements in column one and indent the other statements.

SAS Syntax Rules

- SAS statements are free-format.
- One or more blanks or special characters can be used to separate words.
- They can begin and end in any column.
- A single statement can span multiple lines.
- Several statements can be on the same line.

```
data work.NewSalesEmps;          Unconventional Formatting
length First_Name $ 12
Last_Name $ 18 Job_Title $ 25;
infile 'newemps.csv' dlm=',';
input First_Name $ Last_Name $
Job_Title $ Salary;
run;
proc print data=work.NewSalesEmps; run;
    proc means data   =work.NewSalesEmps;
class Job_Title;   var Salary;run;
```

10

SAS Syntax Rules

- SAS statements are free-format.
- ▸ One or more blanks or special characters can be used to separate words.
- They can begin and end in any column.
- A single statement can span multiple lines.
- Several statements can be on the same line.

```
data work.NewSalesEmps;
length First_Name $ 12
Last_Name $ 18 Job_Title $ 25;
infile 'newemps.csv' dlm=',';
input First_Name $ Last_Name $
Job_Title $ Salary;
run;
proc print data=work.NewSalesEmps; run;
    proc means data  =work.NewSalesEmps;
class Job_Title;   var Salary;run;
```

Unconventional Formatting

11

SAS Syntax Rules

- SAS statements are free-format.
- One or more blanks or special characters can be used to separate words.
- ▸ They can begin and end in any column.
- A single statement can span multiple lines.
- Several statements can be on the same line.

```
data work.NewSalesEmps;
length First_Name $ 12
Last_Name $ 18 Job_Title $ 25;
infile 'newemps.csv' dlm=',';
input First_Name $ Last_Name $
Job_Title $ Salary;
run;
proc print data=work.NewSalesEmps; run;
    proc means data  =work.NewSalesEmps;
class Job_Title;   var Salary;run;
```

Unconventional Formatting

12

SAS Syntax Rules

- SAS statements are free-format.
- One or more blanks or special characters can be used to separate words.
- They can begin and end in any column.
➡ - A single statement can span multiple lines.
- Several statements can be on the same line.

```
data work.NewSalesEmps;                 Unconventional Formatting
length First_Name $ 12
Last_Name $ 18 Job_Title $ 25;
infile 'newemps.csv' dlm=',';
input First_Name $ Last_Name $
Job_Title $ Salary;
run;
proc print data=work.NewSalesEmps; run;
    proc means data  =work.NewSalesEmps;
class Job_Title;  var Salary;run;
```

13

SAS Syntax Rules

- SAS statements are free-format.
- One or more blanks or special characters can be used to separate words.
- They can begin and end in any column.
- A single statement can span multiple lines.
➡ - Several statements can be on the same line.

```
data work.NewSalesEmps;          Unconventional Formatting
length First_Name $ 12
Last_Name $ 18 Job_Title $ 25;
infile 'newemps.csv' dlm=',';
input First_Name $ Last_Name $
Job_Title $ Salary;
run;
proc print data=work.NewSalesEmps; run;
    proc means data  =work.NewSalesEmps;
class Job_Title;   var Salary;run;
```

14

SAS Comments

SAS comments are text that SAS ignores during
processing. You can use comments anywhere in
a SAS program to document the purpose of the
program, explain segments of the program, or
mark SAS code as non-executing text.

Two methods of commenting:

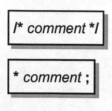

```
/* comment */
```

```
* comment ;
```

15

 Avoid placing the /* comment symbols in columns 1 and 2. On some operating environments,
SAS might interpret these symbols as a request to end the SAS job or session.

SAS Comments

This program contains four comments.

```
*-------------------------------------------*
|    This program creates and uses the      |
|    data set called work.NewSalesEmps.     |
*-------------------------------------------*;
data work.NewSalesEmps;
    length First_Name $ 12 Last_Name $ 18
           Job_Title $ 25;
    infile 'newemps.csv' dlm=',';
    input First_Name $ Last_Name $
          Job_Title $ Salary /*numeric*/;
run;
/*
proc print data=work.NewSalesEmps;
run;
*/
proc means data=work.NewSalesEmps;
    *class Job_Title;
    var Salary;
run;
```

16   p103d02

Setup for the Poll

- Retrieve program **p103a01**.
- Read the comment concerning DATALINES.
- Submit the program and view the log to confirm that the PROC CONTENTS step did not execute.

18

3.02 Multiple Choice Poll

Which statement is true concerning the DATALINES statement based on reading the comment?

a. The DATALINES statement is used when reading data located in a raw data file.

b. The DATALINES statement is used when reading data located directly in the program.

19

3.2   Diagnosing and Correcting Syntax Errors

Objectives

- Identify SAS syntax errors.
- Diagnose and correct a program with errors.
- Save the corrected program.

23

Syntax Errors

Syntax errors occur when program statements
do not conform to the rules of the SAS language.

Examples of syntax errors:

- misspelled keywords
- unmatched quotation marks
- missing semicolons
- invalid options

When SAS encounters a syntax error, SAS prints
a warning or an error message to the log.

```
ERROR 22-322: Syntax error, expecting one of the following:
              a name, a quoted string, (, /, ;, _DATA_, _LAST_,
              _NULL_.
```

24

When SAS encounters a syntax error, SAS underlines the error and the following information is written to the SAS log:

- the word ERROR or WARNING
- the location of the error
- an explanation of the error

3.03 Quiz

This program has three syntax errors.
Any thoughts on what are the errors?

```
daat work.NewSalesEmps;
   length First_Name $ 12
          Last_Name $ 18 Job_Title $ 25;
   infile 'newemps.csv' dlm=',';
   input First_Name $ Last_Name $
         Job_Title $ Salary;
run;

proc print data=work.NewSalesEmps
run;

proc means data=work.NewSalesEmps average max;
   class Job_Title;
   var Salary;
run;
```

26   p103d03

Diagnosing and Correcting Syntax Errors

p103d03

- Submit a SAS program with errors.
- Diagnose and correct the errors.
- Save the corrected program.

Submitting a SAS Program with Errors

```
daat work.NewSalesEmps;
   length First_Name $ 12
          Last_Name $ 18 Job_Title $ 25;
   infile 'newemps.csv' dlm=',';
   input First_Name $ Last_Name $
         Job_Title $ Salary;
run;

proc print data=work.NewSalesEmps
run;

proc means data=work.NewSalesEmps average max;
   class Job_Title;
   var Salary;
run;
```

For z/OS (OS/390), the following INFILE statement is used:

```
   infile '.workshop.rawdata(newemps)' dlm=',';
```

The SAS log contains error messages and warnings.

```
36    daat work.NewSalesEmps;
      ----
      14
WARNING 14-169: Assuming the symbol DATA was misspelled as daat.

37       length First_Name $ 12
38             Last_Name $ 18 Job_Title $ 25;
39       infile 'newemps.csv' dlm=',';
40       input First_Name $ Last_Name $
41            Job_Title $ Salary;
42    run;

NOTE: The infile 'newemps.csv' is:
      Filename=S:\Workshop\newemps.csv,
      RECFM=V,LRECL=256,File Size (bytes)=2604,
      Last Modified=02Apr2008:09:10:12,
      Create Time=02Apr2008:09:10:12

NOTE: 71 records were read from the infile 'newemps.csv'.
```

```
          The minimum record length was 28.
          The maximum record length was 47.
NOTE: The data set WORK.NEWSALESEMPS has 71 observations and 4 variables.


43
44    proc print data=work.NewSalesEmps
45    run;
      ---
      22
      202
ERROR 22-322: Syntax error, expecting one of the following: ;, (, BLANKLINE, DATA, DOUBLE,
              HEADING, LABEL, N, NOOBS, OBS, ROUND, ROWS, SPLIT, STYLE, SUMLABEL, UNIFORM,
              WIDTH.
ERROR 202-322: The option or parameter is not recognized and will be ignored.
46

NOTE: The SAS System stopped processing this step because of errors.


47    proc means data=work.NewSalesEmps average max;
                                         -------
                                         22
                                         202
ERROR 22-322: Syntax error, expecting one of the following: ;, (, ALPHA, CHARTYPE, CLASSDATA,
              CLM, COMPLETETYPES, CSS, CV, DATA, DESCEND, DESCENDING, DESCENDTYPES, EXCLNPWGT,
              EXCLNPWGTS, EXCLUSIVE, FW, IDMIN, KURTOSIS, LCLM, MAX, MAXDEC, MEAN, MEDIAN, MIN,
              MISSING, MODE, N, NDEC, NMISS, NOLABELS, NONOBS, NOPRINT, NOTHREADS, NOTRAP,
              NWAY, ORDER, P1, P10, P25, P5, P50, P75, P90, P95, P99, PCTLDEF, PRINT, PRINTALL,
              PRINTALLTYPES, PRINTIDS, PRINTIDVARS, PROBT, Q1, Q3, QMARKERS, QMETHOD, QNTLDEF,
              QRANGE, RANGE, SKEWNESS, STDDEV, STDERR, SUM, SUMSIZE, SUMWGT, T, THREADS, UCLM,
              USS, VAR, VARDEF.
ERROR 202-322: The option or parameter is not recognized and will be ignored.
48        class Job_Title;
49        var Salary;
50    run;

NOTE: The SAS System stopped processing this step because of errors.
```

Diagnosing and Correcting the Errors

The log indicates that SAS

- assumed the keyword DATA was misspelled and executed the DATA step
- interpreted the word RUN as an option in the PROC PRINT statement (because there was a missing semicolon), so PROC PRINT was not executed
- did not recognize the word AVERAGE as a valid option in the PROC MEANS statement, so the PROC MEANS step was not executed.

1. If you are using the Enhanced Editor, the program remains in the editor.

    However, if you use the Program Editor, the code disappears with each submission. Use the RECALL command or select **Run** ⇨ **Recall Last Submit** to recall the program that you submitted back to the Program Editor. The original program is copied into the Program Editor.

2. Edit the program.

    a. Correct the spelling of DATA.

    b. Put a semicolon at the end of the PROC PRINT statement.

    c. Change the word AVERAGE to MEAN in the PROC MEANS statement.

```
data work.NewSalesEmps;
   length First_Name $ 12
          Last_Name $ 18 Job_Title $ 25;
   infile 'newemps.csv' dlm=',';
   input First_Name $ Last_Name $
         Job_Title $ Salary;
run;

proc print data=work.NewSalesEmps;
run;

proc means data=work.NewSalesEmps mean max;
   class Job_Title;
   var Salary;
run;
```

3. Submit the program. It runs successfully without errors and generates output.

Saving the Corrected Program

You can use the FILE command to save your program to a file. The program must be in the Enhanced Editor or Program Editor before you issue the FILE command. If the code is not in the Program Editor, recall your program before saving the program.

Windows or UNIX	`file 'myprog.sas'`
z/OS (OS/390)	`file '.workshop.sascode(myprog)'`

You can also select **File** ⇨ **Save As**.

A note appears that indicates that the statements are saved to the file.

Diagnosing and Correcting Syntax Errors

p103d04

- Submit a SAS program that contains unbalanced quotation marks.
- Diagnose and correct the error.
- Resubmit the program.

Submitting a SAS Program that Contains Unbalanced Quotation Marks

The closing quotation mark for the DLM= option in the INFILE statement is missing.

```
data work.NewSalesEmps;
   length First_Name $ 12 Last_Name $ 18
          Job_Title $ 25;
   infile 'newemps.csv' dlm=',;
   input First_Name $ Last_Name $
         Job_Title $ Salary;
run;

proc print data=work.NewSalesEmps;
run;

proc means data=work.NewSalesEmps;
   class Job_Title;
   var Salary;
run;
```

SAS Log

```
51    data work.NewSalesEmps;
52       length First_Name $ 12 Last_Name $ 18
53             Job_Title $ 25;
54       infile 'newemps.csv' dlm=',;
55       input First_Name $ Last_Name $
56             Job_Title $ Salary;
57    run;
58
59    proc print data=work.NewSalesEmps;
60    run;
61
62    proc means data=work.NewSalesEmps;
63       class Job_Title;
64       var Salary;
65    run;
```

Diagnosing and Correcting the Errors

There are no notes in the SAS log because all of the SAS statements after the DLM= option became part of the quoted delimiter.

    The banner in the window indicates that the DATA step is still running, and it is still running because the RUN statement was not recognized.

You can correct the unbalanced quotation marks programmatically by adding the following code before your previous statements:

```
*';*";run;
```

If the quotation mark counter within SAS has an uneven number of quotation marks, as seen in the above program, SAS reads the quotation mark in the comment above as the matching quotation mark in the quotation mark counter. SAS then has an even number of quotation marks in the quotation mark counter and runs successfully, assuming no other errors occur. Both single quotation marks and double quotation marks are used in case you submitted double quotation marks instead of single quotation marks.

Point-and-Click Approaches to Balancing Quotation Marks

Windows

1. To correct the problem in the Windows environment, click the break icon [⊕] or press the **CTRL** and **Break** keys.

2. Select **1. Cancel Submitted Statements** in the Tasking Manager window and select **OK**.

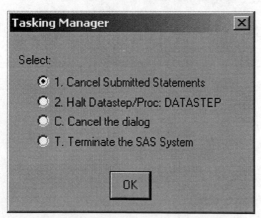

3. Select **Y to cancel submitted statements,** ⇨ **OK**.

UNIX

1. To correct the problem in the UNIX operating environment, open the SAS: Session Management window and select **Interrupt**.

2. Select **1** in the SAS: Tasking Manager window.

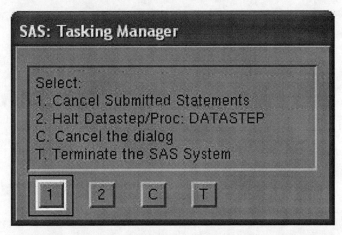

3. Select **Y**.

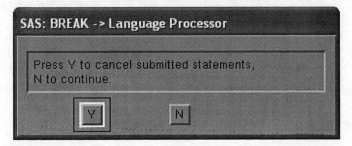

z/OS (OS/390)

1. To correct the problem in the z/OS (OS/390) operating environment, press the **Attention** key or issue the ATTENTION command.

2. Type **1** to select **1. Cancel Submitted Statements** and press the ENTER key.

```
┌Tasking Manager─────────────────────────────────────────
 Select:
 1 ▮. Cancel Submitted Statements
    2. Halt Datastep/Proc: DATASTEP
    C. Cancel the dialog
    T. Terminate the SAS System
```

3. Type **Y** and press ENTER.

```
┌BREAK -> Language Processor──────────────────────────────
 Press Y to cancel submitted statements, N to continue.  y ▮
```

Resubmitting the Program

1. In the appropriate Editor window, add a closing quotation mark to the DLM= option in the INFILE statement.

```
data work.NewSalesEmps;
   length First_Name $ 12 Last_Name $ 18
          Job_Title $ 25;
   infile 'newemps.csv' dlm=',';
   input First_Name $ Last_Name $
         Job_Title $ Salary;
run;

proc print data=work.NewSalesEmps;
run;

proc means data=work.NewSalesEmps;
   class Job_Title;
   var Salary;
run;
```

2. Resubmit the program.

    When you make changes to the program in the Enhanced Editor and have not saved the new version of the program, the window bar and the top border of the window reflect that you changed the program without saving it by putting an asterisk (*) beside the window name. When you save the program, the * disappears.

 **Exercises**

Level 1

1. **Diagnosing and Correcting a Misspelled Word**

    a. With the appropriate Editor window active, include the SAS program **p103e01**.

    b. Submit the program.

    c. Use the notes in the SAS log to identify the error.

    d. Correct the error and resubmit the program.

Level 2

2. **Diagnosing and Correcting a Missing Statement**

    a. With the appropriate Editor window active, include the SAS program **p103e02**.

    b. Submit the program.

    c. Are there any errors in the SAS log?

    d. Notice the message in the title bar of the Editor window.

    e. Why is PROC PRINT running?

    f. Add the missing statement to execute the PROC PRINT step.

    g. Submit the added statement.

    h. Confirm that the output was created for the program by viewing the Log and Output windows.

Level 3

3. **Using the Help Facility to Determine the Types of Errors in SAS**

    a. In the Help facility, type **syntax errors** on the Index tab.

    b. Double-click on **syntax errors** in the results box.

    c. In the Topics Found pop-up box, select **Error Processing and Debugging: Types of Errors in SAS**.

    d. Name the five types of errors.

3.3 Solutions

Solutions to Exercises

1. **Diagnosing and Correcting a Misspelled Word**

    a. Include the SAS program.

    b. Submit the program.

    c. Use the notes in the SAS log to identify the error.

    d. Correct the error.

```
data work.country;
   length Country_Code $ 2 Country_Name $ 48;
   infile 'country.dat' dlm='!';
   input Country_Code $ Country_Name $;
run;

proc print data=work.country;
run;
```

2. **Diagnosing and Correcting a Missing Statement**

    a. Include the SAS program.

    b. Submit the program.

    c. Are there any errors in the SAS log? **No**

    d. Notice the message in the title bar.

    e. Why is PROC PRINT running? **The PROC PRINT step is missing a RUN statement.**

    f. Add the missing statement.

```
data work.donations;
   infile 'donation.dat';
   input Employee_ID Qtr1 Qtr2 Qtr3 Qtr4;
   Total=sum(Qtr1,Qtr2,Qtr3,Qtr4);
run;

proc print data=work.donations;
run;
```

    g. Submit the added statement.

    h. Confirm that the output was created.

3. Using the Help Facility to Determine the Types of Errors in SAS

    a. In the Help facility, type **syntax errors** on the Index tab.

    b. Double-click on <u>syntax errors</u> in the result box.

    c. Select <u>**Error Processing and Debugging: Type of Errors in SAS**</u>.

    d. Name the five types of errors.

        <u>**Syntax: when programming statements do not conform to the rules of the SAS language compile time**</u>

        <u>**Semantic: when the language element is correct, but the element might not be valid for a particular usage compile time**</u>

        <u>**Execution-time: when SAS attempts to execute a program and execution fails execution time**</u>

        <u>**Data: when data values are invalid execution time**</u>

        <u>**Macro-related: when you use the macro facility incorrectly**</u>

Solutions to Student Activities (Polls/Quizzes)

3.01 Quiz – Correct Answer

How many statements are in the DATA step?

  a. 1
  b. 3
  (c.) 5
  d. 7

```
data work.NewSalesEmps;
    length First_Name $ 12
           Last_Name $ 18 Job_Title $ 25;
    infile 'newemps.csv' dlm=',';
    input First_Name $ Last_Name $
          Job_Title $ Salary;
run;
```

8

3.02 Multiple Choice Poll – Correct Answer

Which statement is true concerning the DATALINES statement based on reading the comment?

  a. The DATALINES statement is used when reading data located in a raw data file.

  (b.) The DATALINES statement is used when reading data located directly in the program.

20

3.03 Quiz – Correct Answer

This program has three syntax errors.

Any thoughts on what are the errors?

```
daat work.NewSalesEmps;
   length First_Name $ 12
         Last_Name $ 18 Job_Title $ 25;
   infile 'newemps.csv' dlm=',';
   input First_Name $ Last_Name $
         Job_Title $ Salary;
run;

proc print data=work.NewSalesEmps
run;

proc means data=work.NewSalesEmps average max;
   class Job_Title;
   var Salary;
run;
```

27   p103d03

Chapter 4 Getting Familiar with SAS Data Sets

4.1 Examining Descriptor and Data Portions

Objectives

- Define the components of a SAS data set.
- Define a SAS variable.
- Identify a missing value and a SAS date value.
- State the naming conventions for SAS data sets and variables.
- Browse the descriptor portion of SAS data sets by using the CONTENTS procedure.
- Browse the data portion of SAS data sets by using the PRINT procedure.

3

SAS Data Set

A *SAS data set* is a file that SAS creates and processes.

Partial `work.NewSalesEmps`

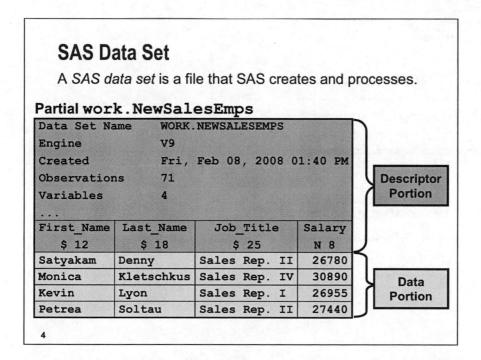

4

Data must be in the form of a SAS data set to be processed by many SAS procedures and some DATA step statements.

A SAS data set is a specially structured file that contains data values.

Descriptor Portion

The *descriptor portion* of a SAS data set contains the following:

- general information about the SAS data set (such as data set name and number of observations)
- variable information (such as name, type, and length)

Partial work.NewSalesEmps

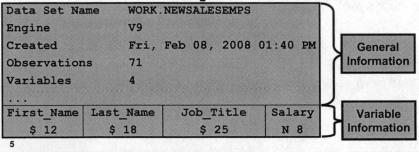

Data Set Name	WORK.NEWSALESEMPS			
Engine	V9			
Created	Fri, Feb 08, 2008 01:40 PM			
Observations	71			
Variables	4			
...				
First_Name	Last_Name	Job_Title	Salary
$ 12	$ 18	$ 25	N 8

General Information

Variable Information

5

Browsing the Descriptor Portion

The *CONTENTS procedure* displays the descriptor portion of a SAS data set.

General form of the CONTENTS procedure:

```
PROC CONTENTS DATA=SAS-data-set;
RUN;
```

Example:

```
proc contents data=work.NewSalesEmps;
run;
```

6   p104d01

Browsing the Descriptor Portion

Partial PROC CONTENTS Output

```
                        The CONTENTS Procedure

Data Set Name      WORK.NEWSALESEMPS      Observations           71
Member Type        DATA                   Variables              4
Engine             V9                     Indexes                0
Created            Wed, Jan 16, 2008      Observation Length     64
                   02:14:20 PM
Last Modified      Wed, Jan 16, 2008      Deleted Observations   0
                   02:14:20 PM
Protection                                Compressed             NO
Data Set Type                             Sorted                 NO
Label


             Alphabetic List of Variables and Attributes

             #     Variable     Type     Len

             1     First_Name   Char      12
             3     Job_Title    Char      25
             2     Last_Name    Char      18
             4     Salary       Num        8
```

7

 This is a partial view of the default PROC CONTENTS output. PROC CONTENTS output also contains information about the physical location of the file and other data set information.

The descriptor portion contains the metadata of the data set.

4.01 Quiz

How many observations are in the data set **work.donations**?

- Retrieve program **p104a01**.
- After the DATA step, add a PROC CONTENTS step to view the descriptor portion of **work.donations**.
- Submit the program and review the results.

9

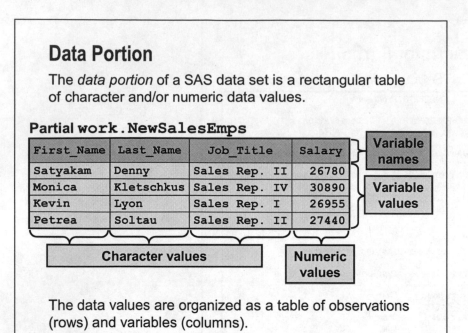

Data Portion

The *data portion* of a SAS data set is a rectangular table of character and/or numeric data values.

Partial `work.NewSalesEmps`

First_Name	Last_Name	Job_Title	Salary
Satyakam	Denny	Sales Rep. II	26780
Monica	Kletschkus	Sales Rep. IV	30890
Kevin	Lyon	Sales Rep. I	26955
Petrea	Soltau	Sales Rep. II	27440

Variable names

Variable values

Character values

Numeric values

The data values are organized as a table of observations (rows) and variables (columns).

11

Variable names are part of the descriptor portion, not the data portion.

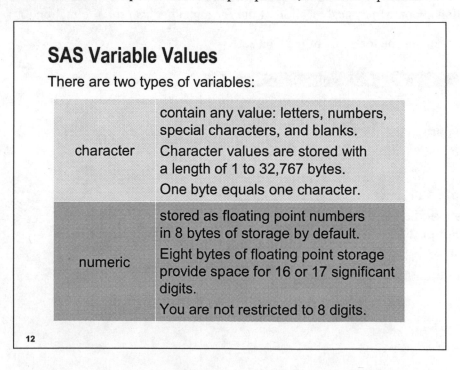

SAS Variable Values

There are two types of variables:

character	contain any value: letters, numbers, special characters, and blanks.
	Character values are stored with a length of 1 to 32,767 bytes.
	One byte equals one character.
numeric	stored as floating point numbers in 8 bytes of storage by default.
	Eight bytes of floating point storage provide space for 16 or 17 significant digits.
	You are not restricted to 8 digits.

12

4.02 Multiple Choice Poll

Which variable type do you think SAS uses to store date values?

a. character
b. numeric

14

SAS Date Values

SAS stores date values as numeric values.

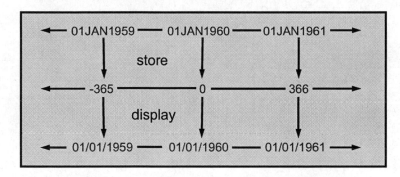

A *SAS date value* is stored as the number of days between January 1, 1960, and a specific date.

18

SAS can perform calculations on dates starting from 1582 A.D.

SAS can read either two- or four-digit year values. If SAS encounters a two-digit year, the YEARCUTOFF= system option is used to specify to which 100-year span the two-digit year should be attributed. For example, by setting the option YEARCUTOFF= option to 1950, the 100-year span from 1950 to 2049 is used for two-digit year values.

4.03 Quiz

What is the numeric value for today's date?

- Submit program **p104a02**.
- View the output to retrieve the current date as a numeric value referencing January 1, 1960.

20

Missing Data Values

A value must exist for every variable for each observation. Missing values are valid values in a SAS data set.

Partial work.NewSalesEmps

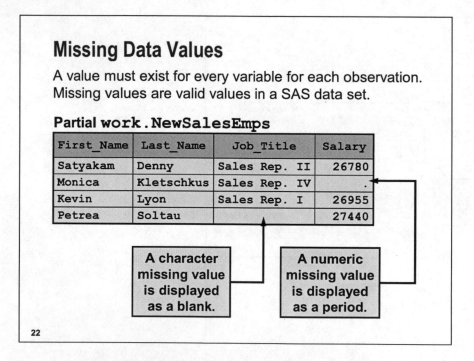

First_Name	Last_Name	Job_Title	Salary
Satyakam	Denny	Sales Rep. II	26780
Monica	Kletschkus	Sales Rep. IV	.
Kevin	Lyon	Sales Rep. I	26955
Petrea	Soltau		27440

A character missing value is displayed as a blank.

A numeric missing value is displayed as a period.

22

A period is the default display for a missing numeric value. The default display can be altered by changing the MISSING= SAS system option.

SAS Data Set and Variable Names

SAS names have these characteristics:

- can be 32 characters long.
- must start with a letter or underscore. Subsequent characters can be letters, underscores, or numerals.
- can be uppercase, lowercase, or mixed case.
- are not case sensitive.

23

Special characters can be used in variable names if you put the name in quotation marks followed immediately by the letter N.

Example: `class 'Flight#'n;`

In order to use special characters in variable names, the VALIDVARNAME option must be set to ANY.

Example: `options validvarname=any;`

4.04 Multiple Answer Poll

Which variable names are valid?

- a. data5mon
- b. 5monthsdata
- c. data#5
- d. five months data
- e. five_months_data
- f. FiveMonthsData

25

SAS Data Set Terminology

Comparable Terminology:

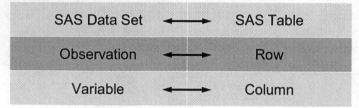

SAS Data Set	←→	SAS Table
Observation	←→	Row
Variable	←→	Column

- The terminology of data set, observation, and variable is specific to SAS.
- The terminology of table, row, and column is common among databases.

27

Browsing the Data Portion

The *PRINT procedure* displays the data portion of a SAS data set.

By default, PROC PRINT displays the following:
- all observations
- all variables
- an Obs column on the left side

28

Browsing the Data Portion

General form of the PRINT procedure:

PROC PRINT DATA=*SAS-data-set* ;
RUN;

Example:

```
proc print data=work.NewSalesEmps;
run;
```

p104d02

Browsing the Data Portion

Partial PROC PRINT Output

Obs	First_Name	Last_Name	Job_Title	Salary
1	Satyakam	Denny	Sales Rep. II	26780
2	Monica	Kletschkus	Sales Rep. IV	30890
3	Kevin	Lyon	Sales Rep. I	26955
4	Petrea	Soltau	Sales Rep. II	27440
5	Marina	Iyengar	Sales Rep. III	29715
6	Shani	Duckett	Sales Rep. I	25795
7	Fang	Wilson	Sales Rep. II	26810
8	Michael	Minas	Sales Rep. I	26970
9	Amanda	Liebman	Sales Rep. II	27465
10	Vincent	Eastley	Sales Rep. III	29695
11	Viney	Barbis	Sales Rep. III	30265
12	Skev	Rusli	Sales Rep. II	26580
13	Narelle	James	Sales Rep. III	29990
14	Gerry	Snellings	Sales Rep. I	26445
15	Leonid	Karavdic	Sales Rep. II	27860

Browsing the Data Portion

Options and statements can be added to the PRINT procedure.

> **PROC PRINT** DATA=*SAS-data-set* **NOOBS**;
>   **VAR** *variable(s)*;
> **RUN**;

- The NOOBS option suppresses the observation numbers on the left side of the report.
- The VAR statement selects variables that appear in the report and determines their order.

31

Browsing the Data Portion

```
proc print data=work.NewSalesEmps noobs;
   var Last_Name First_Name Salary;
run;
```

Partial PROC PRINT Output

Last_Name	First_Name	Salary
Denny	Satyakam	26780
Kletschkus	Monica	30890
Lyon	Kevin	26955
Soltau	Petrea	27440
Iyengar	Marina	29715
Duckett	Shani	25795
Wilson	Fang	26810
Minas	Michael	26970
Liebman	Amanda	27465
Eastley	Vincent	29695

32   p104d03

 **Exercises**

Level 1

1. Examining the Data Portion

a. Retrieve the starter program **p104e01**.

b. After the PROC CONTENTS step, add a PROC PRINT step to display all observations, all variables, and the Obs column for the data set named **work.donations**.

c. Submit the program to create the following PROC PRINT report:

Partial PROC PRINT Output (First 10 of 124 Observations)

Obs	Employee_ID	Qtr1	Qtr2	Qtr3	Qtr4	Total
1	120265	.	.	.	25	25
2	120267	15	15	15	15	60
3	120269	20	20	20	20	80
4	120270	20	10	5	.	35
5	120271	20	20	20	20	80
6	120272	10	10	10	10	40
7	120275	15	15	15	15	60
8	120660	25	25	25	25	100
9	120662	10	.	5	5	20
10	120663	.	.	5	.	5

d. In the PROC PRINT step, add a VAR statement and the NOOBS option to display only the **Employee_ID** and **Total** variables.

e. Submit the program to create the following PROC PRINT report:

Partial PROC PRINT Output (First 10 of 124 Observations)

Employee_ID	Total
120265	25
120267	60
120269	80
120270	35
120271	80
120272	40
120275	60
120660	100
120662	20
120663	5

Level 2

2. Examining the Descriptor and Data Portions

  a. Retrieve the starter program **p104e02**.

  b. After the DATA step, add a PROC CONTENTS step to display the descriptor portion of **work.newpacks**.

  c. Submit the program and answer the following questions:

    How many observations are in the data set?

    How many variables are in the data set?

    What is the length (byte-size) of the variable **Product_Name**?

  d. After the PROC CONTENTS step, add a PROC PRINT step with appropriate statements and options to display part of the data portion of **work.newpacks**.

  e. Submit the program to create the following PROC PRINT report:

```
Product_Name                                      Supplier_Name

Black/Black                                       Top Sports
X-Large Bottlegreen/Black                         Top Sports
Commanche Women's 6000 Q Backpack. Bark           Top Sports
Expedition Camp Duffle Medium Backpack            Miller Trading Inc
Feelgood 55-75 Litre Black Women's Backpack       Toto Outdoor Gear
Jaguar 50-75 Liter Blue Women's Backpack          Toto Outdoor Gear
Medium Black/Bark Backpack                        Top Sports
Medium Gold Black/Gold Backpack                   Top Sports
Medium Olive Olive/Black Backpack                 Top Sports
Trekker 65 Royal Men's Backpack                   Toto Outdoor Gear
Victor Grey/Olive Women's Backpack                Top Sports
Deer Backpack                                     Luna sastreria S.A.
Deer Waist Bag                                    Luna sastreria S.A.
Hammock Sports Bag                                Luna sastreria S.A.
Sioux Men's Backpack 26 Litre.                    Miller Trading Inc
```

Level 3

3. **Working with Times and Datetimes**

    a. Retrieve and submit the starter program **p104e03**.

    b. Notice the values of **CurrentTime** and **CurrentDateTime** in the PROC PRINT output.

    c. Use the Help facility to find documentation on how times and datetimes are stored in SAS.

        Go to the CONTENTS tab in the SAS Help and Documentation and select **SAS Products** ⇨ **Base SAS** ⇨ **SAS 9.2 Language Reference: Concepts** ⇨ **SAS System Concepts** ⇨ **Dates, Times, and Intervals** ⇨ **About SAS Date, Time, and Datetime Values**.

    d. Complete the following sentences:

        A SAS time value is a value representing the number of _____

        _____

        A SAS datetime value is a value representing the number of _____

        _____.

4.2 Accessing SAS Data Libraries

Objectives

- Explain the concept of a SAS data library.
- Assign a library reference name to a SAS data library by using the LIBNAME statement.
- State the difference between a permanent library and a temporary library.
- Browse the contents of a SAS data library by using the SAS Explorer window.
- Investigate a SAS data library by using the CONTENTS procedure.

36

SAS Data Libraries

A *SAS data library* is a collection of SAS files that are recognized as a unit by SAS.

Directory-based System	A SAS data library is a directory.
Windows Example: `s:\workshop`	
UNIX Example: `/users/userid`	

z/OS (OS/390)	A SAS data library is an operating system file.
z/OS (OS/390) Example: `userid.workshop.sasdata`	

37

SAS Data Libraries

You can think of a SAS data library as a drawer in a filing cabinet and a SAS data set as one of the file folders in the drawer.

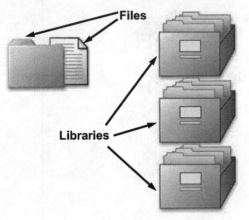

38

Assigning a Libref

Regardless of which host operating system you use, you identify SAS data libraries by assigning a *library reference name (libref)* to each library.

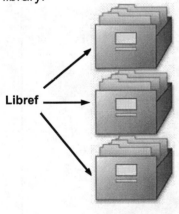

39

SAS Data Libraries

When a SAS session starts, SAS automatically creates
one temporary and at least one permanent SAS data
library that you can access.

work – temporary library

sasuser – permanent library

40

The **work** library and its SAS data files are deleted after your SAS session ends.

SAS data sets in permanent libraries such as the **sasuser** library are saved after
your SAS session ends.

SAS Data Libraries

You can also create and access your own permanent
libraries.

orion – permanent library

41

Assigning a Libref

You can use the *LIBNAME statement* to assign a library reference name (libref) to a SAS data library.

General form of the LIBNAME statement:

> **LIBNAME** *libref* '*SAS-data-library*' *<options>*;

Rules for naming a libref:

- The name must be 8 characters or less.
- The name must begin with a letter or underscore.
- The remaining characters must be letters, numbers, or underscores.

42

For Windows and UNIX, SAS can only make an association between a libref and an existing directory. The LIBNAME statement does not create a new directory.

z/OS (OS/390) users can use a DD statement or TSO ALLOCATE command instead of issuing a LIBNAME statement.

Assigning a Libref

Examples:

Windows

```
libname orion 's:\workshop';
```

UNIX

```
libname orion '/users/userid';
```

z/OS (OS/390)

```
libname orion 'userid.workshop.sasdata';
```

43

Making the Connection

When you submit the LIBNAME statement, a connection is made between a libref in SAS and the physical location of files on your operating system.

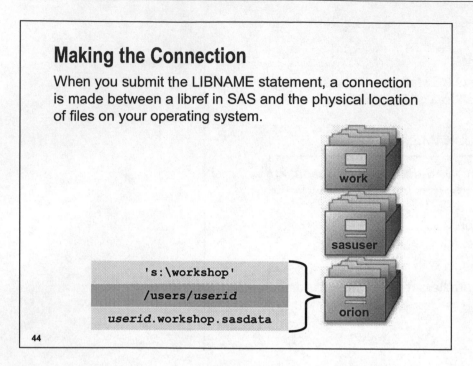

44

When your session ends, the link between the libref and the physical location of your files is broken.

4.05 Poll

During an interactive SAS session, every time you submit a program you must also resubmit the LIBNAME statement.

O True
O False

46

Two-Level SAS Filenames

Every SAS file has a two-level name: *libref.filename*

The data set **orion.sales** is a
SAS file in the **orion** library.

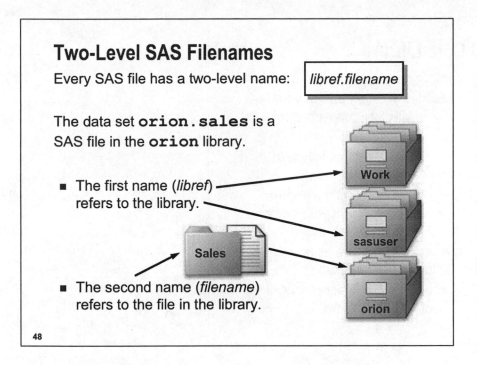

- The first name (*libref*)
  refers to the library.

- The second name (*filename*)
  refers to the file in the library.

48

Temporary SAS Filename

The default libref is **work** if the libref is omitted.

NewSalesEmps ⬌ work.NewSalesEmps

```
data NewSalesEmps;
    length First_Name $ 12
           Last_Name $ 18 Job_Title $ 25;
    infile 'newemps.csv' dlm=',';
    input First_Name $ Last_Name $
          Job_Title $ Salary;
run;

proc print data=work.NewSalesEmps;
run;
```

49

Browsing a SAS Data Library

The *SAS Explorer window* enables you to manage your files in the windowing environment.

In the SAS Explorer window, you can do the following:

- view a list of all the libraries available during your current SAS session
- navigate to see all members of a specific library
- display the descriptor portion of a SAS data set

50

The SAS windowing environment opens the Explorer window by default on many hosts. You can issue the EXPLORER command to invoke this window if it does not appear by default.

The SAS Explorer can be opened by selecting

- **View** ⇨ **Contents Only**

  or

- **View** ⇨ **Explorer**.

In the Contents Only view, the Explorer is a single-paned window that contains the contents of your SAS environment. As you open folders, the folder contents replace the previous contents in the same window.

In the Explorer view of the Explorer window, folders appear in the tree view on the left and folder contents appear in the list view on the right.

Browsing a SAS Data Library

The CONTENTS procedure with the _ALL_ keyword produces a list of all the SAS files in the data library.

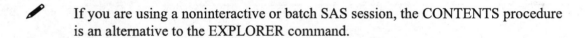

```
PROC CONTENTS DATA=libref._ALL_ NODS;
RUN;
```

- The NODS option suppresses the descriptor portions of the data sets.
- NODS is only used in conjunction with the keyword _ALL_.

51

If you are using a noninteractive or batch SAS session, the CONTENTS procedure is an alternative to the EXPLORER command.

Accessing and Browsing SAS Data Libraries – Windows

p104d04

1. Retrieve and submit the program **p104d04**.

```
libname orion 's:\workshop';

proc contents data=orion._all_ nods;
run;
```

2. Check the log to confirm that the **orion** libref was assigned.

```
1      libname orion 's:\workshop';
NOTE: Libref ORION was successfully assigned as follows:
      Engine:         V9
      Physical Name: s:\workshop
```

3. View the PROC CONTENTS output in the Output window.

Partial PROC CONTENTS Output

```
                       The CONTENTS Procedure


                           Directory


                    Libref        ORION
                    Engine        V9
                    Physical Name s:\workshop
                    File Name     s:\workshop



                              Member    File
         #  Name               Type     Size  Last Modified

         1  BUDGET             DATA      5120  12Feb08:00:57:25
         2  COUNTRY            DATA     17408  12Feb08:00:57:25
            COUNTRY            INDEX    17408  12Feb08:00:57:25
         3  CUSTOMER           DATA     33792  12Feb08:00:57:25
         4  CUSTOMER_DIM       DATA     33792  12Feb08:00:57:25
         5  CUSTOMER_TYPE      DATA     17408  12Feb08:00:57:25
            CUSTOMER_TYPE      INDEX     9216  12Feb08:00:57:25
         6  EMPLOYEE_ADDRESSES DATA     74752  12Feb08:00:57:25
         7  EMPLOYEE_DONATIONS DATA     25600  12Feb08:00:57:25
         8  EMPLOYEE_ORGANIZATION DATA  41984  12Feb08:00:57:25
         9  EMPLOYEE_PAYROLL   DATA     33792  12Feb08:00:57:25
        10  LOOKUP_COUNTRY     DATA     37888  12Feb08:00:57:25
        11  MNTH7_2007         DATA      5120  12Feb08:00:57:25
        12  MNTH8_2007         DATA      5120  12Feb08:00:57:25
        13  MNTH9_2007         DATA      5120  12Feb08:00:57:25
        14  NONSALES           DATA     33792  12Feb08:00:57:25
```

4. Select the Explorer tab on the SAS window bar to activate the SAS Explorer window or select **View** ⇨ **Contents Only**.

5. Double-click on **Libraries** to show all available libraries.

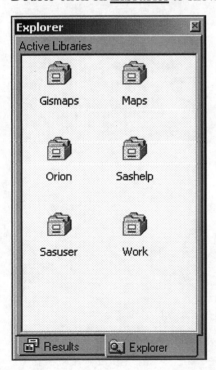

6. Double-click on the **Orion** library to show all members of that library.

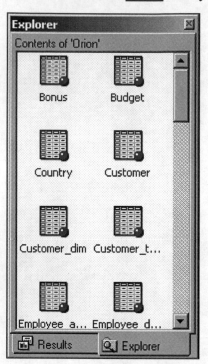

7. Right-click on the **Sales** data set and select **Properties**.

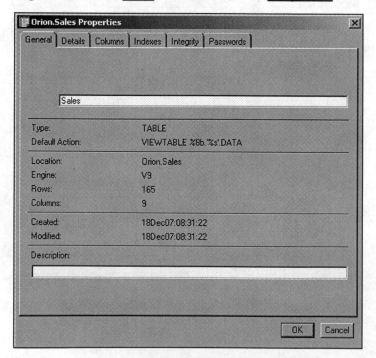

This default view provides general information about the data set, such as the library in which it is stored, the type of information it contains, its creation date, the number of observations and variables, and so on. You can request specific information about the columns in the data table by selecting the **Columns** tab at the top of the Properties window.

8. Select ☒ to close the Properties window.

9. Double-click on the **Sales** data set or right-click on the file and select **Open**.

   This opens the data set in a VIEWTABLE window. A view of `orion.sales` is shown below.

	Employee_ID	First_Name	Last_Name	Gender	Salary	Job_Title	Country	Birth_Date
1	120102	Tom	Zhou	M	108255	Sales Manager	AU	3510
2	120103	Wilson	Dawes	M	87975	Sales Manager	AU	-3998
3	120121	Irenie	Elvish	F	26600	Sales Rep. II	AU	-5630
4	120122	Christina	Ngan	F	27475	Sales Rep. II	AU	-1984
5	120123	Kimiko	Hotstone	F	26190	Sales Rep. I	AU	1732
6	120124	Lucian	Daymond	M	26480	Sales Rep. I	AU	-233
7	120125	Fong	Hofmeister	M	32040	Sales Rep. IV	AU	-1852
8	120126	Satyakam	Denny	M	26780	Sales Rep. II	AU	10490
9	120127	Sharryn	Clarkson	F	28100	Sales Rep. II	AU	6943
10	120128	Monica	Kletschkus	F	30890	Sales Rep. IV	AU	9691
11	120129	Alvin	Roebuck	M	30070	Sales Rep. III	AU	1787
12	120130	Kevin	Lyon	M	26955	Sales Rep. I	AU	9114
13	120131	Marinus	Surawski	M	26910	Sales Rep. I	AU	7207
14	120132	Fancine	Kaiser	F	28525	Sales Rep. III	AU	-3923
15	120133	Petrea	Soltau	F	27440	Sales Rep. II	AU	9608
16	120134	Sian	Shannan	M	28015	Sales Rep. II	AU	-3861
17	120135	Alexei	Platts	M	32490	Sales Rep. IV	AU	3313
18	120136	Atul	Leyden	M	26605	Sales Rep. I	AU	7198
19	120137	Marina	Iyengar	F	29715	Sales Rep. III	AU	7010
20	120138	Shani	Duckett	F	25795	Sales Rep. I	AU	7131
21	120139	Fang	Wilson	F	26810	Sales Rep. II	AU	9726
22	120140	Michael	Minas	M	26970	Sales Rep. I	AU	10442
23	120141	Amanda	Liebman	F	27465	Sales Rep. II	AU	10298
24	120142	Vincent	Eastley	M	29695	Sales Rep. III	AU	9661
25	120143	Phu	Sloey	M	26790	Sales Rep. II	AU	-229
26	120144	Viney	Barbis	M	30265	Sales Rep. III	AU	9562
27	120145	Sandy	Aisbitt	M	26060	Sales Rep. II	AU	1482
28	120146	Wendall	Cederlund	M	25985	Sales Rep. I	AU	-91
29	120147	Skev	Rusli	F	26580	Sales Rep. II	AU	10245
30	120148	Michael	Zubak	M	28480	Sales Rep. III	AU	-3762
31	120149	Judy	Chantharasy	F	26390	Sales Rep. I	AU	5438
32	120150	John	Filo	M	29965	Sales Rep. III	AU	-2002
33	120151	Julianna	Phaiuakounh	F	26520	Sales Rep. II	AU	-5515

In addition to browsing SAS data sets, you can use the VIEWTABLE window to edit data sets, create data sets, and customize your view of a SAS data set. For example, you can do the following:

- sort your data
- change the color and fonts of variables
- display variable labels versus variable names
- remove and add variables

Variable labels are displayed by default. Display variable names instead of variable labels by selecting **View** ⇨ **Column Names**.

10. Select ☒ to close the VIEWTABLE window.

11. With the Explorer window active, select ⬆ to return to **Libraries**.

Accessing and Browsing SAS Data Libraries – UNIX

p104d04

1. Retrieve and submit the program **p104d04**.

```
libname orion '/users/userid';

proc contents data=orion._all_ nods;
run;
```

2. Check the log to confirm that the **orion** libref was assigned.

3. View the PROC CONTENTS output in the Output window.

4. Select **View** ⇨ **Contents Only** to activate the SAS Explorer window.

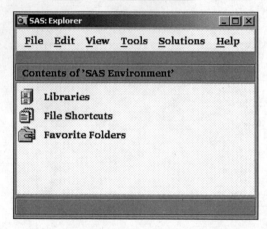

5. Double-click on **Libraries** to show all available libraries.

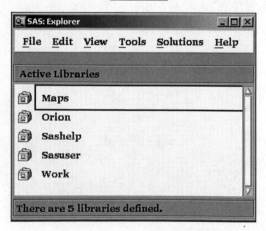

6. Double-click on the **<u>Orion</u>** library to show all members of that library.

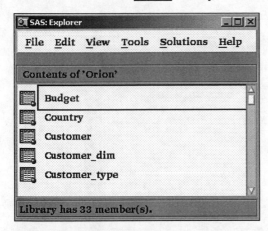

7. Right-click on the **<u>Sales</u>** data set and select **<u>Properties</u>**.

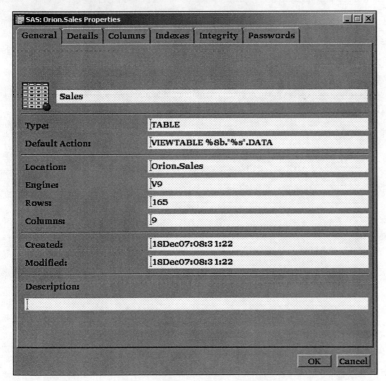

8. Select ☒ to close the Properties window.

9. Double-click on the **Sales** data set or right-click on the file and select **Open**.

    This opens the data set in a VIEWTABLE window. A view of `orion.sales` is shown below.

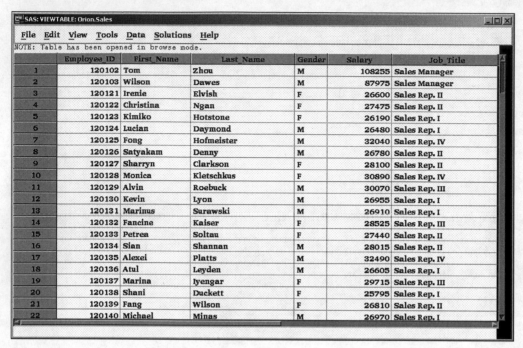

10. Select ✖ to close the VIEWTABLE window.

11. With the Explorer window active, select ⬆ on the Toolbox to return to **Libraries**.

Accessing and Browsing SAS Data Libraries – z/OS (OS/390)

.workshop.sascode(p104d04)

1. Retrieve and submit the program **p104d04**.

```
libname orion '.workshop.sasdata';

proc contents data=orion._all_ nods;
run;
```

2. Check the log to confirm that the **orion** libref was assigned.

3. View the PROC CONTENTS output in the Output window.

4. Type **explorer** on the command line and press ENTER to activate the SAS Explorer window.

5. Type **s** beside `Orion` and press ENTER to show all members of that library.

6. Type **s** beside **Sales** and press ENTER to display the properties.

7. Select **OK** to close the Properties window.

8. Type **?** beside `Sales` and press ENTER.

9. Select **Open** to open FSVIEW window.

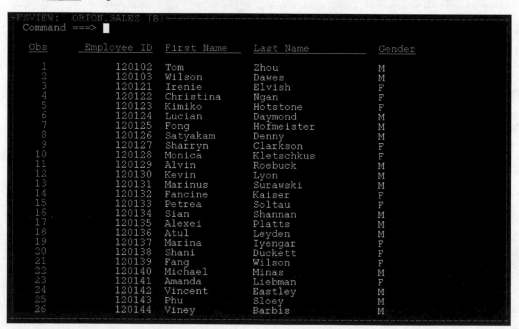

10. Type **end** to close FSVIEW window.

11. Type **end** to close SAS Explorer window.

 **Exercises**

Level 1

4. Accessing a SAS Data Library

   a. Write and submit the appropriate LIBNAME statement to provide access to the **orion** libref.

> Fill in the blank with the location of your SAS data library.
>
> **libname orion '_____';**

Possible location of your SAS data library:

Windows	**s:\workshop**
UNIX	**/users/userid**
z/OS (OS/390)	**.workshop.sasdata**

   b. Check the log to confirm that the SAS data library was assigned.

> NOTE: Libref ORION was successfully assigned as follows:

   c. Add a PROC CONTENTS step to list all the SAS data sets in the **orion** library. Do not display the descriptor portions of the individual data sets.

   d. Add another PROC CONTENTS step to display the descriptor portion of the data set **orion.sales**.

   e. Use the EXPLORER window to view the contents of the **orion** library.

Level 2

5. Reviewing Concepts

   a. SAS statements usually begin with a(n) _____.

   b. Every SAS statement ends with a _____.

   c. The descriptor portion of a SAS data set can be viewed using the _____ procedure.

   d. Character variable values can be up to _____ characters long and use _____ byte(s) of storage per character.

   e. By default, numeric variables are stored in _____ bytes of storage.

   f. The internally stored SAS date value for January 3, 1960, is _____.

g. A SAS variable name has _____ to _____ characters and begins with a

_____ or an _____ .

h. A missing character value is displayed as a _____ .

i. A missing numeric value is displayed as a _____ .

j. When a SAS session starts, SAS automatically creates the temporary library called _____ .

k. A libref name must be _____ characters or less.

l. What are the two kinds of steps?

m. What are the three primary windows in the SAS windowing environment?

n. What are the two portions of every SAS data set?

o. What are the two types of variables?

p. True or False: If a SAS program produces output, then the program ran successfully and there is
    no need to check the SAS log.

q. True or False: There are two methods for commenting in a SAS program.

r. True or False: Omitting a semicolon never causes errors.

s. True or False: A library reference name (libref) references a particular data set.

t. True or False: If a data set is referenced with a one level name, **work** is the implied libref.

u. True or False: The _ALL_ keyword is used with the PRINT procedure.

Level 3

6. **Investigating the LIBNAME Statement**

    a. Use the Help facility to find documentation on the LIBNAME statement.

        Go to the CONTENTS tab in the SAS Help and Documentation and select
        SAS Products ⇨ **Base SAS** ⇨ **SAS 9.2 Language Reference: Dictionary** ⇨
        Dictionary of Language Elements ⇨ **Statements** ⇨ **LIBNAME Statement**.

    b. Answer the following questions:

        What argument disassociates one or more currently assigned librefs?

        What system option allows you the convenience of specifying only a one-level name for
        permanent SAS files?

    c. Write and submit a LIBNAME statement that shows the attributes of all currently assigned
        SAS libraries in the SAS log.

4.3   Accessing Relational Databases (Self-Study)

Objectives

- Assign a library reference name to a relational database by using the LIBNAME statement.
- Reference a relational database table using a SAS two-level name.

62

The LIBNAME Statement (Review)

The *LIBNAME statement* assigns a library reference name (libref) to a SAS data library.

General form of the LIBNAME statement:

> **LIBNAME** *libref* '*SAS-data-library*' <*options*>;

63

The SAS/ACCESS LIBNAME Statement

The *SAS/ACCESS LIBNAME statement* assigns a library reference name (libref) to a relational database.

General form of the SAS/ACCESS LIBNAME statement:

> **LIBNAME** *libref engine-name <SAS/ACCESS-options>*;

After a database is associated with a libref, you can use a SAS two-level name to specify any table in the database and then work with the table as you would with a SAS data set.

64

The SAS/ACCESS interface to relational databases is a family of interfaces (each of which is licensed separately) that enable you to interact with data in other vendors' databases from within SAS.

The *engine-name* such as Oracle or DB2 is the SAS/ACCESS component that reads from and writes to your DBMS. The engine name is required. Because the SAS/ACCESS LIBNAME statement associates a libref with a SAS/ACCESS engine that supports connections to a particular DBMS, it requires a DBMS-specific engine name.

Oracle Example

This example uses the LIBNAME statement as supported in the SAS/ACCESS interface to Oracle.

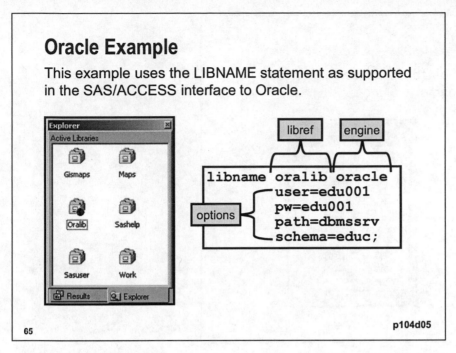

p104d05

USER= specifies an optional Oracle user name. If the user name contains blanks or national characters, enclose it in quotation marks. USER= must be used with PASSWORD=.

PASSWORD= or *PW=* specifies an optional Oracle password that is associated with the Oracle user name.

PATH= specifies the Oracle driver, node, and database. SAS/ACCESS uses the same Oracle path designation that you use to connect to Oracle directly. See your database administrator to determine the databases that have been set up in your operating environment, and to determine the default values if you do not specify a database.

SCHEMA= enables you to read database objects, such as tables and views, in the specified schema. If this option is omitted, you connect to the default schema for your DBMS. The values for SCHEMA= are usually case-sensitive, so use care when you specify this option.

Oracle Example

Any table in this Oracle database can be referenced using a SAS two-level name.

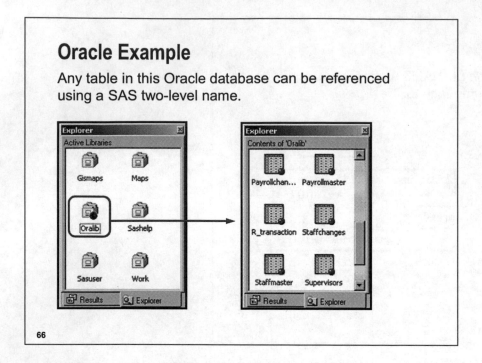

66

Oracle Example

```
libname oralib oracle
        user=edu001 pw=edu001
        path=dbmssrv schema=educ;

proc print data=oralib.supervisors;
run;

data work.staffpay;
   merge oralib.staffmaster
         oralib.payrollmaster;
   by empid;
run;

libname oralib clear;
```

67   p104d05

The CLEAR option in the LIBNAME statement disassociates the libref. Disassociating the libref disconnects the database engine from the database and closes any resources that are associated with that libref's connection.

4.06 Quiz

Which option in the LIBNAME statement specifies a
user's password when accessing an Informix database?

Documentation on SAS/ACCESS for Informix can be found
in the SAS Help and Documentation from the Contents tab
(**SAS Products** ⇨ **SAS/ACCESS** ⇨
SAS/ACCESS 9.2 for Relational Databases Reference ⇨
DBMS-Specific Reference ⇨
SAS/ACCESS for Informix ⇨
LIBNAME Statement Specifics for Informix).

69

4.4 Solutions

Solutions to Exercises

1. **Examining the Data Portion**

   a. Retrieve the starter program.

   b. After the PROC CONTENTS step, add a PROC PRINT step.

```
data work.donations;
   infile 'donation.dat';
   input Employee_ID Qtr1 Qtr2 Qtr3 Qtr4;
   Total=sum(Qtr1,Qtr2,Qtr3,Qtr4);
run;

proc contents data=work.donations;
run;

proc print data=work.donations;
run;
```

   c. Submit the program.

   d. In the PROC PRINT step, add a VAR statement and the NOOBS option.

```
proc print data=work.donations noobs;
   var Employee_ID Total;
run;
```

   e. Submit the program.

2. **Examining the Descriptor and Data Portions**

   a. Retrieve the starter program.

   b. After the DATA step, add a PROC CONTENTS step.

```
data work.newpacks;
   input Supplier_Name $ 1-20 Supplier_Country $ 23-24
         Product_Name $ 28-70;
   datalines;
Top Sports            DK      Black/Black
Top Sports            DK      X-Large Bottlegreen/Black
Top Sports            DK      Commanche Women's 6000 Q Backpack. Bark
Miller Trading Inc    US      Expedition Camp Duffle Medium Backpack
Toto Outdoor Gear     AU      Feelgood 55-75 Litre Black Women's Backpack
Toto Outdoor Gear     AU      Jaguar 50-75 Liter Blue Women's Backpack
Top Sports            DK      Medium Black/Bark Backpack
Top Sports            DK      Medium Gold Black/Gold Backpack
Top Sports            DK      Medium Olive Olive/Black Backpack
Toto Outdoor Gear     AU      Trekker 65 Royal Men's Backpack
Top Sports            DK      Victor Grey/Olive Women's Backpack
Luna sastreria S.A.   ES      Deer Backpack
```

```
Luna sastreria S.A.    ES    Deer Waist Bag
Luna sastreria S.A.    ES    Hammock Sports Bag
Miller Trading Inc     US    Sioux Men's Backpack 26 Litre.
;
run;


proc contents data=work.newpacks;
run;
```

    c. Submit the program and answer the following questions:

       How many observations are in the data set? **15**

       How many variables are in the data set? **3**

       What is the length (byte-size) of the variable **Product_Name**? **43**

    d. After the PROC CONTENTS step, add a PROC PRINT step.

```
proc print data=work.newpacks noobs;
   var Product_Name Supplier_Name;
run;
```

    e. Submit the program.

3. Working with Times and Datetimes

    a. Retrieve and submit the starter program.

    b. Notice the values of **CurrentTime** and **CurrentDateTime** in the PROC PRINT output.

    c. Use the Help facility to find documentation on how times and datetimes are stored in SAS.

    d. Complete the following sentences:

       A SAS time value is a value representing the number of **seconds since midnight of the current day**.

       A SAS datetime value is a value representing the number of **seconds between January 1, 1960 and an hour/minute/second within a specified date**.

4. Accessing a SAS Data Library

    a. Write and submit the appropriate LIBNAME statement.

```
libname orion 'SAS-data-library';
```

    b. Check the log to confirm that the SAS data library was assigned.

    c. Add a PROC CONTENTS step to list all the SAS data sets in the **orion** library.

```
proc contents data=orion._all_ nods;
run;
```

    d. Add another PROC CONTENTS step to display the descriptor portion of **orion.sales**.

```
proc contents data=orion.sales;
run;
```

e. Use the EXPLORER window to view the contents of the **orion** library.

5. **Reviewing Concepts**

a. SAS statements usually begin with an **identifying keyword**.

b. Every SAS statement ends with a **semicolon**.

c. The descriptor portion of a SAS data set can be viewed using the **CONTENTS** procedure.

d. Character variable values can be up to **32,767** characters long and use **1** byte(s) of storage per character.

e. By default, numeric variables are stored in **8** bytes of storage.

f. The internally stored SAS date value for January 3, 1960, is **2**.

g. A SAS variable name has **1** to **32** characters and begins with a **letter** or an **underscore**.

h. A missing character value is displayed as a **blank**.

i. A missing numeric value is displayed as a **period**.

j. When a SAS session starts, SAS automatically creates the temporary library called **work**.

k. A libref name must be **8** characters or less.

l. What are the two kinds of steps? **DATA and PROC**

m. What are the three primary windows in the SAS windowing environment? **Editor, Log, and Output**

n. What are the two portions of every SAS data set? **Descriptor and Data**

o. What are the two types of variables? **Character and Numeric**

p. True or False: If a SAS program produces output, then the program ran successfully and there is no need to check the SAS log. **False**

q. True or False: There are two methods for commenting in a SAS program. **True**

r. True or False: Omitting a semicolon never causes errors. **False**

s. True or False: A library reference name (libref) references a particular data set. **False**

t. True or False: If a data set is referenced with a one level name, **work** is the implied libref. **True**

u. True or False: The _ALL_ keyword is used with the PRINT procedure. **False**

6. Investigating the LIBNAME Statement

   a. Use the Help facility.

   b. Answer the following questions:

      What argument disassociates one or more currently assigned librefs? **<u>CLEAR</u>**

      What system option allows you the convenience of specifying only a one-level name for permanent SAS files? **<u>USER=</u>**

   c. Write and submit a LIBNAME statement.

```
libname _all_ list;
```

Solutions to Student Activities (Polls/Quizzes)

4.01 Quiz – Correct Answer

How many observations are in the data set
work.donations?

124 observations

```
data work.donations;
    infile 'donation.dat';
    input Employee_ID Qtr1 Qtr2 Qtr3 Qtr4;
    Total=sum(Qtr1,Qtr2,Qtr3,Qtr4);
run;

proc contents data=work.donations;
run;
```

10   p104a01s

4.02 Multiple Choice Poll – Correct Answer

Which variable type do you think SAS uses to store date
values?

  a. character
  (b.) numeric

15

4.03 Quiz – Correct Answer

What is the numeric value for today's date?
The answer depends on the current date.

Example:

If the current date is February 1, 2008, the numeric value is 17563.

21

4.04 Multiple Answer Poll – Correct Answer

Which variable names are valid?

(a.) data5mon
 b. 5monthsdata
 c. data#5
 d. five months data
(e.) five_months_data
(f.) FiveMonthsData

26

4.05 Poll – Correct Answer

During an interactive SAS session, every time you submit a program you must also resubmit the LIBNAME statement.

○ True
False

The LIBNAME statement remains in effect until canceled, changed, or your SAS session ends.

47

4.06 Quiz – Correct Answer

Which option in the LIBNAME statement specifies a user's password when accessing an Informix database?

The USING= option specifies the password that is associated with the Informix user. USING= can also be specified with the PASSWORD= and PWD= aliases.

70

Chapter 5   Reading SAS Data Sets

5.1 Introduction to Reading Data

Objectives

- Define the concept of reading from a data source to create a SAS data set.
- Define the business scenario that will be used when reading from a SAS data set, an Excel worksheet, and a raw data file.

3

Business Scenario

An existing data source contains information on Orion Star sales employees from Australia and the United States.

A new SAS data set needs to be created that contains a subset of this existing data source.

This new SAS data set must contain the following:

- only the employees from Australia who are Sales Representatives
- the employee's first name, last name, salary, job title, and hired date
- labels and formats in the descriptor portion

4

Business Scenario

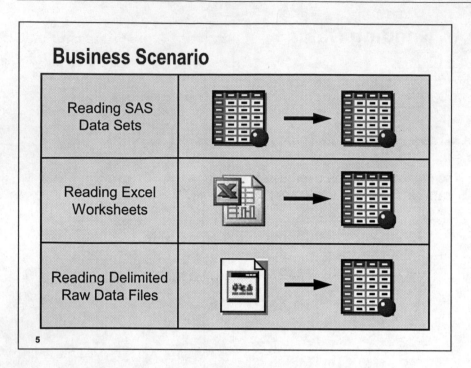

Reading SAS Data Sets	
Reading Excel Worksheets	
Reading Delimited Raw Data Files	

5

Three different input data sources are used to create the new SAS data set.

First, a SAS data set is used as the input data source.

Second, an Excel workbook is used as the input data source.

Third, a raw data file is used as the input data source.

The DATA Statement

The *DATA statement* begins a DATA step and provides the name of the SAS data set being created.

```
LIBNAME libref 'SAS-data-library';

DATA output-SAS-data-set;
    SET input-SAS-data-set;
    <additional SAS statements>
RUN;
```

The DATA statement can create temporary or permanent data sets.

16

The SET Statement

The *SET statement* reads observations from a SAS data set for further processing in the DATA step.

```
LIBNAME libref 'SAS-data-library';

DATA output-SAS-data-set;
    SET input-SAS-data-set;
    <additional SAS statements>
RUN;
```

- By default, the SET statement reads all observations and all variables from the input data set.
- The SET statement can read temporary or permanent data sets.

17

Business Scenario Part 1

Create a temporary SAS data set named **work.subset1**
from the permanent SAS data set named **orion.sales**.

```
libname orion 's:\workshop';

data work.subset1;
   set orion.sales;
run;
```

Partial SAS Log

```
9    data work.subset1;
10     set orion.sales;
11   run;
```

> Both data sets contain 165
> observations and 9 variables

```
NOTE: There were 165 observations read from the data set ORION.SALES.
NOTE: The data set WORK.SUBSET1 has 165 observations and 9 variables.
```

18   p105d01

The LIBNAME statement needs to reference a SAS data library specific to your operating environment.

For example:

Windows	`libname orion 's:\workshop';`
UNIX	`libname orion '/users/userid';`
z/OS (OS/390)	`libname orion '.workshop.sasdata';`

Business Scenario Part 1

```
proc print data=work.subset1;
run;
```

Partial PROC PRINT Output

Obs	Employee_ID	First_ Name	Last_Name	Gender	Salary	Job_Title	Country	Birth_ Date	Hire_ Date
1	120102	Tom	Zhou	M	108255	Sales Manager	AU	3510	10744
2	120103	Wilson	Dawes	M	87975	Sales Manager	AU	-3996	5114
3	120121	Irenie	Elvish	F	26600	Sales Rep. II	AU	-5630	5114
4	120122	Christina	Ngan	F	27475	Sales Rep. II	AU	-1984	6756
5	120123	Kimiko	Hotstone	F	26190	Sales Rep. I	AU	1732	9405
6	120124	Lucian	Daymond	M	26480	Sales Rep. I	AU	-233	6999
7	120125	Fong	Hofmeister	M	32040	Sales Rep. IV	AU	-1852	6999
8	120126	Satyakam	Denny	M	26780	Sales Rep. II	AU	10490	17014
9	120127	Sharryn	Clarkson	F	28100	Sales Rep. II	AU	6943	14184
10	120128	Monica	Kletschkus	F	30890	Sales Rep. IV	AU	9691	17106
11	120129	Alvin	Roebuck	M	30070	Sales Rep. III	AU	1787	9405
12	120130	Kevin	Lyon	M	26955	Sales Rep. I	AU	9114	16922
13	120131	Marinus	Surawski	M	26910	Sales Rep. I	AU	7207	15706
14	120132	Fancine	Kaiser	F	28525	Sales Rep. III	AU	-3923	6848
15	120133	Petrea	Soltau	F	27440	Sales Rep. II	AU	9608	17075

19   p105d01

Setup for the Poll

- Retrieve program **p105a01**.
- Submit the program and confirm that a new SAS data set was created with 77 observations and 12 variables.

21

5.02 Poll

The DATA step reads a temporary SAS data set to create a permanent SAS data set.

O True
O False

22

5.3 Subsetting Observations and Variables

Objectives

- Subset observations by using the WHERE statement.
- Subset variables by using the DROP and KEEP statements.

26

Business Scenario Syntax

Use the following statements to complete the scenario:

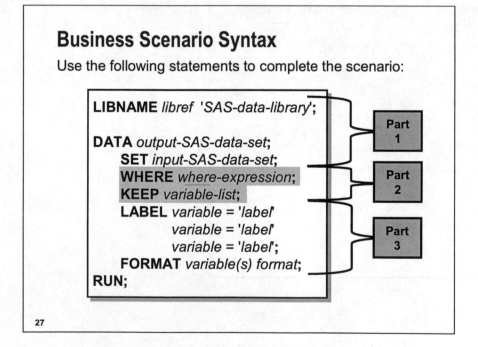

27

Subsetting Observations and Variables

By default, the SET statement reads **all observations** and **all variables** from the input data set.

```
9     data work.subset1;
10       set orion.sales;
11    run;

NOTE: There were 165 observations read from the data set ORION.SALES.
NOTE: The data set WORK.SUBSET1 has 165 observations and 9 variables.
```

By adding statements to the DATA step, the observations and variables can be reduced.

```
NOTE: The data set WORK.SUBSET1 has 61 observations and 5 variables.
```

28

The WHERE Statement

The *WHERE statement* subsets observations that meet a particular condition.

General form of the WHERE statement:

WHERE *where-expression* ;

The *where-expression* is a sequence of operands and operators that form a set of instructions that define a condition for selecting observations.

- Operands include constants and variables.
- Operators are symbols that request a comparison, arithmetic calculation, or logical operation.

29

Operands

A *constant operand* is a fixed value.

- Character values must be enclosed in quotation marks and are case sensitive.
- Numeric values do not use quotation marks.

A *variable operand* must be a variable coming from an input data set.

Examples:

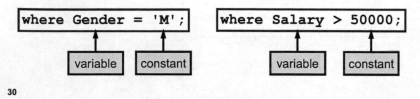

30

Comparison Operators

Comparison operators compare a variable with a value or with another variable.

Symbol	Mnemonic	Definition
=	EQ	equal to
^= ¬= ~=	NE	not equal to
>	GT	greater than
<	LT	less than
>=	GE	greater than or equal
<=	LE	less than or equal
	IN	equal to one of a list

31

Comparison Operators

Examples:

```
where Gender = 'M';
```

```
where Gender eq ' ';
```

```
where Salary ne .;
```

```
where Salary >= 50000;
```

```
where Country in ('AU','US');
```

```
where Country in ('AU' 'US');
```

> values must be separated by commas or blanks

32

Arithmetic Operators

Arithmetic operators indicate that an arithmetic calculation is performed.

Symbol	Definition
**	exponentiation
*	multiplication
/	division
+	addition
-	subtraction

33

Arithmetic Operators

Examples:

```
where Salary / 12 < 6000;
```

```
where Salary / 12 * 1.10 >= 7500;
```

```
where (Salary / 12 ) * 1.10 >= 7500;
```

```
where Salary + Bonus <= 10000;
```

34

Logical Operators

Logical operators combine or modify expressions.

Symbol	Mnemonic	Definition
&	AND	logical and
|	OR	logical or
^ ¬ ~	NOT	logical not

35

Logical Operators

Examples:

```
where Gender ne 'M' and Salary >=50000;
```

```
where Gender ne 'M' or Salary >= 50000;
```

```
where Country = 'AU' or Country = 'US';
```

```
where Country not in ('AU' 'US');
```

36

5.03 Quiz

Which WHERE statement correctly subsets for numeric months May, June, or July and character names with a missing value?

a.
```
where Months in (5-7)
      and Names = .;
```

b.
```
where Months in (5,6,7)
      and Names = ' ';
```

c.
```
where Months in ('5','6','7')
      and Names = '.';
```

38

Special WHERE Operators

Special WHERE operators are operators that can only be used in a where-expression.

Symbol	Mnemonic	Definition
	BETWEEN-AND	an inclusive range
	IS NULL	missing value
	IS MISSING	missing value
?	CONTAINS	a character string
	LIKE	a character pattern

40

BETWEEN-AND Operator

The *BETWEEN-AND operator* selects observations in which the value of a variable falls within an inclusive range of values.

Examples:

```
where salary between 50000 and 100000;
```

```
where salary not between 50000 and 100000;
```

Equivalent Expressions:

```
where salary between 50000 and 100000;
```

```
where 50000 <= salary <= 100000;
```

41

IS NULL and IS MISSING Operators

The *IS NULL* and *IS MISSING operators* select observations in which the value of a variable is missing.

- The operator can be used for both character and numeric variables.
- You can combine the NOT logical operator with IS NULL or IS MISSING to select nonmissing values.

Examples:

```
where Employee_ID is null;
```

```
where Employee_ID is missing;
```

42

CONTAINS Operator

The *CONTAINS (?) operator* selects observations that include the specified substring.

- The position of the substring within the variable's values does not matter.
- The operator is case sensitive when making comparisons.

Example:

```
where Job_Title contains 'Rep';
```

43

5.04 Quiz

Which value will not be returned based on the WHERE statement?

a. Office Rep
b. Sales Rep. IV
c. service rep III
d. Representative

```
where Job_Title contains 'Rep';
```

45

LIKE Operator

The *LIKE operator* selects observations by comparing character values to specified patterns.

There are two special characters available for specifying a pattern:

- A percent sign (%) replaces any number of characters.
- An underscore (_) replaces one character.

Consecutive underscores can be specified.

A percent sign and an underscore can be specified in the same pattern.

The operator is case sensitive.

47

LIKE Operator

Examples:

```
where Name like '%N';
```

This WHERE statement selects observations that begin with any number of characters and end with an N.

```
where Name like 'T_M%';
```

This WHERE statement selects observations that begin with a T, followed by a single character, followed by an M, followed by any number of characters.

48

Starting in SAS 9.2, the LIKE operator supports an escape character, which enables you to search for the percent sign (%) and the underscore (_) characters in values.

An escape character is a single character that in a sequence of characters signifies that what is to follow takes an alternative meaning. For the LIKE operator, an escape character signifies to search for literal instances of the % and _ characters in the variable's values instead of performing the special-character function.

To specify an escape character, you include the character in the pattern-matching expression and then the keyword ESCAPE followed by the escape character expression. When you include an escape character, the pattern-matching expression must be enclosed in quotation marks and it cannot contain a column name. The escape character expression is an expression that evaluates to a single character. The operands must be character or string literals. If it is a single character, it must be enclosed in quotation marks.

For example, if the variable X contains the values abc, a_b, and axb, the following LIKE operator using an escape character selects only the value a_b. The escape character (/) specifies that the pattern search for a literal '_' instead of matching the character b:

```
where x like 'a/_b' escape '/';
```

Without an escape character, the following LIKE operator would select the values a_b and axb. The special character underscore in the search pattern matches any single b character, including the value with the underscore:

```
where x like 'a_b';
```

5.05 Quiz

Which WHERE statement will return the observations that have a first name starting with the letter M for the given values?

a. ```
where Name like '_, M_';
```

b. ```
where Name like '%, M%';
```

c. ```
where Name like '_, M%';
```

d. ```
where Name like '%, M_';
```

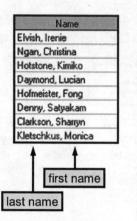

Name
Elvish, Irenie
Ngan, Christina
Hotstone, Kimiko
Daymond, Lucian
Hofmeister, Fong
Denny, Satyakam
Clarkson, Sharryn
Kletschkus, Monica

first name

last name

50

Business Scenario Part 2

Include only the employees from Australia who have the word *Rep* in their job title.

```
data work.subset1;
   set orion.sales;
   where Country='AU' and
         Job_Title contains 'Rep';
run;
```

Partial SAS Log

```
NOTE: There were 61 observations read from the data set ORION.SALES.
      WHERE (Country='AU') and Job_Title contains 'Rep';
NOTE: The data set WORK.SUBSET1 has 61 observations and 9 variables.
```

52

p105d02

Business Scenario Part 2

```
proc print data=work.subset1;
run;
```

Partial PROC PRINT Output

Obs	Employee_ID	First_Name	Last_Name	Gender	Salary	Job_Title	Country	Birth_Date	Hire_Date
1	120121	Irenie	Elvish	F	26600	Sales Rep. II	AU	-5630	5114
2	120122	Christina	Ngan	F	27475	Sales Rep. II	AU	-1984	6756
3	120123	Kimiko	Hotstone	F	26190	Sales Rep. I	AU	1732	9405
4	120124	Lucian	Daymond	M	26480	Sales Rep. I	AU	-233	6999
5	120125	Fong	Hofmeister	M	32040	Sales Rep. IV	AU	-1852	6999
6	120126	Satyakam	Denny	M	26780	Sales Rep. II	AU	10490	17014
7	120127	Sharryn	Clarkson	F	28100	Sales Rep. II	AU	6943	14184
8	120128	Monica	Kletschkus	F	30890	Sales Rep. IV	AU	9691	17106
9	120129	Alvin	Roebuck	M	30070	Sales Rep. III	AU	1787	9405
10	120130	Kevin	Lyon	M	26955	Sales Rep. I	AU	9114	16922
11	120131	Marinus	Surawski	M	26910	Sales Rep. I	AU	7207	15706
12	120132	Fancine	Kaiser	F	28525	Sales Rep. III	AU	-3923	6848
13	120133	Petrea	Soltau	F	27440	Sales Rep. II	AU	9608	17075
14	120134	Sian	Shannan	M	28015	Sales Rep. II	AU	-3861	5114
15	120135	Alexei	Platts	M	32490	Sales Rep. IV	AU	3313	13788

53   p105d02

The DROP and KEEP Statements

The *DROP statement* specifies the names of the variables to omit from the output data set(s).

DROP *variable-list* ;

The *KEEP statement* specifies the names of the variable to write to the output data set(s).

KEEP *variable-list* ;

The *variable-list* specifies the variables to drop or keep, respectively, in the output data set.

55

The DROP and KEEP Statements

Examples:

```
drop Employee_ID Gender
     Country Birth_Date;
```

```
keep First_Name Last_Name
     Salary Job_Title
     Hire_Date;
```

56

Business Scenario Part 2

Include only the employee's first name, last name, salary, job title, and hired date in the data set **work.subset1**.

```
data work.subset1;
   set orion.sales;
   where Country='AU' and
         Job_Title contains 'Rep';
   keep First_Name Last_Name Salary
        Job_Title Hire_Date;
run;
```

Partial SAS Log

```
NOTE: There were 61 observations read from the data set ORION.SALES.
      WHERE (Country='AU') and Job_Title contains 'Rep';
NOTE: The data set WORK.SUBSET1 has 61 observations and 5 variables.
```

57   p105d03

Business Scenario Part 2

```
proc print data=work.subset1;
run;
```

Partial PROC PRINT Output

Obs	First_ Name	Last_Name	Salary	Job_Title	Hire_ Date
1	Irenie	Elvish	26600	Sales Rep. II	5114
2	Christina	Ngan	27475	Sales Rep. II	6756
3	Kimiko	Hotstone	26190	Sales Rep. I	9405
4	Lucian	Daymond	26480	Sales Rep. I	6999
5	Fong	Hofmeister	32040	Sales Rep. IV	6999
6	Satyakam	Denny	26780	Sales Rep. II	17014
7	Sharryn	Clarkson	28100	Sales Rep. II	14184
8	Monica	Kletschkus	30890	Sales Rep. IV	17106
9	Alvin	Roebuck	30070	Sales Rep. III	9405
10	Kevin	Lyon	26955	Sales Rep. I	16922
11	Marinus	Surawski	26910	Sales Rep. I	15706
12	Fancine	Kaiser	28525	Sales Rep. III	6848

58

p105d03

 **Exercises**

Level 1

1. Subsetting Observations and Variables Using the WHERE and KEEP Statements

   a. Retrieve and submit the starter program **p105e01**.

      What is the variable name that contains gender values?

      What are the two possible gender values?

   b. Add a DATA step before the PROC PRINT step to read the data set **orion.customer_dim** to create a new data set called **work.youngadult**.

   c. Modify the PROC PRINT step to refer to the new data set.

   d. Submit the program and confirm that **work.youngadult** was created with 77 observations and 11 variables.

   e. Add a WHERE statement to the DATA step to subset for female customers.

   f. Submit the program and confirm that **work.youngadult** was created with 30 observations and 11 variables.

   g. Modify the WHERE statement to subset for female customers whose **Customer_Age** is between 18 and 36.

   h. Submit the program and confirm that **work.youngadult** was created with 15 observations and 11 variables.

   i. Modify the WHERE statement to subset for female 18- to 36-year-old customers who have the word Gold in their **Customer_Group**.

   j. Submit the program and confirm that **work.youngadult** was created with 5 observations and 11 variables.

   k. Modify the DATA step so that **work.youngadult** contains only **Customer_Name**, **Customer_Age**, **Customer_BirthDate**, **Customer_Gender**, and **Customer_Group**.

   l. Submit the program and confirm that **work.youngadult** was created with 5 observations and 5 variables.

Level 2

2. **Subsetting Observations and Variables Using the WHERE and DROP Statements**

   a. Write a DATA step to read the data set **orion.product_dim** to create a new data set called **work.sports**.

      work.sports should include only those observations with **Supplier_Country** from Great Britain (GB), Spain (ES), or Netherlands (NL) and **Product_Category** values that end in the word Sports.

      work.sports should not include the following variables: **Product_ID**, **Product_Line**, **Product_Group**, **Supplier_Name**, and **Supplier_ID**.

   b. Write a PROC PRINT step to create the following report:

      Partial PROC PRINT Output (First 10 of 30 Observations)

```
              Product_                                         Supplier_
      Obs     Category         Product_Name                    Country

        1     Children Sports  Butch T-Shirt with V-Neck          ES
        2     Children Sports  Children's Knit Sweater            ES
        3     Children Sports  Gordon Children's Tracking Pants   ES
        4     Children Sports  O'my Children's T-Shirt with Logo  ES
        5     Children Sports  Strap Pants BBO                    ES
        6     Indoor Sports    Abdomen Shaper                     NL
        7     Indoor Sports    Fitness Dumbbell Foam 0.90         NL
        8     Indoor Sports    Letour Heart Bike                  NL
        9     Indoor Sports    Letour Trimag Bike                 NL
       10     Indoor Sports    Weight  5.0 Kg                     NL
```

Level 3

3. **Using the SOUNDS-LIKE Operator and the KEEP= Option**

   a. Write a DATA step to read the data set **orion.customer_dim** to create a new data set called **work.tony**.

   b. Add a WHERE statement to the DATA step to subset the observations with **Customer_FirstName** that sound like Tony.

      Documentation on the SOUNDS-LIKE operator can be found in the SAS Help and Documentation from the Index tab by typing *sounds-like operator*.

   c. Add a KEEP= data set option in the SET statement to read only the **Customer_FirstName** and **Customer_LastName** variables.

      Documentation on the KEEP= data set option can be found in the SAS Help and Documentation from the Contents tab (**SAS Products** ⇨ **Base SAS** ⇨ **SAS 9.2 Language Reference: Dictionary** ⇨ **Dictionary of Language Elements** ⇨ **SAS Data Set Options** ⇨ **KEEP= Data Set Option**).

d. Write a PROC PRINT step to create the following report:

```
             Customer_   Customer_
     Obs     FirstName   LastName

      1       Tonie      Asmussen
      2       Tommy      Mcdonald
```

5.4 Adding Permanent Attributes

Objectives

- Add labels to the descriptor portion of a SAS data set by using the LABEL statement.
- Add formats to the descriptor portion of a SAS data set by using the FORMAT statement.

61

Business Scenario Syntax

Use the following statements to complete the scenario:

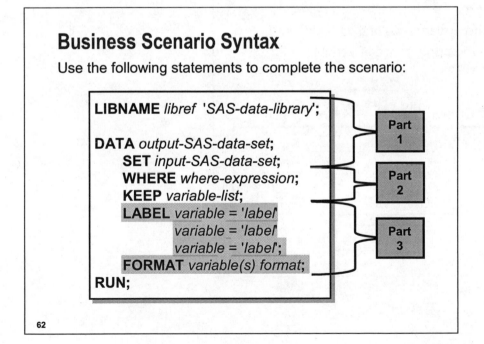

```
LIBNAME libref 'SAS-data-library';

DATA output-SAS-data-set;
    SET input-SAS-data-set;
    WHERE where-expression;
    KEEP variable-list;
    LABEL variable = 'label'
          variable = 'label'
          variable = 'label';
    FORMAT variable(s) format;
RUN;
```

Part 1

Part 2

Part 3

62

Adding Permanent Attributes

The descriptor portion of the SAS data set stores variable attributes including the name, type (character or numeric), and length of the variable.

Labels and formats can also be stored in the descriptor portion.

Partial PROC CONTENTS Output

```
          Alphabetic List of Variables and Attributes

     #    Variable     Type    Len    Format      Label

     1    First_Name   Char     12
     5    Hire_Date    Num       8    DDMMYY10.   Date Hired
     4    Job_Title    Char     25                Sales Title
     2    Last_Name    Char     18
     3    Salary       Num       8    COMMAX8.
```

63

Adding Permanent Attributes

When displaying reports,
- a *label* changes the appearance of a variable name
- a *format* changes the appearance of variable value.

Partial PROC PRINT Output

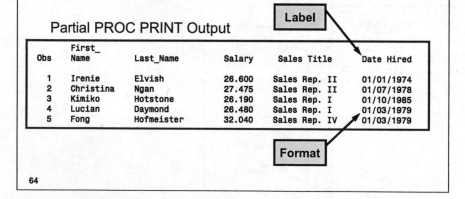

```
          First_
     Obs  Name       Last_Name     Salary   Sales Title   Date Hired

      1   Irenie     Elvish        26.600   Sales Rep. II   01/01/1974
      2   Christina  Ngan          27.475   Sales Rep. II   01/07/1978
      3   Kimiko     Hotstone      26.190   Sales Rep. I    01/10/1985
      4   Lucian     Daymond       26.480   Sales Rep. I    01/03/1979
      5   Fong       Hofmeister    32.040   Sales Rep. IV   01/03/1979
```

Label

Format

64

The LABEL Statement

The *LABEL statement* assigns descriptive labels to variable names.

General form of the LABEL statement:

> **LABEL** *variable = 'label'*
> *variable = 'label'*
> *variable = 'label'*;

- A label can be up to 256 characters.
- Any number of variables can be associated with labels in a single LABEL statement.
- Using a LABEL statement in a DATA step permanently associates labels with variables by storing the label in the descriptor portion of the SAS data set.

65

Business Scenario Part 3

Include labels in the descriptor portion of **work.subset1**.

```
data work.subset1;
   set orion.sales;
   where Country='AU' and
         Job_Title contains 'Rep';
   keep First_Name Last_Name Salary
        Job_Title Hire_Date;
   label Job_Title='Sales Title'
         Hire_Date='Date Hired';
run;
```

66   p105d04

Business Scenario Part 3

```
proc contents data=work.subset1;
run;
```

Partial PROC CONTENTS Output

```
           Alphabetic List of Variables and Attributes

       #     Variable       Type     Len    Label

       1     First_Name     Char      12
       5     Hire_Date      Num        8     Date Hired
       4     Job_Title      Char      25     Sales Title
       2     Last_Name      Char      18
       3     Salary         Num        8
```

67   p105d04

Business Scenario Part 3

In order to use labels in the PRINT procedure, a label
option needs to be added to the PROC PRINT statement.

```
proc print data=work.subset1 label;
run;
```

Partial PROC PRINT Output

```
          First_
    Obs   Name        Last_Name    Salary   Sales Title      Date
                                                             Hired

     1    Irenie      Elvish        26600   Sales Rep. II     5114
     2    Christina   Ngan          27475   Sales Rep. II     6756
     3    Kimiko      Hotstone      26190   Sales Rep. I      9405
     4    Lucian      Daymond       26480   Sales Rep. I      6999
     5    Fong        Hofmeister    32040   Sales Rep. IV     6999
     6    Satyakam    Denny         26780   Sales Rep. II    17014
     7    Sharryn     Clarkson      28100   Sales Rep. II    14184
     8    Monica      Kletschkus    30890   Sales Rep. IV    17106
     9    Alvin       Roebuck       30070   Sales Rep. III    9405
    10    Kevin       Lyon          26955   Sales Rep. I     16922
```

68   p105d04

The FORMAT Statement

The *FORMAT statement* assigns formats to variable values.

General form of the FORMAT statement:

FORMAT *variable(s) format* ;

- A *format* is an instruction that SAS uses to write data values.
- Using a FORMAT statement in a DATA step permanently associates formats with variables by storing the format in the descriptor portion of the SAS data set.

69

SAS Formats

SAS formats have the following form:

<$>*format*<w>.<d>

$	indicates a character format
format	names the SAS format or user-defined format
w	specifies the total format width including decimal places and special characters
.	required delimiter
d	specifies the number of decimal places in numeric formats

70

SAS Formats

Selected SAS formats:

Format	Definition
$w.	Writes standard character data
w.d	Writes standard numeric data
COMMAw.d	Writes numeric values with a comma that separates every three digits and a period that separates the decimal fraction
COMMAXw.d	Writes numeric values with a period that separates every three digits and a comma that separates the decimal fraction
DOLLARw.d	Writes numeric values with a leading dollar sign, a comma that separates every three digits, and a period that separates the decimal fraction
EUROXw.d	Writes numeric values with a leading euro symbol (€), a period that separates every three digits, and a comma that separates the decimal fraction

71

SAS Formats

Selected SAS formats:

Format	Stored Value	Displayed Value
$4.	Programming	Prog
12.	27134.2864	27134
12.2	27134.2864	27134.29
COMMA12.2	27134.2864	27,134.29
COMMAX12.2	27134.2864	27.134,29
DOLLAR12.2	27134.2864	$27,134.29
EUROX12.2	27134.2864	€27.134,29

72

SAS Formats

If you do not specify a format width that is large enough to accommodate a numeric value, the displayed value is automatically adjusted to fit into the width.

Format	Stored Value	Displayed Value
DOLLAR12.2	27134.2864	$27,134.29
DOLLAR9.2	27134.2864	$27134.29
DOLLAR8.2	27134.2864	27134.29
DOLLAR5.2	27134.2864	27134
DOLLAR4.2	27134.2864	27E3

73

5.06 Quiz

Which numeric format writes standard numeric data with leading 0s?

Documentation on formats can be found in the SAS Help and Documentation from the Contents tab (**SAS Products** ⇨ **Base SAS** ⇨ **SAS 9.2 Language Reference: Dictionary** ⇨ **Dictionary of Language Elements** ⇨ **Formats** ⇨ **Formats by Category**).

75

SAS Date Formats

SAS date formats display SAS date values in standard
date forms.

Format	Stored Value	Displayed Value
MMDDYY6.	0	010160
MMDDYY8.	0	01/01/60
MMDDYY10.	0	01/01/1960
DDMMYY6.	365	311260
DDMMYY8.	365	31/12/60
DDMMYY10.	365	31/12/1960

78

SAS Date Formats

Additional date formats:

Format	Stored Value	Displayed Value
DATE7.	-1	31DEC59
DATE9.	-1	31DEC1959
WORDDATE.	0	January 1, 1960
WEEKDATE.	0	Friday, January 1, 1960
MONYY7.	0	JAN1960
YEAR4.	0	1960

79

5.07 Quiz

Which FORMAT statement creates the output?

a.
```
format Birth_Date Hire_Date ddmmyy9.
       Term_Date mmyy7.;
```

b.
```
format Birth_Date Hire_Date ddmmyyyy.
       Term_Date mmmyyyy.;
```

c.
```
format Birth_Date Hire_Date ddmmyy10.
       Term_Date monyy7.;
```

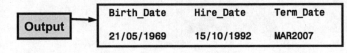

Output →	Birth_Date	Hire_Date	Term_Date
	21/05/1969	15/10/1992	MAR2007

81

SAS Date Formats

The SAS National Language Support (NLS) date formats convert SAS date values to a locale-sensitive date string.

Format	Locale	Example
NLDATE*w.*	English_UnitedStates	January 01, 1960
	German_Germany	01. Januar 1960
NLDATEMN*w.*	English_UnitedStates	January
	German_Germany	Januar
NLDATEW*w.*	English_UnitedStates	Fri, Jan 01, 60
	German_Germany	Fr, 01. Jan 60
NLDATEWN*w.*	English_UnitedStates	Friday
	German_Germany	Freitag

83   p105d05

National Language Support (NLS) is a set of features that enable a software product to function properly in every global market for which the product is targeted. SAS contains NLS features to ensure that SAS applications conform to local language conventions.

A locale reflects the language, local conventions, and culture for a geographical region. Local conventions might include specific formatting rules for dates. Dates have many representations, depending on the conventions that are accepted in a culture.

The LOCALE= system option is used to specify the locale, which reflects the local conventions, language, and culture of a geographical region. For example, a locale value of English_Canada represents the country of Canada with a language of English, and a locale value of French_Canada represents the country of Canada with a language of French. English_UnitedStates represents the country of United States with a language of English. German_Germany represents the country of Germany with a language of German.

The LOCALE= system option can be specified in a configuration file, at SAS invocation, in the OPTIONS statement, or in the SAS System Options window.

For more information, refer to the *SAS 9.2 National Language Support Reference Guide* in SAS Help and Documentation.

5.08 Quiz

How many date and time formats start with EUR?

Documentation on NLS formats can be found in the
SAS Help and Documentation from the Contents tab
(**SAS Products** ⇨ **Base SAS** ⇨ **SAS 9.2 Language
Reference: Dictionary** ⇨ **Dictionary of Language
Elements** ⇨ **Formats** ⇨ **Formats Documented in
Other SAS Publications**).

85

Business Scenario Part 3

Include formats in the descriptor portion of
work.subset1.

```
data work.subset1;
   set orion.sales;
   where Country='AU' and
         Job_Title contains 'Rep';
   keep First_Name Last_Name Salary
        Job_Title Hire_Date;
   label Job_Title='Sales Title'
         Hire_Date='Date Hired';
   format Salary commax8. Hire_Date ddmmyy10.;
run;
```

87

p105d06

Business Scenario Part 3

```
proc contents data=work.subset1;
run;
```

Partial PROC CONTENTS Output

```
           Alphabetic List of Variables and Attributes

    #    Variable      Type    Len    Format        Label

    1    First_Name    Char     12
    5    Hire_Date     Num       8    DDMMYY10.     Date Hired
    4    Job_Title     Char     25                  Sales Title
    2    Last_Name     Char     18
    3    Salary        Num       8    COMMAX8.
```

88   p105d06

Business Scenario Part 3

```
proc print data=work.subset1 label;
run;
```

Partial PROC PRINT Output

```
       First_
Obs    Name         Last_Name      Salary    Sales Title      Date Hired

 1     Irenie       Elvish         26.600    Sales Rep. II    01/01/1974
 2     Christina    Ngan           27.475    Sales Rep. II    01/07/1978
 3     Kimiko       Hotstone       26.190    Sales Rep. I     01/10/1985
 4     Lucian       Daymond        26.480    Sales Rep. I     01/03/1979
 5     Fong         Hofmeister     32.040    Sales Rep. IV    01/03/1979
 6     Satyakam     Denny          26.780    Sales Rep. II    01/08/2006
 7     Sharryn      Clarkson       28.100    Sales Rep. II    01/11/1998
 8     Monica       Kletschkus     30.890    Sales Rep. IV    01/11/2006
 9     Alvin        Roebuck        30.070    Sales Rep. III   01/10/1985
10     Kevin        Lyon           26.955    Sales Rep. I     01/05/2006
11     Marinus      Surawski       26.910    Sales Rep. I     01/01/2003
12     Fancine      Kaiser         28.525    Sales Rep. III   01/10/1978
```

89   p105d06

 **Exercises**

Level 1

4. **Adding Permanent Attributes to `work.youngadult`**

   a. Retrieve and submit the starter program **p105e04**.

   Notice the format and labels stored in the descriptor portion of **`work.youngadult`**.

   b. Add a LABEL statement and a FORMAT statement to the DATA step to create the following PROC PRINT report:

```
                                                                   Customer
Obs   Gender    Customer Name         Date of Birth      Member Level         Age

 1      F      Sandrina Stephano       July 9, 1979    Orion Club Gold members   28
 2      F      Cornelia Krahl      February 27, 1974   Orion Club Gold members   33
 3      F      Dianne Patchin          May 6, 1979    Orion Club Gold members   28
 4      F      Annmarie Leveille      July 16, 1984   Orion Club Gold members   23
 5      F      Sanelisiwe Collier      July 7, 1988   Orion Club Gold members   19
```

   The labels need to be changed for **Customer_Gender**, **Customer_BirthDate**, and **Customer_Group**.

   The format needs to be changed for **Customer_BirthDate**.

   Hint: Do not forget the option in the PROC PRINT step that allows the labels to appear.

   Why do **Customer_Name** and **Customer_Age** appear with a space in the column header but does not need a label?

Level 2

5. **Adding Permanent Attributes to `work.sports`**

   a. Retrieve the starter program **p105e05**.

   b. Add a LABEL statement to the DATA step and a LABEL option to the PROC PRINT step to add the following labels:

Variable	Label
Product_Category	Sports Category
Product_Name	Product Name (Abbrev)
Supplier_Name	Supplier Name (Abbrev)

   c. Add a FORMAT statement to the DATA step to display only the first 15 letters of
`Product_Name` and **`Supplier_Name`**.

   d. Submit the program to create the following PROC PRINT report:

Partial PROC PRINT Output (First 10 of 30 Observations)

Obs	Sports Category	Product Name (Abbrev)	Supplier Country	Supplier Name (Abbrev)
1	Children Sports	Butch T-Shirt w	ES	Luna sastreria
2	Children Sports	Children's Knit	ES	Luna sastreria
3	Children Sports	Gordon Children	ES	Luna sastreria
4	Children Sports	O'my Children's	ES	Luna sastreria
5	Children Sports	Strap Pants BBO	ES	Sportico
6	Indoor Sports	Abdomen Shaper	NL	TrimSport B.V.
7	Indoor Sports	Fitness Dumbbel	NL	TrimSport B.V.
8	Indoor Sports	Letour Heart Bi	NL	TrimSport B.V.
9	Indoor Sports	Letour Trimag B	NL	TrimSport B.V.
10	Indoor Sports	Weight 5.0 Kg	NL	TrimSport B.V.

   e. Add a PROC CONTENTS step to the end of the program to verify that the labels and formats
are stored in the descriptor portion.

Level 3

6. Using the $UPCASE*w*. Format and the SPLIT= Option

   a. Retrieve the starter program **p105e06**.

   b. Add a FORMAT statement to display the **`Customer_FirstName`** and
`Customer_LastName` in uppercase values.

> Documentation on the $UPCASE*w*. format can be found in the SAS Help and
> Documentation from the Contents tab (**SAS Products** ⇨ **Base SAS** ⇨
> **SAS 9.2 Language Reference: Dictionary** ⇨ **Dictionary of Language Elements** ⇨
> **Formats** ⇨ **$UPCASE*w*. Format**).

   c. Add a LABEL statement to add the following labels:

Variable	Label
Customer_FirstName	CUSTOMER*FIRST NAME
Customer_LastName	CUSTOMER*LAST NAME

   d. In the PROC PRINT statement, replace the LABEL option with the SPLIT= option referencing
the asterisk as the split character.

> Documentation on the SPLIT= option can be found in the SAS Help and Documentation
> from the Contents tab (**SAS Products** ⇨ **Base SAS** ⇨
> **Base SAS 9.2 Procedures Guide** ⇨ **Procedures** ⇨ **The PRINT Procedure**).

e. Submit the program to create the following PROC PRINT report:

```
                    CUSTOMER      CUSTOMER
            Obs    FIRST NAME    LAST NAME

             1       TONIE       ASMUSSEN
             2       TOMMY       MCDONALD
```

5.5 Solutions

Solutions to Exercises

1. **Subsetting Observations and Variables Using the WHERE and KEEP Statements**

   a. Retrieve and submit the program.

   What is the variable name that contains gender values? `Customer_Gender`

   What are the two possible gender values? **F** and **M**

   b. Add a DATA step.

```
data work.youngadult;
   set orion.customer_dim;
   where Customer_Gender='F';
run;


proc print data=orion.customer_dim;
run;
```

   c. Modify the PROC PRINT step.

```
proc print data=work.youngadult;
run;
```

   d. Submit the program.

   e. Add a WHERE statement to subset for female customers.

```
data work.youngadult;
   set orion.customer_dim;
   where Customer_Gender='F';
run;
```

   f. Submit the program.

   g. Modify the WHERE statement to subset for female 18- to 36-year-old customers.

```
data work.youngadult;
   set orion.customer_dim;
   where Customer_Gender='F' and
         Customer_Age between 18 and 36;
run;
```

   h. Submit the program.

i. Modify the WHERE statement to subset for female 18- to 36-year-old customers who have the word Gold in their **Customer_Group**.

```
data work.youngadult;
   set orion.customer_dim;
   where Customer_Gender='F' and
         Customer_Age between 18 and 36 and
         Customer_Group contains 'Gold';
run;
```

j. Submit the program.

k. Keep only five variables.

```
data work.youngadult;
   set orion.customer_dim;
   where Customer_Gender='F' and
         Customer_Age between 18 and 36 and
         Customer_Group contains 'Gold';
   keep Customer_Name Customer_Age Customer_BirthDate
         Customer_Gender Customer_Group;
run;
```

l. Submit the program.

2. Subsetting Observations and Variables Using the WHERE and DROP Statements

a. Write a DATA step.

```
data work.sports;
   set orion.product_dim;
   where Supplier_Country in ('GB','ES','NL') and
         Product_Category like '%Sports';
   drop Product_ID Product_Line Product_Group
        Supplier_Name Supplier_ID;
run;
```

b. Write a PROC PRINT step.

```
proc print data=work.sports;
run;
```

3. Using the SOUNDS-LIKE Operator and the KEEP= Option

a. Write a DATA step.

```
data work.tony;
   set orion.customer_dim;
run;
```

b. Add a WHERE statement to the DATA step.

```
data work.tony;
   set orion.customer_dim;
   where Customer_FirstName =* 'Tony';
run;
```

    c. Add a KEEP= data set option in the SET statement.

```
data work.tony;
   set orion.customer_dim(keep=Customer_FirstName Customer_LastName);
   where Customer_FirstName =* 'Tony';
run;
```

    d. Write a PROC PRINT step.

```
proc print data=work.tony;
run;
```

4. **Adding Permanent Attributes to work.youngadult**

    a. Retrieve and submit the starter program.

    b. Add a LABEL statement and a FORMAT statement to the DATA step.

```
data work.youngadult;
   set orion.customer_dim;
   where Customer_Gender='F' and
         Customer_Age between 18 and 35 and
         Customer_Group contains 'Gold';
   keep Customer_Name Customer_Age Customer_BirthDate
        Customer_Gender Customer_Group;
   label Customer_Gender='Gender'
         Customer_BirthDate='Date of Birth'
         Customer_Group='Member Level';
   format Customer_BirthDate worddate.;
run;

proc contents data=work.youngadult;
run;

proc print data=work.youngadult label;
run;
```

    Why do **Customer_Name** and **Customer_Age** appear with a space in the column header but does not need a label? **These variables already have permanent labels assigned in the data set descriptor portion.**

5. **Adding Permanent Attributes to work.sports**

    a. Retrieve the starter program.

b. Add a LABEL statement to the DATA step and a LABEL option to PROC PRINT.

```
data work.sports;
   set orion.product_dim;
   where Supplier_Country in ('GB','ES','NL') and
         Product_Category like '%Sports';
   drop Product_ID Product_Line Product_Group Supplier_ID;
   label Product_Category='Sports Category'
         Product_Name='Product Name (Abbrev)'
         Supplier_Name='Supplier Name (Abbrev)';
run;


proc print data=work.sports label;
run;
```

c. Add a FORMAT statement to the DATA step.

```
data work.sports;
   set orion.product_dim;
   where Supplier_Country in ('GB','ES','NL') and
         Product_Category like '%Sports';
   drop Product_ID Product_Line Product_Group Supplier_ID;
   label Product_Category='Sports Category'
         Product_Name='Product Name (Abbrev)'
         Supplier_Name='Supplier Name (Abbrev)';
   format Product_Name Supplier_Name $15.;
run;
```

d. Submit the program.

e. Add a PROC CONTENTS step.

```
proc contents data=work.sports;
run;
```

6. **Using the $UPCASE*w.* Format and the SPLIT= Option**

   a. Retrieve the starter program.

   b. Add a FORMAT statement.

```
data work.tony;
   set orion.customer_dim(keep=Customer_FirstName Customer_LastName);
   where Customer_FirstName =* 'Tony';
   format Customer_FirstName Customer_LastName $upcase.;
run;


proc print data=work.tony label;
run;
```

c. Add a LABEL statement.

```
data work.tony;
   set orion.customer_dim(keep=Customer_FirstName Customer_LastName);
   where Customer_FirstName =* 'Tony';
   format Customer_FirstName Customer_LastName $upcase.;
   label Customer_FirstName='CUSTOMER*FIRST NAME'
         Customer_LastName='CUSTOMER*LAST NAME';
run;
```

d. Replace the LABEL option with the SPLIT= option.

```
proc print data=work.tony split='*';
run;
```

e. Submit the program.

Solutions to Student Activities (Polls/Quizzes)

5.02 Poll – Correct Answer

The DATA step reads a temporary SAS data set to create a permanent SAS data set.

○ True
◉ False

```
data work.mycustomers;
   set orion.customer;
run;

proc print data=work.mycustomers;
   var Customer_ID Customer_Name
       Customer_Address;
run;
```

23

5.03 Quiz – Correct Answer

Which WHERE statement correctly subsets for numeric months May, June, or July and character names with a missing value?

a.
```
where Months in (5-7)
      and Names = .;
```

(b.)
```
where Months in (5,6,7)
      and Names = ' ';
```

c.
```
where Months in ('5','6','7')
      and Names = '.';
```

39

5.04 Quiz – Correct Answer

Which value will not be returned based on the
WHERE statement?

a. Office Rep
b. Sales Rep. IV
c. service rep III
d. Representative

```
where Job_Title contains 'Rep';
```

46

5.05 Quiz – Correct Answer

Which WHERE statement will return the observations that
have a first name starting with the letter M for the given
values?

a. `where Name like '_, M_';`

b. `where Name like '%, M%';`

c. `where Name like '_, M%';`

d. `where Name like '%, M_';`

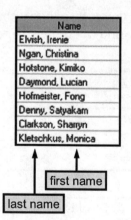

Name
Elvish, Irenie
Ngan, Christina
Hotstone, Kimiko
Daymond, Lucian
Hofmeister, Fong
Denny, Satyakam
Clarkson, Sharryn
Kletschkus, Monica

first name

last name

51

5.06 Quiz – Correct Answer

Which numeric format writes standard numeric data with leading 0s?

Z*w.d*

The Z*w.d* format is similar to the *w.d* format except that Z*w.d* pads right-aligned output with 0s instead of blanks.

76

5.07 Quiz – Correct Answer

Which FORMAT statement creates the output?

a.
```
format Birth_Date Hire_Date ddmmyy9.
       Term_Date mmyy7.;
```

b.
```
format Birth_Date Hire_Date ddmmyyyy.
       Term_Date mmmyyyy.;
```

c.
```
format Birth_Date Hire_Date ddmmyy10.
       Term_Date monyy7.;
```

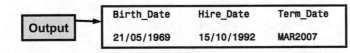

Output	Birth_Date	Hire_Date	Term_Date
	21/05/1969	15/10/1992	MAR2007

82

5.08 Quiz – Correct Answer

How many date and time formats start with EUR?

Nine

Example:

The EURDFDD*w*. format writes international SAS date values in the form dd.mm.yy or dd.mm.yyyy.

Chapter 6   Reading Excel Worksheets

6.1 Using Excel Data as Input

Objectives

- Use the DATA step to create a SAS data set from an Excel worksheet.
- Use the SAS/ACCESS LIBNAME statement to read from an Excel worksheet as though it were a SAS data set.

3

Business Scenario

An existing data source contains information on Orion Star sales employees from Australia and the United States.

A new SAS data set needs to be created that contains a subset of this existing data source.

This new SAS data set must contain the following:

- only the employees from Australia who are Sales Representatives
- the employee's first name, last name, salary, job title, and hired date
- labels and formats in the descriptor portion

4

Business Scenario

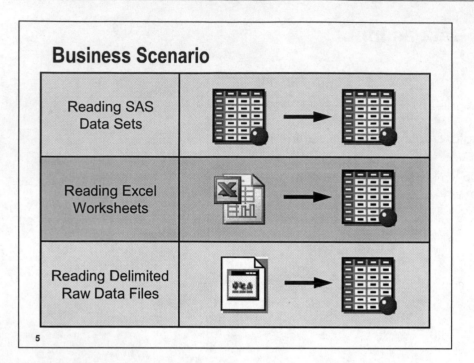

Reading SAS Data Sets	
Reading Excel Worksheets	
Reading Delimited Raw Data Files	

5

Business Scenario

Reading SAS Data Sets	`libname`_____`;`
	`data`_____`;`
	    `set`_____`;`
	    `...`
	`run;`

Reading Excel Worksheets	`libname`_____`;`
	`data`_____`;`
	    `set`_____`;`
	    `...`
	`run;`

Reading Delimited Raw Data Files	`data`_____`;`
	    `infile`_____`;`
	    `input`_____`;`
	    `...`
	`run;`

6

The LIBNAME statement references a SAS data library when reading a SAS data set and an Excel workbook when reading an Excel worksheet.

Business Scenario Syntax

Use the following statements to complete the scenario:

LIBNAME *libref* '*physical-file-name*' ;

DATA *output-SAS-data-set* ;
    SET *input-SAS-data-set* ;
    WHERE *where-expression* ;
    KEEP *variable-list* ;
    LABEL *variable* = '*label*'
            variable = '*label*'
            variable = '*label*' ;
    FORMAT *variable(s) format* ;
RUN;

7

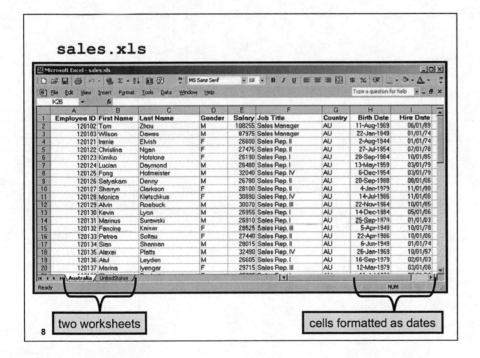

sales.xls

two worksheets   cells formatted as dates

8

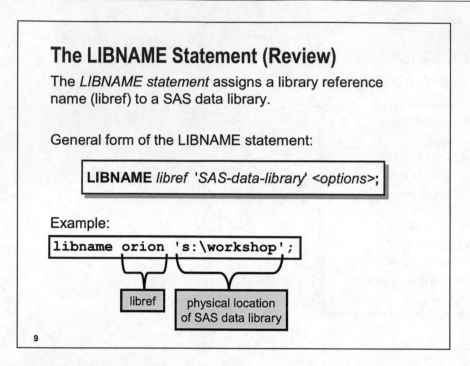

The LIBNAME Statement (Review)

The *LIBNAME statement* assigns a library reference name (libref) to a SAS data library.

General form of the LIBNAME statement:

LIBNAME *libref* '*SAS-data-library*' *<options>*;

Example:

```
libname orion 's:\workshop';
```

libref

physical location of SAS data library

9

The LIBNAME statement needs to reference a SAS data library specific to your operating environment.

The SAS/ACCESS LIBNAME Statement

The *SAS/ACCESS LIBNAME statement* extends the LIBNAME statement to support assigning a library reference name (libref) to Microsoft Excel workbooks.

General form of the SAS/ACCESS LIBNAME statement:

> **LIBNAME** *libref 'physical-file-name' <options>*;

This enables you to reference worksheets directly in a DATA step or SAS procedure, and to read from and write to a Microsoft Excel worksheet as though it were a SAS data set.

10

SAS/ACCESS options can be used in the LIBNAME statement.

For example,

MIXED=YES | NO

> specifies whether to convert numeric data values into character data values for a column with mixed data types.
>
> The default is NO, which means that numeric data will be imported as missing values in a character column. If MIXED=YES, the engine assigns a SAS character type for the column and converts all numeric data values to character data.

The following Technical Support Usage Note addresses column data that gets imported as missing:

http://support.sas.com/kb/6/123.html

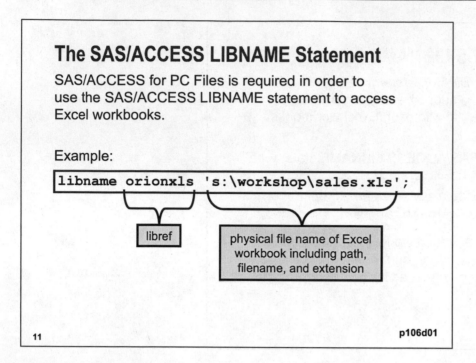

The SAS/ACCESS LIBNAME Statement

SAS/ACCESS for PC Files is required in order to
use the SAS/ACCESS LIBNAME statement to access
Excel workbooks.

Example:

```
libname orionxls 's:\workshop\sales.xls';
```

libref

physical file name of Excel
workbook including path,
filename, and extension

11   p106d01

SAS/ACCESS for PC Files enables you to read data from PC files, to use that data in SAS reports or applications, and to use SAS data sets to create PC files in various formats.

SAS/ACCESS for PC Files gives access to Microsoft Excel, Microsoft Access, dBase, JMP, Lotus 1-2-3, SPSS, Stata, and Paradox.

To determine if you have a license for SAS/ACCESS for PC Files, submit the following step:

```
proc setinit;
run;
```

After submitting, look in the SAS log for the products that are licensed for your site.

    SAS/ACCESS for PC Files on Linux and UNIX allows access to PC files from the Linux and UNIX operating environments. A PC Files Server is used to access the PC data. The PC Files Server runs on a Microsoft Windows server, and SAS/ACCESS to PC Files runs on a Linux or UNIX client server.

SAS Explorer Window

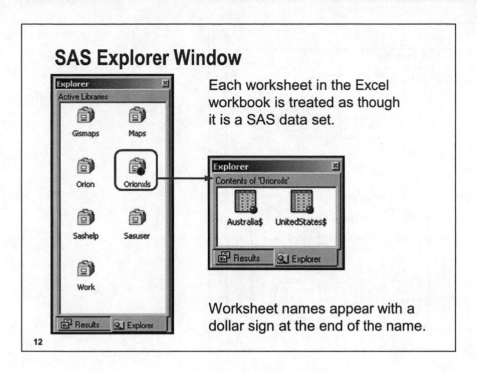

Each worksheet in the Excel workbook is treated as though it is a SAS data set.

Worksheet names appear with a dollar sign at the end of the name.

12

The CONTENTS Procedure

```
proc contents data=orionxls._all_;
run;
```

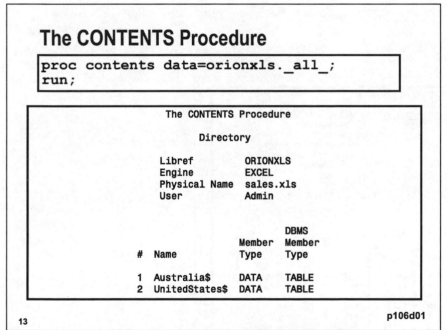

```
                    The CONTENTS Procedure

                          Directory

                 Libref          ORIONXLS
                 Engine          EXCEL
                 Physical Name   sales.xls
                 User            Admin


                                          DBMS
                                Member    Member
            #  Name             Type      Type

            1  Australia$       DATA      TABLE
            2  UnitedStates$    DATA      TABLE
```

13   p106d01

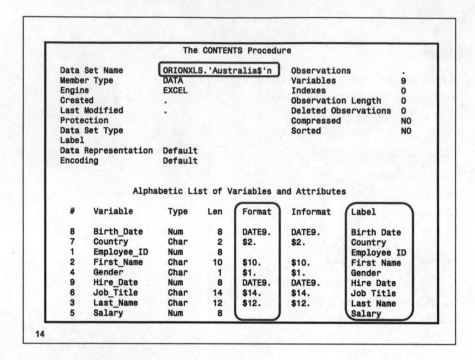

The Excel LIBNAME engine converts worksheet dates to SAS date values and assigns
the DATE9. format.

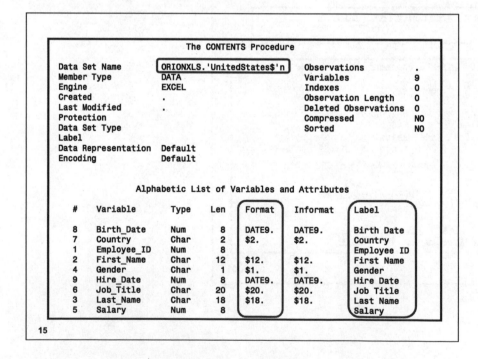

SAS Name Literals

By default, special characters such as the $ are not allowed in data set names.

SAS name literals allow special characters to be included in data set names.

A *SAS name literal* is a name token that is expressed as a string within quotation marks, followed by the letter n.

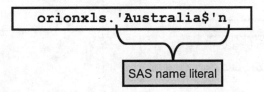

```
orionxls.'Australia$'n
```

SAS name literal

16

The PRINT Procedure

```
proc print data=orionxls.'Australia$'n;
run;
```

Partial PROC PRINT Output

Obs	Employee_ID	First_Name	Last_Name	Gender	Salary	Job_Title	Country	Birth_Date	Hire_Date
1	120102	Tom	Zhou	M	108255	Sales Manager	AU	11AUG1969	01JUN1989
2	120103	Wilson	Dawes	M	87975	Sales Manager	AU	22JAN1949	01JAN1974
3	120121	Irenie	Elvish	F	26600	Sales Rep. II	AU	02AUG1944	01JAN1974
4	120122	Christina	Ngan	F	27475	Sales Rep. II	AU	27JUL1954	01JUL1978
5	120123	Kimiko	Hotstone	F	26190	Sales Rep. I	AU	28SEP1964	01OCT1985
6	120124	Lucian	Daymond	M	26480	Sales Rep. I	AU	13MAY1959	01MAR1979
7	120125	Fong	Hofmeister	M	32040	Sales Rep. IV	AU	06DEC1954	01MAR1979
8	120126	Satyakam	Denny	M	26780	Sales Rep. II	AU	20SEP1988	01AUG2006
9	120127	Sharryn	Clarkson	F	28100	Sales Rep. II	AU	04JAN1979	01NOV1998
10	120128	Monica	Kletschkus	F	30890	Sales Rep. IV	AU	14JUL1986	01NOV2006
11	120129	Alvin	Roebuck	M	30070	Sales Rep. III	AU	22NOV1964	01OCT1985
12	120130	Kevin	Lyon	M	26955	Sales Rep. I	AU	14DEC1984	01MAY2006
13	120131	Marinus	Surawski	M	26910	Sales Rep. I	AU	25SEP1979	01JAN2003
14	120132	Fancine	Kaiser	F	28525	Sales Rep. III	AU	05APR1949	01OCT1978
15	120133	Petrea	Soltau	F	27440	Sales Rep. II	AU	22APR1986	01OCT2006

17   p106d01

6.01 Quiz

Which PROC PRINT step displays the worksheet
containing employees from United States?

a.
```
proc print data=orionxls.'UnitedStates';
run;
```

b.
```
proc print data=orionxls.'UnitedStates$';
run;
```

c.
```
proc print data=orionxls.'UnitedStates'n;
run;
```

d.
```
proc print data=orionxls.'UnitedStates$'n;
run;
```

19

Business Scenario

Create a temporary SAS data set named **work.subset2**
from the Excel workbook named **sales.xls**.

```
libname orionxls 's:\workshop\sales.xls';

data work.subset2;
   set orionxls.'Australia$'n;
   where Job_Title contains 'Rep';
   keep First_Name Last_Name Salary
        Job_Title Hire_Date;
   label Job_Title='Sales Title'
         Hire_Date='Date Hired';
   format Salary comma10. Hire_Date weekdate.;
run;
```

21   p106d02

Business Scenario

```
proc contents data=work.subset2;
run;
```

Partial PROC CONTENTS Output

```
            Alphabetic List of Variables and Attributes

   #   Variable      Type    Len    Format       Informat    Label

   1   First_Name    Char    10     $10.         $10.        First Name
   5   Hire_Date     Num      8     WEEKDATE.    DATE9.      Date Hired
   4   Job_Title     Char    14     $14.         $14.        Sales Title
   2   Last_Name     Char    12     $12.         $12.        Last Name
   3   Salary        Num      8     COMMA10.                 Salary
```

22   p106d02

Business Scenario

```
proc print data=work.subset2 label;
run;
```

Partial PROC PRINT Output

```
Obs First Name Last Name    Salary Sales Title           Date Hired

  1 Irenie    Elvish       26,600 Sales Rep. II     Tuesday, January 1, 1974
  2 Christina Ngan         27,475 Sales Rep. II       Saturday, July 1, 1978
  3 Kimiko    Hotstone     26,190 Sales Rep. I     Tuesday, October 1, 1985
  4 Lucian    Daymond      26,480 Sales Rep. I       Thursday, March 1, 1979
  5 Fong      Hofmeister   32,040 Sales Rep. IV      Thursday, March 1, 1979
  6 Satyakam  Denny        26,780 Sales Rep. II      Tuesday, August 1, 2006
  7 Sharryn   Clarkson     28,100 Sales Rep. II     Sunday, November 1, 1998
  8 Monica    Kletschkus   30,890 Sales Rep. IV Wednesday, November 1, 2006
  9 Alvin     Roebuck      30,070 Sales Rep. III    Tuesday, October 1, 1985
 10 Kevin     Lyon         26,955 Sales Rep. I          Monday, May 1, 2006
 11 Marinus   Surawski     26,910 Sales Rep. I    Wednesday, January 1, 2003
 12 Fancine   Kaiser       28,525 Sales Rep. III     Sunday, October 1, 1978
```

23   p106d02

Disassociating a Libref

If SAS has a libref assigned to an Excel workbook, the workbook cannot be opened in Excel. To disassociate a libref, use a LIBNAME statement, specifying the libref and the CLEAR option.

```
libname orionxls 's:\workshop\sales.xls';

data work.subset2;
   set orionxls.'Australia$'n;
   ...
run;

libname orionxls clear;
```

SAS disconnects from the data source and closes any resources that are associated with that libref's connection.

24   p106d02

Reading Excel Worksheets – Windows

p106d02

1. Submit the following program except for the last LIBNAME statement.

```
libname orionxls 'sales.xls';

data work.subset2;
   set orionxls.'Australia$'n;
   where Job_Title contains 'Rep';
   keep First_Name Last_Name Salary
        Job_Title Hire_Date;
   label Job_Title='Sales Title'
         Hire_Date='Date Hired';
   format Salary comma10. Hire_Date weekdate.;
run;

proc contents data=work.subset2;
run;

proc print data=work.subset2 label;
run;

libname orionxls clear;
```

2. Review the PROC CONTENTS and PROC PRINT results in the Output window.

3. Select the **Explorer** tab on the SAS window bar to activate the SAS Explorer window or select **View** ⇨ **Contents Only**.

4. Double-click on **Libraries** to show all available libraries.

5. Double-click on the **Orionxls** library to show all Excel worksheets of that library.

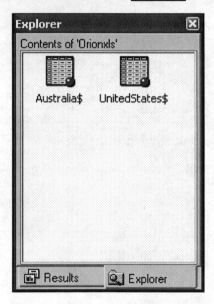

6. Submit the last LIBNAME statement to disassociate the libref.

 **Exercises**

Level 1

1. **Reading an Excel Worksheet**

   a. Retrieve the starter program **p106e01**.

   b. Add a LIBNAME statement before the PROC CONTENTS step to create a *libref* called **CUSTFM** that references the Excel workbook named **custfm.xls**.

   c. Submit the LIBNAME statement and the PROC CONTENTS step to create the following partial PROC CONTENTS report:

   Page 1 of 3

   ```
                            The CONTENTS Procedure

                                  Directory

                    Libref          CUSTFM
                    Engine          EXCEL
                    Physical Name   custfm.xls
                    User            Admin


                                            DBMS
                                  Member    Member
                 #  Name          Type      Type

                 1  Females$      DATA      TABLE
                 2  Males$        DATA      TABLE
   ```

   d. Add a SET statement in the DATA step to read the worksheet containing the male data.

   e. Add a KEEP statement in the DATA step to include only the **First_Name**, **Last_Name**, and **Birth_Date** variables.

   f. Add a FORMAT statement in the DATA step to display the **Birth_Date** as a four-digit year.

   g. Add a LABEL statement to change the column header of **Birth_Date** to **Birth Year**.

h. Submit the program including the last LIBNAME statement and create the following PROC PRINT report:

Partial PROC PRINT Output (First 5 of 47 Observations)

```
                                        Birth
       Obs    First Name    Last Name   Year

        1     James         Kvarniq      1974
        2     David         Black        1969
        3     Markus        Sepke        1988
        4     Ulrich        Heyde        1939
        5     Jimmie        Evans        1954
```

Level 2

2. Reading an Excel Worksheet

a. Write a LIBNAME statement to create a *libref* called **PROD** that references the Excel workbook named **products.xls**.

b. Write a PROC CONTENTS step to view all of the contents of **PROD**.

c. Submit the program to determine the names of the four worksheets in **products.xls**.

d. Write a DATA step to read the worksheet containing sports data to create a new data set called **work.golf**.

The data set **work.golf** should

- include only the observations where **Category** is equal to Golf

- not include the **Category** variable

- include a label of Golf Products for the **Name** variable.

e. Write a LIBNAME to clear the **PROD** *libref*.

f. Write a PROC PRINT step to create the following report:

Partial PROC PRINT Output (First 10 of 56 Observations)

```
        Obs    Golf Products

         1     Ball Bag
         2     Red/White/Black Staff 9 Bag
         3     Tee Holder
         4     Bb Softspikes - Xp 22-pack
         5     Bretagne Performance Tg Men's Golf Shoes L.
         6     Bretagne Soft-Tech Men's Glove, left
         7     Bretagne St2 Men's Golf Glove, left
         8     Bretagne Stabilites 2000 Goretex Shoes
         9     Bretagne Stabilities Tg Men's Golf Shoes
        10     Bretagne Stabilities Women's Golf Shoes
```

Level 3

3. Reading a Range of an Excel Worksheet

a. Write a LIBNAME statement to create a *libref* called **XLSDATA** that references the Excel workbook named **custcaus.xls**. The worksheets in this Excel workbook do not have column names. Add the appropriate option to the LIBNAME statement that specifies not to use the first row of data as column names.

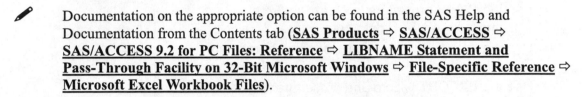 Documentation on the appropriate option can be found in the SAS Help and Documentation from the Contents tab (**SAS Products** ⇨ **SAS/ACCESS** ⇨ **SAS/ACCESS 9.2 for PC Files: Reference** ⇨ **LIBNAME Statement and Pass-Through Facility on 32-Bit Microsoft Windows** ⇨ **File-Specific Reference** ⇨ **Microsoft Excel Workbook Files**).

b. Write a PROC CONTENTS step to view all of the contents of **XLSDATA**.

c. Submit the program. Any member not containing a dollar sign in the name is an Excel range.

d. Write a DATA step to read the range containing Germany (DE) data to create a new data set called **work.germany**. Add appropriate labels and formats based on the desired report.

e. Write a LIBNAME to clear the **XLSDATA** *libref*.

f. Write a PROC PRINT step to create the following report:

Obs	Customer ID	Country	Gender	First Name	Last Name	Birth Date
1	9	DE	F	Cornelia	Krahl	27/02/74
2	11	DE	F	Elke	Wallstab	16/08/74
3	13	DE	M	Markus	Sepke	21/07/88
4	16	DE	M	Ulrich	Heyde	16/01/39
5	19	DE	M	Oliver S.	Füßling	23/02/64
6	33	DE	M	Rolf	Robak	24/02/39
7	42	DE	M	Thomas	Leitmann	09/02/79
8	50	DE	M	Gert-Gunter	Mendler	16/01/34
9	61	DE	M	Carsten	Maestrini	08/07/44
10	65	DE	F	Ines	Deisser	20/07/69

6.2 Doing More with Excel Worksheets (Self-Study)

Objectives

- Use the DATA step to create an Excel worksheet from a SAS data set.
- Use the COPY procedure to create an Excel worksheet from a SAS data set.
- Use the IMPORT wizard and procedure to read an Excel worksheet.
- Use the EXPORT wizard and procedure to create an Excel worksheet.

29

Creating Excel Worksheets

In addition to reading an Excel worksheet, the SAS/ACCESS LIBNAME statement with the DATA step can be used to create an Excel worksheet.

```
libname orionxls
        's:\workshop\qtr2007a.xls';

data orionxls.qtr1_2007;
   set orion.qtr1_2007;
run;

data orionxls.qtr2_2007;
   set orion.qtr2_2007;
run;

proc contents data=orionxls._all_;
run;

libname orionxls clear;
```

30   p106d03

Creating Excel Worksheets

Partial SAS Log

```
70   data orionxls.qtr1_2007;
71      set orion.qtr1_2007;
72
73   run;

NOTE: SAS variable labels, formats, and lengths are not written to DBMS tables.
NOTE: There were 22 observations read from the data set ORION.QTR1_2007.
NOTE: The data set ORIONXLS.qtr1_2007 has 22 observations and 5 variables.


74   data orionxls.qtr2_2007;
75      set orion.qtr2_2007;
76   run;

NOTE: SAS variable labels, formats, and lengths are not written to DBMS tables.
NOTE: There were 36 observations read from the data set ORION.QTR2_2007.
NOTE: The data set ORIONXLS.qtr2_2007 has 36 observations and 6 variables.
```

31

Creating Excel Worksheets

Partial PROC CONTENTS Output

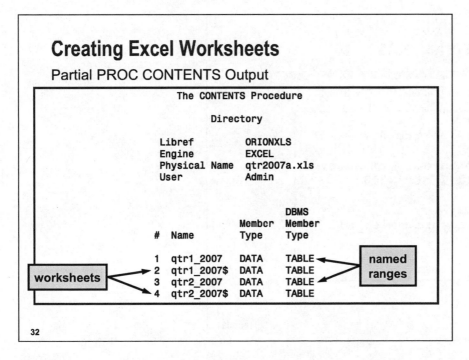

32

In Excel, a named range is a descriptive name for a range of cells.

Creating Excel Worksheets

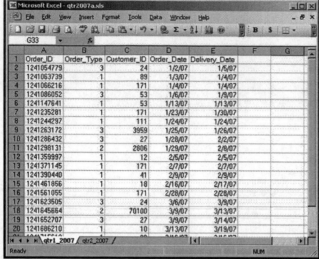

33

Creating Excel Worksheets

As an alternative to the DATA step, the COPY procedure can be used to create an Excel worksheet.

```
libname orionxls
        's:\workshop\qtr2007b.xls';

proc copy  in=orion out=orionxls;
   select qtr1_2007 qtr2_2007;
run;

proc contents data=orionxls._all_;
run;

libname orionxls clear;
```

34   p106d03

Creating Excel Worksheets

Partial SAS Log

```
82   proc copy  in=orion out=orionxls;
83      select qtr1_2007 qtr2_2007;
84   run;

NOTE: Copying ORION.QTR1_2007 to ORIONXLS.QTR1_2007 (memtype=DATA).
NOTE: SAS variable labels, formats, and lengths are not written to DBMS tables.
NOTE: There were 22 observations read from the data set ORION.QTR1_2007.
NOTE: The data set ORIONXLS.QTR1_2007 has 22 observations and 5 variables.
NOTE: Copying ORION.QTR2_2007 to ORIONXLS.QTR2_2007 (memtype=DATA).
NOTE: SAS variable labels, formats, and lengths are not written to DBMS tables.
NOTE: There were 36 observations read from the data set ORION.QTR2_2007.
NOTE: The data set ORIONXLS.QTR2_2007 has 36 observations and 6 variables.
```

35

Import/Export Wizards and Procedures

The Import/Export wizards and IMPORT/EXPORT
procedures enable you to read and write data between
SAS data sets and external PC files.

The Import/Export wizards and procedures are part of
Base SAS and allow access to delimited files. If you
have a license to SAS/ACCESS to PC Files, you can
also access Microsoft Excel, Microsoft Access, dBASE,
JMP, Lotus 1-2-3, SPSS, Stata, and Paradox files.

36

Import/Export Wizards and Procedures

The wizards and procedures have similar capabilities; the wizards are point-and-click interfaces and the procedures are code-based.

To invoke the wizards from the SAS windowing environment, select **File** and **Import Data** or **Export Data**.

37

The Import Wizard

The Import wizard enables you to read data from an external data source and write it to a SAS data set.

Steps of the Import wizard:
1. Select the type of file you are importing.
2. Locate the input file.
3. Select the table range or worksheet from which to import data.
4. Select a location to store the imported file.
5. Save the generated PROC IMPORT code. (Optional)

38

The Import Wizard

1. Select the type of file you are importing.

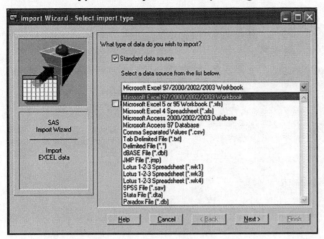

39

The Import Wizard

2. Locate the input file.

40

The Import Wizard

3. Select the table range or worksheet from which to import data.

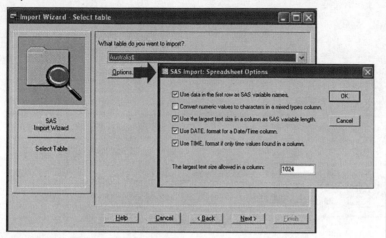

41

The Import Wizard

4. Select a location to store the imported file.

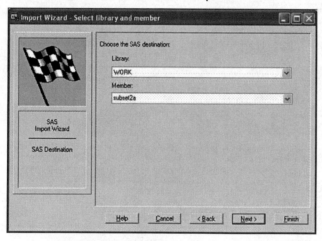

42

The Import Wizard

5. Save the generated PROC IMPORT code. (Optional)

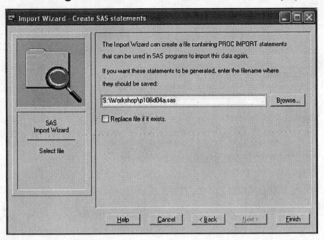

43

The Import Wizard

SAS Log

NOTE: WORK.SUBSET2A data set was successfully created.

```
proc print data=work.subset2a;
run;
```

Partial PROC PRINT Output

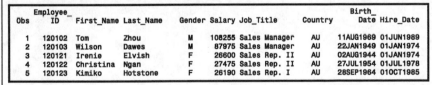

Obs	Employee_ID	First_Name	Last_Name	Gender	Salary	Job_Title	Country	Birth_Date	Hire_Date
1	120102	Tom	Zhou	M	108255	Sales Manager	AU	11AUG1969	01JUN1989
2	120103	Wilson	Dawes	M	87975	Sales Manager	AU	22JAN1949	01JAN1974
3	120121	Irenie	Elvish	F	26600	Sales Rep. II	AU	02AUG1944	01JAN1974
4	120122	Christina	Ngan	F	27475	Sales Rep. II	AU	27JUL1954	01JUL1978
5	120123	Kimiko	Hotstone	F	26190	Sales Rep. I	AU	28SEP1964	01OCT1985

44   p106d04

The Import Wizard

```
proc contents data=work.subset2a;
run;
```

Partial PROC CONTENTS Output

```
                   Alphabetic List of Variables and Attributes

     #   Variable      Type   Len   Format    Informat   Label

     8   Birth_Date    Num     8    DATE9.    DATE9.     Birth Date
     7   Country       Char    2    $2.       $2.        Country
     1   Employee_ID   Num     8                         Employee ID
     2   First_Name    Char   10    $10.      $10.       First Name
     4   Gender        Char    1    $1.       $1.        Gender
     9   Hire_Date     Num     8    DATE9.    DATE9.     Hire Date
     6   Job_Title     Char   14    $14.      $14.       Job Title
     3   Last_Name     Char   12    $12.      $12.       Last Name
     5   Salary        Num     8                         Salary
```

45   p106d04

The IMPORT Procedure

p106d04a was created from the Import wizard.

```
PROC IMPORT OUT= WORK.subset2a
            DATAFILE= "S:\Workshop\sales.xls"
            DBMS=EXCEL REPLACE;
     RANGE="Australia$";
     GETNAMES=YES;
     MIXED=NO;
     SCANTEXT=YES;
     USEDATE=YES;
     SCANTIME=YES;
RUN;
```

46   **p106d04a**

OUT=*<libref.>SAS-data-set*

idcntifies the output SAS data set.

DATAFILE="*filename*"

specifies the complcte path and filename or a fileref for the input PC file, spreadsheet, or delimited external file.

DBMS=*identifier*

specifies the type of data to import. To import a DBMS table, you must specify DBMS= using a valid database identifier. For example, DBMS=EXCEL specifies to import a Microsoft Excel worksheet.

REPLACE

overwrites an existing SAS data set. If you do not specify REPLACE, PROC IMPORT does not overwrite an existing data set.

RANGE="*range-name | absolute-range*"

subsets a spreadsheet by identifying the rectangular set of cells to import from the specified spreadsheet.

GETNAMES=YES | NO

for spreadsheets and delimited external files, determines whether to generate SAS variable names from the column names in the input file's first row of data. Note that if a column name contains special characters that are not valid in a SAS name, such as a blank, SAS converts the character to an underscore.

MIXED=YES | NO

> converts numeric data values into character data values for a column that contains mixed data types. The default is NO, which means that numeric data will be imported as missing values in a character column. If MIXED=YES, then the engine will assign a SAS character type for the column and convert all numeric data values to character data values.

SCANTEXT=YES | NO

> scans the length of text data for a data source column and uses the length of the longest string data that it finds as the SAS column width.

USEDATE=YES | NO

> specifies which format to use. If USEDATE=YES, then DATE. format is used for date/time columns in the data source table while importing data from Excel workbook. If USEDATE=NO, then DATETIME. format is used for date/time.

SCANTIME=YES | NO

> scans all row values for a DATETIME data type field and automatically determines the TIME data type if only time values (that is, no date or datetime values) exist in the column.

The Export Wizard

The Export wizard reads data from a SAS data set and writes it to an external file source.

Steps of the Export wizard:
1. Select the data set from which you want to export data.
2. Select the type of data source to which you want to export files.
3. Assign the output file.
4. Assign the table name.
5. Save the generated PROC EXPORT code. (Optional)

47

The Export Wizard

1. Select the data set from which you want to export data.

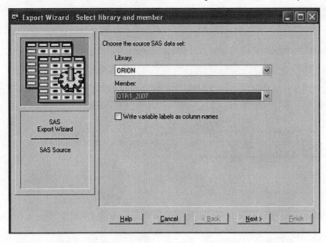

48

The Export Wizard

2. Select the type of data source to which you want to export files.

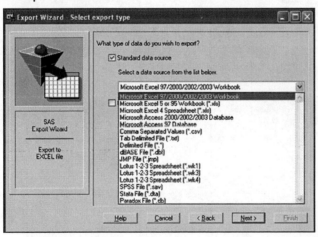

49

The Export Wizard

3. Assign the output file.

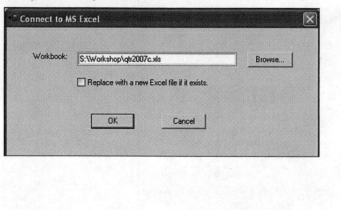

50

The Export Wizard

4. Assign the table name.

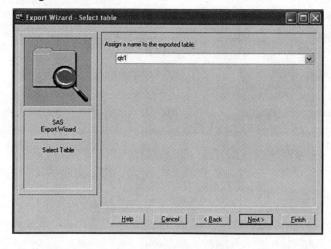

51

The Export Wizard

5. Save the generated PROC EXPORT code. (Optional)

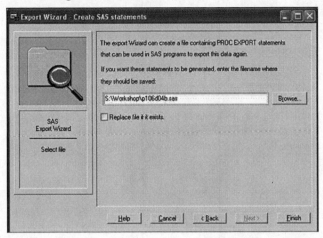

52

The Export Wizard

SAS Log

```
NOTE: File "S:\Workshop\qtr2007c.xls" will be created if the export
      process succeeds.
NOTE: "qtr1" table was successfully created.
```

53

The Export Wizard

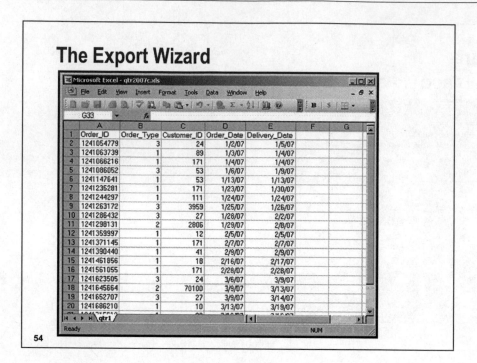

The EXPORT Procedure

p106d04b was created from the Export wizard.

```
PROC EXPORT DATA= ORION.QTR1_2007
             OUTFILE= "S:\Workshop\qtr2007c.xls"
             DBMS=EXCEL REPLACE;
      RANGE="qtr1";
RUN;
```

✎ The RANGE statement is not supported and is
ignored in the EXPORT procedure.

55   **p106d04b**

DATA=<*libref.*>*SAS-data-set*

identifies the input SAS data set.

OUTFILE="*filename*"

specifies the complete path and filename or a fileref for the output PC file, spreadsheet, or
delimited external file.

DBMS=*identifier*

specifies the type of data to export. To export a DBMS table, you must specify DBMS= by
using a valid database identifier. For example, DBMS=EXCEL specifies to export a table
into a Microsoft Excel worksheet.

 **Exercises**

Level 1

4. **Using PROC COPY to Create an Excel Worksheet**

   a. Write a LIBNAME statement to create a *libref* called **MNTH** that references a new Excel workbook named **mnth2007.xls**.

   b. Write a PROC COPY step that copies **orion.mnth7_2007**, **orion.mnth8_2007**, and **orion.mnth9_2007** to the new Excel workbook.

   c. Write a PROC CONTENTS step to view all of the contents of **MNTH**.

   d. Write a LIBNAME statement to clear the **MNTH** *libref*.

Level 2

5. **Using the Import Wizard to Read an Excel Worksheet**

   a. Use the Import wizard to read the **products.xls** workbook.

      Select the worksheet containing children data.

      Name the new data set **work.children**.

      Save the generated PROC IMPORT code to a file called **children.sas**.

   b. Write a PROC PRINT step to create a report of the new data set.

   c. Open **children.sas** to view the PROC IMPORT code.

Level 3

6. **Using the EXPORT Procedure to Create an Excel Worksheet**

   a. Write a PROC EXPORT step to export the data set **orion.mnth7_2007** to an Excel workbook called **mnth7.xls**.

   b. Submit and confirm in the log that **MNTH7_2007** was successfully created.

6.3 Solutions

Solutions to Exercises

1. **Reading an Excel Worksheet**

   a. Retrieve the starter program.

   b. Add a LIBNAME statement.

```
libname custfm 'custfm.xls';

proc contents data=custfm._all_;
run;

data work.males;

run;

proc print data=work.males label;
run;

libname custfm clear;
```

   c. Submit the LIBNAME statement and the PROC CONTENTS step.

   d. Add a SET statement in the DATA step.

```
data work.males;
   set custfm.'Males$'n;
run;
```

   e. Add a KEEP statement in the DATA step.

```
data work.males;
   set custfm.'Males$'n;
   keep First_Name Last_Name Birth_Date;
run;
```

   f. Add a FORMAT statement in the DATA step.

```
data work.males;
   set custfm.'Males$'n;
   keep First_Name Last_Name Birth_Date;
   format Birth_Date year4.;
run;
```

   g. Add a LABEL statement.

```
data work.males;
   set custfm.'Males$'n;
   keep First_Name Last_Name Birth_Date;
   format Birth_Date year4.;
   label Birth_Date='Birth Year';
run;
```

    h. Submit the program.

2. **Reading an Excel Worksheet**

    a. Write a LIBNAME statement.

```
libname prod 'products.xls';
```

    b. Write a PROC CONTENTS step.

```
proc contents data=prod._all_;
run;
```

    c. Submit the program.

    d. Write a DATA step.

```
data work.golf;
   set prod.'Sports$'n;
   where Category='Golf';
   drop Category;
   label Name='Golf Products';
run;
```

    e. Write a LIBNAME statement.

```
libname prod clear;
```

    f. Write a PROC PRINT step.

```
proc print data=work.golf label;
run;
```

3. **Reading a Range of an Excel Worksheet**

    a. Write a LIBNAME statement.

```
libname xlsdata 'custcaus.xls' header=no;
```

    b. Write a PROC CONTENTS step.

```
proc contents data=xlsdata._all_;
run;
```

    c. Submit the program.

    d. Write a DATA step.

```
data work.germany;
   set xlsdata.DE;
   label F1='Customer ID'
         F2='Country'
         F3='Gender'
         F4='First Name'
         F5='Last Name'
         F6='Birth Date';
   format F6 ddmmyy8.;
run;
```

e. Write a LIBNAME statement.

```
libname xlsdata clear;
```

f. Write a PROC PRINT step.

```
proc print data=work.germany label;
run;
```

4. Using PROC COPY to Create an Excel Worksheet

a. Write a LIBNAME statement.

```
libname mnth 'mnth2007.xls';
```

b. Write a PROC COPY step.

```
proc copy  in=orion out=mnth;
   select mnth7_2007 mnth8_2007 mnth9_2007;
run;
```

c. Write a PROC CONTENTS step.

```
proc contents data=mnth._all_;
run;
```

d. Write a LIBNAME statement.

```
libname mnth clear;
```

5. Using the Import Wizard to Read an Excel Worksheet

a. Use the IMPORT wizard.

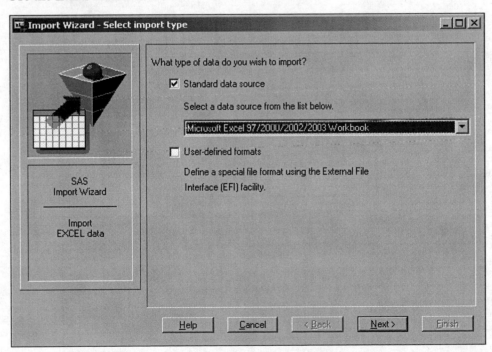

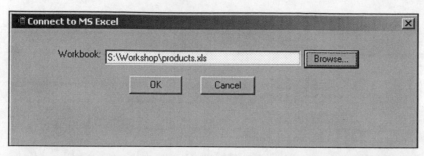

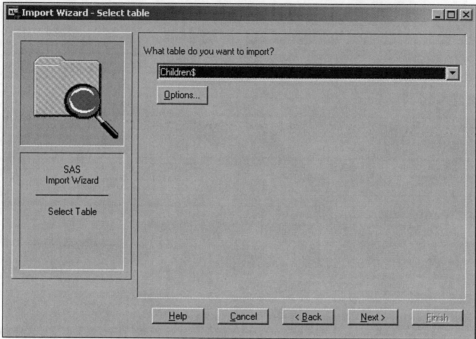

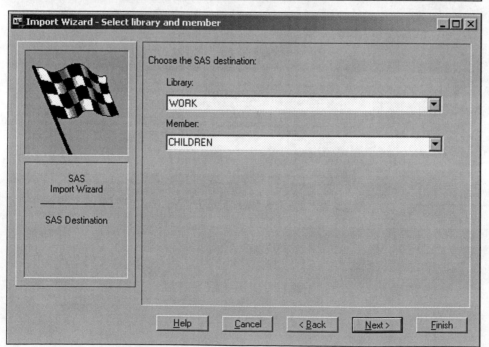

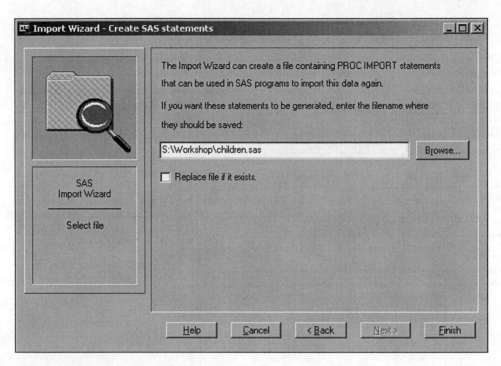

b. Write a PROC PRINT step.

```
proc print data=work.children;
run;
```

c. Open **children.sas**.

```
PROC IMPORT OUT= WORK.children
            DATAFILE= "S:\Workshop\products.xls"
            DBMS=EXCEL REPLACE;
     RANGE="Children$";
     GETNAMES=YES;
     MIXED=NO;
     SCANTEXT=YES;
     USEDATE=YES;
     SCANTIME=YES;
RUN;
```

6. Using the EXPORT Procedure to Create an Excel Worksheet

a. Write a PROC EXPORT step.

```
proc export data=orion.mnth7_2007
            outfile='mnth7.xls'
            dbms=excel replace;
run;
```

b. Submit the program.

Solutions to Student Activities (Polls/Quizzes)

6.01 Quiz – Correct Answer

Which PROC PRINT step displays the worksheet containing employees from United States?

a.
```
proc print data=orionxls.'UnitedStates';
run;
```

b.
```
proc print data=orionxls.'UnitedStates$';
run;
```

c.
```
proc print data=orionxls.'UnitedStates'n;
run;
```

(d.)
```
proc print data=orionxls.'UnitedStates$'n;
run;
```

20

Chapter 7 Reading Delimited Raw Data Files

7.1   Using Standard Delimited Data as Input

Objectives

- Use the DATA step to create a SAS data set from a delimited raw data file.
- Examine the compilation and execution phases of the DATA step when reading a raw data file.
- Explicitly define the length of a variable by using the LENGTH statement.

3

Business Scenario

An existing data source contains information on Orion Star sales employees from Australia and the United States.

A new SAS data set needs to be created that contains a subset of this existing data source.

This new SAS data set must contain the following:

- only the employees from Australia who are Sales Representatives
- the employee's first name, last name, salary, job title, and hired date
- labels and formats in the descriptor portion

4

Business Scenario

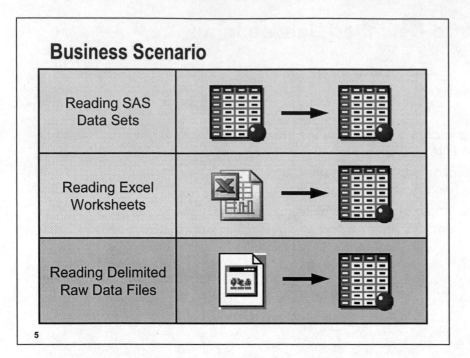

Reading SAS Data Sets	
Reading Excel Worksheets	
Reading Delimited Raw Data Files	

5

Business Scenario

Reading SAS Data Sets	`libname _____ ;`
	`data _____ ;`
	`   set _____ ;`
	`   ...`
	`run;`

Reading Excel Worksheets	`libname _____ ;`
	`data _____ ;`
	`   set _____ ;`
	`   ...`
	`run;`

Reading Delimited Raw Data Files	`data _____ ;`
	`   infile _____ ;`
	`   input _____ ;`
	`   ...`
	`run;`

6

```
sales.csv
```

Partial `sales.csv`   comma delimited

```
120102,Tom,Zhou,M,108255,Sales Manager,AU,11AUG1969,06/01/1989
120103,Wilson,Dawes,M,87975,Sales Manager,AU,22JAN1949,01/01/1974
120121,Irenie,Elvish,F,26600,Sales Rep. II,AU,02AUG1944,01/01/1974
120122,Christina,Ngan,F,27475,Sales Rep. II,AU,27JUL1954,07/01/1978
120123,Kimiko,Hotstone,F,26190,Sales Rep. I,AU,28SEP1964,10/01/1985
120124,Lucian,Daymond,M,26480,Sales Rep. I,AU,13MAY1959,03/01/1979
120125,Fong,Hofmeister,M,32040,Sales Rep. IV,AU,06DEC1954,03/01/1979
120126,Satyakam,Denny,M,26780,Sales Rep. II,AU,20SEP1988,08/01/2006
120127,Sharryn,Clarkson,F,28100,Sales Rep. II,AU,04JAN1979,11/01/1998
120128,Monica,Kletschkus,F,30890,Sales Rep. IV,AU,14JUL1986,11/01/2006
120129,Alvin,Roebuck,M,30070,Sales Rep. III,AU,22NOV1964,10/01/1985
120130,Kevin,Lyon,M,26955,Sales Rep. I,AU,14DEC1984,05/01/2006
120131,Marinus,Surawski,M,26910,Sales Rep. I,AU,25SEP1979,01/01/2003
120132,Fancine,Kaiser,F,28525,Sales Rep. III,AU,05APR1949,10/01/1978
120133,Petrea,Soltau,F,27440,Sales Rep. II,AU,22APR1986,10/01/2006
120134,Sian,Shannan,M,28015,Sales Rep. II,AU,06JUN1949,01/01/1974
120135,Alexei,Platts,M,32490,Sales Rep. IV,AU,26JAN1969,10/01/1997
```

7

The raw data filename needs to be specific to your operating environment.

Business Scenario Syntax

Use the following statements to complete the scenario:

```
DATA output-SAS-data-set;
      LENGTH variable(s) $ length;
      INFILE 'raw-data-file-name';
      INPUT specifications;
      KEEP variable-list;
      LABEL variable = 'label'
                variable = 'label'
                variable = 'label';
      FORMAT variable(s) format;
RUN;
```

8

The DATA Statement (Review)

The *DATA statement* begins a DATA step and provides the name of the SAS data set being created.

```
DATA output-SAS-data-set;
      INFILE 'raw-data-file-name';
      INPUT specifications;
      <additional SAS statements>
RUN;
```

The DATA statement can create temporary or permanent data sets.

9

The INFILE Statement

The *INFILE statement* identifies the physical name of the raw data file to read with an INPUT statement.

```
DATA output-SAS-data-set;
      INFILE 'raw-data-file-name';
      INPUT specifications;
      <additional SAS statements>
RUN;
```

The physical name is the name that the operating environment uses to access the file.

10

The INFILE Statement

Examples:

Windows	`infile 's:\workshop\sales.csv';`
UNIX	`infile '/users/`*userid*`/sales.csv';`
z/OS (OS/390)	`infile '.workshop.rawdata(sales)';`

11

The INPUT Statement

The *INPUT statement* describes the arrangement of values in the raw data file and assigns input values to the corresponding SAS variables.

```
DATA output-SAS-data-set;
    INFILE 'raw-data-file-name';
    INPUT specifications;
    <additional SAS statements>
RUN;
```

The following are input specifications:

- column input
- formatted input
- list input

12

Column input enables you to read standard data values that are aligned in columns in the raw data file.

Formatted input combines the flexibility of using informats with many of the features of column input. By using formatted input, you can read nonstandard data for which SAS requires additional instructions.

List input uses a scanning method for locating data values. Data values are not required to be aligned in columns, but must be separated by at least one blank or other defined delimiter.

7.01 Multiple Answer Poll

Which types of raw data files do you read?

a. delimited raw data files
b. raw data files aligned in columns
c. other
d. none
e. not sure

14

List Input

To read with list input, data values
- must be separated with a delimiter
- can be in standard or nonstandard form.

Partial `sales.csv`

```
120102,Tom,Zhou,M,108255,Sales Manager,AU,11AUG1969,06/01/1989
120103,Wilson,Dawes,M,87975,Sales Manager,AU,22JAN1949,01/01/1974
120121,Irenie,Elvish,F,26600,Sales Rep. II,AU,02AUG1944,01/01/1974
120122,Christina,Ngan,F,27475,Sales Rep. II,AU,27JUL1954,07/01/1978
120123,Kimiko,Hotstone,F,26190,Sales Rep. I,AU,28SEP1964,10/01/1985
120124,Lucian,Daymond,M,26480,Sales Rep. I,AU,13MAY1959,03/01/1979
120125,Fong,Hofmeister,M,32040,Sales Rep. IV,AU,06DEC1954,03/01/1979
120126,Satyakam,Denny,M,26780,Sales Rep. II,AU,20SEP1988,08/01/2006
120127,Sharryn,Clarkson,F,28100,Sales Rep. II,AU,04JAN1979,11/01/1998
```

15

Delimiter

A space (blank) is the default delimiter.

The *DLM= option* can be added to the INFILE statement
to specify an alternate delimiter.

DATA *output-SAS-data-set*;
    INFILE '*raw-data-file-name*' dlm='*delimiter*';
    INPUT *specifications*;
    <additional SAS statements>
RUN;

16

The DLM= option is an alias for the DELIMITER= option.

To specify a tab delimiter on Windows or UNIX, type `dlm='09'x`.

To specify a tab delimiter on z/OS (OS/390), type `dlm='05'x`.

The DSD (delimiter-sensitive data) option changes how SAS treats delimiters when you use LIST input and sets the default delimiter to a comma. When you specify DSD, SAS treats two consecutive delimiters as a missing value and removes quotation marks from character values. The DSD option specifies that when data values are enclosed in quotation marks, delimiters within the value be treated as character data.

Standard and Nonstandard Data

- *Standard data* is data that SAS can read without
  any special instructions.

  Examples of standard numeric data:
  58   -23   67.23   00.99   5.67E5   1.2E-2

- *Nonstandard data* is any data that SAS cannot read
  without a special instruction.

  Examples of nonstandard numeric data:
  5,823   (23) $67.23   01/12/1999   12MAY2006

17

List Input for Standard Data

List input specification:

> **INPUT** *variable* <$>;

- Variables must be specified in the order they appear in the raw data file, left to right.
- $ indicates to store a variable value as a character value rather than as a numeric value.
- The default length for character and numeric variables is eight bytes.

18

List Input for Standard Data

Partial **sales.csv**

```
120102,Tom,Zhou,M,108255,Sales Manager,AU,11AUG1969,06/01/1989
120103,Wilson,Dawes,M,87975,Sales Manager,AU,22JAN1949,01/01/1974
120121,Irenie,Elvish,F,26600,Sales Rep. II,AU,02AUG1944,01/01/1974
120122,Christina,Ngan,F,27475,Sales Rep. II,AU,27JUL1954,07/01/1978
120123,Kimiko,Hotstone,F,26190,Sales Rep. I,AU,28SEP1964,10/01/1985
120124,Lucian,Daymond,M,26480,Sales Rep. I,AU,13MAY1959,03/01/1979
120125,Fong,Hofmeister,M,32040,Sales Rep. IV,AU,06DEC1954,03/01/1979
120126,Satyakam,Denny,M,26780,Sales Rep. II,AU,20SEP1988,08/01/2006
120127,Sharryn,Clarkson,F,28100,Sales Rep. II,AU,04JAN1979,11/01/1998
```

```
input Employee_ID First_Name $ Last_Name $
      Gender $ Salary Job_Title $ Country $;
```

19

Business Scenario

Create a temporary SAS data set named **work.subset3**
from the delimited raw data file named **sales.csv**.

```
data work.subset3;
   infile 'sales.csv' dlm=',';
   input Employee_ID First_Name $ Last_Name $
         Gender $ Salary Job_Title $ Country $;
run;
```

20   p107d01

Business Scenario

```
281   data work.subset3;
282      infile 'sales.csv' dlm=',';
283      input Employee_ID First_Name $ Last_Name $
284            Gender $ Salary Job_Title $ Country $;
285   run;

NOTE: The infile 'sales.csv' is:
      File Name=S:\Workshop\sales.csv,
      RECFM=V,LRECL=256

NOTE: 165 records were read from the infile 'sales.csv'.
      The minimum record length was 61.
      The maximum record length was 80.
NOTE: The data set WORK.SUBSET3 has 165 observations and 7 variables.
```

21

Business Scenario

```
proc print data=work.subset3;
run;
```

Partial PROC PRINT Output

Obs	Employee_ ID	First_ Name	Last_ Name	Gender	Salary	Job_ Title	Country
1	120102	Tom	Zhou	M	108255	Sales Ma	AU
2	120103	Wilson	Dawes	M	87975	Sales Ma	AU
3	120121	Irenie	Elvish	F	26600	Sales Re	AU
4	120122	Christin	Ngan	F	27475	Sales Re	AU
5	120123	Kimiko	Hotstone	F	26190	Sales Re	AU
6	120124	Lucian	Daymond	M	26480	Sales Re	AU
7	120125	Fong	Hofmeist	M	32040	Sales Re	AU
8	120126	Satyakam	Denny	M	26780	Sales Re	AU
9	120127	Sharryn	Clarkson	F	28100	Sales Re	AU
10	120128	Monica	Kletschk	F	30890	Sales Re	AU
11	120129	Alvin	Roebuck	M	30070	Sales Re	AU
12	120130	Kevin	Lyon	M	26955	Sales Re	AU

22   p107d01

DATA Step Processing

The DATA step is processed in two phases:

- compilation
- execution

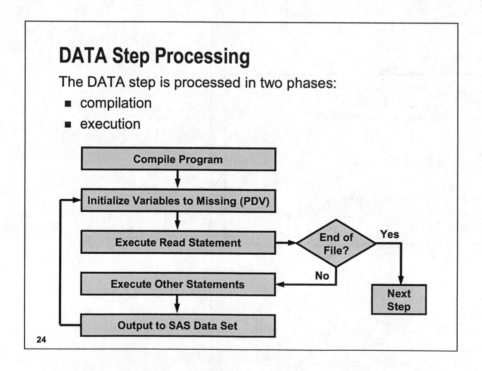

24

Compilation

During the compilation phase, SAS

- checks the syntax of the DATA step statements
- creates an input buffer to hold the current raw data file record that is being processed
- creates a program data vector (PDV) to hold the current SAS observation
- creates the descriptor portion of the output data set.

25

Compilation

```
data work.subset3;
    infile 'sales.csv' dlm=',';
    input Employee_ID First_Name $ Last_Name $
          Gender $ Salary Job_Title $ Country $;
run;
```

26   ...

Compilation

```
data work.subset3;
   infile 'sales.csv' dlm=',';
   input Employee_ID First_Name $ Last_Name $
         Gender $ Salary Job_Title $ Country $;
run;
```

Input Buffer

									1										2				
1	2	3	4	5	6	7	8	9	0	1	2	3	4	5	6	7	8	9	0	1	2	3	4	5

27

...

Compilation

```
data work.subset3;
   infile 'sales.csv' dlm=',';
   input Employee_ID First_Name $ Last_Name $
         Gender $ Salary Job_Title $ Country $;
run;
```

Input Buffer

									1										2				
1	2	3	4	5	6	7	8	9	0	1	2	3	4	5	6	7	8	9	0	1	2	3	4	5

PDV

Employee _ID
N 8

The default length for numeric
variables is eight bytes.

28

...

Compilation

```
data work.subset3;
   infile 'sales.csv' dlm=',';
   input Employee_ID First_Name $ Last_Name $
         Gender $ Salary Job_Title $ Country $;
run;
```

Input Buffer

									1										2					
1	2	3	4	5	6	7	8	9	0	1	2	3	4	5	6	7	8	9	0	1	2	3	4	5

PDV

Employee _ID N 8	First_ Name $ 8

For list input, the default length for character variables is eight bytes.

29   ...

Compilation

```
data work.subset3;
   infile 'sales.csv' dlm=',';
   input Employee_ID First_Name $ Last_Name $
         Gender $ Salary Job_Title $ Country $;
run;
```

Input Buffer

									1										2					
1	2	3	4	5	6	7	8	9	0	1	2	3	4	5	6	7	8	9	0	1	2	3	4	5

PDV

Employee _ID N 8	First_ Name $ 8	Last _Name $ 8	Gender $ 8	Salary N 8	Job_ Title $ 8	Country $ 8

30   ...

Compilation

```
data work.subset3;
   infile 'sales.csv' dlm=',';
   input Employee_ID First_Name $ Last_Name $
         Gender $ Salary Job_Title $ Country $;
run;
```

Descriptor Portion work.subset3

Employee_ID	First_Name	Last_Name	Gender	Salary	Job_Title	Country
N 8	$ 8	$ 8	$ 8	N 8	$ 8	$ 8

31   ...

7.02 Multiple Choice Poll

Which statement is true?

a. An input buffer is only created if reading data from a raw data file.

b. The PDV at compile time holds the variable name, type, byte size, and initial value.

c. The descriptor portion is the first item that gets created at compile time.

33

Execution

Partial `sales.csv`

```
120102,Tom,Zhou, ...
120103,Wilson,Dawes, ...
120121,Irenie,Elvish, ...
120122,Christina,Ngan, ...
120123,Kimiko,Hotstone, ...
120124,Lucian,Daymond, ...
120125,Fong,Hofmeister, ...
```

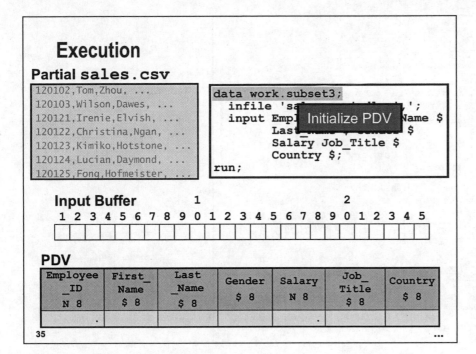

```
data work.subset3;
   infile 'sa          ';
   input Empl          Name $
         Last_         $
         Salary Job_Title $
         Country $;
run;
```

Initialize PDV

Input Buffer

									1										2				
1	2	3	4	5	6	7	8	9	0	1	2	3	4	5	6	7	8	9	0	1	2	3	4	5

PDV

Employee_ID N 8	First_Name $ 8	Last_Name $ 8	Gender $ 8	Salary N 8	Job_Title $ 8	Country $ 8
.				.		

35   ...

Execution

Partial `sales.csv`

```
120102,Tom,Zhou, ...
120103,Wilson,Dawes, ...
120121,Irenie,Elvish, ...
120122,Christina,Ngan, ...
120123,Kimiko,Hotstone, ...
120124,Lucian,Daymond, ...
120125,Fong,Hofmeister, ...
```

```
data work.subset3;
   infile 'sales.csv' dlm=',';
   input Employee_ID First_Name $
         Last_Name $ Gender $
         Salary Job_Title $
         Country $;
run;
```

Input Buffer

									1										2				
1	2	3	4	5	6	7	8	9	0	1	2	3	4	5	6	7	8	9	0	1	2	3	4	5

PDV

Employee_ID N 8	First_Name $ 8	Last_Name $ 8	Gender $ 8	Salary N 8	Job_Title $ 8	Country $ 8
.				.		

36   ...

Execution

Partial `sales.csv`

```
120102,Tom,Zhou, ...
120103,Wilson,Dawes, ...
120121,Irenie,Elvish, ...
120122,Christina,Ngan, ...
120123,Kimiko,Hotstone, ...
120124,Lucian,Daymond, ...
120125,Fong,Hofmeister, ...
```

```
data work.subset3;
   infile 'sales.csv' dlm=',';
   input Employee_ID First_Name $
         Last_Name $ Gender $
         Salary Job_Title $
         Country $;
run;
```

Input Buffer

| | | | | | | | | | 1 | | | | | | | | | | 2 | | | | | |
|1|2|3|4|5|6|7|8|9|0|1|2|3|4|5|6|7|8|9|0|1|2|3|4|5|

| 1 | 2 | 0 | 1 | 0 | 2 | , | T | o | m | , | Z | h | o | u | , | M | , | 1 | 0 | 8 | 2 | 5 | 5 | , |

PDV

Employee _ID N 8	First_ Name $ 8	Last _Name $ 8	Gender $ 8	Salary N 8	Job_ Title $ 8	Country $ 8
.				.		

37   ...

Execution

Partial `sales.csv`

```
120102,Tom,Zhou, ...
120103,Wilson,Dawes, ...
120121,Irenie,Elvish, ...
120122,Christina,Ngan, ...
120123,Kimiko,Hotstone, ...
120124,Lucian,Daymond, ...
120125,Fong,Hofmeister, ...
```

```
data work.subset3;
   infile 'sales.csv' dlm=',';
   input Employee_ID First_Name $
         Last_Name $ Gender $
         Salary Job_Title $
         Country $;
run;
```

Input Buffer

| | | | | | | | | | 1 | | | | | | | | | | 2 | | | | | |
|1|2|3|4|5|6|7|8|9|0|1|2|3|4|5|6|7|8|9|0|1|2|3|4|5|

| 1 | 2 | 0 | 1 | 0 | 2 | , | T | o | m | , | Z | h | o | u | , | M | , | 1 | 0 | 8 | 2 | 5 | 5 | , |

PDV

Employee _ID N 8	First_ Name $ 8	Last _Name $ 8	Gender $ 8	Salary N 8	Job_ Title $ 8	Country $ 8
120102	Tom	Zhou	M	108255	Sales Ma	AU

38   ...

Execution

Partial `sales.csv`

```
120102,Tom,Zhou, ...
120103,Wilson,Dawes, ...
120121,Irenie,Elvish, ...
120122,Christina,Ngan, ...
120123,Kimiko,Hotstone, ...
120124,Lucian,Daymond, ...
120125,Fong,Hofmeister, ...
```

```
data work.subset3;
   infile 'sales.csv' dlm=',';
   input Employee_ID First_Name $
         Last_Name $ Gender $
         Salary Job_Title $
         Country $;
run;
```

Implicit OUTPUT;
Implicit RETURN;

Input Buffer   1

1	2	3	4	5	6	7	8	9	0	1	2	3	4	5	6	7	8	9	0	1	2	3	4	5
1	2	0	1	0	2	,	T	o	m	,	Z	h	o	u	,	M	,	1	0	8	2	5	5	,

PDV

Employee _ID N 8	First_ Name $ 8	Last_ Name $ 8	Gender $ 8	Salary N 8	Job_ Title $ 8	Country $ 8
120102	Tom	Zhou	M	108255	Sales Ma	AU

39   ...

Execution

Output SAS Data Set after First Iteration of DATA Step

`work.subset3`

Employee _ID	First_ Name	Last_ Name	Gender	Salary	Job_ Title	Country
120102	Tom	Zhou	M	108255	Sales Ma	AU

40   ...

Execution

Partial `sales.csv`

```
120102,Tom,Zhou, ...
120103,Wilson,Dawes, ...
120121,Irenie,Elvish, ...
120122,Christina,Ngan, ...
120123,Kimiko,Hotstone, ...
120124,Lucian,Daymond, ...
120125,Fong,Hofmeister, ...
```

```
data work.subset3;
   infile 'sa              ;
   input Empl            me $
          Las
          Salary Job_Title $
          Country $;
run;
```

Reinitialize PDV

Input Buffer

									1										2					
1	2	3	4	5	6	7	8	9	0	1	2	3	4	5	6	7	8	9	0	1	2	3	4	5
1	2	0	1	0	2	,	T	o	m	,	Z	h	o	u	,	M	,	1	0	8	2	5	5	,

PDV

Employee _ID N 8	First_ Name $ 8	Last_ Name $ 8	Gender $ 8	Salary N 8	Job_ Title $ 8	Country $ 8
.				.		

41   ...

Execution

Partial `sales.csv`

```
120102,Tom,Zhou, ...
120103,Wilson,Dawes, ...
120121,Irenie,Elvish, ...
120122,Christina,Ngan, ...
120123,Kimiko,Hotstone, ...
120124,Lucian,Daymond, ...
120125,Fong,Hofmeister, ...
```

```
data work.subset3;
   infile 'sales.csv' dlm=',';
   input Employee_ID First_Name $
          Last_Name $ Gender $
          Salary Job_Title $
          Country $;
run;
```

Input Buffer

									1										2					
1	2	3	4	5	6	7	8	9	0	1	2	3	4	5	6	7	8	9	0	1	2	3	4	5
1	2	0	1	0	2	,	T	o	m	,	Z	h	o	u	,	M	,	1	0	8	2	5	5	,

PDV

Employee _ID N 8	First_ Name $ 8	Last_ Name $ 8	Gender $ 8	Salary N 8	Job_ Title $ 8	Country $ 8
.				.		

42   ...

Execution

Partial sales.csv

```
120102,Tom,Zhou, ...
120103,Wilson,Dawes, ...
120121,Irenie,Elvish, ...
120122,Christina,Ngan, ...
120123,Kimiko,Hotstone, ...
120124,Lucian,Daymond, ...
120125,Fong,Hofmeister, ...
```

```
data work.subset3;
   infile 'sales.csv' dlm=',';
   input Employee_ID First_Name $
         Last_Name $ Gender $
         Salary Job_Title $
         Country $;
run;
```

Input Buffer

									1										2					
1	2	3	4	5	6	7	8	9	0	1	2	3	4	5	6	7	8	9	0	1	2	3	4	5
1	2	0	1	0	3	,	W	i	l	s	o	n	,	D	a	w	e	s	,	8	7	9	7	5

PDV

Employee _ID N 8	First_ Name $ 8	Last_ Name $ 8	Gender $ 8	Salary N 8	Job_ Title $ 8	Country $ 8
.				.		

43   ...

Execution

Partial sales.csv

```
120102,Tom,Zhou, ...
120103,Wilson,Dawes, ...
120121,Irenie,Elvish, ...
120122,Christina,Ngan, ...
120123,Kimiko,Hotstone, ...
120124,Lucian,Daymond, ...
120125,Fong,Hofmeister, ...
```

```
data work.subset3;
   infile 'sales.csv' dlm=',';
   input Employee_ID First_Name $
         Last_Name $ Gender $
         Salary Job_Title $
         Country $;
run;
```

Input Buffer

									1										2					
1	2	3	4	5	6	7	8	9	0	1	2	3	4	5	6	7	8	9	0	1	2	3	4	5
1	2	0	1	0	3	,	W	i	l	s	o	n	,	D	a	w	e	s	,	8	7	9	7	5

PDV

Employee _ID N 8	First_ Name $ 8	Last_ Name $ 8	Gender $ 8	Salary N 8	Job_ Title $ 8	Country $ 8
120103	Wilson	Dawes	M	87975	Sales Ma	AU

44   ...

Execution

Partial `sales.csv`

```
120102,Tom,Zhou, ...
120103,Wilson,Dawes, ...
120121,Irenie,Elvish, ...
120122,Christina,Ngan, ...
120123,Kimiko,Hotstone, ...
120124,Lucian,Daymond, ...
120125,Fong,Hofmeister, ...
```

```
data work.subset3;
   infile 'sales.csv' dlm=',';
   input Employee_ID First_Name $
         Last_Name $ Gender $
         Salary Job_Title $
         Country $;
run;
```

Implicit OUTPUT;
Implicit RETURN;

Input Buffer   1

1	2	3	4	5	6	7	8	9	0	1	2	3	4	5	6	7	8	9	0	1	2	3	4	5
1	2	0	1	0	3	,	W	i	l	s	o	n	,	D	a	w	e	s	,	8	7	9	7	5

PDV

Employee _ID N 8	First_ Name $ 8	Last _Name $ 8	Gender $ 8	Salary N 8	Job_ Title $ 8	Country $ 8
120103	Wilson	Dawes	M	87975	Sales Ma	AU

45

...

Execution

Output SAS Data Set after Second Iteration of DATA Step

`work.subset3`

Employee ID	First_ Name	Last _Name	Gender	Salary	Job_ Title	Country
120102	Tom	Zhou	M	108255	Sales Ma	AU
120103	Wilson	Dawes	M	87975	Sales Ma	AU

46

...

Execution

Partial `sales.csv`

```
120102,Tom,Zhou, ...
120103,Wilson,Dawes, ...
120121,Irenie,Elvish, ...
120122,Christina,Ngan, ...
120123,Kimiko,Hotstone, ...
120124,Lucian,Daymond, ...
120125,Fong,Hofmeister, ...
```

Continue until EOF

```
infile 'sales.csv' dlm=',';
input Employee_ID First_Name $
      Last_Name $ Gender $
      Salary Job_Title $
      Country $;
run;
```

Input Buffer

									1										2					
1	2	3	4	5	6	7	8	9	0	1	2	3	4	5	6	7	8	9	0	1	2	3	4	5
1	2	0	1	0	3	,	W	i	l	s	o	n	,	D	a	w	e	s	,	8	7	9	7	5

PDV

Employee _ID N 8	First_ Name $ 8	Last_ Name $ 8	Gender $ 8	Salary N 8	Job_ Title $ 8	Country $ 8
120103	Wilson	Dawes	M	87975	Sales Ma	AU

47

7.03 Multiple Choice Poll

Which statement is true?

a. Data is read directly from the raw data file to the PDV.

b. At the bottom of the DATA step, the contents of the PDV are output to the output SAS data set.

c. When SAS returns to the top of the DATA step, any variable coming from a SAS data set is set to missing.

49

The LENGTH Statement

The *LENGTH statement* defines the length of a variable explicitly.

General form of the LENGTH statement:

LENGTH *variable(s)* $ *length*;

Example:

```
length First_Name Last_Name $ 12
       Gender $ 1;
```

52

Business Scenario

Create a temporary SAS data set named **work.subset3** from the delimited raw data file named **sales.csv**.

```
data work.subset3;
   length First_Name $ 12 Last_Name $ 18
          Gender $ 1 Job_Title $ 25
          Country $ 2;
   infile 'sales.csv' dlm=',';
   input Employee_ID First_Name $ Last_Name $
         Gender $ Salary Job_Title $ Country $;
run;
```

53   p107d02

Business Scenario

```
proc print data=work.subset3;
run;
```

Partial PROC PRINT Output

Obs	First_Name	Last_Name	Gender	Job_Title	Country	Employee_ID	Salary
1	Tom	Zhou	M	Sales Manager	AU	120102	108255
2	Wilson	Dawes	M	Sales Manager	AU	120103	87975
3	Irenie	Elvish	F	Sales Rep. II	AU	120121	26600
4	Christina	Ngan	F	Sales Rep. II	AU	120122	27475
5	Kimiko	Hotstone	F	Sales Rep. I	AU	120123	26190
6	Lucian	Daymond	M	Sales Rep. I	AU	120124	26480
7	Fong	Hofmeister	M	Sales Rep. IV	AU	120125	32040
8	Satyakam	Denny	M	Sales Rep. II	AU	120126	26780
9	Sharryn	Clarkson	F	Sales Rep. II	AU	120127	28100
10	Monica	Kletschkus	F	Sales Rep. IV	AU	120128	30890
11	Alvin	Roebuck	M	Sales Rep. III	AU	120129	30070
12	Kevin	Lyon	M	Sales Rep. I	AU	120130	26955

54

p107d02

Compilation

```
data work.subset3;
   length First_Name $ 12 Last_Name $ 18
          Gender $ 1 Job_Title $ 25
          Country $ 2;
   infile 'sales.csv' dlm=',';
   input Employee_ID First_Name $ Last_Name $
         Gender $ Salary Job_Title $ Country $;
run;
```

PDV

First _Name $ 12	Last _Name $ 18	Gender $ 1	Job_ Title $ 25	Country $ 2

55

...

Compilation

```
data work.subset3;
   length First_Name $ 12 Last_Name $ 18
          Gender $ 1 Job_Title $ 25
          Country $ 2;
   infile 'sales.csv' dlm=',';
   input Employee_ID First_Name $ Last_Name $
         Gender $ Salary Job_Title $ Country $;
run;
```

PDV

First _Name $ 12	Last _Name $ 18	Gender $ 1	Job_ Title $ 25	Country $ 2	Employee _ID N 8	Salary N 8

56

 **Exercises**

Level 1

1. **Reading a Comma Delimited Raw Data File**

   a. Retrieve the starter program **p107e01**.

   b. Add the appropriate LENGTH, INFILE, and INPUT statements to read the comma delimited raw data file named the following:

Windows or UNIX	**newemps.csv**
z/OS (OS/390)	**.workshop.rawdata(newemps)**

   Partial Raw Data File

   ```
   Satyakam,Denny,Sales Rep. II,26780
   Monica,Kletschkus,Sales Rep. IV,30890
   Kevin,Lyon,Sales Rep. I,26955
   Petrea,Soltau,Sales Rep. II,27440
   Marina,Iyengar,Sales Rep. III,29715
   ```

   The following variables should be read into the program data vector:

Name	Type	Length
First	Character	12
Last	Character	18
Title	Numeric	25
Salary	Numeric	8

   c. Submit the program to create the following PROC PRINT report:

   Partial PROC PRINT Output (First 5 of 71 Observations)

   ```
   Obs    First        Last                  Title         Salary

     1    Satyakam     Denny            Sales Rep. II      26780
     2    Monica       Kletschkus       Sales Rep. IV      30890
     3    Kevin        Lyon             Sales Rep. I       26955
     4    Petrea       Soltau           Sales Rep. II      27440
     5    Marina       Iyengar          Sales Rep. III     29715
   ```

Level 2

2. Reading a Space Delimited Raw Data File

a. Write a DATA step to create a new data set named **work.QtrDonation** by reading the space delimited raw data file named the following:

Windows or UNIX	**donation.dat**
z/OS (OS/390)	**.workshop.rawdata(donation)**

Partial Raw Data File

```
120265 . . . 25
120267 15 15 15 15
120269 20 20 20 20
120270 20 10 5 .
120271 20 20 20 20
```

The following variables should be read into the program data vector:

Name	Type	Length
IDNum	Character	6
Qtr1	Numeric	8
Qtr2	Numeric	8
Qtr3	Numeric	8
Qtr4	Numeric	8

b. Write a PROC PRINT step to create the following report:

Partial PROC PRINT Output (First 10 of 124 Observations)

Obs	IDNum	Qtr1	Qtr2	Qtr3	Qtr4
1	120265	.	.	.	25
2	120267	15	15	15	15
3	120269	20	20	20	20
4	120270	20	10	5	.
5	120271	20	20	20	20
6	120272	10	10	10	10
7	120275	15	15	15	15
8	120660	25	25	25	25
9	120662	10	.	5	5
10	120663	.	.	5	.

Level 3

3. Using Column Input to Read a Fixed Column Raw Data File

a. Write a DATA step to create a new data set named **work.supplier_info** by reading the fixed column raw data file named the following:

Windows or UNIX	**supplier.dat**
z/OS (OS/390)	**.workshop.rawdata(supplier)**

Use column input in the INPUT statement to read the fixed column data.

 Documentation on column input can be found in the SAS Help and Documentation from the Contents tab (**SAS Products** ⇨ **Base SAS** ⇨ **SAS 9.2 Language Reference: Dictionary** ⇨ **Dictionary of Language Elements** ⇨ **Statements** ⇨ **INPUT Statement, Column**).

Partial Raw Data File

```
50    Scandinavian Clothing A/S      NO
109   Petterson AB                   SE
316   Prime Sports Ltd               GB
755   Top Sports                     DK
772   AllSeasons Outdoor Clothing    US
```

The following is the layout of the raw data file:

Name	Starting Column	Ending Column
ID	1	5
Name	8	37
Country	40	41

b. Write a PROC PRINT step to create the following report:

Partial PROC PRINT Output (First 10 of 52 Observations)

```
          Obs      ID   Name                           Country

            1      50   Scandinavian Clothing A/S      NO
            2     109   Petterson AB                   SE
            3     316   Prime Sports Ltd               GB
            4     755   Top Sports                     DK
            5     772   AllSeasons Outdoor Clothing    US
            6     798   Sportico                       ES
            7    1280   British Sports Ltd             GB
            8    1303   Eclipse Inc                    US
            9    1684   Magnifico Sports               PT
           10    1747   Pro Sportswear Inc             US
```

7.2 Using Nonstandard Delimited Data as Input

Objectives

- Use informats to read nonstandard data.
- Add additional SAS statements to perform further processing in the DATA step.

60

Standard and Nonstandard Data

- *Standard data* is data that SAS can read without any special instructions.

  Examples of standard numeric data:

  58   -23   67.23   00.99   5.67E5   1.2E-2

- *Nonstandard data* is any data that SAS cannot read without a special instruction.

  Examples of nonstandard numeric data:

  5,823   (23) $67.23   01/12/1999   12MAY2006

61

List Input for Nonstandard Data

List input specification:

> **INPUT** *variable* <$> *variable* < :*informat* >;

- An informat is an instruction that SAS uses to read data values into a variable.
- The **:** modifier informs SAS to ignore the width associated with the informat and treat the file as delimited.

62

SAS Informats

SAS informats have the following form:

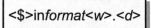

> <$>in*format*<*w*>.<*d*>

$	indicates a character informat
informat	names the SAS informat or user-defined informat
w	specifies the number of columns to read in the input data
.	required delimiter
d	specifies an optional decimal scaling factor in the numeric informats

63

SAS Informats

Selected SAS Informats:

Informat	Definition
$w.	Reads standard character data.
w.d	Reads standard numeric data.
COMMAw.d DOLLARw.d	Reads nonstandard numeric data and removes embedded commas, blanks, dollar signs, percent signs, and dashes.
COMMAXw.d DOLLARXw.d	Reads nonstandard numeric data and removes embedded periods, blanks, dollar signs, percent signs, and dashes.
EUROXw.d	Reads nonstandard numeric data and removes embedded characters in European currency.

64

SAS Informats

In list input, informats are used to convert nonstandard numeric data to SAS numeric values.

Informat	Raw Data Value	SAS Data Value
COMMA7.0 DOLLAR7.0	$12,345	12345
COMMAX7.0 DOLLARX7.0	$12.345	12345
EUROX7.0	€12.345	12345

65

SAS Informats

| <$>informat<w>.<d> |

The *d* specifies the power of 10 by which to divide the value.

Informat	Raw Data Value	SAS Data Value
COMMA6.2 DOLLAR6.2	$12345	123.45
COMMA10.2 DOLLAR10.2	$12345.567	12345.567

If the data value contains a decimal point, the *d* is ignored.

66

SAS Informats

SAS uses date informats to read and convert dates to SAS date values.

Informat	Raw Data Value	SAS Data Value
MMDDYY6.	010160	0
MMDDYY8.	01/01/60	0
MMDDYY10.	01/01/1960	0
DDMMYY6.	311260	365
DDMMYY8.	31/12/60	365
DDMMYY10.	31/12/1960	365
DATE7.	31DEC59	-1
DATE9.	31DEC1959	-1

67

: Modifier

The : modifier informs SAS to ignore the width associated with the informat and treat the file as delimited.

For example,   `:mmddyy10.`

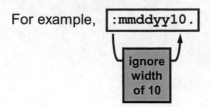

`:mmddyy10.` can read all of the following values:

- 01/07/2008
- 1/07/2008
- 01/7/2008
- 1/7/2008
- 01/07/08
- 1/7/08

68

List Input for Nonstandard Data

Partial **sales.csv**

```
120102,Tom,Zhou,M,108255,Sales Manager,AU,11AUG1969,06/01/1989
120103,Wilson,Dawes,M,87975,Sales Manager,AU,22JAN1949,01/01/1974
120121,Irenie,Elvish,F,26600,Sales Rep. II,AU,02AUG1944,01/01/1974
120122,Christina,Ngan,F,27475,Sales Rep. II,AU,27JUL1954,07/01/1978
120123,Kimiko,Hotstone,F,26190,Sales Rep. I,AU,28SEP1964,10/01/1985
120124,Lucian,Daymond,M,26480,Sales Rep. I,AU,13MAY1959,03/01/1979
120125,Fong,Hofmeister,M,32040,Sales Rep. IV,AU,06DEC1954,03/01/1979
120126,Satyakam,Denny,M,26780,Sales Rep. II,AU,20SEP1988,08/01/2006
120127,Sharryn,Clarkson,F,28100,Sales Rep. II,AU,04JAN1979,11/01/1998
```

```
input Employee_ID First_Name $ Last_Name $
      Gender $ Salary Job_Title $ Country $
      Birth_Date :date9.
      Hire_Date :mmddyy10. ;
```

69

7.04 Quiz

Which INPUT statement correctly reads the space-delimited raw data file?

Raw Data

```
Donny 5MAY2008 25 FL $43,132.50
Margaret 20FEB2008 43 NC 65,150
```

a.
```
input name $ hired date9. age
      state $ salary comma10.;
```

b.
```
input name $ hired :date9. age
      state $ salary :comma10.;
```

71

Business Scenario

Create a temporary SAS data set named **work.subset3** from the delimited raw data file named **sales.csv**.

```
data work.subset3;
   length First_Name $ 12 Last_Name $ 18
          Gender $ 1 Job_Title $ 25
          Country $ 2;
   infile 'sales.csv' dlm=',';
   input Employee_ID First_Name $ Last_Name $
         Gender $ Salary Job_Title $ Country $
         Birth_Date :date9.
         Hire_Date :mmddyy10.;
run;
```

73   p107d03

Business Scenario

```
proc print data=work.subset3;
run;
```

Partial PROC PRINT Output

Obs	First_Name	Last_Name	Gender	Job_Title	Country	Employee_ID	Salary	Birth_Date	Hire_Date
1	Tom	Zhou	M	Sales Manager	AU	120102	108255	3510	10744
2	Wilson	Dawes	M	Sales Manager	AU	120103	87975	-3996	5114
3	Irenie	Elvish	F	Sales Rep. II	AU	120121	26600	-5630	5114
4	Christina	Ngan	F	Sales Rep. II	AU	120122	27475	-1984	6756
5	Kimiko	Hotstone	F	Sales Rep. I	AU	120123	26190	1732	9405
6	Lucian	Daymond	M	Sales Rep. I	AU	120124	26480	-233	6999
7	Fong	Hofmeister	M	Sales Rep. IV	AU	120125	32040	-1852	6999
8	Satyakam	Denny	M	Sales Rep. II	AU	120126	26780	10490	17014
9	Sharryn	Clarkson	F	Sales Rep. II	AU	120127	28100	6943	14184
10	Monica	Kletschkus	F	Sales Rep. IV	AU	120128	30890	9691	17106
11	Alvin	Roebuck	M	Sales Rep. III	AU	120129	30070	1787	9405
12	Kevin	Lyon	M	Sales Rep. I	AU	120130	26955	9114	16922
13	Marinus	Surawski	M	Sales Rep. I	AU	120131	26910	7207	15706
14	Fancine	Kaiser	F	Sales Rep. III	AU	120132	28525	-3923	6848

74   p107d03

Additional SAS Statements

Additional SAS statements can be added to perform
further processing in the DATA step.

```
data work.subset3;
   length First_Name $ 12 Last_Name $ 18
          Gender $ 1 Job_Title $ 25
          Country $ 2;
   infile 'sales.csv' dlm=',';
   input Employee_ID First_Name $ Last_Name $
         Gender $ Salary Job_Title $ Country $
         Birth_Date :date9.
         Hire_Date :mmddyy10.;
   keep First_Name Last_Name Salary
        Job_Title Hire_Date;
   label Job_Title='Sales Title'
         Hire_Date='Date Hired';
   format Salary dollar12. Hire_Date monyy7.;
run;
                                              p107d04
```

Additional SAS Statements

```
proc print data=work.subset3 label;
run;
```

Partial PROC PRINT Output

Obs	First_ Name	Last_Name	Sales Title	Salary	Date Hired
1	Tom	Zhou	Sales Manager	$108,255	JUN1989
2	Wilson	Dawes	Sales Manager	$87,975	JAN1974
3	Irenie	Elvish	Sales Rep. II	$26,600	JAN1974
4	Christina	Ngan	Sales Rep. II	$27,475	JUL1978
5	Kimiko	Hotstone	Sales Rep. I	$26,190	OCT1985
6	Lucian	Daymond	Sales Rep. I	$26,480	MAR1979
7	Fong	Hofmeister	Sales Rep. IV	$32,040	MAR1979
8	Satyakam	Denny	Sales Rep. II	$26,780	AUG2006
9	Sharryn	Clarkson	Sales Rep. II	$28,100	NOV1998
10	Monica	Kletschkus	Sales Rep. IV	$30,890	NOV2006

76   p107d04

Additional SAS Statements

- The WHERE statement is used to obtain a subset of observations from an input data set.
- The WHERE statement cannot be used to select records from a raw data file.

The subsetting IF, which can subset data that is in the PDV, is discussed in a later chapter.

77

Exercises

Level 1

4. Reading a Comma Delimited Raw Data File

a. Retrieve the starter program **p107e04**.

b. Add the appropriate LENGTH, INFILE, and INPUT statements to read the comma delimited raw data file named the following:

Windows or UNIX	`custca.csv`
z/OS (OS/390)	`.workshop.rawdata(custca)`

Partial Raw Data File

```
Bill,Cuddy,11171,M,16/10/1986,21,15-30 years
Susan,Krasowski,17023,F,09/07/1959,48,46-60 years
Andreas,Rennie,26148,M,18/07/1934,73,61-75 years
Lauren,Krasowski,46966,F,24/10/1986,21,15-30 years
Lauren,Marx,54655,F,18/08/1969,38,31-45 years
```

The following variables should be read into the program data vector:

Name	Type	Length
First	Character	20
Last	Character	20
ID	Numeric	8
Gender	Character	1
BirthDate	Numeric	8
Age	Numeric	8
AgeGroup	Character	12

c. Add a FORMAT statement and a DROP statement in the DATA step to create a data set that looks like the following when used in the PROC PRINT step:

Partial PROC PRINT Output (First 5 of 15 Observations)

```
                                                     Birth
   Obs    First     Last        Gender   AgeGroup     Date

     1    Bill      Cuddy         M      15-30 years  OCT1986
     2    Susan     Krasowski     F      46-60 years  JUL1959
     3    Andreas   Rennie        M      61-75 years  JUL1934
     4    Lauren    Krasowski     F      15-30 years  OCT1986
     5    Lauren    Marx          F      31-45 years  AUG1969
```

Level 2

5. Reading an Asterisk Delimited Raw Data File

a. Write a DATA step to create a new data set named **work.prices** by reading the asterisk delimited raw data file named the following:

Windows or UNIX	**prices.dat**
z/OS (OS/390)	**.workshop.rawdata(prices)**

Partial Raw Data File

```
210200100009*09JUN2007*31DEC9999*$15.50*$34.70
210200100017*24JAN2007*31DEC9999*$17.80*$40.00
210200200023*04JUL2007*31DEC9999*$8.25*$19.80
210200600067*27OCT2007*31DEC9999*$28.90*$67.00
210200600085*28AUG2007*31DEC9999*$17.85*$39.40
```

The following variables should be read into the program data vector:

Name	Type	Length
ProductID	Numeric	8
StartDate	Numeric	8
EndDate	Numeric	8
UnitCostPrice	Numeric	8
UnitSalesPrice	Numeric	8

b. Write a PROC PRINT step and add a LABEL and a FORMAT statement in the DATA step to create a data set that looks like the following when used in the PROC PRINT step:

Partial PROC PRINT Output (First 10 of 259 Observations)

Obs	Product ID	Start of Date Range	End of Date Range	Cost Price per Unit	Sales Price per Unit
1	210200100009	06/09/2007	12/31/9999	15.50	34.70
2	210200100017	01/24/2007	12/31/9999	17.80	40.00
3	210200200023	07/04/2007	12/31/9999	8.25	19.80
4	210200600067	10/27/2007	12/31/9999	28.90	67.00
5	210200600085	08/28/2007	12/31/9999	17.85	39.40
6	210200600112	01/04/2007	12/31/9999	9.25	21.80
7	210200900033	09/17/2007	12/31/9999	6.45	14.20
8	210200900038	02/01/2007	12/31/9999	9.30	20.30
9	210201000050	04/02/2007	12/31/9999	9.00	19.60
10	210201000126	04/22/2007	12/31/9999	2.30	6.50

Level 3

6. Reading a Space Delimited Raw Data File with Spaces in Data Values

a. Write a DATA step to create a new data set named **work.us_customers** by reading the space delimited raw data named the following:

Windows or UNIX	**custus.dat**
z/OS (OS/390)	**.workshop.rawdata(custus)**

Use an option in the INFILE statement to specify that when data values are enclosed in quotation marks, delimiters within the value are treated as part of the data value.

    Documentation on the INFILE statement options can be found in the SAS Help and Documentation from the Contents tab (**SAS Products** ⇨ **Base SAS** ⇨ **SAS 9.2 Language Reference: Dictionary** ⇨ **Dictionary of Language Elements** ⇨ **Statements** ⇨ **INFILE Statement**).

Partial Raw Data File

```
"James Kvarniq" 4 M 27JUN1974 33 "31-45 years"
"Sandrina Stephano" 5 F 09JUL1979 28 "15-30 years"
"Karen Ballinger" 10 F 18OCT1984 23 "15-30 years"
"David Black" 12 M 12APR1969 38 "31-45 years"
"Jimmie Evans" 17 M 17AUG1954 53 "46-60 years"
```

The following variables should be created in data set **work.us_customers**:

Name	Type	Length
Name	Character	20
ID	Numeric	8
Gender	Character	1
BirthDate	Numeric	8
Age	Numeric	8
AgeGroup	Character	12

b. Add a FORMAT statement in the DATA step to make the **BirthDate** look like a three-character month with a four-digit year.

c. Write a PROC PRINT step with a VAR statement to create the following report:

Partial PROC PRINT Output (First 7 of 28 Observations)

```
                                          Birth
        Obs    Name              Gender    Date     AgeGroup     Age

          1    James Kvarniq       M      JUN1974   31-45 years   33
          2    Sandrina Stephano   F      JUL1979   15-30 years   28
          3    Karen Ballinger     F      OCT1984   15-30 years   23
          4    David Black         M      APR1969   31-45 years   38
          5    Jimmie Evans        M      AUG1954   46-60 years   53
          6    Tonie Asmussen      M      FEB1954   46-60 years   53
          7    Michael Dineley     M      APR1959   46-60 years   48
```

7.3 Solutions

Solutions to Exercises

1. **Reading a Comma Delimited Raw Data File**

   a. Retrieve the starter program.

   b. Add the appropriate LENGTH, INFILE, and INPUT statements.

```
data work.NewEmployees;
   length First $ 12 Last $ 18 Title $ 25;
   infile 'newemps.csv' dlm=',';
   input First $ Last $ Title $ Salary;
run;

proc print data=work.NewEmployees;
run;
```

   For z/OS (OS/390), the following INFILE statement is used:

```
   infile '.workshop.rawdata(newemps)' dlm=',';
```

   c. Submit the program.

2. **Reading a Space Delimited Raw Data File**

   a. Write a DATA step.

```
data work.QtrDonation;
   length IDNum $ 6;
   infile 'donation.dat';
   input IDNum $ Qtr1 Qtr2 Qtr3 Qtr4;
run;
```

   For z/OS (OS/390), the following INFILE statement is used:

```
   infile '.workshop.rawdata(donation)';
```

   b. Write a PROC PRINT step.

```
proc print data=work.QtrDonation;
run;
```

3. **Using Column Input to Read a Fixed Column Raw Data File**

   a. Write a DATA step.

```
data work.supplier_info;
   infile 'supplier.dat';
   input ID 1-5 Name $ 8-37 Country $ 40-41;
run;
```

   For z/OS (OS/390), the following INFILE statement is used:

```
   infile '.workshop.rawdata(supplier)';
```

b. Write a PROC PRINT step.

```
proc print data=work.supplier_info;
run;
```

4. Reading a Comma Delimited Raw Data File

a. Retrieve the starter program.

b. Add the appropriate LENGTH, INFILE, and INPUT statements.

```
data work.canada_customers;
   length First Last $ 20 Gender $ 1 AgeGroup $ 12;
   infile 'custca.csv' dlm=',';
   input First $ Last $ ID Gender $
         BirthDate :ddmmyy10. Age AgeGroup $;
run;

proc print data=work.canada_customers;
run;
```

For z/OS (OS/390), the following INFILE statement is used:

```
   infile '.workshop.rawdata(custca)' dlm=',';
```

c. Add a FORMAT statement and a DROP statement.

```
data work.canada_customers;
   length First Last $ 20 Gender $ 1 AgeGroup $ 12;
   infile 'custca.csv' dlm=',';
   input First $ Last $ ID Gender $
         BirthDate :ddmmyy10. Age AgeGroup $;
   format BirthDate monyy7.;
   drop ID Age;
run;
```

5. Reading an Asterisk Delimited Raw Data File

a. Write a DATA step.

```
data work.prices;
   infile 'prices.dat' dlm='*';
   input ProductID StartDate :date9. EndDate :date9.
         UnitCostPrice :dollar8. UnitSalesPrice :dollar8.;
run;
```

For z/OS (OS/390), the following INFILE statement is used:

```
   infile '.workshop.rawdata(prices)' dlm='*';
```

b. Write a PROC PRINT step and add a LABEL and a FORMAT statement in the DATA step.

```
data work.prices;
   infile 'prices.dat' dlm='*';
   input ProductID StartDate :date9. EndDate :date9.
         UnitCostPrice :dollar8. UnitSalesPrice :dollar8.;
   label ProductID='Product ID'
         StartDate='Start of Date Range'
         EndDate='End of Date Range'
         UnitCostPrice='Cost Price per Unit'
         UnitSalesPrice='Sales Price per Unit';
   format StartDate EndDate mmddyy10.
          UnitCostPrice UnitSalesPrice 8.2;
run;


proc print data=work.prices label;
run;
```

6. Reading a Space Delimited Raw Data File with Spaces in Data Values

    a. Write a DATA step.

```
data work.us_customers;
   length Name $ 20 Gender $ 1 AgeGroup $ 12;
   infile 'custus.dat' dlm=' ' dsd;
   input Name $ ID Gender $ BirthDate :date9.
         Age AgeGroup $;
run;
```

    For z/OS (OS/390), the following INFILE statement is used:

```
   infile '.workshop.rawdata(custus)' dlm=' ' dsd;
```

    b. Add a FORMAT statement.

```
data work.us_customers;
   length Name $ 20 Gender $ 1 AgeGroup $ 12;
   infile 'custus.dat' dlm=' ' dsd;
   input Name $ ID Gender $ BirthDate :date9.
         Age AgeGroup $;
   format BirthDate monyy7.;
run;
```

    c. Write a PROC PRINT step.

```
proc print data=work.us_customers;
   var Name Gender BirthDate AgeGroup Age;
run;
```

Solutions to Student Activities (Polls/Quizzes)

7.02 Multiple Choice Poll – Correct Answer

Which statement is true?

(a.) An input buffer is only created if reading data from a raw data file.

b. The PDV at compile time holds the variable name, type, byte size, and initial value.

c. The descriptor portion is the first item that gets created at compile time.

34

7.03 Multiple Choice Poll – Correct Answer

Which statement is true?

a. Data is read directly from the raw data file to the PDV.

(b.) At the bottom of the DATA step, the contents of the PDV are output to the output SAS data set.

c. When SAS returns to the top of the DATA step, any variable coming from a SAS data set is set to missing.

50

7.04 Quiz – Correct Answer

Which INPUT statement correctly reads the space-delimited raw data file?

Raw Data

```
Donny 5MAY2008 25 FL $43,132.50
Margaret 20FEB2008 43 NC 65,150
```

a.
```
input name $ hired date9. age
      state $ salary comma10.;
```

b.
```
input name $ hired :date9. age
      state $ salary :comma10.;
```

72

Chapter 8   Validating and Cleaning Data

8.1 Introduction to Validating and Cleaning Data

Objectives

- Define data errors in a raw data file.
- Identify procedures for validating data.
- Identify techniques for cleaning data.
- Define the business scenario that will be used with validating and cleaning data.

3

Business Scenario

A delimited raw data file containing information on Orion Star non-sales employees from Australia and the United States needs to be read to create a data set.

Requirements of non-sales employee data:

- `Employee_ID`, `Salary`, `Birth_Date`, and `Hire_Date` must be numeric variables.

- `First`, `Last`, `Gender`, `Job_Title`, and `Country` must be character variables.

4

8.01 Quiz

What problems will SAS have reading the numeric data
Salary and **Hire_Date**?

Partial nonsales.csv

```
120101,Patrick,Lu,M,163040,Director,AU,18AUG1976,01JUL2003
120104,Kareen,Billington,F,46230,Administration Manager,au,11MAY1954,01JAN1981
120105,Liz,Povey,F,27110,Secretary I,AU,21DEC1974,01MAY1999
120106,John,Hornsey,M,unknown,Office Assistant II,AU,23DEC1944,01JAN1974
120107,Sherie,Sheedy,F,30475,Office Assistant III,AU,01FEB1978,21JAN1953
120108,Gladys,Gromek,F,27660,Warehouse Assistant II,AU,23FEB1984,01AUG2006
120108,Gabriele,Baker,F,26495,Warehouse Assistant I,AU,15DEC1986,01OCT2006
120110,Dennis,Entwisle,M,28615,Warehouse Assistant III,AU,20NOV1949,01NOV1979
120111,Ubaldo,Spillane,M,26895,Security Guard II,AU,23JUL1949,99NOV1978
120112,Ellis,Glattback,F,26550, ,AU,17FEB1969,01JUL1990
120113,Riu,Horsey,F,26870,Security Guard II,AU,10MAY1944,01JAN1974
120114,Jeannette,Buddery,G,31285,Security Manager,AU,08FEB1944,01JAN1974
120115,Hugh,Nichollas,M,2650,Service Assistant I,AU,08MAY1984,01AUG2005
,,Austen,Ralston,M,29250,Service Assistant II,AU,13JUN1959,01FEB1980
120117,Bill,Mccleary,M,31670,Cabinet Maker III,AU,11SEP1964,01APR1986
```

6

Data Errors

Data errors occur when data values are not appropriate
for the SAS statements that are specified in a program.

- SAS detects data errors during program execution.
- When a data error is detected, SAS continues to
  execute the program.

```
NOTE: Invalid data for Salary in line 4 23-29.
RULE:     ----+----1----+----2----+----3----+----4----+----5----+----6
4         120106,John,Hornsey,M,unknown,Office Assistant II,AU,23DEC19
      61  44,01JAN1974 72
Employee_ID=120106 First=John Last=Hornsey Gender=M Salary=.
Job_Title=Office Assistant II Country=AU Birth_Date=23/12/1944
Hire_Date=01/01/1974 _ERROR_=1 _N_=4
NOTE: Invalid data for Hire_Date in li
9         120111,Ubaldo,Spillane,M,268                              94
      61  9,99NOV1978 71
Employee_ID=120111 First=Ubaldo Last=S
Job_Title=Security Guard II Country=AU
Hire_Date=. _ERROR_=1 _N_=9
```

A data error example is
defining a variable as
numeric, but the data value
is actually character.

8

Business Scenario

Additional requirements of non-sales employee data:

- **Employee_ID** must be unique and not missing.
- **Gender** must have a value of F or M.
- **Salary** must be in the numeric range of 24000 – 500000.
- **Job_Title** must not be missing.
- **Country** must have a value of AU or US.
- **Birth_Date** value must occur before **Hire_Date** value.
- **Hire_Date** must have a value of 01/01/1974 or later.

9

8.02 Quiz

What problems exist with the data in this partial data set?

	Employee_ID	First	Last	Gender	Salary	Job_Title	Country	Birth_Date	Hire_Date
1	120101	Patrick	Lu	M	163E3	Director	AU	18/08/1976	01/07/2003
2	120104	Kareen	Billington	F	46230	Administration Manager	au	11/05/1954	01/01/1981
3	120105	Liz	Povey	F	27110	Secretary I	AU	21/12/1974	01/05/1999
4	120106	John	Hornsey	M	.	Office Assistant II	AU	23/12/1944	01/01/1974
5	120107	Sherie	Sheedy	F	30475	Office Assistant III	AU	01/02/1978	21/01/1953
6	120108	Gladys	Gromek	F	27660	Warehouse Assistant II	AU	23/02/1984	01/08/2006
7	120108	Gabriele	Baker	F	26495	Warehouse Assistant I	AU	15/12/1986	01/10/2006
8	120110	Dennis	Entwisle	M	28615	Warehouse Assistant III	AU	20/11/1949	01/11/1979
9	120111	Ubaldo	Spillane	M	26895	Security Guard II	AU	23/07/1949	.
10	120112	Ellis	Glattback	F	26550		AU	17/02/1969	01/07/1990
11	120113	Riu	Horsey	F	26870	Security Guard II	AU	10/05/1944	01/01/1974
12	120114	Jeannette	Buddery	G	31285	Security Manager	AU	08/02/1944	01/01/1974
13	120115	Hugh	Nichollas	M	2650	Service Assistant I	AU	08/05/1984	01/08/2005
14	.	Austen	Ralston	M	29250	Service Assistant II	AU	13/06/1959	01/02/1980
15	120117	Bill	Mccleary	M	31670	Cabinet Maker III	AU	11/09/1964	01/04/1986
16	120118	Darshi	Hartshorn	M	29090	Cabinet Maker II	AU	03/06/1959	01/07/1984

Hint: There are nine data problems.

11

Validating the Data

In general, SAS procedures analyze data, produce output, or manage SAS files.

In addition, SAS procedures can be used to detect invalid data.

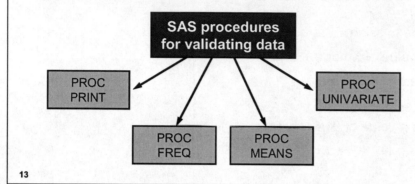

13

The PRINT Procedure

The PRINT procedure can show the job titles that are missing and the hire dates that occur before the birth dates.

```
         Employee_
Obs         ID         Job_Title          Birth_Date      Hire_Date

  5       120107    Office Assistant III   01/02/1978     21/01/1953
  9       120111    Security Guard II      23/07/1949         .
 10       120112                           17/02/1969     01/07/1990
```

14   p108d01

The FREQ Procedure

The FREQ procedure can show if any genders are not F or M and if any countries are not AU or US.

```
                      The FREQ Procedure

                                      Cumulative    Cumulative
Gender    Frequency    Percent        Frequency      Percent

F             110       47.01            110          47.01
G               1        0.43            111          47.44
M             123       52.56            234         100.00

                 Frequency Missing = 1


                                      Cumulative    Cumulative
Country   Frequency    Percent        Frequency      Percent

AU             33       14.04             33          14.04
US            196       83.40            229          97.45
au              3        1.28            232          98.72
us              3        1.28            235         100.00
```

15

The MEANS Procedure

The MEANS procedure can show if any salaries are not in the range of 24000 to 500000.

```
                   The MEANS Procedure

                Analysis Variable : Salary

             N
     N     Miss      Minimum          Maximum

    234      1       2401.00        433800.00
```

16

p108d01

The UNIVARIATE Procedure

The UNIVARIATE procedure can show if any salaries are not in the range of 24000 to 500000.

Partial PROC UNIVARIATE Output

```
              The UNIVARIATE Procedure
                 Variable:  Salary

                 Extreme Observations

      -----Lowest----        -----Highest----

      Value     Obs          Value      Obs

       2401      20         163040        1
       2650      13         194885      231
      24025      25         207885       28
      24100      19         268455       29
      24390     228         433800       27
```

17   p108d01

Cleaning the Data

After the data has been validated, the invalid data needs to be cleaned up.

Techniques for cleaning data:
- Editing raw data file outside of SAS
- Interactively editing data set using VIEWTABLE
- Programmatically editing data set using the DATA step
- Programmatically editing data set using the SQL procedure
- Using SAS's DataFlux product dfPower Studio

18

Ideally, invalid data should be cleaned in the original data source and not in the SAS data set.

Integrity constraints can be placed on a data set to eliminate the possibility of invalid data in the data set. Integrity constraints are a set of data validation rules that you can specify in order to restrict the data values that can be stored for a variable in a SAS data file. Integrity constraints help you preserve the validity and consistency of your data. SAS enforces the integrity constraints when the values associated with an integrity constraint variable are added, updated, or deleted.

Section 8.5 addresses the situation where you have no choice but to correct the data in the SAS data set.

8.2 Examining Data Errors When Reading Raw Data Files

Objectives

- Identify data errors.
- Demonstrate what happens when a data error is encountered.
- Direct the observations with data errors to a different data set than the observations without data errors. (Self-Study)

21

Business Scenario

A delimited raw data file containing information on Orion Star non-sales employees from Australia and the United States needs to be read to create a data set.

Requirements of non-sales employee data:

- `Employee_ID`, `Salary`, `Birth_Date`, and `Hire_Date` must be numeric variables.
- `First`, `Last`, `Gender`, `Job_Title`, and `Country` must be character variables.

22

8.03 Multiple Choice Poll

Which statements are used to read a delimited
raw data file and create a SAS data set?

a. DATA and SET only
b. DATA and INFILE only
c. DATA, SET, and INPUT only
d. DATA, INFILE, and INPUT only

24

Data Errors

One type of data error is when the INPUT statement
encounters invalid data in a field.

When SAS encounters a data error, these events occur:
- A note that describes the error is printed in the
  SAS log.
- The input record (contents of the input buffer) being
  read is displayed in the SAS log.
- The values in the SAS observation (contents of the
  PDV) being created are displayed in the SAS log.
- A missing value is assigned to the appropriate
  SAS variable.
- Execution continues.

26

Data Errors

A note that describes the error is printed in the
SAS log.

Partial SAS Log

```
NOTE: Invalid data for Salary in line 4 23-29.
RULE:     ----+----1----+----2----+----3----+----4----+----5----+----6
4         120106,John,Hornsey,M,unknown,Office Assistant II,AU,23DEC19
     61   44,01JAN1974 72
Employee_ID=120106 First=John Last=Hornsey Gender=M Salary=.
Job_Title=Office Assistant II Country=AU Birth_Date=23/12/1944
Hire_Date=01/01/1974 _ERROR_=1 _N_=4
```

This note indicates that invalid data was found for variable
Salary in line 4 of the raw data file in columns 23-29.

27

Data Errors

The input record (contents of the input buffer) being read
is displayed in the SAS log.

Partial SAS Log

```
NOTE: Invalid data for Salary in line 4 23-29.
RULE:     ----+----1----+----2----+----3----+----4----+----5----+----6
4         120106,John,Hornsey,M,unknown,Office Assistant II,AU,23DEC19
     61   44,01JAN1974 72
Employee_ID=120106 First=John Last=Hornsey Gender=M Salary=.
Job_Title=Office Assistant II Country=AU Birth_Date=23/12/1944
Hire_Date=01/01/1974 _ERROR_=1 _N_=4
```

A ruler is drawn above the raw data record that contains
the invalid data.

28

Data Errors

The values in the SAS observation (contents of the PDV) being created are displayed in the SAS log.

Partial SAS Log

```
NOTE: Invalid data for Salary in line 4 23-29.
RULE:      ----+----1----+----2----+----3----+----4----+----5----+----6
4          120106,John,Hornsey,M,unknown,Office Assistant II,AU,23DEC19
       61  44,01JAN1974 72
Employee_ID=120106 First=John Last=Hornsey Gender=M Salary=.
Job_Title=Office Assistant II Country=AU Birth_Date=23/12/1944
Hire_Date=01/01/1974 _ERROR_=1 _N_=4
```

29

Data Errors

A missing value is assigned to the appropriate SAS variable.

Partial SAS Log

```
NOTE: Invalid data for Salary in line 4 23-29.
RULE:      ----+----1----+----2----+----3----+----4----+----5----+----6
4          120106,John,Hornsey,M,unknown,Office Assistant II,AU,23DEC19
       61  44,01JAN1974 72
Employee_ID=120106 First=John Last=Hornsey Gender=M Salary=.
Job_Title=Office Assistant II Country=AU Birth_Date=23/12/1944
Hire_Date=01/01/1974 _ERROR_=1 _N_=4
```

30

Data Errors

During the processing of every DATA step, SAS automatically creates the following temporary variables:

- the _N_ variable, which counts the number of times the DATA step begins to iterate

- the _ERROR_ variable, which signals the occurrence of an error caused by the data during execution

  0 indicates no errors exist.

  1 indicates one or more errors occurred.

```
NOTE: Invalid data for Salary in line 4 23-29.
RULE:     ----+----1----+----2----+----3----+----4----+----5----+----6
4           120106,John,Hornsey,M,unknown,Office Assistant II,AU,23DEC19
      61  44,01JAN1974 72
Employee_ID=120106 First=John Last=Hornsey Gender=M Salary=.
Job_Title=Office Assistant II Country=AU Birth_Date=23/12/1944
Hire_Date=01/01/1974  ERROR_=1  _N_=4
```

31

Examining Data Errors

p108d02

Submit the following program and review the results in the Output and Log windows.

```
data work.nonsales;
   length Employee_ID 8 First $ 12 Last $ 18
          Gender $ 1 Salary 8 Job_Title $ 25 Country $ 2
          Birth_Date Hire_Date 8;
   infile 'nonsales.csv' dlm=',';
   input Employee_ID First $ Last $
         Gender $ Salary Job_Title $ Country $
         Birth_Date :date9.
         Hire_Date :date9.;
   format Birth_Date Hire_Date ddmmyy10.;
run;

proc print data=work.nonsales;
run;
```

For z/OS (OS/390), the following INFILE statement is used:

```
infile '.workshop.rawdata(nonsales)' dlm=',';
```

Partial PROC PRINT Output

Obs	Employee_ID	First	Last	Gender	Salary	Job_Title	Country	Birth_Date	Hire_Date
1	120101	Patrick	Lu	M	163040	Director	AU	18/08/1976	01/07/2003
2	120104	Kareen	Billington	F	46230	Administration Manager	au	11/05/1954	01/01/1981
3	120105	Liz	Povey	F	27110	Secretary I	AU	21/12/1974	01/05/1999
4	120106	John	Hornsey	M	.	Office Assistant II	AU	23/12/1944	01/01/1974
5	120107	Sherie	Sheedy	F	30475	Office Assistant III	AU	01/02/1978	21/01/1953
6	120108	Gladys	Gromek	F	27660	Warehouse Assistant II	AU	23/02/1984	01/08/2006
7	120108	Gabriele	Baker	F	26495	Warehouse Assistant I	AU	15/12/1986	01/10/2006
8	120110	Dennis	Entwisle	M	28615	Warehouse Assistant III	AU	20/11/1949	01/11/1979
9	120111	Ubaldo	Spillane	M	26895	Security Guard II	AU	23/07/1949	.
10	120112	Ellis	Glattback	F	26550		AU	17/02/1969	01/07/1990
11	120113	Riu	Horsey	F	26870	Security Guard II	AU	10/05/1944	01/01/1974
12	120114	Jeannette	Buddery	G	31285	Security Manager	AU	08/02/1944	01/01/1974
13	120115	Hugh	Nichollas	M	2650	Service Assistant I	AU	08/05/1984	01/08/2005
14	.	Austen	Ralston	M	29250	Service Assistant II	AU	13/06/1959	01/02/1980
15	120117	Bill	Mccleary	M	31670	Cabinet Maker III	AU	11/09/1964	01/04/1986

Partial SAS Log

```
181  data work.nonsales;
182     length Employee_ID 8 First $ 12 Last $ 18
183            Gender $ 1 Salary 8 Job_Title $ 25 Country $ 2
184            Birth_Date Hire_Date 8;
185     infile 'nonsales.csv' dlm=',';
186     input Employee_ID First $ Last $
187            Gender $ Salary Job_Title $ Country $
188            Birth_Date :date9.
189            Hire_Date :date9.;
190     format Birth_Date Hire_Date ddmmyy10.;
191  run;

NOTE: The infile 'nonsales.csv' is:
      File Name=s:\workshop\nonsales.csv,
      RECFM=V,LRECL=256

NOTE: Invalid data for Salary in line 4 23-29.
RULE:      ----+----1----+----2----+----3----+----4----+----5----+----6----+----7----+----8----+
4          120106,John,Hornsey,M,unknown,Office Assistant II,AU,23DEC1944,01JAN1974 72
Employee_ID=120106 First=John Last=Hornsey Gender=M Salary=. Job_Title=Office Assistant II
Country=AU Birth_Date=23/12/1944 Hire_Date=01/01/1974 _ERROR_=1 _N_=4
NOTE: Invalid data for Hire_Date in line 9 63-71.
9          120111,Ubaldo,Spillane,M,26895,Security Guard II,AU,23JUL1949,99NOV1978 71
Employee_ID=120111 First=Ubaldo Last=Spillane Gender=M Salary=26895 Job_Title=Security Guard II
Country=AU Birth_Date=23/07/1949 Hire_Date=. _ERROR_=1 _N_=9
NOTE: 235 records were read from the infile 'nonsales.csv'.
      The minimum record length was 55.
      The maximum record length was 82.
NOTE: The data set WORK.NONSALES has 235 observations and 9 variables.
```

Setup for the Poll

- Submit program **p108a01**.
- Determine the reason for the invalid data that appears in the SAS log.

34

8.04 Multiple Choice Poll

Which statement best describes the invalid data?

a. The data in the raw data file is bad.
b. The programmer incorrectly read the data.

35

Outputting to Multiple Data Sets (Self-Study)

The DATA statement can specify multiple output data sets.

```
data work.baddata work.gooddata;
   length Employee_ID 8 First $ 12 Last $ 18
          Gender $ 1 Salary 8 Job_Title $ 25
          Country $ 2 Birth_Date Hire_Date 8;
   infile 'nonsales.csv' dlm=',';
   input Employee_ID First $ Last $
         Gender $ Salary Job_Title $ Country $
         Birth_Date :date9.
         Hire_Date :date9.;
   format Birth_Date Hire_Date ddmmyy10.;
   if _error_=1 then output work.baddata;
   else output work.gooddata;
run;
```

38   p108d03

The raw data filename specified in the INFILE statement needs to be specific to your operating environment.

Outputting to Multiple Data Sets (Self-Study)

An OUTPUT statement can be used in a conditional statement to write the current observation to a specific data set that is listed in the DATA statement.

```
data work.baddata work.gooddata;
   length Employee_ID 8 First $ 12 Last $ 18
          Gender $ 1 Salary 8 Job_Title $ 25
          Country $ 2 Birth_Date Hire_Date 8;
   infile 'nonsales.csv' dlm=',';
   input Employee_ID First $ Last $
         Gender $ Salary Job_Title $ Country $
         Birth_Date :date9.
         Hire_Date :date9.;
   format Birth_Date Hire_Date ddmmyy10.;
   if _error_=1 then output work.baddata;
   else output work.gooddata;
run;
```

39   p108d03

Outputting to Multiple Data Sets (Self-Study)

Partial SAS Log

```
NOTE: Invalid data for Salary in line 4 23-29.
RULE:       ----+----1----+----2----+----3----+----4----+----5----+----6
4          120106,John,Hornsey,M,unknown,Office Assistant II,AU,23DEC19
     61  44,01JAN1974 72
Employee_ID=120106 First=John Last=Hornsey Gender=M Salary=.
Job_Title=Office Assistant II Country=AU Birth_Date=23/12/1944
Hire_Date=01/01/1974 _ERROR_=1 _N_=4
NOTE: Invalid data for Hire_Date in line 9 63-71.
9          120111,Ubaldo,Spillane,M,26895,Security Guard II,AU,23JUL194
     61  9,99NOV1978 71
Employee_ID=120111 First=Ubaldo Last=Spillane Gender=M Salary=26895
Job_Title=Security Guard II Country=AU Birth_Date=23/07/1949
Hire_Date=. _ERROR_=1 _N_=9
NOTE: 235 records were read from the infile
      's:\workshop\nonsales.csv'.
      The minimum record length was 55.
      The maximum record length was 82.
NOTE: The data set WORK.BADDATA has 2 observations and 9 variables.
NOTE: The data set WORK.GOODDATA has 233 observations and 9 variables.
```

40

8.3 Validating Data with the PRINT and FREQ Procedures

Objectives

- Validate data by using the PRINT procedure with the WHERE statement.
- Validate data by using the FREQ procedure with the TABLES statement.

42

Business Scenario

Additional requirements of non-sales employee data:

- **Employee_ID** must be unique and not missing.
- **Gender** must have a value of F or M.
- **Salary** must be in the numeric range of 24000 – 500000.
- **Job_Title** must not be missing.
- **Country** must have a value of AU or US.
- **Birth_Date** value must occur before **Hire_Date** value.
- **Hire_Date** must have a value of 01/01/1974 or later.

43

SAS Procedures for Validating Data

SAS procedures can be used to detect invalid data.

PROC PRINT step with VAR and WHERE statements	Detects invalid character and numeric values by subsetting observations based on conditions
PROC FREQ step with TABLES statement	Detects invalid character and numeric values by looking at distinct values
PROC MEANS step with VAR statement	Detects invalid numeric values by using summary statistics
PROC UNIVARIATE step with VAR statement	Detects invalid numeric values by looking at extreme values

44

The PRINT Procedure

The PRINT procedure produces detail reports based on SAS data sets.

General form of the PRINT procedure:

```
PROC PRINT DATA=SAS-data-set ;
     VAR variable(s) ;
     WHERE where-expression ;
RUN;
```

- The VAR statement selects variables to include in the report and their order in the report.
- The WHERE statement is used to obtain a subset of observations.

45

The WHERE Statement

For validating data, the WHERE statement is used to retrieve the observations that do not meet the data requirements.

General form of the WHERE statement:

> **WHERE** *where-expression* ;

The *where-expression* is a sequence of operands and operators that form a set of instructions that define a condition for selecting observations.

- Operands include constants and variables.
- Operators are symbols that request a comparison, arithmetic calculation, or logical operation.

46

The WHERE Statement

The following PROC PRINT step retrieves observations that have missing values for **Job_Title**.

```
proc print data=orion.nonsales;
   var Employee_ID Last Job_Title;
   where Job_Title = ' ';
run;
```

Obs	Employee_ID	Last	Job_Title
10	120112	Glattback	

p108d04

47

The WHERE Statement

A WHERE statement might need to reference
a SAS date value.

For example, the PRINT procedure needs to retrieve
observations that have values of **Hire_Date** less
than January 1, 1974.

> **What is the numeric SAS date value for January 1, 1974?**

A *SAS date constant* is used to convert a calendar date
to a SAS date value.

48

SAS Date Constant

To write a SAS date constant, enclose a date in quotation
marks in the form **ddMMMyyyy** and immediately follow
the final quotation mark with the letter **d**.

dd	is a one- or two-digit value for the day.
MMM	is a three-letter abbreviation for the month.
yyyy	is a four-digit value for the year.
d	is required to convert the quoted string to a SAS date.

Example:
Date constant for January 1, 1974, is `'01JAN1974'd`

49

SAS Date Constant

The following PROC PRINT step retrieves observations that have values of **Hire_Date** less than January 1, 1974.

```
proc print data=orion.nonsales;
   var Employee_ID Birth_Date Hire_Date;
   where Hire_Date < '01JAN1974'd;
run;
```

Obs	Employee_ID	Birth_Date	Hire_Date
5	120107	01/02/1978	21/01/1953
9	120111	23/07/1949	.
214	121011	11/03/1944	01/01/1968

p108d04

50

8.05 Multiple Choice Poll

Which data requirement can not be achieved with the PRINT procedure using a WHERE statement?

a. **Employee_ID** must be unique and not missing.
b. **Gender** must have a value of F or M.
c. **Salary** must be in the numeric range of 24000 – 500000.
d. **Job_Title** must not be missing.
e. **Country** must have a value of AU or US.
f. **Birth_Date** value must occur before **Hire_Date** value.
g. **Hire_Date** must have a value of 01/01/1974 or later.

52

Data Requirements

Data Requirement	*where-expression* to obtain invalid data
Employee_ID must be unique and not missing.	`Employee_ID = .` **Does not account for uniqueness.**
Gender must have a value of F or M.	`Gender not in ('F','M')`
Salary must be in the range of 24000 – 500000.	`Salary not between 24000 and 500000`
Job_Title must not be missing.	`Job_Title = ' '`
Country must have a value of AU or US.	`Country not in ('AU','US')`
Birth_Date must occur before **Hire_Date**.	`Birth_Date > Hire_Date`
Hire_Date must have a value of 01/01/1974 or later.	`Hire_Date < '01JAN1974'd`

54

Data Requirements

The following PROC PRINT step accounts for all of the data requirements except the **Employee_ID** being unique.

```
proc print data=orion.nonsales;
   var Employee_ID Gender Salary Job_Title
       Country Birth_Date Hire_Date;
   where Employee_ID = . or
         Gender not in ('F','M') or
         Salary not between 24000 and 500000 or
         Job_Title = ' ' or
         Country not in ('AU','US') or
         Birth_Date > Hire_Date or
         Hire_Date < '01JAN1974'd;
run;
```

✎   The OR operator is used between expressions. Only one expression needs to be true to account for an observation with invalid data.

55   p108d04

Data Requirements

Sixteen observations need data cleaned.

Obs	Employee_ID	Gender	Salary	Job_Title	Country	Birth_Date	Hire_Date
2	120104	F	46230	Administration Manager	au	11/05/1954	01/01/1981
4	120106	M	.	Office Assistant II	AU	23/12/1944	01/01/1974
5	120107	F	30475	Office Assistant III	AU	01/02/1978	21/01/1953
9	120111	M	26895	Security Guard II	AU	23/07/1949	.
10	120112	F	26550		AU	17/02/1969	01/07/1990
12	120114	G	31285	Security Manager	AU	08/02/1944	01/01/1974
13	120115	M	2650	Service Assistant I	AU	08/05/1984	01/08/2005
14	.	M	29250	Service Assistant II	AU	13/06/1959	01/02/1980
20	120191	F	2401	Trainee	AU	17/01/1959	01/01/2003
84	120695	M	28180	Warehouse Assistant II	au	13/07/1964	01/07/1989
87	120698	M	26160	Warehouse Assistant I	au	17/05/1954	01/08/1976
101	120723		33950	Corp. Comm. Specialist II	US	10/08/1949	01/01/1974
125	120747	F	43590	Financial Controller I	us	20/06/1974	01/08/1995
197	120994	F	31645	Office Administrator I	us	16/06/1974	01/11/1994
200	120997	F	27420	Shipping Administrator I	us	21/11/1974	01/09/1996
214	121011	M	25735	Service Assistant I	US	11/03/1944	01/01/1968

56

The FREQ Procedure

The FREQ procedure produces one-way to *n*-way
frequency tables.

General form of the FREQ procedure:

```
PROC FREQ DATA=SAS-data-set <NLEVELS> ;
    TABLES variable(s) ;
RUN;
```

- The TABLES statement specifies the frequency tables
  to produce.
- The NLEVELS option displays a table that provides
  the number of distinct values for each variable named
  in the TABLES statement.

57

The FREQ Procedure

The following PROC FREQ step will show if there
are any invalid values for **Gender** and **Country**.

```
proc freq data=orion.nonsales;
   tables Gender Country;
run;
```

✐ Without the TABLES statement, PROC FREQ
produces a frequency table for each variable.

58   p108d05

The FREQ Procedure

Two observations need data cleaned for **Gender** and
six observations need data cleaned for **Country**.

```
                        The FREQ Procedure

                                      Cumulative    Cumulative
   Gender     Frequency     Percent    Frequency     Percent

   F             110        47.01         110        47.01
   G               1         0.43         111        47.44
   M             123        52.56         234       100.00

                   Frequency Missing = 1


                                      Cumulative    Cumulative
   Country    Frequency     Percent    Frequency     Percent

   AU             33        14.04          33        14.04
   US            196        83.40         229        97.45
   au              3         1.28         232        98.72
   us              3         1.28         235       100.00
```

59

If a format is permanently assigned to a variable, PROC FREQ automatically groups
the report by the formatted values.

The FREQ Procedure

This PROC FREQ step will show if there are any duplicates for **Employee_ID**.

```
proc freq data=orion.nonsales;
   tables Employee_ID;
run;
```

60   p108d05

The FREQ Procedure

Partial PROC FREQ Output

```
                        The FREQ Procedure

                                    Cumulative    Cumulative
Employee_ID   Frequency    Percent   Frequency      Percent

    120101        1         0.43          1          0.43      ative
    120104        1         0.43          2          0.86      cent
    120105        1         0.43          3          1.29
    120106        1         0.43          4          1.72
    120107        1         0.43          5          2.15     .57
    120108        2         0.86          7          3.00     .00
    120110        1         0.43          8          3.43     .42
    120111        1         0.43          9          3.86     .85
    120112        1         0.43         10          4.29     .28
    120113        1         0.43         11          4.72     .71
    121146        1         0.43        231         99.14
    121147        1         0.43        232         99.57
    121148        1         0.43        233        100.00

                        Frequency Missing = 1
```

61

The NLEVELS Option

If the number of desired distinct values is known, the NLEVELS option can help determine if there are any duplicates.

```
proc freq data=orion.nonsales nlevels;
   tables Gender Country Employee_ID;
run;
```

The *NLEVELS option* displays a table that provides the number of distinct values for each variable named in the TABLES statement.

62   p108d05

To display the number of levels without displaying the frequency counts, add the NOPRINT option to the TABLES statement.

```
proc freq data=orion.nonsales nlevels;
   tables Gender Country Employee_ID / noprint;
run;
```

To display the number of levels for all variables without displaying any frequency counts, use the _ALL_ keyword and the NOPRINT option in the TABLES statement.

```
proc freq data=orion.nonsales nlevels;
   tables _all_ / noprint;
run;
```

The NLEVELS Option

The Number of Variable Levels table appears before the individual frequency tables.

Partial PROC FREQ Output

```
             The FREQ Procedure

          Number of Variable Levels

                            Missing    Nonmissing
Variable         Levels     Levels       Levels

Gender              4          1            3
Country             4          0            4
Employee_ID       234          1          233
```

There are 235 employees but there are only 234 distinct **Employee_ID** values. Therefore, there is one duplicate value for **Employee_ID**.

63

   **Exercises**

Level 1

1. **Validating `orion.shoes_tracker` with the PRINT and FREQ Procedures**

    a. Retrieve the starter program **p108e01**.

    b. The data in **`orion.shoes_tracker`** should meet the following requirements:

    *   **`Product_Category`** must not be missing.

    *   **`Supplier_Country`** must have a value of GB or US.

    Add a WHERE statement to the PROC PRINT step to find any observations that do **not** meet the above requirements.

    c. Add a VAR statement to create the following PROC PRINT report:

Obs	Product_ Category	Supplier_Name	Supplier_ Country	Supplier_ID
1	Shoes	3Top Sports	us	.
2		3Top Sports	US	2963
5	Shoes	3Top Sports	UT	2963
10	Shoes	Greenline Sports Ltd	gB	14682

    How many observations have missing **`Product_Category`**?

    How many observations have invalid values of **`Supplier_Country`**?

    d. Add a PROC FREQ step with a TABLES statement to create frequency tables for **`Supplier_Name`** and **`Supplier_ID`** of **`orion.shoes_tracker`**. Include the NLEVELS option.

    The data in **`orion.shoes_tracker`** should meet the following requirements:

    *   **`Supplier_Name`** must be 3Top Sports or Greenline Sports Ltd.

    *   **`Supplier_ID`** must be 2963 or 14682.

    What invalid data exist for **`Supplier_Name`** and **`Supplier_ID`**?

Level 2

2. **Validating `orion.qtr2_2007` with the PRINT and FREQ Procedures**

    a. Write a PROC PRINT step with a WHERE statement to validate the data in
    `orion.qtr2_2007`.

    The data in `orion.qtr2_2007` should meet the following requirements:

    - **`Delivery_Date`** values must be equal to or greater than **`Order_Date`** values.
    - **`Order_Date`** values must be in the range of April 1, 2007 – June 30, 2007.

    The WHERE statement should find any observations that do **not** meet the above requirements.

    b. Submit the program to create the following PROC PRINT report:

Obs	Order_ID	Order_Type	EmployeeID	Customer_ID	Order_Date	Delivery_Date
5	1242012259	1	121040	10	18APR2007	12APR2007
22	1242449327	3	99999999	27	26JUL2007	26JUL2007

    How many observations have **`Delivery_Date`** values occurring before **`Order_Date`** values?

    How many observations have **`Order_Date`** values out of the range of April 1, 2007 – June 30, 2007?

    c. Add a PROC FREQ step with a TABLES statement to create frequency tables for **`Order_ID`** and **`Order_Type`** of `orion.qtr2_2007`. Include the NLEVELS option.

    d. Submit the PROC FREQ step.

    The data in `orion.qtr2_2007` should meet the following requirements:

    - **`Order_ID`** must be unique (36 distinct values) and not missing.
    - **`Order_Type`** must have a value of 1, 2, or 3.

    What invalid data exist for **`Order_ID`** and **`Order_Type`**?

Level 3

3. **Using the PROPCASE Function, Two-Way Frequency Table, and MISSING Option**

    a. Write a PROC PRINT step with a WHERE statement to validate the data in
    `orion.shoes_tracker`. All **`Product_Name`** values should be written in proper case.

    > 📝 Documentation on the PROPCASE function can be found in the SAS Help
    > and Documentation from the Contents tab (**SAS Products** ⇨ **Base SAS** ⇨
    > **SAS 9.2 Language Reference: Dictionary** ⇨ **Dictionary of Language Elements** ⇨
    > **Functions and CALL Routines** ⇨ **PROPCASE Function**).

b. Add a VAR statement to create the following PROC PRINT report:

```
      Obs       Product_ID                   Product_Name

        3     220200300015     men's running shoes piedmont
        6     220200300096     Mns.raptor Precision Sg Football
```

c. Add a PROC FREQ step with a TABLES statement to create the following two-way frequency table with **Supplier_Name** and **Supplier_ID** of **orion.shoes_tracker**:

```
                       The FREQ Procedure

               Table of Supplier_Name by Supplier_ID

            Supplier_Name(Supplier Name)       Supplier_ID(Supplier ID)

            Frequency      |
            Percent        |
            Row Pct        |
            Col Pct        |      .      2963      14682|  Total
            ---------------+------+------+------+
            3Top Sports    |    1 |    5 |    1 |    7
                           |10.00 |50.00 |10.00 |70.00
                           |14.29 |71.43 |14.29 |
                           |100.00|71.43 |50.00 |
            ---------------+------+------+------+
            3op Sports     |    0 |    2 |    0 |    2
                           | 0.00 |20.00 | 0.00 |20.00
                           | 0.00 |100.00| 0.00 |
                           | 0.00 |28.57 | 0.00 |
            ---------------+------+------+------+
            Greenline Sports|   0 |    0 |    1 |    1
             Ltd           | 0.00 | 0.00 |10.00 |10.00
                           | 0.00 | 0.00 |100.00|
                           | 0.00 | 0.00 |50.00 |
            ---------------+------+------+------+
            Total               1      7      2      10
                            10.00  70.00  20.00  100.00
```

🖉   Documentation on two-way frequency tables and the MISSING option can be found in the SAS Help and Documentation from the Contents tab (**SAS Products** ⇨ **Base SAS** ⇨ **Base SAS Procedures Guide: Statistical Procedures** ⇨ **The FREQ Procedure** ⇨ **Syntax: FREQ Procedure** ⇨ **TABLES Statement**).

The data in **orion.shoes_tracker** should meet the following requirements:

- A **Supplier_Name** of 3Top Sports must have a **Supplier_ID** of 2963.

- A **Supplier_Name** of Greenline Sports Ltd must have a **Supplier_ID** of 14682.

What invalid data exist for **Supplier_Name** and **Supplier_ID**?

8.4 Validating Data with the MEANS and UNIVARIATE Procedures

Objectives

- Validate data by using the MEANS procedure with the VAR statement.
- Validate data by using the UNIVARIATE procedure with the VAR statement.

67

The MEANS Procedure

The MEANS procedure produces summary reports displaying descriptive statistics.

General form of the MEANS procedure:

```
PROC MEANS DATA=SAS-data-set <statistics> ;
    VAR variable(s) ;
RUN;
```

- The VAR statement specifies the analysis variables and their order in the results.
- The statistics to display can be specified in the PROC MEANS statement.

68

The MEANS Procedure

This PROC MEANS step shows default descriptive statistics for **Salary**.

```
proc means data=orion.nonsales;
   var Salary;
run;
```

```
                    The MEANS Procedure

                 Analysis Variable : Salary

    N          Mean         Std Dev        Minimum        Maximum

   234      43954.60       38354.77        2401.00      433800.00
```

✎   Without the VAR statement, PROC MEANS
    analyses all numeric variables in the data set.   p108d06

69

The MEANS Procedure

By default, the MEANS procedure creates a report with N (number of non-missing values), MEAN, STDDEV, MIN, and MAX.

For validating data, the following descriptive statistics are beneficial:

- N, number of non-missing values
- NMISS, number of missing values
- MIN
- MAX

70

The MEANS Procedure

The following PROC MEANS step shows if there are
any **Salary** values not in the range of 24000 through
500000.

```
proc means data=orion.nonsales n nmiss min max;
   var Salary;
run;
```

```
                    The MEANS Procedure

                 Analysis Variable : Salary

               N
      N      Miss        Minimum          Maximum

     234       1         2401.00         433800.00
```

71   p108d06

The UNIVARIATE Procedure

The UNIVARIATE procedure produces summary reports
displaying descriptive statistics.

General form of the UNIVARIATE procedure:

> **PROC UNIVARIATE DATA=**_SAS-data-set_ **;**
>   **VAR** _variable(s)_ **;**
> **RUN;**

The VAR statement specifies the analysis variables and
their order in the results.

72

The UNIVARIATE Procedure

The following PROC UNIVARIATE step shows default descriptive statistics for **Salary**.

```
proc univariate data=orion.nonsales;
   var Salary;
run;
```

✎ Without the VAR statement, SAS will analyze all numeric variables.

73   p108d06

The UNIVARIATE Procedure

The UNIVARIATE procedure can produce the following sections of output:

- Moments
- Basic Statistical Measures
- Tests for Locations
- Quantiles
➤ - Extreme Observations
➤ - Missing Values

For validating data, the Extreme Observations and Missing Values sections are beneficial.

74

The UNIVARIATE Procedure

Partial PROC UNIVARIATE Output

```
                      Extreme Observations

          -----Lowest----          -----Highest----

         Value      Obs             Value      Obs

          2401       20            163040        1
          2650       13            194885      231
         24025       25            207885       28
         24100       19            268455       29
         24390      228            433800       27


                       Missing Values

                                 -----Percent Of-----
         Missing                              Missing
          Value      Count      All Obs          Obs

            .          1          0.43         100.00
```

75

NEXTROBS=*n*

specifies the number of extreme observations that PROC UNIVARIATE lists in the table of extreme observations. The table lists the *n* lowest observations and the *n* highest observations. The default value is 5, and *n* can range between 0 and half the maximum number of observations. You can specify NEXTROBS=0 to suppress the table of extreme observations.

For example:

```
proc univariate data=orion.nonsales nextrobs=8;
   var Salary;
run;
```

 **Exercises**

Level 1

4. **Validating `orion.price_current` with the MEANS and UNIVARIATE Procedures**

   a. Retrieve the starter program **p108e04**.

   b. Add a VAR statement to the PROC MEANS step to validate `Unit_Cost_Price`, `Unit_Sales_Price`, and `Factor`.

   c. Add statistics to the PROC MEANS statement to create the following PROC MEANS report:

   ```
                          The MEANS Procedure

   Variable          Label                      N      Minimum       Maximum
   ───────────────────────────────────────────────────────────────────────────
   Unit_Cost_Price   Unit Cost Price          171    2.3000000   315.1500000
   Unit_Sales_Price  Unit Sales Price         170    6.5000000       5730.00
   Factor            Yearly increase in Price 171    0.0100000   100.0000000
   ───────────────────────────────────────────────────────────────────────────
   ```

   The data in **orion.price_current** should meet the following requirements:

   • **Unit_Cost_Price** must be in the numeric range of 1 – 400.

   • **Unit_Sales_Price** must be in the numeric range of 3 – 800.

   • **Factor** must be in the numeric range of 1 – 1.05.

   What variables have invalid data?

   d. Add a PROC UNIVARIATE step with a VAR statement to validate `Unit_Sales_Price` and `Factor`.

   e. Submit the PROC UNIVARIATE step and find the Extreme Observations output.

   How many values of `Unit_Sales_Price` are over the maximum of 800?

   How many values of `Factor` are under the minimum of 1?

   How many values of `Factor` are over the maximum of 1.05?

Level 2

5. **Validating `orion.shoes_tracker` with the MEANS and UNIVARIATE Procedures**

   a. Write a PROC MEANS step with a VAR statement to validate `Product_ID` of `orion.shoes_tracker`.

   b. Add the MIN, MAX, and RANGE statistics to the PROC MEANS statement.

c. Add **FW=15** to the PROC MEANS statement. The FW= option specifies the field width to display the statistics in printed or displayed output.

d. Add the following CLASS statement to group the data by **Supplier_Name**.

```
class Supplier_Name;
```

 Documentation on the FW= option and the CLASS statement can be found in the SAS Help and Documentation from the Contents tab (**SAS Products** ⇨ **Base SAS** ⇨ **Base SAS 9.2 Procedures Guide** ⇨ **Procedures** ⇨ **The MEANS Procedure**).

e. Submit the program to create the following PROC MEANS report:

```
                           The MEANS Procedure

                   Analysis Variable : Product_ID Product ID

                               N
Supplier Name          Obs         Minimum          Maximum             Range

3Top Sports              7       22020030007   2202003001290    2179982971283

3op Sports               2      220200300015    220200300116      101.00000000

Greenline Sports Ltd     1      220200300157    220200300157                0
```

Which **Supplier_Name** has invalid **Product_ID** values assuming **Product_ID** must have only twelve digits?

f. Add a PROC UNIVARIATE step with a VAR statement to validate **Product_ID** of **orion.shoes_tracker**.

g. Submit the PROC UNIVARIATE step and find the Extreme Observations output.

How many values of **Product_ID** are too small?

How many values of **Product_ID** are too large?

Level 3

6. Selecting Only the Extreme Observations Output from the UNIVARIATE Procedure

a. Write a PROC UNIVARIATE step with a VAR statement to validate **Product_ID** of **orion.shoes_tracker**.

b. Before the PROC UNIVARIATE step add the following ODS statement:

```
ods trace on;
```

c. After the PROC UNIVARIATE step add the following ODS statement:

```
ods trace off;
```

d. Submit the program and notice the trace information in the SAS log.

What is the name of the last Output Added in the SAS log?

e. Add an ODS SELECT statement immediately before the PROC UNIVARIATE step to select only the Extreme Observation output object.

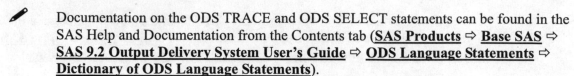 Documentation on the ODS TRACE and ODS SELECT statements can be found in the SAS Help and Documentation from the Contents tab (**SAS Products** ⇨ **Base SAS** ⇨ **SAS 9.2 Output Delivery System User's Guide** ⇨ **ODS Language Statements** ⇨ **Dictionary of ODS Language Statements**).

f. Submit the program to create the following PROC UNIVARIATE report:

```
                    The UNIVARIATE Procedure
                Variable:  Product_ID  (Product ID)

                        Extreme Observations

        --------Lowest-------        -------Highest------

              Value       Obs             Value       Obs

          2.20200E+10       4        2.2020E+11         6
          2.20200E+11       1        2.2020E+11         7
          2.20200E+11       2        2.2020E+11         9
          2.20200E+11       3        2.2020E+11        10
          2.20200E+11       5        2.2020E+12         8
```

8.5 Cleaning Invalid Data

Objectives

- Clean data by using the Viewtable window.
- Clean data by using assignment statements in the DATA step.
- Clean data by using IF-THEN / ELSE statements in the DATA step.

79

Invalid Data to Clean

The **orion.nonsales** data set contains invalid data that needs to be cleaned.

	Employee_ID	First	Last	Gender	Salary	Job_Title	Country	Birth_Date	Hire_Date
1	120101	Patrick	Lu	M	163E3	Director	AU	18/08/1976	01/07/2003
2	120104	Kareen	Billington	F	46230	Administration Manager	au	11/05/1954	01/01/1981
3	120105	Liz	Povey	F	27110	Secretary I	AU	21/12/1974	01/05/1999
4	120106	John	Hornsey	M		Office Assistant II	AU	23/12/1944	01/01/1974
5	120107	Sherie	Sheedy	F	30475	Office Assistant III	AU	01/02/1978	21/01/1953
6	120108	Gladys	Gromek	F	27660	Warehouse Assistant II	AU	23/02/1984	01/08/2006
7	120108	Gabriele	Baker	F	26495	Warehouse Assistant I	AU	15/12/1986	01/10/2006
8	120110	Dennis	Entwisle	M	28615	Warehouse Assistant III	AU	20/11/1949	01/11/1979
9	120111	Ubaldo	Spillane	M	26895	Security Guard II	AU	23/07/1949	,
10	120112	Ellis	Glattback	F	2655		AU	17/02/1969	01/07/1990
11	120113	Riu	Horsey	F	26870	Security Guard II	AU	10/05/1944	01/01/1974
12	120114	Jeannette	Buddery	G	31285	Security Manager	AU	08/02/1944	01/01/1974
13	120115	Hugh	Nichollas	M	2650	Service Assistant I	AU	08/05/1984	01/08/2005
14	.	Austen	Ralston	M	29250	Service Assistant II	AU	13/06/1959	01/02/1980
15	120117	Bill	Mccleary	M	31670	Cabinet Maker III	AU	11/09/1964	01/04/1986
16	120118	Darshi	Hartshorn	M	28090	Cabinet Maker II	AU	02/06/1959	01/07/1984

After validating the data and finding the invalid data, the correct data values are needed.

80

Variable	Obs	Invalid Value	Correct Value
Employee_ID	7	120108	120109
	14	.	120116
Gender	12	G	F
	101		F
Job_Title	10		Security Guard I
Country	2, 84, 87, 125, 197, and 200	au or us	AU or US
Salary	4	.	26960
	13	2650	26500
	20	2401	24015
Hire_Date	5	21/01/1953	21/01/1995
	9	.	01/11/1978
	214	01/01/1968	01/01/1998

81

Interactively Cleaning Data

If using the SAS windowing environment, the Viewtable window can be used to interactively clean data.

Use the Viewtable window to interactively clean the following five observations:

Variable	Obs	Invalid Value	Correct Value
Employee_ID	7	120108	120109
	14	.	120116
Gender	12	G	F
	101		F
Job_Title	10		Security Guard I

82

For z/OS (OS/390), the FSEDIT window is used to clean data.

Interactively Cleaning Data

The Viewtable window enables you to browse, edit, or create SAS data sets.

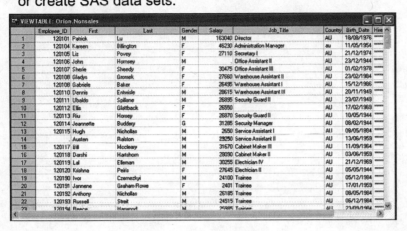

Using the Viewtable Window to Clean Data – Windows

1. Select the **Explorer** tab on the SAS window bar to activate the SAS Explorer window or select **View** ⇨ **Contents Only**.

2. Double-click on **Libraries** to show all available libraries.

3. Double-click on the **Orion** library to show all members of that library.

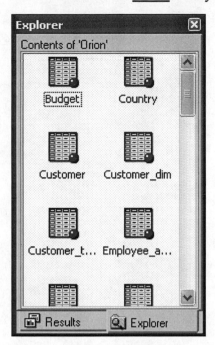

4. Double-click on the **Nonsales** data set to open the data set in the Viewtable window.

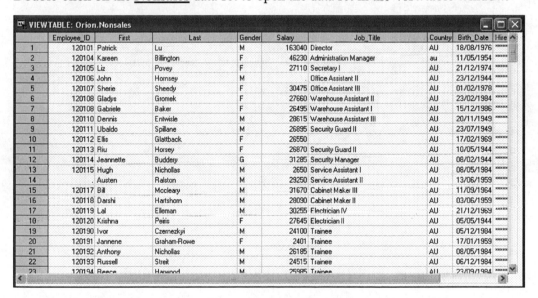

5. Select **<u>Edit Mode</u>** from the Edit pull-down menu.

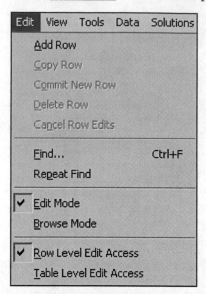

6. Go to the following observations and make the desired changes:

Obs	Variable	Correct Value
7	Employee_ID	120109
12	Gender	F
14	Employee_ID	120116
101	Gender	F

7. Select ☒ to close the Viewtable window. The changes are saved to the data set.

Using the Viewtable Window to Clean Data – UNIX

1. Select **View** ⇨ **Contents Only** to activate the SAS Explorer window.

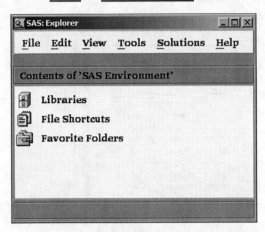

2. Double-click on **Libraries** to show all available libraries.

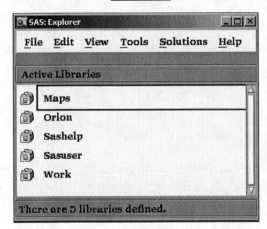

3. Double-click on the **Orion** library to show all members of that library.

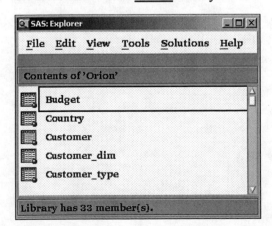

4. Double-click on the **Nonsales** data set to open the data set in the Viewtable window.

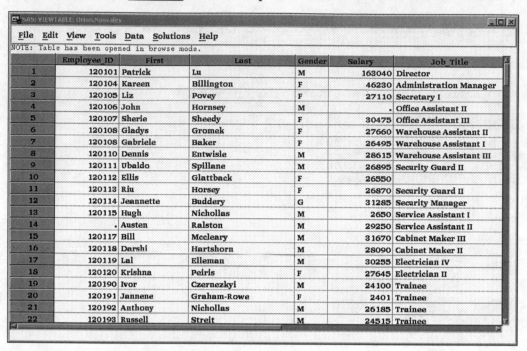

5. Select **Edit Mode** from the Edit pull-down menu.

6. Go to the following observations and make the desired changes:

Obs	Variable	Correct Value
7	Employee_ID	120109
12	Gender	F
14	Employee_ID	120116
101	Gender	F

7. Select ☒ to close the Viewtable window. The changes are saved to the data set.

Using the FSEDIT Window to Clean Data – z/OS (OS/390)

1. Type **fsedit orion.nonsales** on the command line and press ENTER to activate the FSEDIT window.

2. Go to the following observations and make the desired changes:

Obs	Variable	Correct Value
7	**Employee_ID**	120109
12	**Gender**	F
14	**Employee_ID**	120116
101	**Gender**	F

Type the observation number on the command line and press ENTER to go to an observation.

3. Type **end** on the command line and press ENTER to close the FSEDIT window. The changes are saved to the data set.

8.06 Quiz

- Open the Viewtable window for **orion.nonsales**.
- Use the Viewtable window to interactively clean the following observation:

Variable	Obs	Invalid Value	Correct Value
Job_Title	10		Security Guard I

86

Programmatically Cleaning Data

The DATA step can be used to programmatically clean the invalid data.

Use the DATA step to clean the following observations:

Variable	Obs	Invalid Value	Correct Value
Country	2, 84, 87, 125, 197, and 200	au or us	AU or US
Salary	4	.	26960
	13	2650	26500
	20	2401	24015
Hire_Date	5	21/01/1953	21/01/1995
	9	.	01/11/1978
	214	01/01/1968	01/01/1998

89

The Assignment Statement

The *assignment statement* evaluates an expression and assigns the resulting value to a variable.

General form of the assignment statement:

> *variable = expression* ;

- *variable* names an existing or new variable.
- *expression* is a sequence of operands and operators that form a set of instructions that produce a value.

90

Assignment statements evaluate the expression on the right side of the equal sign and store the result in the variable that is specified on the left side of the equal sign.

The Assignment Statement Expression

Operands are
- character constants
- numeric constants
- date constants
- character variables
- numeric variables.

Operators are
- symbols that represent an arithmetic calculation
- SAS functions.

91

A SAS function is a routine that returns a value that is determined from specified arguments.

The Assignment Statement Expression

Examples:

```
Salary = 26960;
```
← numeric constant

```
Gender = 'F';
```
← character constant

```
Hire_Date = '21JAN1995'd;
```
← date constant

```
Country = upcase(Country);
```
function   variable

92

SAS Functions

A SAS *function* is a a routine that returns a value that is determined from specified arguments.

The *UPCASE function* converts all letters in an argument to uppercase.

General form of the UPCASE function:

UPCASE(*argument***)**

The *argument* specifies any SAS character expression.

93

The Assignment Statement

All the values of **Country** in the data set
orion.nonsales need to be uppercase.

```
data work.clean;
   set orion.nonsales;
   Country=upcase(Country);
run;
```

PDV

Employee_ID		Job_Title	Country	
120101	...	Director	AU	...

94   p108d07
...

The Assignment Statement

All the values of **Country** in the data set
orion.nonsales need to be uppercase.

```
data work.clean;
   set orion.nonsales;
   Country=upcase(Country);
run;
```

PDV

Employee_ID		Job_Title	Country	
120101	...	Director	AU	...

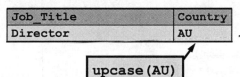

upcase(AU)

95   ...

The Assignment Statement

All the values of **Country** in the data set
orion.nonsales need to be uppercase.

```
data work.clean;
    set orion.nonsales;
    Country=upcase(Country);
run;
```

PDV

Employee_ID		Job_Title	Country	
120104	...	Administration Manager	au	...

96

...

The Assignment Statement

All the values of **Country** in the data set
orion.nonsales need to be uppercase.

```
data work.clean;
    set orion.nonsales;
    Country=upcase(Country);
run;
```

PDV

Employee_ID		Job_Title	Country	
120104	...	Administration Manager	AU	...

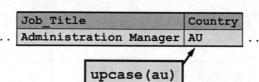

upcase(au)

97

The Assignment Statement

```
proc print data=work.clean;
   var Employee_ID Job_Title Country;
run;
```

Partial PROC PRINT Output

```
          Employee_
  Obs        ID      Job_Title                 Country

  84       120695    Warehouse Assistant II       AU
  85       120696    Warehouse Assistant I        AU
  86       120697    Warehouse Assistant IV       AU
  87       120698    Warehouse Assistant I        AU
  88       120710    Business Analyst II          US
  89       120711    Business Analyst III         US
  90       120712    Marketing Manager            US
  91       120713    Marketing Assistant III      US
```

The assignment statement executed for every observation regardless of whether the value needed to be uppercased or not.

98

Programmatically Cleaning Data

The DATA step can be used to programmatically clean the invalid data.

Use the DATA step to clean the following observations:

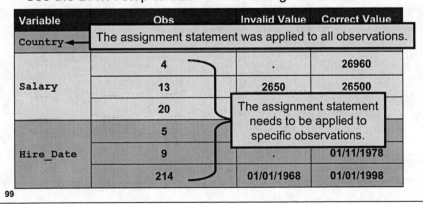

Variable	Obs	Invalid Value	Correct Value
Country	The assignment statement was applied to all observations.		
Salary	4	.	26960
	13	2650	26500
	20		
Hire_Date	5		
	9	.	01/11/1978
	214	01/01/1968	01/01/1998

The assignment statement needs to be applied to specific observations.

99

8.07 Quiz

Which variable could be used to specifically identify
the observations with invalid salary values?

```
Obs  Employee_ID Gender Salary Job_Title              Country Birth_Date Hire_Date

 2      120104    F      46230 Administration Manager   au     11/05/1954 01/01/1981
 4      120106    M          . Office Assistant II      AU     23/12/1944 01/01/1974
 5      120107    F      30475 Office Assistant III     AU     01/02/1978 21/01/1953
 9      120111    M      26895 Security Guard II        AU     23/07/1949          .
10      120112    F      26550                          AU     17/02/1969 01/07/1990
12      120114    G      31285 Security Manager         AU     08/02/1944 01/01/1974
13      120115    M       2650 Service Assistant I      AU     08/05/1984 01/08/2005
14           .    M      29250 Service Assistant II     AU     13/06/1959 01/02/1980
20      120191    F       2401 Trainee                  AU     17/01/1959 01/01/2003
84      120695    M      28180 Warehouse Assistant II   au     13/07/1964 01/07/1989
87      120698    M      26160 Warehouse Assistant I    au     17/05/1954 01/08/1976
101     120723           33950 Corp. Comm. Specialist II US    10/08/1949 01/01/1974
125     120747    F      43590 Financial Controller I   us     20/06/1974 01/08/1995
197     120994    F      31645 Office Administrator I   us     16/06/1974 01/11/1994
200     120997    F      27420 Shipping Administrator I us     21/11/1974 01/09/1996
214     121011    M      25735 Service Assistant I      US     11/03/1944 01/01/1968
```

101

Programmatically Cleaning Data

The DATA step can be used to programmatically clean
the invalid data.

Use the DATA step to clean the following observations:

Variable	Obs	Invalid Value	Correct Value
Country	2, 84, 87, 125, 197, and 200	au or us	AU or US
Salary	4	.	26960
	13	2650	26500
	20	2401	24015
Hire_Date	5	21/01/1953	21/01/1995
	9	.	01/11/1978
	214	01/01/1968	01/01/1998

103

IF-THEN Statements

The *IF-THEN statement* executes a SAS statement
for observations that meet specific conditions.

General form of the IF-THEN statement:

> **IF** *expression* **THEN** *statement* ;

- *expression* is a sequence of operands and operators
  that form a set of instructions that define a condition
  for selecting observations.
- *statement* is any executable statement such as the
  assignment statement.

104

If the condition in the IF clause is met, the IF-THEN statement executes a SAS statement
for that observation.

IF-THEN Statements

All the values of **Salary** must be in the range
of 24000 – 500000.

```
data work.clean;
   set orion.nonsales;
   if Employee_ID=120106 then Salary=26960;
   if Employee_ID=120115 then Salary=26500;
   if Employee_ID=120191 then Salary=24015;
run;
```

PDV

Employee_ID		Salary	Job_Title	
120105	...	27110	Secretary I	...

105

p108d07
...

IF-THEN Statements

All the values of **Salary** must be in the range
of 24000 – 500000.

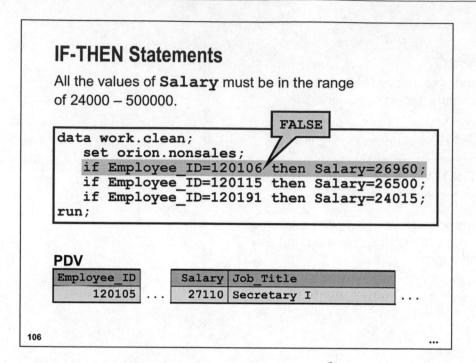

```
data work.clean;
   set orion.nonsales;
   if Employee_ID=120106 then Salary=26960;
   if Employee_ID=120115 then Salary=26500;
   if Employee_ID=120191 then Salary=24015;
run;
```

FALSE

PDV

Employee_ID		Salary	Job_Title	
120105	...	27110	Secretary I	...

106

IF-THEN Statements

All the values of **Salary** must be in the range
of 24000 – 500000.

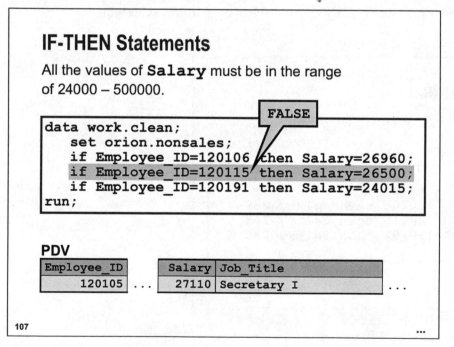

```
data work.clean;
   set orion.nonsales;
   if Employee_ID=120106 then Salary=26960;
   if Employee_ID=120115 then Salary=26500;
   if Employee_ID=120191 then Salary=24015;
run;
```

FALSE

PDV

Employee_ID		Salary	Job_Title	
120105	...	27110	Secretary I	...

107

IF-THEN Statements

All the values of **Salary** must be in the range
of 24000 – 500000.

```
data work.clean;
   set orion.nonsales;
   if Employee_ID=120106 then Salary=26960;
   if Employee_ID=120115 then Salary=26500;
   if Employee_ID=120191 then Salary=24015;
run;
```

FALSE

PDV

Employee_ID		Salary	Job_Title	
120105	...	27110	Secretary I	...

108

IF-THEN Statements

All the values of **Salary** must be in the range
of 24000 – 500000.

```
data work.clean;
   set orion.nonsales;
   if Employee_ID=120106 then Salary=26960;
   if Employee_ID=120115 then Salary=26500;
   if Employee_ID=120191 then Salary=24015;
run;
```

PDV

Employee_ID		Salary	Job_Title	
120106	...	.	Office Assistant II	...

109

IF-THEN Statements

All the values of **Salary** must be in the range
of 24000 – 500000.

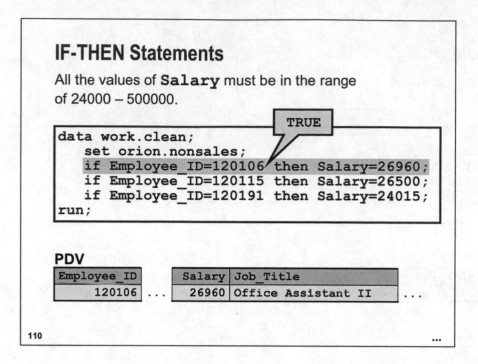

```
data work.clean;
   set orion.nonsales;
   if Employee_ID=120106 then Salary=26960;
   if Employee_ID=120115 then Salary=26500;
   if Employee_ID=120191 then Salary=24015;
run;
```

PDV

Employee_ID		Salary	Job_Title	
120106	...	26960	Office Assistant II	...

110

...

IF-THEN Statements

All the values of **Salary** must be in the range
of 24000 – 500000.

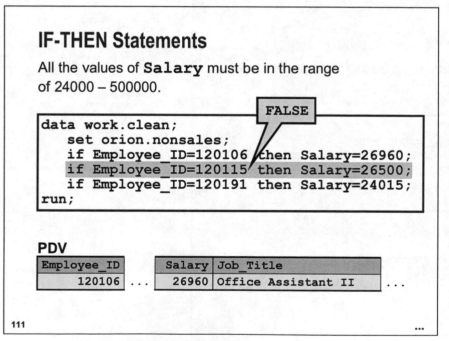

```
data work.clean;
   set orion.nonsales;
   if Employee_ID=120106 then Salary=26960;
   if Employee_ID=120115 then Salary=26500;
   if Employee_ID=120191 then Salary=24015;
run;
```

PDV

Employee_ID		Salary	Job_Title	
120106	...	26960	Office Assistant II	...

111

...

IF-THEN Statements

All the values of **Salary** must be in the range
of 24000 – 500000.

```
data work.clean;
    set orion.nonsales;
    if Employee_ID=120106  then Salary=26960;
    if Employee_ID=120115  then Salary=26500;
    if Employee_ID=120191 then Salary=24015;
run;
```

FALSE

PDV

Employee_ID		Salary	Job_Title	
120106	...	26960	Office Assistant II	...

112

IF-THEN Statements

When an IF expression is TRUE in this IF-THEN
statement series, there is no reason to check the
remaining IF-THEN statements when checking
Employee_ID.

TRUE

```
data work.clean;
    set orion.nonsales;
    if Employee_ID=120106  then Salary=26960;
    if Employee_ID=120115  then Salary=26500;
    if Employee_ID=120191  then Salary=24015;
run;
```

The word ELSE can be placed before the word IF,
causing SAS to execute conditional statements until it
encounters the first true statement.

113

When a series of IF expressions represent mutually exclusive events, then it is not necessary
to check all expressions when one is found to be true.

IF-THEN / ELSE Statements

All the values of **Salary** must be in the range
of 24000 – 500000.

```
data work.clean;
  set orion.nonsales;
  if Employee_ID=120106 then Salary=26960;
  else if Employee_ID=120115 then Salary=26500;
  else if Employee_ID=120191 then Salary=24015;
run;
```

PDV

Employee_ID		Salary	Job_Title	
120106	...	.	Office Assistant II	...

114   p108d07
...

IF-THEN / ELSE Statements

All the values of **Salary** must be in the range
of 24000 – 500000.

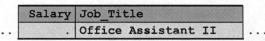

```
data work.clean;
  set orion.nonsales;
  if Employee_ID=120106 then Salary=26960;
  else if    SKIP   ee_ID=120115 then Salary=26500;
  else if         ee_ID=120191 then Salary=24015;
run;
```

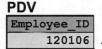

PDV

Employee_ID		Salary	Job_Title	
120106	...	26960	Office Assistant II	...

115

Programmatically Cleaning Data

The DATA step can be used to programmatically clean the invalid data.

Use the DATA step to clean the following observations:

Variable	Obs	Invalid Value	Correct Value
Country	2, 84, 87, 125, 197, and 200	au or us	AU or US
Salary	4	.	26960
	13	2650	26500
	20	2401	24015
Hire_Date	5	21/01/1953	21/01/1995
	9	.	01/11/1978
	214	01/01/1968	01/01/1998

116

IF-THEN / ELSE Statements

All the values of **Hire_Date** must have a value of 01/01/1974 or later.

```
data work.clean;
  set orion.nonsales;
  Country=upcase(Country);
  if Employee_ID=120106 then  Salary=26960;
  else if Employee_ID=120115  then Salary=26500;
  else if Employee_ID=120191  then Salary=24015;
  else if Employee_ID=120107  then
        Hire_Date='21JAN1995'd;
  else if Employee_ID=120111  then
        Hire_Date='01NOV1978'd;
  else if Employee_ID=121011  then
        Hire_Date='01JAN1998'd;
run;
```

117   p108d07

 **Exercises**

Level 1

7. **Cleaning Data from `orion.qtr2_2007`**

   a. Retrieve the starter program **p108e07**.

   b. Add two conditional statements to the DATA step to correct the following invalid data:

Variable	Obs	Invalid Value	Correct Value	Reference Variable
`Delivery_Date`	5	12APR2007	12MAY2007	`Order_ID=1242012259`
`Order_Date`	22	26JUL2007	26JUN2007	`Order_ID=1242449327`

   c. Submit the program. Verify that 0 observations were returned from the PROC PRINT step.

Level 2

8. **Cleaning Data from `orion.price_current`**

   a. Retrieve the starter program **p108e08**.

   b. Add a DATA step prior to the PROC steps to read **`orion.price_current`** to create **`work.price_current`**. In the DATA step, include two conditional IF-THEN statements to correct the following invalid data:

Variable	Obs	Invalid Value	Correct Value	Reference Variable
`Unit_Sales_Price`	41	5730	57.30	`Product_ID=220200200022`
`Unit_Sales_Price`	103	.	41.20	`Product_ID=240200100056`

   c. Submit the program. Verify that the **`Unit_Sales_Price`** is in the numeric range of 3 – 800.

Level 3

9. **Cleaning Data from `orion.shoes_tracker`**

   a. Retrieve the starter program **p108e09**.

   b. Add a DATA step prior to the PROC steps to read **orion.shoes_tracker** to create **work.shoes_tracker**. In the DATA step, include statements to correct the following invalid data:

Variable	Obs	Invalid Value	Correct Value	Reference Variable
Supplier_Country		*mixed case*	*upper case*	
Supplier_Country	5	UT	US	Supplier_Country='UT'
Product_Category	2		Shoes	Product_Category=' '
Supplier_ID	1	.	2963	Supplier_ID=.
Supplier_Name	3, 7	3op Sports	3Top Sports	Supplier_Name = '3op Sports'
Product_ID	4	22020030007	220200300079	_N_=4
Product_ID	8	2202003001290	220200300129	_N_=8
Product_Name		*not proper case*	*proper case*	
Supplier_Name	9	3Top Sports	Greenline Sports Ltd	Supplier_ID=14682 and Supplier_Name = '3Top Sports'

   c. Submit the program. Verify that the data requirements are all met.
   - **Product_Category** must not be missing.
   - **Supplier_Country** must have a value of GB or US.
   - **Supplier_Name** must be 3Top Sports or Greenline Sports Ltd.
   - **Supplier_ID** must be 2963 or 14682.
   - A **Supplier_Name** of 3Top Sports must have a **Supplier_ID** of 2963.
   - A **Supplier_Name** of Greenline Sports Ltd must have a **Supplier_ID** of 14682.
   - **Product_ID** must have only twelve digits.

8.6 Solutions

Solutions to Exercises

1. **Validating orion.shoes_tracker with the PRINT and FREQ Procedures**

   a. Retrieve the starter program.

   b. Add a WHERE statement to the PROC PRINT step.

```
proc print data=orion.shoes_tracker;
   where Product_Category=' ' or
         Supplier_Country not in ('GB','US');
run;
```

   c. Add a VAR statement.

```
proc print data=orion.shoes_tracker;
   where Product_Category=' ' or
         Supplier_Country not in ('GB','US');
   var Product_Category Supplier_Name Supplier_Country Supplier_ID;
run;
```

   How many observations have missing **Product_Category**? **One (observation 2)**

   How many observations have invalid values of **Supplier_Country**? **Three (observations 1, 5, and 10)**

   d. Add a PROC FREQ step with a TABLES statement.

```
proc freq data=orion.shoes_tracker nlevels;
   tables Supplier_Name Supplier_ID;
run;
```

   What invalid data exist for **Supplier_Name** and **Supplier_ID**?

   - **two invalid values for Supplier_Name (3op Sports)**
   - **one missing value for Supplier_ID**

2. **Validating orion.qtr2_2007 with the PRINT and FREQ Procedures**

   a. Write a PROC PRINT step with a WHERE statement.

```
proc print data=orion.qtr2_2007;
   where Order_Date>Delivery_Date or
         Order_Date<'01APR2007'd or
         Order_Date>'30JUN2007'd;
run;
```

   b. Submit the program.

   How many observations have **Delivery_Date** values occurring before **Order_Date** values? **One (observation 5)**

   How many observations have **Order_Date** values out of the range of April 1, 2007 – June 30, 2007? **One (observation 22)**

c. Add a PROC FREQ step with a TABLES statement.

```
proc freq data=orion.qtr2_2007 nlevels;
   tables Order_ID Order_Type;
run;
```

d. Submit the PROC FREQ step.

What invalid data exist for `Order_ID` and `Order_Type`?

- **two missing values for Order_ID**
- **one value of 0 for Order_Type**
- **one value of 4 for Order_Type**

3. **Using the PROPCASE Function, Two-Way Frequency Table, and MISSING Option**

   a. Write a PROC PRINT step with a WHERE statement.

```
proc print data=orion.shoes_tracker;
   where propcase(Product_Name) ne Product_Name;
run;
```

   b. Add a VAR statement.

```
proc print data=orion.shoes_tracker;
   where propcase(Product_Name) ne Product_Name;
   var Product_ID Product_Name;
run;
```

   c. Add a PROC FREQ step with a TABLES statement.

```
proc freq data=orion.shoes_tracker;
   tables Supplier_Name*Supplier_ID / missing;
run;
```

What invalid data exist for `Supplier_Name` and `Supplier_ID`?

- **two invalid values for Supplier_Name (3op Sports should be 3Top Sports)**
- **one missing value for Supplier_ID (. should be 2963)**
- **one wrong value for Supplier_ID (14682 should be 2963)**

4. **Validating `orion.price_current` with the MEANS and UNIVARIATE Procedures**

   a. Retrieve the starter program.

   b. Add a VAR statement to the PROC MEANS step.

```
proc means data=orion.price_current;
   var Unit_Cost_Price Unit_Sales_Price Factor;
run;
```

    c. Add statistics to the PROC MEANS statement.

```
proc means data=orion.price_current n min max;
   var Unit_Cost_Price Unit_Sales_Price Factor;
run;
```

        What variables have invalid data?

- **The maximum value of Unit_Sales_Price is out of range and one value of Unit_Sales_Price is missing.**

- **The minimum and maximum values of Factor are out of range.**

    d. Add a PROC UNIVARIATE step with a VAR statement.

```
proc univariate data=orion.price_current;
   var Unit_Sales_Price Factor;
run;
```

    e. Find the Extreme Observations output.

        How many values of **Unit_Sales_Price** are over the maximum of 800? **One (5730)**

        How many values of **Factor** are under the minimum of 1? **One (0.01)**

        How many values of **Factor** are over the maximum of 1.05? **Two (10.20 and 100.00)**

5. **Validating orion.shoes_tracker with the MEANS and UNIVARIATE Procedures**

    a. Write a PROC MEANS step with a VAR statement.

```
proc means data=orion.shoes_tracker;
   var Product_ID;
run;
```

    b. Add the MIN, MAX, and RANGE statistics to the PROC MEANS statement.

```
proc means data=orion.shoes_tracker min max range;
   var Product_ID;
run;
```

    c. Add FW=15 to the PROC MEANS statement.

```
proc means data=orion.shoes_tracker min max range fw=15;
   var Product_ID;
run;
```

    d. Add the CLASS statement.

```
proc means data=orion.shoes_tracker min max range fw=15;
   var Product_ID;
   class Supplier_Name;
run;
```

    e. Submit the program.

        Which **Supplier_Name** has invalid **Product_ID** values assuming **Product_ID** must have only twelve digits? **3Top Sports**

f. Add a PROC UNIVARIATE step with a VAR statement.

```
proc univariate data=orion.shoes_tracker;
   var Product_ID;
run;
```

g. Submit the PROC UNIVARIATE step.

How many values of **Product_ID** are too small? **One (2.20200E+10)**

How many values of **Product_ID** are too large? **One (2.2020E+12)**

6. **Selecting Only the Extreme Observations Output from the UNIVARIATE Procedure**

a. Write a PROC UNIVARIATE step with a VAR statement.

```
proc univariate data=orion.shoes_tracker;
   var Product_ID;
run;
```

b. Before the PROC UNIVARIATE step, add an ODS statement.

```
ods trace on;

proc univariate data=orion.shoes_tracker;
   var Product_ID;
run;
```

c. After the PROC UNIVARIATE step, add an ODS statement.

```
ods trace on;

proc univariate data=orion.shoes_tracker;
   var Product_ID;
run;

ods trace off;
```

d. Submit the program.

What is the name of the last Output Added in the SAS log? **ExtremeObs**

e. Add an ODS SELECT statement.

```
ods trace on;

ods select ExtremeObs;
proc univariate data=orion.shoes_tracker;
   var Product_ID;
run;

ods trace off;
```

f. Submit the program.

7. **Cleaning Data from orion.qtr2_2007**

a. Retrieve the starter program.

b. Add two conditional statements to the DATA step.

```
data work.qtr2_2007;
   set orion.qtr2_2007;
   if Order_ID=1242012259 then Delivery_Date='12MAY2007'd;
   else if Order_ID=1242449327 then Order_Date='26JUN2007'd;
run;

proc print data=work.qtr2_2007;
   where Order_Date>Delivery_Date or
         Order_Date<'01APR2007'd or
         Order_Date>'30JUN2007'd;
run;
```

c. Submit the program.

8. Cleaning Data from `orion.price_current`

a. Retrieve the starter program.

b. Add a DATA step.

```
data work.price_current;
   set orion.price_current;
   if Product_ID=220200200022 then Unit_Sales_Price=57.30;
   else if Product_ID=240200100056 then Unit_Sales_Price=41.20;
run;

proc means data=work.price_current n min max;
   var Unit_Sales_Price;
run;

proc univariate data=work.price_current;
   var Unit_Sales_Price;
run;
```

c. Submit the program.

9. Cleaning Data from `orion.shoes_tracker`

   a. Retrieve the starter program.

   b. Add a DATA step.

```
data work.shoes_tracker;
   set orion.shoes_tracker;
   Supplier_Country=upcase(Supplier_Country);
   if Supplier_Country='UT' then Supplier_Country='US';
   if Product_Category=' ' then Product_Category='Shoes';
   if Supplier_ID=. then Supplier_ID=2963;
   if Supplier_Name='3op Sports' then Supplier_Name='3Top Sports';
   if _n_=4 then Product_ID=220200300079;
   else if _n_=8 then Product_ID=220200300129;
   Product_Name=propcase(Product_Name);
   if Supplier_ID=14682 and Supplier_Name='3Top Sports'
      then Supplier_Name='Greenline Sports Ltd';
run;

proc print data=work.shoes_tracker;
   where Product_Category=' ' or
         Supplier_Country not in ('GB','US') or
         propcase(Product_Name) ne Product_Name;
run;

proc freq data=work.shoes_tracker;
   tables Supplier_Name*Supplier_ID / missing;
run;

proc means data=work.shoes_tracker min max range fw=15;
   var Product_ID;
   class Supplier_Name;
run;

proc univariate data=work.shoes_tracker;
   var Product_ID;
run;
```

   c. Submit the program.

Solutions to Student Activities (Polls/Quizzes)

8.01 Quiz – Correct Answer

What problems will SAS have reading the numeric data
Salary and **Hire_Date**?

Partial nonsales.csv

```
120101,Patrick,Lu,M,163040,Director,AU,18AUG1976,01JUL2003
120104,Kareen,Billington,F,46230,Administration Manager,au,11MAY1954,01JAN1981
120105,Liz,Povey,F,27110,Secretary I,AU,21DEC1974,01MAY1999
120106,John,Hornsey,M,unknown,Office Assistant II,AU,23DEC1944,01JAN1974
120107,Sherie,Sheedy,F,30475,Office Assistant III,AU,01FEB1978,21JAN1953
120108,Gladys,Gromek,F,27660,Warehouse Assistant II,AU,23FEB1984,01AUG2006
120108,Gabriele,Baker,F,26495,Warehouse Assistant I,AU,15DEC1986,01OCT2006
120110,Dennis,Entwisle,M,28615,Warehouse Assistant III,AU,20NOV1949,01NOV1979
120111,Ubaldo,Spillane,M,26895,Security Guard II,AU,23JUL1949,99NOV1978
120112,Ellis,Glattback,F,26550, ,AU,17FEB1969,01JUL1990
120113,Riu,Horsey,F,26870,Security Guard II,AU,10MAY1944,01JAN1974
120114,Jeannette,Buddery,G,31285,Security Manager,AU,08FEB1944,01JAN1974
120115,Hugh,Nichollas,M,2650,Service Assistant I,AU,08MAY1984,01AUG2005
,,Austen,Ralston,M,29250,Service Assistant II,AU,13JUN1959,01FEB1980
120117,Bill,Mccleary,M,31670,Cabinet Maker III,AU,11SEP1964,01APR1986
```

7

8.02 Quiz – Correct Answer

What problems exist with the data in this partial data set?

	Employee_ID	First	Last	Gender	Salary	Job_Title	Country	Birth_Date	Hire_Date
1	120101	Patrick	Lu	M	163E3	Director	AU	18/08/1976	01/07/2003
2	120104	Kareen	Billington	F	46230	Administration Manager	au	11/05/1954	01/01/1981
3	120105	Liz	Povey	F	27110	Secretary I	AU	21/12/1974	01/05/1999
4	120106	John	Hornsey	M		Office Assistant II	AU	23/12/1944	01/01/1974
5	120107	Sherie	Sheedy	F	30475	Office Assistant III	AU	01/02/1978	21/01/1953
6	120108	Gladys	Gromek	F	27660	Warehouse Assistant II	AU	23/02/1984	01/08/2006
7	120108	Gabriele	Baker	F	26495	Warehouse Assistant I	AU	15/12/1986	01/10/2006
8	120110	Dennis	Entwisle	M	28615	Warehouse Assistant III	AU	20/11/1949	01/11/1979
9	120111	Ubaldo	Spillane	M	26895	Security Guard II	AU	23/07/1949	.
10	120112	Ellis	Glattback	F	26550		AU	17/02/1969	01/07/1990
11	120113	Riu	Horsey	F	26870	Security Guard II	AU	10/05/1944	01/01/1974
12	120114	Jeannette	Buddery	G	31285	Security Manager	AU	08/02/1944	01/01/1974
13	120115	Hugh	Nichollas	M	2650	Service Assistant I	AU	08/05/1984	01/08/2005
14		Austen	Ralston	M	29250	Service Assistant II	AU	13/06/1959	01/02/1980
15	120117	Bill	Mccleary	M	31670	Cabinet Maker III	AU	11/09/1964	01/04/1986
16	120118	Darahi	Hutchon	M	28090	Cabinet Maker II	AU	03/06/1959	01/07/1984

Hint: There are nine data problems.

12

8.03 Multiple Choice Poll – Correct Answer

Which statements are used to read a delimited
raw data file and create a SAS data set?

a. DATA and SET only
b. DATA and INFILE only
c. DATA, SET, and INPUT only
d. DATA, INFILE, and INPUT only

25

8.04 Multiple Choice Poll – Correct Answer

Which statement best describes the invalid data?

a. The data in the raw data file is bad.
b. The programmer incorrectly read the data.

Partial SAS Log

> **Last** was read as numeric but needs to be read as character.

```
404      input Employee_ID First $ Last;
405  run;

NOTE: Invalid data for Last in line 1 16-17.
RULE:      ----+----1----+----2----+----3----+----4----+----5----+----6
1         120101,Patrick,Lu,M,163040,Director,AU,18AUG1976,01JUL2003 58
Employee_ID=120101 First=Patrick Last=. _ERROR_=1 _N_=1
NOTE: Invalid data for Last in line 2 15-24.
2         120104,Kareen,Billington,F,46230,Administration Manager,au,1
     61  1MAY1954,01JAN1981 78
Employee_ID=120104 First=Kareen Last=. _ERROR_=1 _N_=2
```

36

8.05 Multiple Choice Poll – Correct Answer

Which data requirement can not be achieved with
the PRINT procedure using a WHERE statement?

a. `Employee_ID` must be unique and not missing.
b. `Gender` must have a value of `F` or `M`.
c. `Salary` must be in the numeric range of 24000 – 500000.
d. `Job_Title` must not be missing.
e. `Country` must have a value of `AU` or `US`.
f. `Birth_Date` value must occur before `Hire_Date` value.
g. `Hire_Date` must have a value of 01/01/1974 or later.

53

8.06 Quiz – Correct Answer

- Open the Viewtable window for `orion.nonsales`.
- Use the Viewtable window to interactively clean the
following observation:

	Employee_ID	First	Last	Gender	Salary	Job_Title
1	120101	Patrick	Lu	M	163040	Director
2	120104	Kareen	Billington	F	46230	Administration Manager
3	120105	Liz	Povey	F	27110	Secretary I
4	120106	John	Hornsey	M		Office Assistant II
5	120107	Sherie	Sheedy	F	30475	Office Assistant III
6	120108	Gladys	Gromek	F	27660	Warehouse Assistant II
7	120109	Gabriele	Baker	F	26495	Warehouse Assistant I
8	120110	Dennis	Entwisle	M	28615	Warehouse Assistant III
9	120111	Ubaldo	Spillane	M	26895	Security Guard II
10	120112	Ellis	Glattback	F	26550	Security Guard I

VIEWTABLE: Orion.Nonsales

87

8.07 Quiz – Correct Answer

Which variable could be used to specifically identify
the observations with invalid salary values?

Obs	Employee_ID	Gender	Salary	Job_Title	Country	Birth_Date	Hire_Date
2	120104	F	46230	Administration Manager	au	11/05/1954	01/01/1981
4	120106	M		Office Assistant II	AU	23/12/1944	01/01/1974
5	120107	F	30475	Office Assistant III	AU	01/02/1978	21/01/1953
9	120111	M	26895	Security Guard II	AU	23/07/1949	.
10	120112	F	26550		AU	17/02/1969	01/07/1990
12	120114	G	31285	Security Manager	AU	08/02/1944	01/01/1974
13	120115	M	2650	Service Assistant I	AU	08/05/1984	01/08/2005
14	.	M	29250	Service Assistant II	AU	13/06/1959	01/02/1980
20	120191	F	2401	Trainee	AU	17/01/1959	01/01/2003
84	120695	M	28180	Warehouse Assistant II	au	13/07/1964	01/07/1989
87	120698	M	26160	Warehouse Assistant I	au	17/05/1954	01/08/1976
101	120723		33950	Corp. Comm. Specialist II	US	10/08/1949	01/01/1974
125	120747	F	43590	Financial Controller I	us	20/06/1974	01/08/1995
197	120994	F	31645	Office Administrator I	us	16/06/1974	01/11/1994
200	120997	F	27420	Shipping Administrator I	us	21/11/1974	01/09/1996
214	121011	M	25735	Service Assistant I	US	11/03/1944	01/01/1968

Employee_ID because the values are unique.

102

Chapter 9 Manipulating Data

9.1 Creating Variables

Objectives

- Create SAS variables with the assignment statement in the DATA step.
- Create data values by using operators including SAS functions.
- Subset variables by using the DROP and KEEP statements.
- Examine the compilation and execution phases of the DATA step when reading a SAS data set.
- Subset variables by using the DROP= and KEEP= options. (Self-Study)

3

Business Scenario

A new SAS data set named **work.comp** needs to be created by reading the **orion.sales** data set.

work.comp must include the following new variables:

- **Bonus**, which is equal to a constant 500.
- **Compensation**, which is the combination of the employee's salary and bonus.
- **BonusMonth**, which is equal to the month the employee was hired.

work.comp must not include the **Gender**, **Salary**, **Job_Title**, **Country**, **Birth_Date**, and **Hire_Date** variables from **orion.sales**.

4

Business Scenario

Partial `orion.sales`

Employee_ID	First_Name	Last_Name	Gender	Salary	Job_ Title	Country	Birth_Date	Hire_Date
120102	Tom	Zhou	M	108255	Sales Manager	AU	3510	10744
120103	Wilson	Dawes	M	87975	Sales Manager	AU	-3996	5114
120121	Irenie	Elvish	F	26600	Sales Rep. II	AU	-5630	5114

Partial `work.comp`

Employee_ID	First_Name	Last_Name	Bonus	Compensation	Bonus Month
120102	Tom	Zhou	500	108755	6
120103	Wilson	Dawes	500	88475	1
120121	Irenie	Elvish	500	27100	1

5

Assignment Statements (Review)

Assignment statements are used in the DATA step
to update existing variables or create new variables.

```
DATA output-SAS-data-set ;
    SET input-SAS-data-set ;
    variable = expression ;
RUN;
```

defn. of datastep

(closes off data step)

name output you're creating

```
DATA output-SAS-data-set ;
    INFILE 'raw-data-file-name' ;
    INPUT specifications ;
    variable = expression ;
RUN;
```

6

Assignment Statements (Review)

The *assignment statement* evaluates an expression and assigns the resulting value to a variable.

General form of the assignment statement:

> *variable = expression* ;

- *variable* names an existing or new variable.
- *expression* is a sequence of operands and operators that form a set of instructions that produce a value.

7

An assignment statement evaluates the expression on the right side of the equal sign and stores the result in the variable that is specified on the left side of the equal sign.

Operands (Review)

Operands are constants (character, numeric, or date) and variables (character or numeric).

Examples:

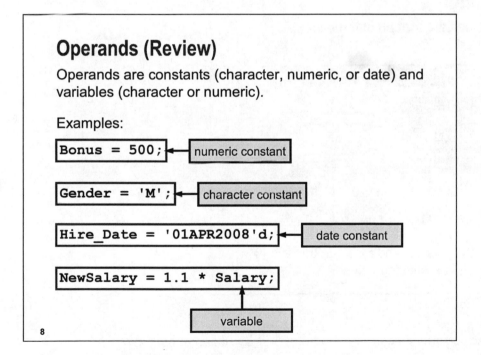

```
Bonus = 500;          numeric constant

Gender = 'M';         character constant

Hire_Date = '01APR2008'd;    date constant

NewSalary = 1.1 * Salary;
                           variable
```

8

Operators (Review)

Operators are symbols that represent an arithmetic calculation and SAS functions.

Examples:

```
Revenue = Quantity * Price;
```

```
NewCountry = upcase(Country);
```

9

Arithmetic Operators

Arithmetic operators indicate that an arithmetic calculation is performed.

Symbol	Definition	Priority
**	exponentiation	I
-	negative prefix	I
*	multiplication	II
/	division	II
+	addition	III
-	subtraction	III

✎ If a missing value is an operand for an arithmetic operator, the result is a missing value.

10

Rules for Operators

- Operations of priority I are performed before operations of priority II, and so on.
- Consecutive operations with the same priority are performed in this sequence:
  - from right to left within priority I
  - from left to right within priority II and III
- Parentheses can be used to control the order of operations.

9.01 Quiz

What is the result of the assignment statement?

a. . (missing)
b. 0

```
num = 4 + 10 / 2;
```

c. 7
d. 9

12

9.02 Quiz

What is the result of the assignment statement given the values of **var1** and **var2**?

a. . (missing)
b. 0
c. 5
d. 10

```
num = var1 + var2 / 2;
```

var1	var2
.	10

15

SAS Functions (Review)

A SAS *function* is a a routine that returns a value that is determined from specified arguments.

Some SAS functions manipulate character values, compute descriptive statistics, or manipulate SAS date values.

General form of a SAS function:

> *function-name***(***argument1***,** *argument2***, ...)**

- Depending on the function, zero, one, or many arguments are used.
- Arguments are separated with commas.

17

Descriptive Statistics Function

The *SUM function* returns the sum of the arguments.

General form of the SUM function:

> **SUM(***argument1,argument2***, ...)**

- The arguments must be numeric values.
- Missing values are ignored in all descriptive statistics functions.

Example:

```
Compensation=sum(Salary,Bonus);
```

18

Date Functions

SAS date functions can be used to

- extract information from SAS date values
- create SAS date values.

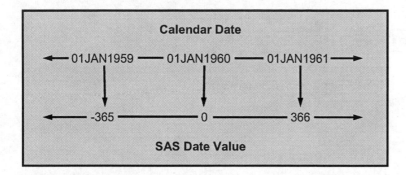

19

Date Functions – Extracting Information

YEAR(*SAS-date*)	extracts the year from a SAS date and returns a four-digit value for year
QTR(*SAS-date*)	extracts the quarter from a SAS date and returns a number from 1 to 4
MONTH(*SAS-date*)	extracts the month from a SAS date and returns a number from 1 to 12
DAY(*SAS-date*)	extracts the day of the month from a SAS data and returns a number from 1 to 31
WEEKDAY(*SAS-date*)	extracts the day of the week from a SAS date and returns a number from 1 to 7, where 1 represents Sunday, and so on

Example:

```
BonusMonth=month(Hire_Date);
```

20

Date Functions – Creating SAS Dates

TODAY()	returns the current date as a SAS date value
MDY(*month,day,year*)	returns a SAS date value from numeric month, day, and year values

Example:

```
AnnivBonus=mdy(month(Hire_Date),15,2008);
```

21

Business Scenario

Create **Bonus**, **Compensation**, and **BonusMonth**.

```
data work.comp;
   set orion.sales;
   Bonus=500;
   Compensation=sum(Salary,Bonus);
   BonusMonth=month(Hire_Date);
run;
```

```
1700   data work.comp;
1701      set orion.sales;
1702      Bonus=500;
1703      Compensation=sum(Salary,Bonus);
1704      BonusMonth=month(Hire_Date);
1705   run;
```

`orion.sales`
has 9 variables

```
NOTE: There were 165 observations read from the data set ORION.SALES.
NOTE: The data set WORK.COMP has 165 observations and 12 variables.
```

23   p109d01

9.03 Quiz

What statement needs to be added to the DATA step
to eliminate six of the twelve variables?

25

The DROP and KEEP Statements (Review)

The *DROP statement* specifies the names of the variables
to omit from the output data set(s).

> **DROP** *variable-list* ;

The *KEEP statement* specifies the names of the variable
to write to the output data set(s).

> **KEEP** *variable-list* ;

The *variable-list* specifies the variables to drop or keep,
respectively, in the output data set.

27

Business Scenario

Drop **Gender**, **Salary**, **Job_Title**, **Country**, **Birth_Date**, and **Hire_Date**.

```
data work.comp;
   set orion.sales;
   Bonus=500;
   Compensation=sum(Salary,Bonus);
   BonusMonth=month(Hire_Date);
   drop Gender Salary Job_Title
        Country Birth_Date Hire_Date;
run;
```

no commas

Partial SAS Log

```
NOTE: There were 165 observations read from the data set ORION.SALES.
NOTE: The data set WORK.COMP has 165 observations and 6 variables.
```

28   p109d01

Business Scenario

```
proc print data=work.comp;
run;
```

Partial PROC PRINT Output

Obs	Employee_ID	First_Name	Last_Name	Bonus	Compensation	Bonus Month
1	120102	Tom	Zhou	500	108755	6
2	120103	Wilson	Dawes	500	88475	1
3	120121	Irenie	Elvish	500	27100	1
4	120122	Christina	Ngan	500	27975	7
5	120123	Kimiko	Hotstone	500	26690	10
6	120124	Lucian	Daymond	500	26980	3
7	120125	Fong	Hofmeister	500	32540	3
8	120126	Satyakam	Denny	500	27280	8
9	120127	Sharryn	Clarkson	500	28600	11
10	120128	Monica	Kletschkus	500	31390	11

29   p109d01

Setup for the Poll

- Submit program **p109a01**.
- Verify the results.

```
data work.comp;
   set orion.sales;
   drop Gender Salary Job_Title
        Country Birth_Date Hire_Date;
   Bonus=500;
   Compensation=sum(Salary,Bonus);
   BonusMonth=month(Hire_Date);
run;
```

31

9.04 Poll

Are the correct results produced when the DROP statement is placed after the SET statement?

- ◑ Yes
- ○ No

32

NOOBS → removes rows

☆ P 4-12 procprint

Processing the DROP and KEEP Statements

The DROP and KEEP statements select variables **after** they are brought into the program data vector.

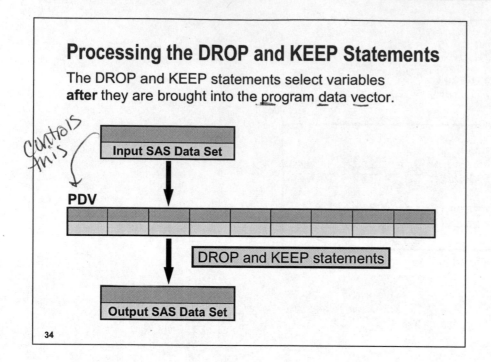

controls this

Input SAS Data Set

PDV

DROP and KEEP statements

Output SAS Data Set

34

Compilation

```
data work.comp;
   set orion.sales;
   drop Gender Salary Job_Title
        Country Birth_Date Hire_Date;
   Bonus=500;
   Compensation=sum(Salary,Bonus);
   BonusMonth=month(Hire_Date);
run;
```

35   ...

Compilation

```
data work.comp;
    set orion.sales;
    drop Gender Salary Job_Title
         Country Birth_Date Hire_Date;
    Bonus=500;
    Compensation=sum(Salary,Bonus);
    BonusMonth=month(Hire_Date);
run;
```

PDV

Employee_ID	First_Name	Last_Name	Gender	Salary	Job_Title
N 8	$ 12	$ 18	$ 1	N 8	$ 25

Country	Birth_Date	Hire_Date
$ 2	N 8	N 8

36   ...

Compilation

```
data work.comp;
    set orion.sales;
    drop Gender Salary Job_Title
         Country Birth_Date Hire_Date;
    Bonus=500;        → added
    Compensation=sum(Salary,Bonus);
    BonusMonth=month(Hire_Date);
run;
```

PDV

Employee_ID	First_Name	Last_Name	Gender	Salary	Job_Title
N 8	$ 12	$ 18	$ 1	N 8	$ 25

Country	Birth_Date	Hire_Date	Bonus
$ 2	N 8	N 8	N 8

37   ...

Compilation

```
data work.comp;
   set orion.sales;
   drop Gender Salary Job_Title
        Country Birth_Date Hire_Date;
   Bonus=500;
   Compensation=sum(Salary,Bonus);   added
   BonusMonth=month(Hire_Date);
run;
```

PDV

Employee_ID	First_Name	Last_Name	Gender	Salary	Job_Title
N 8	$ 12	$ 18	$ 1	N 8	$ 25

Country	Birth_Date	Hire_Date	Bonus	Compensation
$ 2	N 8	N 8	N 8	N 8

38   ...

Compilation

```
data work.comp;
   set orion.sales;
   drop Gender Salary Job_Title
        Country Birth_Date Hire_Date;
   Bonus=500;
   Compensation=sum(Salary,Bonus);
   BonusMonth=month(Hire_Date);   added
run;
```

PDV

Employee_ID	First_Name	Last_Name	Gender	Salary	Job_Title
N 8	$ 12	$ 18	$ 1	N 8	$ 25

Country	Birth_Date	Hire_Date	Bonus	Compensation	BonusMonth
$ 2	N 8	N 8	N 8	N 8	N 8

39   ...

Compilation

```
data work.comp;
   set orion.sales;
   drop Gender Salary Job_Title
        Country Birth_Date Hire_Date;
   Bonus=500;
   Compensation=sum(Salary,Bonus);
   BonusMonth=month(Hire_Date);
run;
```

PDV

Employee_ID	First_Name	Last_Name	Gender	Salary	Job_Title
N 8	$ 12	$ 18	D▶ $ 1	D▶ N 8	D▶ $ 25

Country	Birth_Date	Hire_Date	Bonus	Compensation	BonusMonth
D▶ $ 2	D▶ N 8	D▶ N 8	N 8	N 8	N 8

40   ...

Compilation

```
data work.comp;
   set orion.sales;
   drop Gender Salary Job_Title
        Country Birth_Date Hire_Date;
   Bonus=500;
   Compensation=sum(Salary,Bonus);
   BonusMonth=month(Hire_Date);
run;
```

PDV

Employee_ID	First_Name	Last_Name	Gender	Salary	Job_Title
N 8	$ 12	$ 18	D▶ $ 1	D▶ N 8	D▶ $ 25

Country	Birth_Date	Hire_Date	Bonus	Compensation	BonusMonth
D▶ $ 2	D▶ N 8	D▶ N 8	N 8	N 8	N 8

Descriptor Portion work.comp

Employee_ID	First_Name	Last_Name	Bonus	Compensation	BonusMonth
N 8	$ 12	$ 18	N 8	N 8	N 8

Execution

Partial `orion.sales`

Employee ID		Hire_Date
120102		10744
120103	...	5114
120121		5114
120122		6756

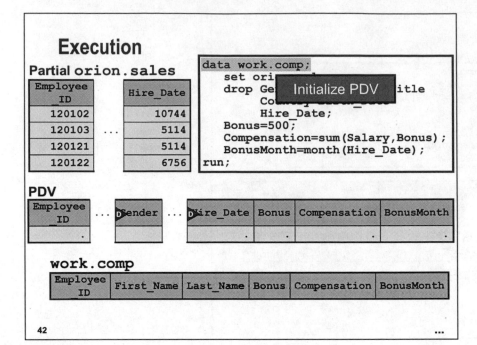

```
data work.comp;
    set ori
    drop Ge          Initialize PDV   itle
              Co
              Hire_Date;
    Bonus=500;
    Compensation=sum(Salary,Bonus);
    BonusMonth=month(Hire_Date);
run;
```

PDV

Employee ID		Gender		Hire_Date	Bonus	Compensation	BonusMonth
.	...		...		.	.	.

`work.comp`

Employee ID	First_Name	Last_Name	Bonus	Compensation	BonusMonth

42   ...

Execution

Partial `orion.sales`

Employee ID		Hire_Date
120102		10744
120103	...	5114
120121		5114
120122		6756

```
data work.comp;
    set orion.sales;
    drop Gender Salary Job_Title
         Country Birth_Date
         Hire_Date;
    Bonus=500;
    Compensation=sum(Salary,Bonus);
    BonusMonth=month(Hire_Date);
run;
```

PDV

Employee ID		Gender		Hire_Date	Bonus	Compensation	BonusMonth
120102	...	M	...	10744	.	.	.

`work.comp`

Employee ID	First_Name	Last_Name	Bonus	Compensation	BonusMonth

43   ...

Execution

Partial `orion.sales`

Employee ID		Hire_Date
120102		10744
120103	...	5114
120121		5114
120122		6756

```
data work.comp;
    set orion.sales;
    drop Gender Salary Job_Title
        Country Birth_Date
        Hire_Date;
    Bonus=500;
    Compensation=sum(Salary,Bonus);
    BonusMonth=month(Hire_Date);
run;
```

PDV

Employee ID		Gender		Hire_Date	Bonus	Compensation	BonusMonth
120102	...	M	...	10744	500	.	.

`work.comp`

Employee ID	First_Name	Last_Name	Bonus	Compensation	BonusMonth

44   ...

Execution

Partial `orion.sales`

Employee ID		Hire_Date
120102		10744
120103	...	5114
120121		5114
120122		6756

```
data work.comp;
    set orion.sales;
    drop Gender Salary Job_Title
        Country Birth_Date
        Hire_Date;
    Bonus=500;
    Compensation=sum(Salary,Bonus);
    BonusMonth=month(Hire_Date);
run;
```

PDV

Employee ID		Gender		Hire_Date	Bonus	Compensation	BonusMonth
120102	...	M	...	10744	500	108755	.

`work.comp`

Employee ID	First_Name	Last_Name	Bonus	Compensation	BonusMonth

45   ...

Execution

Partial `orion.sales`

Employee ID		Hire_Date
120102		10744
120103	...	5114
120121		5114
120122		6756

```
data work.comp;
    set orion.sales;
    drop Gender Salary Job_Title
        Country Birth_Date
        Hire_Date;
    Bonus=500;
    Compensation=sum(Salary,Bonus);
    BonusMonth=month(Hire_Date);
run;
```

PDV

Employee ID		D Gender		D Hire_Date	Bonus	Compensation	BonusMonth
120102	...	M	...	10744	500	108755	6

`work.comp`

Employee ID	First_Name	Last_Name	Bonus	Compensation	BonusMonth

46   ...

Execution

Partial `orion.sales`

Employee ID		Hire_Date
120102		10744
120103	...	5114
120121		5114
120122		6756

```
data work.comp;
    set orion.sales;
    drop Gender Salary Job_Title
        Country Birth_Date
        Hire_Date;
    Bonus=500;
    Compensation=sum(Salary,Bonus);
    BonusMon                          ;
run;
```

Implicit OUTPUT;
Implicit RETURN;

PDV

Employee ID		D Gender		D Hire_Date	Bonus	Compensation	BonusMonth
120102	...	M	...	10744	500	108755	6

`work.comp`

Employee ID	First_Name	Last_Name	Bonus	Compensation	BonusMonth
120102	Tom	Zhou	500	108755	6

47   ...

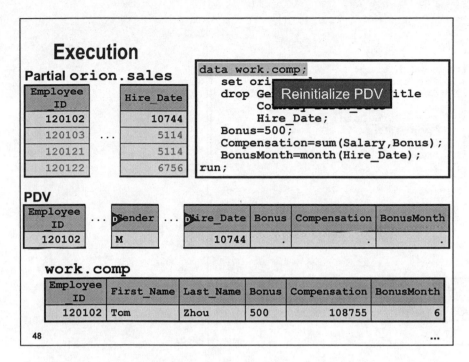

SAS reinitializes variables in the PDV at the start of every DATA step iteration. Variables created by an assignment statement are reset to missing but variables that are read with a SET statement are not reset to missing.

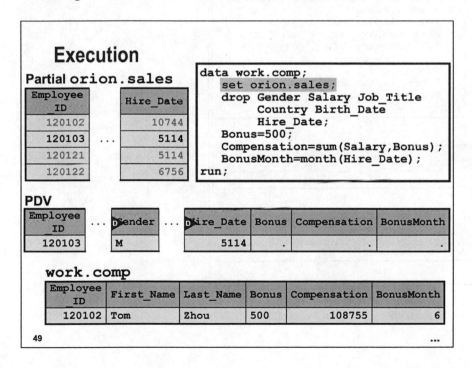

Execution

Partial `orion.sales`

Employee ID		Hire_Date
120102	...	10744
120103		5114
120121		5114
120122		6756

```
data work.comp;
    set orion.sales;
    drop Gender Salary Job_Title
        Country Birth_Date
        Hire_Date;
    Bonus=500;
    Compensation=sum(Salary,Bonus);
    BonusMonth=month(Hire_Date);
run;
```

PDV

Employee ID		D Gender		D Hire_Date	Bonus	Compensation	BonusMonth
120103	...	M	...	5114	500	.	.

`work.comp`

Employee ID	First_Name	Last_Name	Bonus	Compensation	BonusMonth
120102	Tom	Zhou	500	108755	6

50 ...

Execution

Partial `orion.sales`

Employee ID		Hire_Date
120102	...	10744
120103		5114
120121		5114
120122		6756

```
data work.comp;
    set orion.sales;
    drop Gender Salary Job_Title
        Country Birth_Date
        Hire_Date;
    Bonus=500;
    Compensation=sum(Salary,Bonus);
    BonusMonth=month(Hire_Date);
run;
```

PDV

Employee ID		D Gender		D Hire_Date	Bonus	Compensation	BonusMonth
120103	...	M	...	5114	500	88475	.

`work.comp`

Employee ID	First_Name	Last_Name	Bonus	Compensation	BonusMonth
120102	Tom	Zhou	500	108755	6

51 ...

Execution

Partial orion.sales

Employee ID		Hire_Date
120102		10744
120103	...	5114
120121		5114
120122		6756

```
data work.comp;
    set orion.sales;
    drop Gender Salary Job_Title
        Country Birth_Date
        Hire_Date;
    Bonus=500;
    Compensation=sum(Salary,Bonus);
    BonusMonth=month(Hire_Date);
run;
```

PDV

Employee ID		Gender		Hire_Date	Bonus	Compensation	BonusMonth
120103	...	M	...	5114	500	88475	1

work.comp

Employee ID	First_Name	Last_Name	Bonus	Compensation	BonusMonth
120102	Tom	Zhou	500	108755	6

52 ...

Execution

Partial orion.sales

Employee ID		Hire_Date
120102		10744
120103	...	5114
120121		5114
120122		6756

```
data work.comp;
    set orion.sales;
    drop Gender Salary Job_Title
        Country Birth_Date
        Hire_Date;
    Bonus=500;
    Compensation=sum(Salary,Bonus);
    BonusMon             ;
run;
```

Implicit OUTPUT;
Implicit RETURN;

PDV

Employee ID		Gender		Hire_Date	Bonus	Compensation	BonusMonth
120103	...	M	...	5114	500	88475	1

work.comp

Employee ID	First_Name	Last_Name	Bonus	Compensation	BonusMonth
120102	Tom	Zhou	500	108755	6
120103	Wilson	Dawes	500	88475	1

53

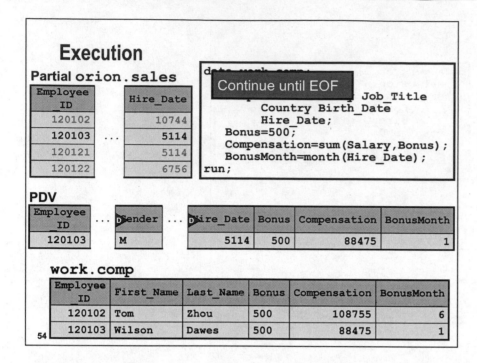

Execution

Partial `orion.sales`

Employee ID		Hire_Date
120102	...	10744
120103	...	5114
120121	...	5114
120122	...	6756

```
data work.comp;
                              Job_Title
         Country Birth_Date
         Hire_Date;
   Bonus=500;
   Compensation=sum(Salary,Bonus);
   BonusMonth=month(Hire_Date);
run;
```

Continue until EOF

PDV

Employee ID	...	Gender	...	Hire_Date	Bonus	Compensation	BonusMonth
120103		M		5114	500	88475	1

`work.comp`

Employee ID	First_Name	Last_Name	Bonus	Compensation	BonusMonth
120102	Tom	Zhou	500	108755	6
120103	Wilson	Dawes	500	88475	1

54

DROP= and KEEP= Options (Self-Study)

Alternatives to the DROP and KEEP statements are the DROP= and KEEP= data set options placed in the DATA statement.

- The *DROP= data set option* in the DATA statement excludes the variables for writing to the output data set.

  DATA *output-SAS-data-set* (DROP = *variable-list*) ;

- The *KEEP= data set option* in the DATA statement specifies the variables for writing to the output data set.

  DATA *output-SAS-data-set* (KEEP = *variable-list*) ;

56

When specified for a data set named in the DATA statement, the DROP= and KEEP= data set options are similar to DROP and KEEP statements. However, the DROP= and KEEP= data set options can be used in situations where the DROP and KEEP statements cannot. For example, the DROP= and KEEP= data set options can be used in a PROC step to control which variables are available for processing by the procedure.

DROP= and KEEP= Options (Self-Study)

The DROP= and KEEP= data set options can also be placed in the SET statement to control which variables are read from the input data set.

- The *DROP= data set option* in the SET statement excludes the variables for processing in the PDV.

> **SET** *input-SAS-data-set* (DROP = *variable-list*) ;

- The *KEEP= data set option* in the SET statement specifies the variables for processing in the PDV.

> **SET** *input-SAS-data-set* (KEEP = *variable-list*) ;

57

DROP= and KEEP= Options (Self-Study)

```
data work.comp(drop=Salary Hire_Date);
   set orion.sales(keep=Employee_ID First_Name
                        Last_Name Salary Hire_Date);
   Bonus=500;
   Compensation=sum(Salary,Bonus);
   BonusMonth=month(Hire_Date);
run;
```

orion.sales

Employee_ ID	First_ Name	Last_ Name	Gender	Salary	Job_ Title	Country	Birth_ Date	Hire_ Date

PDV

Employee_ ID	First_ Name	Last_ Name	Salary	Hire_ Date	Bonus	Compensation	BonusMonth

work.comp

Employee_ ID	First_ Name	Last_ Name	Bonus	Compensation	BonusMonth

58   p109d02

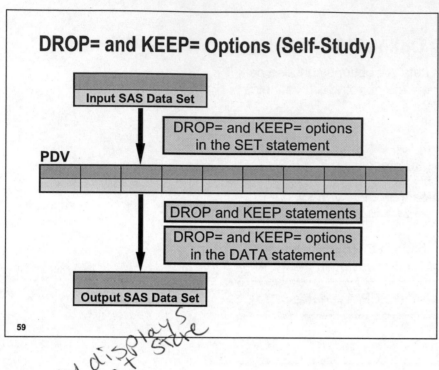

DROP= and KEEP= Options (Self-Study)

Input SAS Data Set

DROP= and KEEP= options
in the SET statement

PDV

DROP and KEEP statements

DROP= and KEEP= options
in the DATA statement

Output SAS Data Set

59

* → only displays
    doesn't store

* Format
    comma10.

* label ___ = ' ';   *
                        also include in
                        proc print work.label;

bday2009=mdy(munth(birtn_date),day(birth-date),2009);
bday dow 2009=weekday (bday 2009);
age2009=(bday2009-birth_date)/36.5.25;
keep .
format age2009.2;)

 **Exercises**

Level 1

1. **Creating Two New Variables**

    a. Retrieve the starter program **p109e01**.

    b. In the DATA step, create two new variables, **Increase** and **NewSalary**.

    - **Increase** is the **Salary** multiplied by 0.10.
    - **NewSalary** is **Salary** added with **Increase**.

    c. The data set should include only the following variables: **Employee_ID**, **Salary**, **Increase**, and **NewSalary**.

    d. Formats displaying commas should be stored for **Salary**, **Increase**, and **NewSalary**.

    e. Submit the program to create the following PROC PRINT report:

    Partial PROC PRINT Output (First 10 of 424 Observations)

Obs	Employee_ID	Employee Annual Salary	Increase	NewSalary
1	120101	163,040	16,304	179,344
2	120102	108,255	10,826	119,081
3	120103	87,975	8,798	96,773
4	120104	46,230	4,623	50,853
5	120105	27,110	2,711	29,821
6	120106	26,960	2,696	29,656
7	120107	30,475	3,048	33,523
8	120108	27,660	2,766	30,426
9	120109	26,495	2,650	29,145
10	120110	28,615	2,862	31,477

Level 2

2. **Creating Three New Variables**

    a. Write a DATA step to read **orion.customer** to create **work.birthday**.

    b. In the DATA step, create three new variables, **Bday2009**, **BdayDOW2009**, and **Age2009**.
    - **Bday2009** is the combination of the month of **Birth_Date**, the day of **Birth_Date**, and the constant of 2009 in the MDY function.
    - **BdayDOW2009** is the day of week of **Bday2009**.
    - **Age2009** is the age of the customer in 2009. Subtract **Birth_Date** from **Bday2009** and then divide by 365.25.

c. The data set should include only the following variables: **Customer_Name**, **Birth_Date**, **Bday2009**, **BdayDOW2009**, and **Age2009**.

d. **Bday2009** should be formatted to look like a two-digit day, a three-letter month, and a four-digit year. **Age2009** should be formatted to display with no digits after the decimal point.

e. Write a PROC PRINT step to create the following report:

Partial PROC PRINT Output (First 10 of 77 Observations)

Obs	Customer_Name	Birth_ Date	Bday2009	Bday DOW2009	Age2009
1	James Kvarniq	27JUN1974	27JUN2009	7	35
2	Sandrina Stephano	09JUL1979	09JUL2009	5	30
3	Cornelia Krahl	27FEB1974	27FEB2009	6	35
4	Karen Ballinger	18OCT1984	18OCT2009	1	25
5	Elke Wallstab	16AUG1974	16AUG2009	1	35
6	David Black	12APR1969	12APR2009	1	40
7	Markus Sepke	21JUL1988	21JUL2009	3	21
8	Ulrich Heyde	16JAN1939	16JAN2009	6	70
9	Jimmie Evans	17AUG1954	17AUG2009	2	55
10	Tonie Asmussen	02FEB1954	02FEB2009	2	55

Level 3

3. Using the CATX and INTCK Functions to Create Variables

a. Write a DATA step to read **orion.sales** to create **work.employees**.

b. In the DATA step, create the new variable **FullName**, which is the combination of **First_Name**, a space, and **Last_Name**. Use the CATX function.

> Documentation on the CATX function can be found in the SAS Help and Documentation from the Contents tab (**SAS Products** ⇨ **Base SAS** ⇨ **SAS 9.2 Language Reference: Dictionary** ⇨ **Dictionary of Language Elements** ⇨ **Functions and CALL Routines** ⇨ **CATX Function**).

c. In the DATA step, create the new variable **Yrs2012**, which is the number of years between January 1, 2012 and **Hire_Date**. Use the INTCK function.

> Documentation on the INTCK function can be found in the SAS Help and Documentation from the Contents tab (**SAS Products** ⇨ **Base SAS** ⇨ **SAS 9.2 Language Reference: Dictionary** ⇨ **Dictionary of Language Elements** ⇨ **Functions and CALL Routines** ⇨ **INTCK Function**).

d. **Hire_Date** should be formatted to look like a two-digit day, a two-digit month, and a four-digit year.

e. **Yrs2012** should have a label of Years of Employment in 2012.

f. Write a PROC PRINT step with a VAR statement to create the following report:

Partial PROC PRINT Output (First 10 of 165 Observations)

```
                                              Years of
                                             Employment
            Obs    FullName          Hire_Date    in 2012

              1    Tom Zhou          01/06/1989      23
              2    Wilson Dawes      01/01/1974      38
              3    Irenie Elvish     01/01/1974      38
              4    Christina Ngan    01/07/1978      34
              5    Kimiko Hotstone   01/10/1985      27
              6    Lucian Daymond    01/03/1979      33
              7    Fong Hofmeister   01/03/1979      33
              8    Satyakam Denny    01/08/2006       6
              9    Sharryn Clarkson  01/11/1998      14
             10    Monica Kletschkus 01/11/2006       6
```

9.2 Creating Variables Conditionally

Objectives

- Execute statements conditionally by using IF-THEN and IF-THEN DO statements.
- Give alternate actions if the previous THEN clause is not executed by using the ELSE statement.
- Control the length of character variables by using the LENGTH statement.

62

Business Scenario

A new SAS data set named **work.bonus** needs to be created by reading the **orion.sales** data set.

work.bonus must include a new variable named **Bonus** that is equal to

- 500 for United States employees
- 300 for Australian employees.

63

IF-THEN Statements (Review)

The *IF-THEN statement* executes a SAS statement for observations that meet specific conditions.

General form of the IF-THEN statement:

> **IF** *expression* **THEN** *statement* **;**

- *expression* is a sequence of operands and operators that form a set of instructions that define a condition for selecting observations.
- *statement* is any executable statement such as the assignment statement.

64

If the condition in the IF clause is met, the IF-THEN statement executes a SAS statement for that observation.

IF-THEN / ELSE Statements (Review)

The optional *ELSE statement* gives an alternate action if the previous THEN clause is not executed.

General form of the IF-THEN / ELSE statements:

> **IF** *expression* **THEN** *statement* **;**
> **ELSE IF** *expression* **THEN** *statement* **;**

can only followed by 1 sas statement

- Using IF-THEN statements **without** the ELSE statement causes SAS to evaluate all IF-THEN statements.
- Using IF-THEN statements **with** the ELSE statement causes SAS to execute IF-THEN statements until it encounters the first true statement.

65

*pg- operators
5-14*

Conditional logic can include one or more ELSE IF statements.

For greater efficiency, construct your IF-THEN / ELSE statements with conditions of decreasing probability.

Business Scenario

Create the new variable **Bonus**.

```
data work.bonus;
   set orion.sales;
   if Country='US' then Bonus=500;
   else if Country='AU' then Bonus=300;
run;
```

```
1819  data work.bonus;
1820     set orion.sales;
1821     if Country='US' then Bonus=500;
1822     else if Country='AU' then Bonus=300;
1823  run;

NOTE: There were 165 observations read from the data set ORION.SALES.
NOTE: The data set WORK.BONUS has 165 observations and 10 variables
```

66   p109d03

Business Scenario

```
proc print data=work.bonus;
   var First_Name Last_Name Country Bonus;
run;
```

Partial PROC PRINT Output

Obs	First_Name	Last_Name	Country	Bonus
60	Billy	Plested	AU	300
61	Matsuoka	Wills	AU	300
62	Vino	George	AU	300
63	Meera	Body	AU	300
64	Harry	Highpoint	US	500
65	Julienne	Magolan	US	500
66	Scott	Desanctis	US	500
67	Cherda	Ridley	US	500
68	Priscilla	Farren	US	500
69	Robert	Stevens	US	500

67   p109d03

9.05 Quiz

Why are some of the **Bonus** values missing in
the PROC PRINT output for `orion.nonsales`?

- Submit program **p109a02**.
- Review the results.

69

ELSE Statements

The conditional clause does not have to be in an
ELSE statement.

For example:

```
data work.bonus;
   set orion.sales;
   if Country='US' then Bonus=500;
   else Bonus=300;
run;
```

 All observations not equal to US get a bonus of 300.

71   **p109d03**

Business Scenario

A new SAS data set named `work.bonus` needs to be created by reading the `orion.sales` data set.

`work.bonus` must include a new variable named **Bonus** that is equal to

- 500 for United States employees
- 300 for Australian employees.

`work.bonus` must include another new variable named **Freq** that is equal to

- `Once a Year` for United States employees
- `Twice a Year` for Australian employees.

72

IF-THEN / ELSE Statements

Only **one** executable statement is allowed in IF-THEN / ELSE statements.

```
IF expression THEN statement ;
ELSE IF expression THEN statement ;
ELSE statement ;
```

For the given business scenario, two statements need to be executed per each true expression.

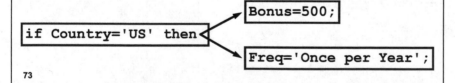

```
if Country='US' then
```
```
Bonus=500;
```
```
Freq='Once per Year';
```

73

IF-THEN DO / ELSE DO Statements

Multiple executable statements are allowed in
IF-THEN DO / ELSE DO statements.

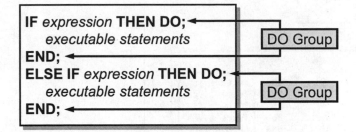

```
IF expression THEN DO;
    executable statements          DO Group
END;
ELSE IF expression THEN DO;
    executable statements          DO Group
END;
```

- Each DO group can contain multiple statements
  that apply to the expression.
- Each DO group ends with an END statement.

74

Business Scenario

Create another new variable named **Freq**.

```
data work.bonus;
   set orion.sales;
   if Country='US' then do;
      Bonus=500;
      Freq='Once a Year';
   end;
   else if Country='AU' then do;
      Bonus=300;
      Freq='Twice a Year';
   end;
run;
```

75   p109d04

Business Scenario

```
proc print data=work.bonus;
    var First_Name Last_Name
        Country Bonus Freq;
run;
```

Partial PROC PRINT Output

Obs	First_Name	Last_Name	Country	Bonus	Freq
60	Billy	Plested	AU	300	Twice a Yea
61	Matsuoka	Wills	AU	300	Twice a Yea
62	Vino	George	AU	300	Twice a Yea
63	Meera	Body	AU	300	Twice a Yea
64	Harry	Highpoint	US	500	Once a Year
65	Julienne	Magolan	US	500	Once a Year
66	Scott	Desanctis	US	500	Once a Year
67	Cherda	Ridley	US	500	Once a Year
68	Priscilla	Farren	US	500	Once a Year
69	Robert	Stevens	US	500	Once a Year

76   p109d04

Compilation

```
data work.bonus;
    set orion.sales;
    if Country='US' then do;
        Bonus=500;
        Freq='Once a Year';
    end;
    else if Country='AU' then do;
        Bonus=300;
        Freq='Twice a Year';
    end;
run;
```

PDV

Employee_ID	First_Name	...	Hire_Date
N 8	$ 12		N 8

77   ...

Compilation

```
data work.bonus;
   set orion.sales;
   if Country='US' then do;
      Bonus=500;
      Freq='Once a Year';
   end;
   else if Country='AU' then do;
      Bonus=300;
      Freq='Twice a Year';
   end;
run;
```

PDV

Employee_ID	First_Name	...	Hire_Date	Bonus
N 8	$ 12		N 8	N 8

78

...

Compilation

```
data work.bonus;
   set orion.sales;
   if Country='US' then do;
      Bonus=500;
      Freq='Once a Year';
   end;
   else if                    then do;
      Bonus=300;
      Freq='Twice a Year';
   end;
run;
```

11 characters

PDV

Employee_ID	First_Name	...	Hire_Date	Bonus	Freq
N 8	$ 12		N 8	N 8	$ 11

79

9.06 Quiz

How would you prevent **Freq** from being truncated?

81

The LENGTH Statement (Review)

The *LENGTH statement* defines the length of a variable explicitly.

General form of the LENGTH statement:

> **LENGTH** *variable(s)* $ *length* ;

Example:

```
length First_Name Last_Name $ 12
       Gender $ 1;
```

83

Business Scenario

Set the length of the variable **Freq** to avoid truncation.

```
data work.bonus;
   set orion.sales;
   length Freq $ 12;
   if Country='US' then do;
      Bonus=500;
      Freq='Once a Year';
   end;
   else if Country='AU' then do;
      Bonus=300;
      Freq='Twice a Year';
   end;
run;
```

84   p109d04

Business Scenario

```
proc print data=work.bonus;
   var First_Name Last_Name
       Country Bonus Freq;
run;
```

Partial PROC PRINT Output

Obs	First_Name	Last_Name	Country	Bonus	Freq
60	Billy	Plested	AU	300	Twice a Year
61	Matsuoka	Wills	AU	300	Twice a Year
62	Vino	George	AU	300	Twice a Year
63	Meera	Body	AU	300	Twice a Year
64	Harry	Highpoint	US	500	Once a Year
65	Julienne	Magolan	US	500	Once a Year
66	Scott	Desanctis	US	500	Once a Year
67	Cherda	Ridley	US	500	Once a Year
68	Priscilla	Farren	US	500	Once a Year
69	Robert	Stevens	US	500	Once a Year

85   p109d04

ELSE Statements

The conditional clause does not have to be in an
ELSE statement.

```
data work.bonus;
   set orion.sales;
   length Freq $ 12;
   if Country='US' then do;
      Bonus=500;
      Freq='Once a Year';
   end;
   else do;
      Bonus=300;
      Freq='Twice a Year';
   end;
run;
```

⚠ All observations not equal to US execute the
statements in the second DO group.

86   p109d04

 **Exercises**

Level 1

4. Creating Variables Conditionally

a. Retrieve the starter program **p109e04**.

b. In the DATA step, create three new variables, **Discount**, **DiscountType**, and **Region**.

If **Country** is equal to CA or US,

- **Discount** is equal to 0.10.
- **DiscountType** is equal to Required.
- **Region** is equal to North America.

If **Country** is equal to any other value,

- **Discount** is equal to 0.05.
- **DiscountType** is equal to Optional.
- **Region** is equal to Not North America.

c. The data set should include only the following variables: **Supplier_Name**, **Country**, **Discount**, **DiscountType**, and **Region**.

d. Submit the program to create the following PROC PRINT report:

Partial PROC PRINT Output (First 10 of 52 Observations)

Obs	Supplier_Name	Country	Region	Discount	Discount Type
1	Scandinavian Clothing A/S	NO	Not North America	0.05	Optional
2	Petterson AB	SE	Not North America	0.05	Optional
3	Prime Sports Ltd	GB	Not North America	0.05	Optional
4	Top Sports	DK	Not North America	0.05	Optional
5	AllSeasons Outdoor Clothing	US	North America	0.10	Required
6	Sportico	ES	Not North America	0.05	Optional
7	British Sports Ltd	GB	Not North America	0.05	Optional
8	Eclipse Inc	US	North America	0.10	Required
9	Magnifico Sports	PT	Not North America	0.05	Optional
10	Pro Sportswear Inc	US	North America	0.10	Required

Level 2

5. **Creating Variables Unconditionally and Conditionally**

   a. Write a DATA step to read **orion.orders** to create **work.ordertype**.

   b. Create the new variable **DayOfWeek**, which is equal to the week day of **Order_Date**.

   c. Create the new variable **Type**, which is equal to
      - Catalog Sale if **Order_Type** is equal to 1
      - Internet Sale if **Order_Type** is equal to 2
      - Retail Sale if **Order_Type** is equal to 3.

   d. Create the new variable **SaleAds**, which is equal to
      - Mail if **Order_Type** is equal to 1
      - Email if **Order_Type** is equal to 2.

   e. The data set should not include **Order_Type**, **Employee_ID**, and **Customer_ID**.

   f. Write a PROC PRINT step to create the following report:

   Partial PROC PRINT Output (First 20 of 490 Observations)

Obs	Order_ID	Order_ Date	Delivery_ Date	Type	Sale Ads	Day Of Week
1	1230058123	11JAN2003	11JAN2003	Catalog Sale	Mail	7
2	1230080101	15JAN2003	19JAN2003	Internet Sale	Email	4
3	1230106883	20JAN2003	22JAN2003	Internet Sale	Email	2
4	1230147441	28JAN2003	28JAN2003	Catalog Sale	Mail	3
5	1230315085	27FEB2003	27FEB2003	Catalog Sale	Mail	5
6	1230333319	02MAR2003	03MAR2003	Internet Sale	Email	1
7	1230338566	03MAR2003	08MAR2003	Internet Sale	Email	2
8	1230371142	09MAR2003	11MAR2003	Internet Sale	Email	1
9	1230404278	15MAR2003	15MAR2003	Catalog Sale	Mail	7
10	1230440481	22MAR2003	22MAR2003	Catalog Sale	Mail	7
11	1230450371	24MAR2003	26MAR2003	Internet Sale	Email	2
12	1230453723	24MAR2003	25MAR2003	Internet Sale	Email	2
13	1230455630	25MAR2003	25MAR2003	Catalog Sale	Mail	3
14	1230478006	28MAR2003	30MAR2003	Internet Sale	Email	6
15	1230498538	01APR2003	01APR2003	Catalog Sale	Mail	3
16	1230500669	02APR2003	03APR2003	Retail Sale		4
17	1230503155	02APR2003	03APR2003	Internet Sale	Email	4
18	1230591673	18APR2003	23APR2003	Internet Sale	Email	6
19	1230591675	18APR2003	20APR2003	Retail Sale		6
20	1230591684	18APR2003	18APR2003	Catalog Sale	Mail	6

Level 3

6. **Using WHEN Statements in a SELECT Group to Create Variables Conditionally**

   a. Write a DATA step to read **orion.nonsales** to create **work.gifts**.

   b. Create two new variables, **Gift1** and **Gift2**, using a SELECT group with WHEN statements.

      If **Gender** is equal to F,
      - **Gift1** is equal to Perfume.
      - **Gift2** is equal to Cookware.

      If **Gender** is equal to M,
      - **Gift1** is equal to Cologne.
      - **Gift2** is equal to Lawn Equipment.

      If **Gender** is not equal to F or M,
      - **Gift1** is equal to Coffee.
      - **Gift2** is equal to Lawn Calendar.

      🖉   Documentation on the SELECT group with WHEN statements can be found in the SAS Help and Documentation from the Contents tab (**SAS Products** ⇨ **Base SAS** ⇨ **SAS 9.2 Language Reference: Dictionary** ⇨ **Dictionary of Language Elements** ⇨ **Statements** ⇨ **SELECT Statement**).

   c. The data set should include only the following variables: **Employee_ID**, **First**, **Last**, **Gift1**, and **Gift2**.

   d. Write a PROC PRINT step to create the following report:

   Partial PROC PRINT Output (First 15 of 235 Observations)

Obs	Employee_ID	First	Last	Gift1	Gift2
1	120101	Patrick	Lu	Cologne	Lawn Equipment
2	120104	Kareen	Billington	Perfume	Cookware
3	120105	Liz	Povey	Perfume	Cookware
4	120106	John	Hornsey	Cologne	Lawn Equipment
5	120107	Sherie	Sheedy	Perfume	Cookware
6	120108	Gladys	Gromek	Perfume	Cookware
7	120108	Gabriele	Baker	Perfume	Cookware
8	120110	Dennis	Entwisle	Cologne	Lawn Equipment
9	120111	Ubaldo	Spillane	Cologne	Lawn Equipment
10	120112	Ellis	Glattback	Perfume	Cookware
11	120113	Riu	Horsey	Perfume	Cookware
12	120114	Jeannette	Buddery	Coffee	Calendar
13	120115	Hugh	Nichollas	Cologne	Lawn Equipment
14	.	Austen	Ralston	Cologne	Lawn Equipment
15	120117	Bill	Mccleary	Cologne	Lawn Equipment

9.3 Subsetting Observations

Objectives

- Subset observations by using the WHERE statement.
- Subset observations by using the subsetting IF statement.
- Subset observations by using the IF-THEN DELETE statement. (Self-Study)

90

Business Scenario

A new SAS data set named **work.december** needs to be created by reading the **orion.sales** data set.

work.december must include the following new variables:

- **Bonus**, which is equal to a constant 500.
- **Compensation**, which is the combination of the employee's salary and bonus.
- **BonusMonth**, which is equal to the month the employee was hired.

work.december must include only the employees from Australia who have a bonus month in December.

91

The WHERE Statement (Review)

The *WHERE statement* subsets observations that meet a particular condition.

General form of the WHERE statement:

> **WHERE** *where-expression* **;**

The *where-expression* is a sequence of operands and operators that form a set of instructions that define a condition for selecting observations.

- Operands include constants and variables.
- Operators are symbols that request a comparison, arithmetic calculation, or logical operation.

92

Processing the WHERE Statement

The WHERE statement selects observations **before** they are brought into the program data vector.

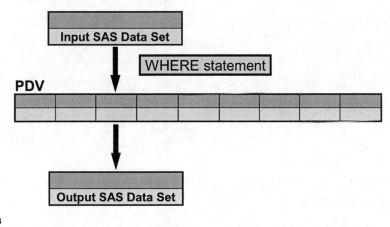

93

9.07 Quiz

Why does the WHERE statement not work in this
DATA step?

```
data work.december;
   set orion.sales;
   BonusMonth=month(Hire_Date);
   Bonus=500;
   Compensation=sum(Salary,Bonus);
   where Country='AU' and BonusMonth=12;
run;
```

not in data set

95   p109d05

The Subsetting IF Statement

The *subsetting IF statement* continues processing
only those observations that meet the condition.

General form of the subsetting IF statement:

> **IF** *expression* ;

The *expression* is a sequence of operands and operators
that form a set of instructions that define a condition for
selecting observations.

- Operands include constants and variables.
- Operators are symbols that request a comparison,
  arithmetic calculation, or logical operation.

97

The Subsetting IF Statement

Examples:

```
if Salary > 50000;
```

```
if Last_Name='Smith' and First_Name='Joe';
```

```
if Country not in ('GB', 'FR', 'NL');
```

```
if Hire_Date = '15APR2008'd;
```

```
if BirthMonth = 5 or BirthMonth = 6;
```

```
if upcase(Gender)='M';
```

```
if 40000 <= Compensation <= 80000;
```

```
if sum(Salary,Bonus) < 43000;
```

98

Special WHERE operators such as BETWEEN-AND, IS NULL, IS MISSING, CONTAINS, and LIKE cannot be used with the subsetting IF statement.

Processing the Subsetting IF Statement

The subsetting IF statement determines if observations continue being processed in the program data vector.

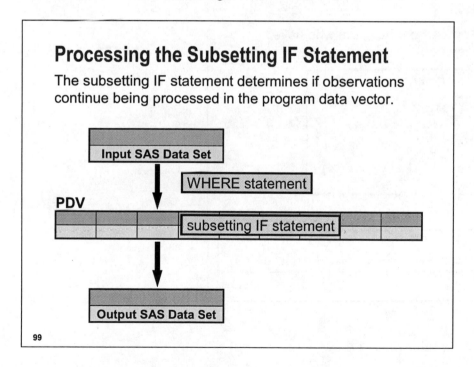

99

Processing the Subsetting IF Statement

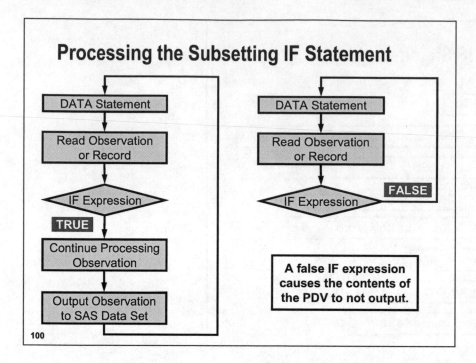

DATA Statement

Read Observation or Record

IF Expression

TRUE

Continue Processing Observation

Output Observation to SAS Data Set

DATA Statement

Read Observation or Record

IF Expression

FALSE

A false IF expression causes the contents of the PDV to not output.

100

Business Scenario

Include only the employees from Australia who have a bonus month in December.

```
data work.december;
    set orion.sales;
    where Country='AU';
    BonusMonth=month(Hire_Date);
    if BonusMonth=12;
    Bonus=500;
    Compensation=sum(Salary,Bonus);
run;
```

Partial SAS Log

```
NOTE: There were 63 observations read from the data set ORION.SALES.
      WHERE Country='AU';
NOTE: The data set WORK.DECEMBER has 3 observations and 12 variables.
```

101   p109d05

9.08 Quiz

Could you have written just an IF statement?

Ⓞ Yes

Ⓞ No

more efficient ←

```
data work.december;
   set orion.sales;
   where Country='AU';
   BonusMonth=month(Hire_Date);
   if BonusMonth=12;
   Bonus=500;
   Compensatio
run;
```

```
data work.december;
   set orion.sales;
   BonusMonth=month(Hire_Date);
   if BonusMonth=12 and Country='AU';
   Bonus=500;
   Compensation=sum(Salary,Bonus);
run;
```

103   p109d05

WHERE Statement vs. Subsetting IF Statement

Step and Usage	WHERE	IF
PROC step	Yes	No
DATA step (source of variable)		
INPUT statement	No	Yes
assignment statement	No	Yes
SET statement (single data set)	Yes	Yes
SET/MERGE statement (multiple data sets)		
Variable in ALL data sets	Yes	Yes
Variable not in ALL data sets	No	Yes

105

The IF-THEN DELETE Statement (Self-Study)

An alternative to the subsetting IF statement is the DELETE statement on an IF-THEN statement.

General form of the IF-THEN DELETE statement:

> **IF** *expression* **THEN DELETE ;**

The *DELETE statement* stops processing the current observation.

107

When DELETE executes, the current observation is not written to a data set, and SAS returns immediately to the beginning of the DATA step for the next iteration.

The IF-THEN DELETE Statement (Self-Study)

```
data work.december;
   set orion.sales;
   where Country='AU';
   BonusMonth=month(Hire_Date);
   if BonusMonth ne 12 then delete;
   Bonus=500;
   Compensation=sum(Salary,Bonus);
run;
```

equivalent

```
data work.december;
   set orion.sales;
   where Country='AU';
   BonusMonth=month(Hire_Date);
   if BonusMonth=12;   then continue;
   Bonus=500;
   Compensation=sum(Salary,Bonus);
run;
```

108   p109d06

 **Exercises**

Level 1

7. Subsetting Observations Based on Two Conditions

   a. Retrieve the starter program **p109e07**.

   b. In the DATA step, write a statement to select only the observations that have **Emp_Hire_Date** greater than or equal to July 1, 2006. Subset the observations as they are being read into the program data vector.

   c. In the DATA step, write another statement to select only the observations that have an increase greater than 3000.

   d. Submit the program to create the following PROC PRINT report:

Obs	Employee ID	Employee Annual Salary	Employee Hire Date	Increase	NewSalary
1	120128	30,890	01NOV2006	3,089	33,979
2	120144	30,265	01OCT2006	3,027	33,292
3	120161	30,785	01OCT2006	3,079	33,864
4	120264	37,510	01DEC2006	3,751	41,261
5	120761	30,960	01JUL2006	3,096	34,056
6	120995	34,850	01AUG2006	3,485	38,335
7	121055	30,185	01AUG2006	3,019	33,204
8	121062	30,305	01AUG2006	3,031	33,336
9	121085	32,235	01JAN2007	3,224	35,459
10	121107	31,380	01JUL2006	3,138	34,518

Level 2

8. Subsetting Observations Based on Three Conditions

   a. Write a DATA step to read **orion.orders** to create **work.delays**.

   b. Create the new variable **Order_Month**, which is equal to the month of **Order_Date**.

   c. Use a WHERE statement and a subsetting IF statement to select only the observations that meet all of the following conditions:

   - **Delivery_Date** values that are more than four days beyond **Order_Date**
   - **Employee_ID** values that are equal to 99999999
   - **Order_Month** values occurring in August

d. Write a PROC PRINT step to create the following report:

Obs	Order_ID	Order_Type	Employee_ID	Customer_ID	Order_Date	Delivery_Date	Order_Month
1	1231227910	2	99999999	70187	13AUG2003	18AUG2003	8
2	1231270767	3	99999999	52	20AUG2003	26AUG2003	8
3	1231305521	2	99999999	16	27AUG2003	04SEP2003	8
4	1231317443	2	99999999	61	29AUG2003	03SEP2003	8
5	1233484749	3	99999999	2550	10AUG2004	15AUG2004	8
6	1233514453	3	99999999	70201	15AUG2004	20AUG2004	8
7	1236673732	3	99999999	9	10AUG2005	15AUG2005	8
8	1240051245	3	99999999	71	30AUG2006	05SEP2006	8
9	1243165497	3	99999999	70201	24AUG2007	29AUG2007	8

Level 3

9. Using an IF-THEN DELETE Statement to Subset Observations

a. Write a DATA step to read **orion.employee_donations** to create
work.bigdonations.

b. Create the new variable **Total**, which is equal to sum of **Qtr1**, **Qtr2**, **Qtr3**, and **Qtr4**.

c. Create the new variable **NoDonation**, which is equal to the count of missing values in **Qtr1**,
Qtr2, **Qtr3**, and **Qtr4**. Use the NMISS function.

> Documentation on the NMISS function can be found in the SAS Help and
> Documentation from the Contents tab (**SAS Products** ⇨ **Base SAS** ⇨
> **SAS 9.2 Language Reference: Dictionary** ⇨ **Dictionary of Language Elements** ⇨
> **Functions and CALL Routines** ⇨ **NMISS Function**).

d. The final data set should contain only observations meeting the following two conditions:

- **Total** values greater than or equal to 50

- **NoDonation** values equal to 0.

Use an IF-THEN DELETE statement to eliminate the observations where the conditions are not
met.

> The IF-THEN DELETE statement is mentioned at the end of this section in a self-study
> section.

e. Write a PROC PRINT step with a VAR statement to create the following report:

Partial PROC PRINT Output (First 7 of 50 Observations)

Obs	Employee_ID	Qtr1	Qtr2	Qtr3	Qtr4	Total	No Donation
1	120267	15	15	15	15	60	0
2	120269	20	20	20	20	80	0
3	120271	20	20	20	20	80	0
4	120275	15	15	15	15	60	0
5	120660	25	25	25	25	100	0
6	120669	15	15	15	15	60	0
7	120671	20	20	20	20	80	0

9.4 Solutions

Solutions to Exercises

1. **Creating Two New Variables**

    a. Retrieve the starter program.

    b. Create two new variables.

```
data work.increase;
   set orion.staff;
   Increase=Salary*0.10;
   NewSalary=sum(Salary,Increase);
run;

proc print data=work.increase label;
run;
```

    c. Include only four variables.

```
data work.increase;
   set orion.staff;
   Increase=Salary*0.10;
   NewSalary=sum(Salary,Increase);
   keep Employee_ID Salary Increase NewSalary;
run;

proc print data=work.increase label;
run;
```

    d. Format three variables.

```
data work.increase;
   set orion.staff;
   Increase=Salary*0.10;
   NewSalary=sum(Salary,Increase);
   keep Employee_ID Salary Increase NewSalary;
   format Salary Increase NewSalary comma10.;
run;

proc print data=work.increase label;
run;
```

    e. Submit the program.

2. **Creating Three New Variables**

    a. Write a DATA step.

```
data work.birthday;
   set orion.customer;
run;
```

b. Create three new variables.

```
data work.birthday;
   set orion.customer;
   Bday2009=mdy(month(Birth_Date),day(Birth_Date),2009);
   BdayDOW2009=weekday(Bday2009);
   Age2009=(Bday2009-Birth_Date)/365.25;
run;
```

c. Include only five variables.

```
data work.birthday;
   set orion.customer;
   Bday2009=mdy(month(Birth_Date),day(Birth_Date),2009);
   BdayDOW2009=weekday(Bday2009);
   Age2009=(Bday2009-Birth_Date)/365.25;
   keep Customer_Name Birth_Date Bday2009 BdayDOW2009 Age2009;
run;
```

d. Format two variables.

```
data work.birthday;
   set orion.customer;
   Bday2009=mdy(month(Birth_Date),day(Birth_Date),2009);
   BdayDOW2009=weekday(Bday2009);
   Age2009=(Bday2009-Birth_Date)/365.25;
   keep Customer_Name Birth_Date Bday2009 BdayDOW2009 Age2009;
   format Bday2009 date9. Age2009 3.;
run;
```

e. Write a PROC PRINT step.

```
proc print data=work.birthday;
run;
```

3. Using the CATX and INTCK Functions to Create Variables

a. Write a DATA step.

```
data work.employees;
   set orion.sales;
run;
```

b. Create the new variable **FullName**.

```
data work.employees;
   set orion.sales;
   FullName=catx(' ',First_Name,Last_Name);
run;
```

c. Create the new variable **Yrs2012**.

```
data work.employees;
   set orion.sales;
   FullName=catx(' ',First_Name,Last_Name);
   Yrs2012=intck('year',Hire_Date,'01JAN2012'd);
run;
```

    d. Format **Hire_Date**.

```
data work.employees;
   set orion.sales;
   FullName=catx(' ',First_Name,Last_Name);
   Yrs2012=intck('year',Hire_Date,'01JAN2012'd);
   format Hire_Date ddmmyy10.;
run;
```

    e. Add a label.

```
data work.employees;
   set orion.sales;
   FullName=catx(' ',First_Name,Last_Name);
   Yrs2012=intck('year',Hire_Date,'01JAN2012'd);
   format Hire_Date ddmmyy10.;
   label Yrs2012='Years of Employment in 2012';
run;
```

    f. Write a PROC PRINT step.

```
proc print data=work.employees label;
   var FullName Hire_Date Yrs2012;
run;
```

4. Creating Variables Conditionally

    a. Retrieve the starter program.

    b. Create three new variables.

```
data work.region;
   set orion.supplier;
   length Region $ 17;
   if Country in ('CA','US') then do;
      Discount=0.10;
      DiscountType='Required';
      Region='North America';
   end;
   else do;
      Discount=0.05;
      DiscountType='Optional';
      Region='Not North America';
   end;
run;

proc print data=work.region;
run;
```

c. Include only five variables.

```
data work.region;
   set orion.supplier;
   length Region $ 17;
   if Country in ('CA','US') then do;
      Discount=0.10;
      DiscountType='Required';
      Region='North America';
   end;
   else do;
      Discount=0.05;
      DiscountType='Optional';
      Region='Not North America';
   end;
   keep Supplier_Name Country
        Discount DiscountType Region ;
run;


proc print data=work.region;
run;
```

d. Submit the program.

5. Creating Variables Unconditionally and Conditionally

a. Write a DATA step.

```
data work.ordertype;
   set orion.orders;
run;
```

b. Create the new variable **DayOfWeek**.

```
data work.ordertype;
   set orion.orders;
   DayOfWeek=weekday(Order_Date);
run;
```

c. Create the new variable **Type**.

```
data work.ordertype;
   set orion.orders;
   length Type $ 13;
   DayOfWeek=weekday(Order_Date);
   if Order_Type=1 then do;
      Type='Catalog Sale';
   end;
   else if Order_Type=2 then do;
      Type='Internet Sale';
   end;
   else if Order_Type=3 then do;
      Type='Retail Sale';
   end;
run;
```

d. Create the new variable **SaleAds**.

```
data work.ordertype;
   set orion.orders;
   length Type $ 13 SaleAds $ 5;
   DayOfWeek=weekday(Order_Date);
   if Order_Type=1 then do;
      Type='Catalog Sale';
      SaleAds='Mail';
   end;
   else if Order_Type=2 then do;
      Type='Internet Sale';
      SaleAds='Email';
   end;
   else if Order_Type=3 then do;
      Type='Retail Sale';
   end;
run;
```

e. Do not include three variables.

```
data work.ordertype;
   set orion.orders;
   length Type $ 13 SaleAds $ 5;
   DayOfWeek=weekday(Order_Date);
   if Order_Type=1 then do;
      Type='Catalog Sale';
      SaleAds='Mail';
   end;
   else if Order_Type=2 then do;
      Type='Internet Sale';
      SaleAds='Email';
   end;
   else if Order_Type=3 then do;
      Type='Retail Sale';
   end;
   drop Order_Type Employee_ID Customer_ID;
run;
```

f. Write a PROC PRINT step.

```
proc print data=work.ordertype;
run;
```

6. Using WHEN Statements in a SELECT Group to Create Variables Conditionally

a. Write a DATA step.

```
data work.gifts;
   set orion.nonsales;
run;
```

b. Create two new variables.

```
data work.gifts;
   set orion.nonsales;
   length Gift1 Gift2 $ 15;
   select(Gender);
     when('F') do;
       Gift1='Perfume';
       Gift2='Cookware';
     end;
     when('M') do;
       Gift1='Cologne';
       Gift2='Lawn Equipment';
     end;
     otherwise do;
       Gift1='Coffee';
       Gift2='Calendar';
     end;
   end;
run;
```

c. Include only five variables.

```
data work.gifts;
   set orion.nonsales;
   length Gift1 Gift2 $ 15;
   select(Gender);
     when('F') do;
       Gift1='Perfume';
       Gift2='Cookware';
     end;
     when('M') do;
       Gift1='Cologne';
       Gift2='Lawn Equipment';
     end;
     otherwise do;
       Gift1='Coffee';
       Gift2='Calendar';
     end;
   end;
   keep Employee_ID First Last Gift1 Gift2;
run;
```

d. Write a PROC PRINT step.

```
proc print data=gifts;
run;
```

7. Subsetting Observations Based on Two Conditions

    a. Retrieve the starter program.

    b. Write a statement to select only the observations based on **Emp_Hire_Date**.

```
data work.increase;
   set orion.staff;
   where Emp_Hire_Date>='01JUL2006'd;
   Increase=Salary*0.10;
   NewSalary=sum(Salary,Increase);
   keep Employee_ID Emp_Hire_Date Salary Increase NewSalary;
   format Salary Increase NewSalary comma10.;
run;

proc print data=work.increase label;
run;
```

    c. Write another statement to select only the observations based on **Increase**.

```
data work.increase;
   set orion.staff;
   where Emp_Hire_Date>='01JUL2006'd;
   Increase=Salary*0.10;
   if Increase>3000;
   NewSalary=sum(Salary,Increase);
   keep Employee_ID Emp_Hire_Date Salary Increase NewSalary;
   format Salary Increase NewSalary comma10.;
run;

proc print data=work.increase label;
run;
```

    d. Submit the program.

8. Subsetting Observations Based on Three Conditions

    a. Write a DATA step.

```
data work.delays;
   set orion.orders;
run;
```

    b. Create a new variable.

```
data work.delays;
   set orion.orders;
   Order_Month=month(Order_Date);
run;
```

c. Use a WHERE statement and a subsetting IF statement.

```
data work.delays;
   set orion.orders;
   where Order_Date+4<Delivery_Date
         and Employee_ID=99999999;
   Order_Month=month(Order_Date);
   if Order_Month=8;
run;
```

d. Write a PROC PRINT step.

```
proc print data=work.delays;
run;
```

9. Using an IF-THEN DELETE Statement to Subset Observations

a. Write a DATA step.

```
data work.bigdonations;
   set orion.employee_donations;
run;
```

b. Create the new variable **Total**.

```
data work.bigdonations;
   set orion.employee_donations;
   Total=sum(Qtr1,Qtr2,Qtr3,Qtr4);
run;
```

c. Create the new variable **NoDonation**.

```
data work.bigdonations;
   set orion.employee_donations;
   Total=sum(Qtr1,Qtr2,Qtr3,Qtr4);
   NoDonation=nmiss(Qtr1,Qtr2,Qtr3,Qtr4);
run;
```

d. Use an IF-THEN DELETE statement.

```
data work.bigdonations;
   set orion.employee_donations;
   Total=sum(Qtr1,Qtr2,Qtr3,Qtr4);
   NoDonation=nmiss(Qtr1,Qtr2,Qtr3,Qtr4);
   if Total < 50 or NoDonation > 0 then delete;
run;
```

e. Write a PROC PRINT step.

```
proc print data=work.bigdonations;
   var Employee_ID Qtr1 Qtr2 Qtr3 Qtr4 Total NoDonation;
run;
```

Solutions to Student Activities (Polls/Quizzes)

9.01 Quiz – Correct Answer

What is the result of the assignment statement?

a. . (missing)
b. 0
c. 7
(d.) 9

```
num = 4 + 10 / 2;
```

The order of operations from left to right is division and multiplication followed by addition and subtraction.

Parentheses can be used to control the order of operations.

```
num = (4 + 10) / 2;
```

13

9.02 Quiz – Correct Answer

What is the result of the assignment statement given the values of **var1** and **var2**?

(a.) . (missing)
b. 0
c. 5
d. 10

```
num = var1 + var2 / 2;
```

var1	var2
.	10

If an operand is missing for an arithmetic operator, the result is missing.

16

9.03 Quiz – Correct Answer

What statement needs to be added to the DATA step to eliminate six of the twelve variables?

the DROP or KEEP statement

26

9.04 Poll – Correct Answer

Are the correct results produced when the DROP statement is placed after the SET statement?

◉ Yes
○ No

Yes, the DROP statement specifies the names of the variables to omit from the output data set.

33

9.05 Quiz – Correct Answer

Why are some of the **Bonus** values missing in
the PROC PRINT output for `orion.nonsales`?

`Country` has mixed case values in the
`orion.nonsales` data set.

The UPCASE function will correct the issue.

```
data work.bonus;
    set orion.nonsales;
    if upcase(Country)='US'
        then Bonus=500;
    else if upcase(Country)='AU'
        then Bonus=300;
run;
```

70   p109a02s

9.06 Quiz – Correct Answer

How would you prevent **Freq** from being truncated?

Possible solutions:

- **Pad the first occurrence of the Freq value with blanks to be the length of the longest possible value.**
- **Switch conditional statements to place the longest value of Freq in the first conditional statement.**
- **Add a LENGTH statement to declare the byte size of the variable upfront.**

82

9.07 Quiz – Correct Answer

Why does the WHERE statement not work in this
DATA step?

```
data work.december;
   set orion.sales;
   BonusMonth=month(Hire_Date);
   Bonus=500;
   Compensation=sum(Salary,Bonus);
   where Country='AU' and BonusMonth=12;
run;
```

**The WHERE statement can only subset variables that
are coming from an existing data set.**

```
ERROR: Variable BonusMonth is not on file ORION.SALES.
```

96   p109d05

9.08 Quiz – Correct Answer

Could you have written just an IF statement?

 Yes

○ No

**Yes, but the program using both the
WHERE and IF statements is more efficient.**

**Both methods create a data set with 3 observations.
The program using both statements reads 63
observations into the PDV. The program using just
the IF statement reads 165 observations
into the PDV.**

104   p109d05

Chapter 10   Combining SAS Data Sets

10.1 Introduction to Combining Data Sets

Objectives

- Define the methods for combining SAS data sets.

3

Appending and Concatenating

Appending and concatenating involves combining SAS data sets, one after the other, into a single SAS data set.

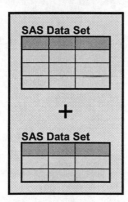

- *Appending* adds the observations in the second data set directly to the end of the original data set.

- *Concatenating* copies all observations from the first data set and then copies all observations from one or more successive data sets into a new data set.

4

Merging

Merging involves combining observations from two or more SAS data sets into a single observation in a new SAS data set.

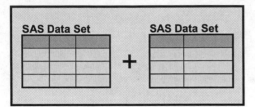

Observations can be merged based on their positions in the original data sets or merged by one or more common variables.

5

Example: Appending a Data Set

One data set is appended to a master data set.

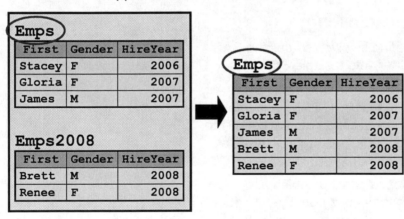

6

Example: Concatenating Data Sets

Two data sets are concatenated to create a new data set.

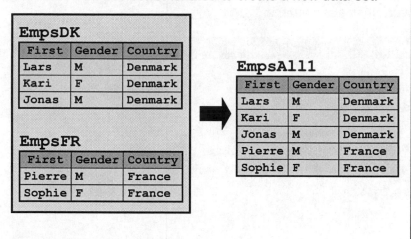

EmpsDK

First	Gender	Country
Lars	M	Denmark
Kari	F	Denmark
Jonas	M	Denmark

EmpsFR

First	Gender	Country
Pierre	M	France
Sophie	F	France

EmpsAll1

First	Gender	Country
Lars	M	Denmark
Kari	F	Denmark
Jonas	M	Denmark
Pierre	M	France
Sophie	F	France

7

Example: Merging Data Sets

Two data sets are merged to create a new data set.

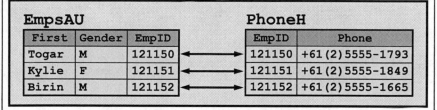

EmpsAU

First	Gender	EmpID
Togar	M	121150
Kylie	F	121151
Birin	M	121152

PhoneH

EmpID	Phone
121150	+61 (2) 5555-1793
121151	+61 (2) 5555-1849
121152	+61 (2) 5555-1665

EmpsAUH

First	Gender	EmpID	Phone
Togar	M	121150	+61 (2) 5555-1793
Kylie	F	121151	+61 (2) 5555-1849
Birin	M	121152	+61 (2) 5555-1665

8

10.01 Quiz

Which method (appending, concatenating, or merging) should be used for the given business scenario?

	Business Scenario	Method
1	The **JanSales**, **FebSales**, and **MarSales** data sets need to be combined to create the **Qtr1Sales** data set.	
2	The **Sales** data set needs to be combined with the **Target** data set by **month** to compare the sales data to the target data.	
3	The **OctSales** data sets need to be added to the **YTD** data set.	

10

10.2 Appending a Data Set

Objectives

- Append one SAS data set to another SAS data set by using the APPEND procedure.
- Append a SAS data set containing additional variables to another SAS data set by using the FORCE option with the APPEND procedure.

14

Appending and Concatenating

Appending and concatenating involves combining SAS data sets, one after the other, into a single SAS data set.

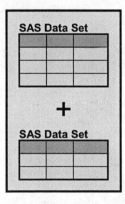

➡ Appending adds the observations in the second data set directly to the end of the original data set.

- Concatenating copies all observations from the first data set and then copies all observations from one or more successive data sets into a new data set.

15

The APPEND Procedure

The *APPEND procedure* adds the observations from
one SAS data set to the end of another SAS data set.

General form of the APPEND procedure:

```
PROC APPEND  BASE = SAS-data-set
             DATA = SAS-data-set ;
RUN;
```

what you want to add

BASE= names the data set to which observations
are added.

DATA= names the data set containing observations
that are added to the base data set.

16

The APPEND Procedure

Requirements:

- Only two data sets can be used at a time in one step.
- The observations in the base data set are not read.
- The variable information in the descriptor portion of
  the base data set cannot change.

17

Business Scenario

Emps is a master data set that contains employees hired in 2006 and 2007.

Emps

First	Gender	HireYear
Stacey	F	2006
Gloria	F	2007
James	M	2007

18

Business Scenario

Emps is a master data set that contains employees hired in 2006 and 2007.

Emps

First	Gender	HireYear
Stacey	F	2006
Gloria	F	2007
James	M	2007

The employees hired in 2008, 2009, and 2010 need to be appended.

Emps2008

First	Gender	HireYear
Brett	M	2008
Renee	F	2008

Emps2009

First	HireYear
Sara	2009
Dennis	2009

Emps2010

First	HireYear	Country
Rose	2010	Spain
Eric	2010	Spain

19

10.02 Quiz

How many observations will be in **Emps** after appending the three data sets?

Emps2008

First	Gender	HireYear
Brett	M	2008
Renee	F	2008

Emps2009

First	HireYear
Sara	2009
Dennis	2009

Emps

First	Gender	HireYear
Stacey	F	2006
Gloria	F	2007
James	M	2007

Emps2010

First	HireYear	Country
Rose	2010	Spain
Eric	2010	Spain

21

10.03 Quiz

How many variables will be in **Emps** after appending the three data sets?

Emps2008

First	Gender	HireYear
Brett	M	2008
Renee	F	2008

Emps2009

First	HireYear
Sara	2009
Dennis	2009

Emps

First	Gender	HireYear
Stacey	F	2006
Gloria	F	2007
James	M	2007

Emps2010

First	HireYear	Country
Rose	2010	Spain
Eric	2010	Spain

24

Like-Structured Data Sets

Emps

First	Gender	HireYear
Stacey	F	2006
Gloria	F	2007
James	M	2007

Emps2008

First	Gender	HireYear
Brett	M	2008
Renee	F	2008

The data sets contain the same variables.

```
proc append base=Emps
            data=Emps2008;
run;
```

26

p110d01

Like-Structured Data Sets

```
84    proc append base=Emps
85                data=Emps2008;
86    run;

NOTE: Appending WORK.EMPS2008 to WORK.EMPS.
NOTE: There were 2 observations read from the data set
      WORK.EMPS2008.
NOTE: 2 observations added.
NOTE: The data set WORK.EMPS has 5 observations and 3 variables.
```

Emps

First	Gender	HireYear
Stacey	F	2006
Gloria	F	2007
James	M	2007
Brett	M	2008
Renee	F	2008

27

Unlike-Structured Data Sets

Emps

First	Gender	HireYear
Stacey	F	2006
Gloria	F	2007
James	M	2007
Brett	M	2008
Renee	F	2008

Emps2009

First	HireYear
Sara	2009
Dennis	2009

The BASE= data set has a variable that is not in the DATA= data set.

```
proc append base=Emps
             data=Emps2009;
run;
```

28   p110d01

Unlike-Structured Data Sets

```
90    proc append base=Emps
91                data=Emps2009;
92    run;

NOTE: Appending WORK.EMPS2009 to WORK.EMPS.
WARNING: Variable Gender was not found on DATA file.
NOTE: There were 2 observations read from the data set
      WORK.EMPS2009.
NOTE: 2 observations added.
NOTE: The data set WORK.EMPS has 7 observations and 3 variables.
```

Emps

First	Gender	HireYear
Stacey	F	2006
Gloria	F	2007
James	M	2007
Brett	M	2008
Renee	F	2008
Sara		2009
Dennis		2009

29

Unlike-Structured Data Sets

Emps

First	Gender	HireYear
Stacey	F	2006
Gloria	F	2007
James	M	2007
Brett	M	2008
Renee	F	2008
Sara		2009
Dennis		2009

Emps2010

First	HireYear	Country
Rose	2010	Spain
Eric	2010	Spain

The DATA= data set has a variable that is not in the
BASE= data set.

```
proc append base=Emps
             data=Emps2010;
run;
```

30   p110d01

Unlike-Structured Data Sets

```
96    proc append base=Emps
97                data=Emps2010;
98    run;

NOTE: Appending WORK.EMPS2010 to WORK.EMPS.
WARNING: Variable Country was not found on BASE file. The
         variable will not be added to the BASE file.
WARNING: Variable Gender was not found on DATA file.
ERROR: No appending done because of anomalies listed above.
       Use FORCE option to append these files.
NOTE: 0 observations added.
NOTE: The data set WORK.EMPS has 7 observations and 3 variables.
NOTE: Statements not processed because of errors noted above.

NOTE: The SAS System stopped processing this step because of
      errors.
```

31

Unlike-Structured Data Sets

The *FORCE option* forces the observations to be appended when the DATA= data set contains variables that are not in the BASE= data set.

General form of the FORCE option:

PROC APPEND BASE = *SAS-data-set*
                 DATA = *SAS-data-set* FORCE;
RUN;

The FORCE option causes the extra variables to be dropped and issues a warning message.

```
proc append base=Emps
            data=Emps2010 force;
run;
```

32   p110d01

The FORCE option is needed when the DATA= data set contains variables that either

- are not in the BASE= data set
- do not have the same type as the variables in the BASE= data set
- are longer than the variables in the BASE= data set.

If the length of a variable is longer in the DATA= data set than in the BASE=data set, SAS truncates values from the DATA= data set to fit them into the length that is specified in the BASE= data set.

If the type of a variable in the DATA= data set is different than in the BASE= data set, SAS replaces all values for the variable in the DATA= data set with missing values and keeps the variable type of the variable specified in the BASE= data set.

Unlike-Structured Data Sets

```
100   proc append base=Emps
101              data=Emps2010 force;
102   run;

NOTE: Appending WORK.EMPS2010 to WORK.EMPS.
WARNING: Variable Country was not found on BASE file. The
         variable will not be added to the BASE file.
WARNING: Variable Gender was not found on DATA file.
NOTE: FORCE is specified, so dropping/truncating will occur.
NOTE: There were 2 observations read from the data set
      WORK.EMPS2010.
NOTE: 2 observations added.
NOTE: The data set WORK.EMPS has 9 observations and 3 variables.
```

33

Unlike-Structured Data Sets

Emps

First	Gender	HireYear
Stacey	F	2006
Gloria	F	2007
James	M	2007
Brett	M	2008
Renee	F	2008
Sara		2009
Dennis		2009
Rose		2010
Eric		2010

34

Unlike-Structured Data Sets

Situation	Action
BASE= data set contains a variable that is not in the DATA= data set	The observations are appended, but the observations from the DATA= data set have a missing value for the variable that was not present in the DATA= data set. The FORCE option is not necessary in this case.
DATA= data set contains a variable that is not in the BASE= data set	Use the FORCE option in the PROC APPEND statement to force the concatenation of the two data sets. The statement drops the extra variable and issues a warning message.

35

10.04 Quiz

How many observations will be in **Emps** if the program is submitted a second time?

Submitting this program once appends six observations to the **Emps** data set, which results in a total of nine observations.

is

```
proc append base=Emps
            data=Emps2008;      3 obs + 2 obs = 5 obs
run;
proc append base=Emps
            data=Emps2009;      5 obs + 2 obs = 7 obs
run;
proc append base=Emps
            data=Emps2010 force;
run;                            7 obs + 2 obs = 9 obs
```

37

proc copy in=orion out=work;
select sales;
run;

 **Exercises**

Level 1

1. **Appending Like-Structured Data Sets**

    a. Retrieve the starter program **p110e01**.

    b. Submit the two PROC CONTENTS steps to compare the variables in the two data sets.

    How many variables are in **orion.price_current**?

    How many variables are in **orion.price_new**?

    Does **orion.price_new** contain any variables that are not in **orion.price_current**?

    c. Add a PROC APPEND step after the PROC CONTENTS steps to append **orion.price_new** to **orion.price_current**. The FORCE option is not needed.

    Why is the FORCE option not needed?

    d. Submit the program and confirm that 88 observations from **orion.price_new** were added to **orion.price_current**, which should now have 259 observations (171 original observations plus 88 appended observations).

Level 2

2. **Appending Unlike-Structured Data Sets**

    a. Write and submit two PROC CONTENTS steps to compare the variables in **orion.qtr1_2007** and **orion.qtr2_2007**.

    How many variables are in **orion.qtr1_2007**?

    How many variables are in **orion.qtr2_2007**?

    Which variable is not in both data sets?

    b. Write a PROC APPEND step to append **orion.qtr1_2007** to non-existing data set called **work.ytd**.

    c. Submit the PROC APPEND step and confirm that 22 observations were copied to **work.ytd**.

    d. Write another PROC APPEND step to append **orion.qtr2_2007** to **work.ytd**. The FORCE option is needed.

    Why is the FORCE option needed?

    e. Submit the second PROC APPEND step and confirm that 36 observations from
`orion.qtr2_2007` were added to `work.ytd`, which should now have 58 observations.

Level 3

3. Using the Append Statement

    a. Write and submit three PROC CONTENTS steps to compare the variables in
`orion.shoes_eclipse`, `orion.shoes_tracker`, and `orion.shoes`.

    b. Write a PROC DATASETS step with two APPEND statements to append
`orion.shoes_eclipse` and `orion.shoes_tracker` to `orion.shoes`.

        ✎   Documentation on the DATASETS procedure can be found in the SAS Help
and Documentation from the Contents tab (**SAS Products** ⇨ **Base SAS** ⇨
Base SAS 9.2 Procedures Guide ⇨ **Procedures** ⇨ **The DATASETS Procedure**).

    c. Submit the PROC DATASETS step and confirm that `orion.shoes` contains 34 observations
(10 original observations plus 14 observations from `orion.shoes_eclispe` and 10
observations from `orion.shoes_tracker`).

10.3 Concatenating Data Sets

Objectives

- Concatenate two or more SAS data sets by using the SET statement in a DATA step.
- Change the names of variables by using the RENAME= data set option.
- Compare the APPEND procedure to the SET statement.
- Interleave two or more SAS data sets by using the SET and BY statements in a DATA step. (Self-Study)

42

Appending and Concatenating

Appending and concatenating involves combining SAS data sets, one after the other, into a single SAS data set.

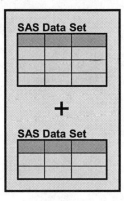

- Appending adds the observations in the second data set directly to the end of the original data set.

➡ Concatenating copies all observations from the first data set and then copies all observations from one or more successive data sets into a new data set.

43

The SET Statement

The *SET statement* in a DATA step reads observations from one or more SAS data sets.

```
DATA SAS-data-set ;
     SET SAS-data-set1 SAS-data-set2 . . . ;
     <additional SAS statements>
RUN;
```

- Any number of data sets can be in the SET statement.
- The observations from the first data set in the SET statement appear first in the new data set. The observations from the second data set follow those from the first data set, and so on.

44

You must know your data. By default, a compile-time error occurs if the same variable is not the same type in all SAS data sets in the SET statement.

Like-Structured Data Sets

Concatenate **EmpsDK** and **EmpsFR** to create a new data set named **EmpsAll1**.

EmpsDK

First	Gender	Country
Lars	M	Denmark
Kari	F	Denmark
Jonas	M	Denmark

EmpsFR

First	Gender	Country
Pierre	M	France
Sophie	F	France

The data sets contain the same variables.

```
data EmpsAll1;
   set EmpsDK EmpsFR;
run;
```

45   p110d02

Compilation

EmpsDK

First	Gender	Country
Lars	M	Denmark
Kari	F	Denmark
Jonas	M	Denmark

EmpsFR

First	Gender	Country
Pierre	M	France
Sophie	F	France

```
data EmpsAll1;
    set EmpsDK EmpsFR;
run;
```

PDV

First	Gender	Country

EmpsAll1

First	Gender	Country

46   ...

Execution

EmpsDK

First	Gender	Country
Lars	M	Denmark
Kari	F	Denmark
Jonas	M	Denmark

EmpsFR

First	Gender	Country
Pierre	M	France
Sophie	F	France

```
data EmpsAll1;
    set EmpsD
run;
```

 Initialize PDV

PDV

First	Gender	Country

EmpsAll1

First	Gender	Country

47   ...

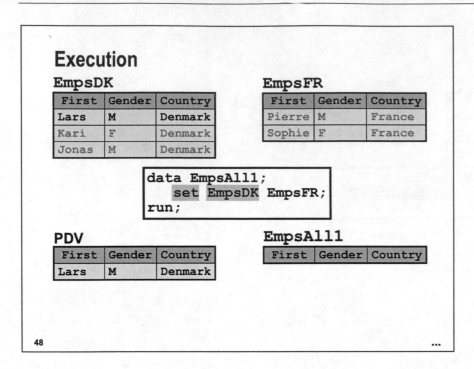

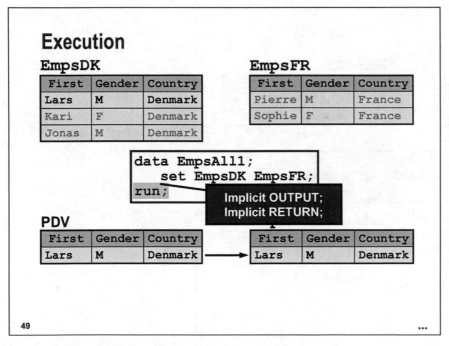

SAS reinitializes variables in the PDV at the start of every DATA step iteration. Variables created by an assignment statement are reset to missing but variables that are read with a SET statement are not reset to missing.

Execution

EmpsDK

First	Gender	Country
Lars	M	Denmark
Kari	F	Denmark
Jonas	M	Denmark

EmpsFR

First	Gender	Country
Pierre	M	France
Sophie	F	France

```
data EmpsAll1;
    set EmpsDK EmpsFR;
run;
```

PDV

First	Gender	Country
Kari	F	Denmark

EmpsAll1

First	Gender	Country
Lars	M	Denmark

50   ...

Execution

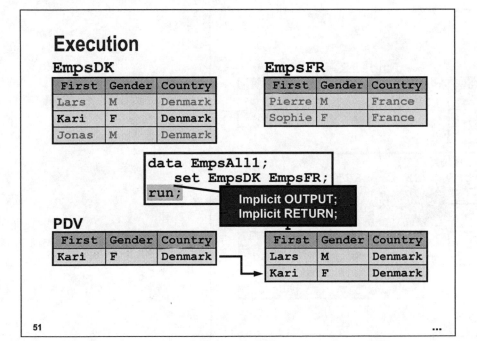

EmpsDK

First	Gender	Country
Lars	M	Denmark
Kari	F	Denmark
Jonas	M	Denmark

EmpsFR

First	Gender	Country
Pierre	M	France
Sophie	F	France

```
data EmpsAll1;
    set EmpsDK EmpsFR;
run;
```

Implicit OUTPUT;
Implicit RETURN;

PDV

First	Gender	Country
Kari	F	Denmark

First	Gender	Country
Lars	M	Denmark
Kari	F	Denmark

51   ...

Execution

EmpsDK

First	Gender	Country
Lars	M	Denmark
Kari	F	Denmark
Jonas	M	Denmark

EmpsFR

First	Gender	Country
Pierre	M	France
Sophie	F	France

```
data EmpsAll1;
    set EmpsDK EmpsFR;
run;
```

PDV

First	Gender	Country
Jonas	M	Denmark

EmpsAll1

First	Gender	Country
Lars	M	Denmark
Kari	F	Denmark

52

...

Execution

EmpsDK

First	Gender	Country
Lars	M	Denmark
Kari	F	Denmark
Jonas	M	Denmark

EmpsFR

First	Gender	Country
Pierre	M	France
Sophie	F	France

```
data EmpsAll1;
    set EmpsDK EmpsFR;
run;
```

Implicit OUTPUT;
Implicit RETURN;

PDV

First	Gender	Country
Jonas	M	Denmark

First	Gender	Country
Lars	M	Denmark
Kari	F	Denmark
Jonas	M	Denmark

53

...

Execution

EmpsDK

First	Gender	Country
Lars	M	Denmark
Kari	F	Denmark
nas	M	Denmark

EmpsFR

First	Gender	Country
Pierre	M	France
Sophie	F	France

```
data EmpsAll1;
    set EmpsDK EmpsFR;
run;
```

PDV

First	Gender	Country
Jonas	M	Denmark

EmpsAll1

First	Gender	Country
Lars	M	Denmark
Kari	F	Denmark
Jonas	M	Denmark

54   ...

Execution

EmpsDK

First	Gender	Country
Lars	M	Denmark
Kari	F	Denmark
Jonas	M	Denmark

EmpsFR

First	Gender	Country
Pierre	M	France
Sophie	F	France

```
data EmpsAll1;
    set EmpsD  Reinitialize PDV
run;
```

PDV

First	Gender	Country

EmpsAll1

First	Gender	Country
Lars	M	Denmark
Kari	F	Denmark
Jonas	M	Denmark

55   ...

Execution

EmpsDK

First	Gender	Country
Lars	M	Denmark
Kari	F	Denmark
Jonas	M	Denmark

EmpsFR

First	Gender	Country
Pierre	M	France
Sophie	F	France

```
data EmpsAll1;
    set EmpsDK EmpsFR;
run;
```

PDV

First	Gender	Country
Pierre	M	France

EmpsAll1

First	Gender	Country
Lars	M	Denmark
Kari	F	Denmark
Jonas	M	Denmark

56

...

Execution

EmpsDK

First	Gender	Country
Lars	M	Denmark
Kari	F	Denmark
Jonas	M	Denmark

EmpsFR

First	Gender	Country
Pierre	M	France
Sophie	F	France

```
data EmpsAll1;
    set EmpsDK EmpsFR;
run;
```

Implicit OUTPUT;
Implicit RETURN;

PDV

First	Gender	Country
Pierre	M	France

First	Gender	Country
Lars	M	Denmark
Kari	F	Denmark
Jonas	M	Denmark
Pierre	M	France

57

...

Execution

EmpsDK

First	Gender	Country
Lars	M	Denmark
Kari	F	Denmark
Jonas	M	Denmark

EmpsFR

First	Gender	Country
Pierre	M	France
Sophie	F	France

```
data EmpsAll1;
    set EmpsDK EmpsFR;
run;
```

PDV

First	Gender	Country
Sophie	F	France

EmpsAll1

First	Gender	Country
Lars	M	Denmark
Kari	F	Denmark
Jonas	M	Denmark
Pierre	M	France

58   ...

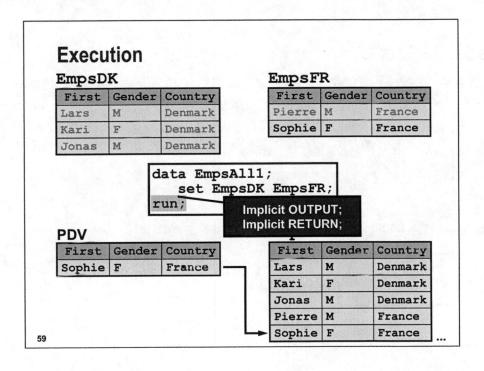

Execution

EmpsDK

First	Gender	Country
Lars	M	Denmark
Kari	F	Denmark
Jonas	M	Denmark

EmpsFR

First	Gender	Country
Pierre	M	France
Sophie	F	France

```
data EmpsAll1;
    set EmpsDK EmpsFR;
run;
```

Implicit OUTPUT;
Implicit RETURN;

PDV

First	Gender	Country
Sophie	F	France

First	Gender	Country
Lars	M	Denmark
Kari	F	Denmark
Jonas	M	Denmark
Pierre	M	France
Sophie	F	France

59   ...

Execution

EmpsDK

First	Gender	Country
Lars	M	Denmark
Kari	F	Denmark
Jonas	M	Denmark

EmpsFR

First	Gender	Country
Pierre	M	France
EOF ohie	F	France

```
data EmpsAll1;
    set EmpsDK EmpsFR;
run;
```

PDV

First	Gender	Country
Sophie	F	France

EmpsAll1

First	Gender	Country
Lars	M	Denmark
Kari	F	Denmark
Jonas	M	Denmark
Pierre	M	France
Sophie	F	France

60

Unlike-Structured Data Sets

Concatenate **EmpsCN** and **EmpsJP** to create a new data set named **EmpsAll2**.

EmpsCN

First	Gender	Country
Chang	M	China
Li	M	China
Ming	F	China

EmpsJP

First	Gender	Region
Cho	F	Japan
Tomi	M	Japan

The data sets do not contain the same variables.

```
data EmpsAll2;
    set EmpsCN EmpsJP;
run;
```

61

p110d03

10.05 Quiz

How many variables will be in **EmpsAll2** after concatenating **EmpsCN** and **EmpsJP**?

EmpsCN

First	Gender	Country
Chang	M	China
Li	M	China
Ming	F	China

EmpsJP

First	Gender	Region
Cho	F	Japan
Tomi	M	Japan

```
data EmpsAll2;
   set EmpsCN EmpsJP;
run;
```

63

Compilation

EmpsCN

First	Gender	Country
Chang	M	China
Li	M	China
Ming	F	China

EmpsJP

First	Gender	Region
Cho	F	Japan
Tomi	M	Japan

```
data EmpsAll2;
   set EmpsCN EmpsJP;
run;
```

PDV

First	Gender	Country

65   ...

Compilation

EmpsCN

First	Gender	Country
Chang	M	China
Li	M	China
Ming	F	China

EmpsJP

First	Gender	Region
Cho	F	Japan
Tomi	M	Japan

```
data EmpsAll2;
   set EmpsCN EmpsJP;
run;
```

PDV

First	Gender	Country	Region

66   ...

Final Results

EmpsAll2

First	Gender	Country	Region
Chang	M	China	
Li	M	China	
Ming	F	China	
Cho	F		Japan
Tomi	M		Japan

67

The RENAME= Data Set Option

The *RENAME= data set option* changes the name
of a variable.

General form of the RENAME= data set option:

> *SAS-data-set* (RENAME = (*old-name-1 = new-name-1*
>   *old-name-2 = new-name-2*
>   ...
>   *old-name-n = new-name-n*))

- The RENAME= option must be specified in
  parentheses immediately after the appropriate
  SAS data set name.
- If the RENAME= option is associated with an input
  data set in the SET statement, the action applies
  to the data set that is being read.

68

The RENAME= Data Set Option

SET statement examples:

```
set EmpsCN(rename=(Country=Region))
    EmpsJP;
```

```
set EmpsCN(rename=(First=Fname
                   Country=Region))
    EmpsJP(rename=(First=Fname));
```

```
set EmpsCN
    EmpsJP(rename=(Region=Country));
```

69

10.06 Quiz

Which statement has correct syntax?

a.
```
set EmpsCN(rename(Country=Location))
    EmpsJP(rename(Region=Location));
```

b.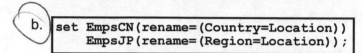
```
set EmpsCN(rename=(Country=Location))
    EmpsJP(rename=(Region=Location));
```

c.
```
set EmpsCN rename=(Country=Location)
    EmpsJP rename=(Region=Location);
```

71

Compilation

EmpsCN

First	Gender	Country
Chang	M	China
Li	M	China
Ming	F	China

EmpsJP

First	Gender	Region
Cho	F	Japan
Tomi	M	Japan

```
data EmpsAll2;
   set EmpsCN EmpsJP(rename=(Region=Country);
run;
```

PDV

First	Gender	Country

73   p110d03

Compilation

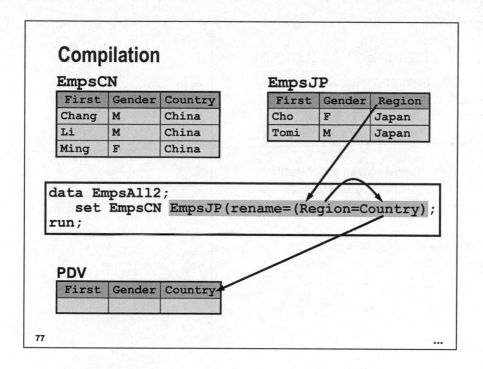

EmpsCN

First	Gender	Country
Chang	M	China
Li	M	China
Ming	F	China

EmpsJP

First	Gender	Region
Cho	F	Japan
Tomi	M	Japan

```
data EmpsAll2;
   set EmpsCN EmpsJP(rename=(Region=Country);
run;
```

PDV

First	Gender	Country

77 ...

Final Results

EmpsAll2

First	Gender	Country
Chang	M	China
Li	M	China
Ming	F	China
Cho	F	Japan
Tomi	M	Japan

78

APPEND Procedure versus SET Statement

- The data set that results from concatenating two data sets with the SET statement is the same data set that results from concatenating them with the APPEND procedure if the two data sets contain the same variables.
- The APPEND procedure concatenates much faster than the SET statement because the APPEND procedure does not process the observations from the BASE= data set.
- The two methods are significantly different when the variables differ between data sets.

79

APPEND Procedure versus SET Statement

Criterion	APPEND Procedure	SET Statement
Number of data sets that you can concatenate	Uses two data sets.	Uses any number of data sets.
Handling of data sets that contain different variables	Uses all variables in the BASE= data set and assigns missing values to observations from the DATA= data set where appropriate. Cannot include variables found only in the DATA= data set.	Uses all variables and assigns missing values where appropriate.

80

10.07 Multiple Choice Poll

Which method would you use if you wanted to create
a new variable at the time of concatenation?

a. APPEND procedure

 b. SET statement

82

Interleaving (Self-Study)

Interleaving intersperses observations from two or more
data sets, based on one or more common variables.

The SET statement with a BY statement in a DATA step
interleaves SAS data sets.

```
DATA SAS-data-set ;
    SET SAS-data-set1 SAS-data-set2 . . . ;
    BY <DESCENDING> by-variable(s) ;
    <additional SAS statements>
RUN;
```

The data sets must
be sorted by the
by-variable.

Use the SORT procedure to sort
the data sets by the *by-variable*.

85

Typically, it is more efficient to sort small SAS data sets and then interleave them as opposed
to concatenating several SAS data sets and then sorting the resultant larger file.

Interleaving (Self-Study)

EmpsCN

First	Gender	Country
Chang	M	China
Li	M	China
Ming	F	China

EmpsJP

First	Gender	Region
Cho	F	Japan
Tomi	M	Japan

Which value comes first?

Chang

```
data EmpsAll2;
   set EmpsCN EmpsJP(rename=(Region=Country);
   by First;
run;
```

PDV

First	Gender	Country
Chang	M	China

86

p110d03
...

Interleaving (Self-Study)

EmpsCN

First	Gender	Country
Chang	M	China
Li	M	China
Ming	F	China

EmpsJP

First	Gender	Region
Cho	F	Japan
Tomi	M	Japan

Which value comes first?

Cho

```
data EmpsAll2;
   set EmpsCN  Reinitialize PDV  (Region=Country);
   by First;
run;
```

PDV

First	Gender	Country

87

...

Interleaving (Self-Study)

EmpsCN

First	Gender	Country
Chang	M	China
Li	M	China
Ming	F	China

EmpsJP

First	Gender	Region
Cho	F	Japan
Tomi	M	Japan

Which value comes first?

Cho

```
data EmpsAll2;
   set EmpsCN EmpsJP(rename=(Region=Country);
   by First;
run;
```

PDV

First	Gender	Country
Cho	F	Japan

88   ...

Interleaving (Self-Study)

EmpsCN

First	Gender	Country
Chang	M	China
Li	M	China
Ming	F	China

EmpsJP

First	Gender	Region
Cho	F	Japan
Tomi	M	Japan

Which value comes first?

Li

```
data EmpsAll2;
   set EmpsCN           (Region=Country);
   by First;
run;
```

Reinitialize PDV

PDV

First	Gender	Country

89   ...

Interleaving (Self-Study)

EmpsCN

First	Gender	Country
Chang	M	China
Li	M	China
Ming	F	China

EmpsJP

First	Gender	Region
Cho	F	Japan
Tomi	M	Japan

Which value comes first?

Li

```
data EmpsAll2;
   set EmpsCN EmpsJP(rename=(Region=Country);
   by First;
run;
```

PDV

First	Gender	Country
Li	M	China

90   ...

Interleaving (Self-Study)

EmpsCN

First	Gender	Country
Chang	M	China
Li	M	China
Ming	F	China

EmpsJP

First	Gender	Region
Cho	F	Japan
Tomi	M	Japan

Which value comes first?

Ming

```
data EmpsAll2;
   set EmpsCN EmpsJP(rename=(Region=Country);
   by First;
run;
```

PDV

First	Gender	Country
Ming	F	China

91   ...

Interleaving (Self-Study)

EmpsCN

First	Gender	Country
Chang	M	China
Li	M	China
EOF ng	F	China

EmpsJP

First	Gender	Region
Cho	F	Japan
Tomi	M	Japan

Which value comes first?

Tomi

```
data EmpsAll2;
   set EmpsCN  Reinitialize PDV  (Region=Country);
   by First;
run;
```

PDV

First	Gender	Country

92   ...

Interleaving (Self-Study)

EmpsCN

First	Gender	Country
Chang	M	China
Li	M	China
EOF ng	F	China

EmpsJP

First	Gender	Region
Cho	F	Japan
Tomi	M	Japan

Which value comes first?

Tomi

```
data EmpsAll2;
   set EmpsCN EmpsJP(rename=(Region=Country);
   by First;
run;
```

PDV

First	Gender	Country
Tomi	M	Japan

93   ...

Interleaving (Self-Study)

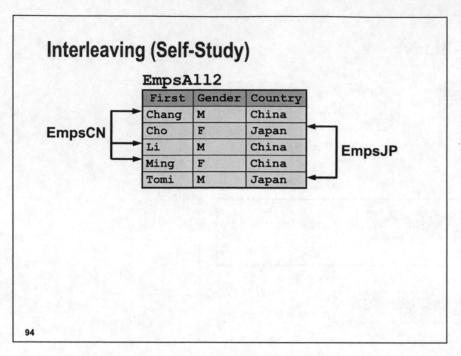

94

In the case where the data values are equal, the observation is always read first from the first data set listed in the SET statement.

 **Exercises**

Level 1

4. Concatenating Like-Structured Data Sets

a. Write and submit a DATA step to concatenate **orion.mnth7_2007**, **orion.mnth8_2007**, and **orion.mnth9_2007** to create a new data set called **work.thirdqtr**.

How many observations in **work.thirdqtr** are from **orion.mnth7_2007**? *10*

How many observations in **work.thirdqtr** are from **orion.mnth8_2007**? *12*

How many observations in **work.thirdqtr** are from **orion.mnth9_2007**? *10*

b. Write and submit a <u>PROC PRINT</u> step to create the following report:

Partial PROC PRINT Output (First 10 of 32 Observations)

Obs	Order_ID	Order_ Type	Employee_ID	Customer_ID	Order_ Date	Delivery_ Date
1	1242691897	2	99999999	90	02JUL2007	04JUL2007
2	1242736731	1	121107	10	07JUL2007	07JUL2007
3	1242773202	3	99999999	24	11JUL2007	14JUL2007
4	1242782701	3	99999999	27	12JUL2007	17JUL2007
5	1242827683	1	121105	10	17JUL2007	17JUL2007
6	1242836878	1	121027	10	18JUL2007	18JUL2007
7	1242838815	1	120195	41	19JUL2007	19JUL2007
8	1242848557	2	99999999	2806	19JUL2007	23JUL2007
9	1242923327	3	99999999	70165	28JUL2007	29JUL2007
10	1242938120	1	120124	171	30JUL2007	30JUL2007

Level 2

5. Concatenating Unlike-Structured Data Sets

a. Retrieve the starter program **p110e05**.

b. Submit the two PROC CONTENTS steps to compare the variables in the two data sets.

What are the names of the two variables that are different in the two data sets?

orion.sales	orion.nonsales
first-name	*first*
Last-name	*last*

c. Add a DATA step after the PROC CONTENTS steps to concatenate `orion.sales` and `orion.nonsales` to create a new data set called `work.allemployees`.

Use a RENAME= data set option to change the names of the different variables in `orion.nonsales`.

The new data set should include only the following five variables: `Employee_ID`, `First_Name`, `Last_Name`, `Job_Title`, and `Salary`.

d. Add a PROC PRINT step to create the following report:

Partial PROC PRINT Output (First 10 of 400 Observations)

```
                    First_
     Obs   Employee_ID   Name        Last_Name    Salary    Job_Title

      1      120102     Tom         Zhou         108255    Sales Manager
      2      120103     Wilson      Dawes         87975    Sales Manager
      3      120121     Irenie      Elvish        26600    Sales Rep. II
      4      120122     Christina   Ngan          27475    Sales Rep. II
      5      120123     Kimiko      Hotstone      26190    Sales Rep. I
      6      120124     Lucian      Daymond       26480    Sales Rep. I
      7      120125     Fong        Hofmeister    32040    Sales Rep. IV
      8      120126     Satyakam    Denny         26780    Sales Rep. II
      9      120127     Sharryn     Clarkson      28100    Sales Rep. II
     10      120128     Monica      Kletschkus    30890    Sales Rep. IV
```

Level 3

6. Interleaving Data Sets

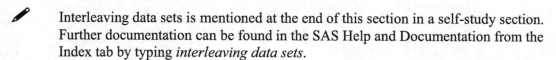 Interleaving data sets is mentioned at the end of this section in a self-study section. Further documentation can be found in the SAS Help and Documentation from the Index tab by typing *interleaving data sets*.

a. Retrieve the starter program **p110e06**.

b. Add a PROC SORT step after the PROC SORT step in the starter program. The PROC SORT step needs to sort `orion.shoes_tracker` by `Product_Name` to create a new data set called `work.trackersort`.

📝 Documentation on the SORT procedure can be found in the SAS Help and Documentation from the Contents tab (**SAS Products** ⇨ **Base SAS** ⇨ **Base SAS 9.2 Procedures Guide** ⇨ **Procedures** ⇨ **The SORT Procedure**).

c. Add a DATA step after the two PROC SORT steps to interleave the two sorted data sets by `Product_Name` to create a new data set called `work.e_t_shoes`.

The new data set should include only the following three variables: `Product_Group`, `Product_Name`, and `Supplier_ID`.

d. Add a PROC PRINT step to create the following report:

Partial PROC PRINT Output (First 10 of 24 Observations)

```
 Obs    Product_Group    Product_Name                                Supplier_ID

   1    Eclipse Shoes    Atmosphere Imara Women's Running Shoes              1303
   2    Eclipse Shoes    Atmosphere Shatter Mid Shoes                        1303
   3    Eclipse Shoes    Big Guy Men's Air Deschutz Viii Shoes               1303
   4    Eclipse Shoes    Big Guy Men's Air Terra Reach Shoes                 1303
   5    Eclipse Shoes    Big Guy Men's Air Terra Sebec Shoes                 1303
   6    Eclipse Shoes    Big Guy Men's International Triax Shoes              1303
   7    Eclipse Shoes    Big Guy Men's Multicourt Ii Shoes                   1303
   8    Eclipse Shoes    Cnv Plus Men's Off Court Tennis                     1303
   9    Tracker Shoes    Hardcore Junior/Women's Street Shoes Large         14682
  10    Tracker Shoes    Hardcore Men's Street Shoes Large                  14682
```

   The order of the observations will be different for z/OS (OS/390).

10.4 Merging Data Sets One-to-One

Objectives

- Define the different types of match-merging.
- Prepare data sets for merging using the SORT procedure.
- Merge SAS data sets one-to-one based on a common variable by using the MERGE and BY statements in a DATA step.
- Eliminate duplicate observations using the SORT procedure. (Self-Study)

97

Merging

Merging involves combining observations from two or more SAS data sets into a single observation in a new SAS data set.

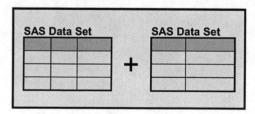

Observations can be merged based on their positions in the original data sets or merged by one or more common variables.

98

Match-Merging

Match-merging combines observations from two or more SAS data sets into a single observation in a new data set based on the values of one or more common variables.

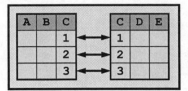

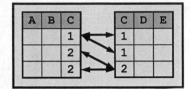

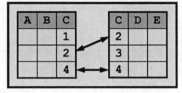

99

Match-Merging

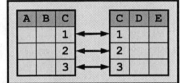

One-to-One

a single observation in one data set is related to one and only one observation from another data set based on the values of one or more selected variables

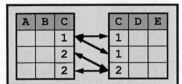

One-to-Many or Many-to-One

a single observation in one data set is related to more than one observation from another data set based on the values of one or more selected variables and vice versa

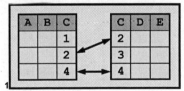

Non-Matches

at least one single observation in one data set is unrelated to any observation from another data set based on the values of one or more selected variables

1

Match-Merging

In order to perform match-merging, the observations in each data set must be sorted by the one or more common variables that are being matched.

General form of the SORT procedure:

```
PROC SORT  DATA=input-SAS-data-set
              <OUT=output-SAS-data-set> ;
    BY <DESCENDING> by-variable(s) ;
RUN;
```

The *SORT procedure* orders SAS data set observations by the values of one or more variables.

101

The SORT Procedure

```
PROC SORT  DATA=input-SAS-data-set
              <OUT=output-SAS-data-set> ;
    BY <DESCENDING> by-variable(s) ;
RUN;
```

The SORT procedure
- rearranges the observations in a SAS data set
- either replaces the original data set or creates a new data set
- can sort on multiple variables
- can sort in ascending (default) or descending order
- does not generate printed output.

102

10.08 Quiz

Which step is sorting the observations in a SAS data set and overwriting the same SAS data set?

a.
```
proc sort data=work.EmpsAU
           out=work.sorted;
   by First ;
run;
```

b.
```
proc sort data=work.EmpsAU
           out=orion.EmpsAU;
   by First ;
run;
```

c.
```
proc sort data=work.EmpsAU;
   by First ;
run;
```

104

The BY Statement

The *BY statement* specifies the sorting variables.

- PROC SORT first arranges the data set by the values in ascending order, by default, of the first BY variable.
- PROC SORT then arranges any observations that have the same value of the first BY variable by the values of the second BY variable in ascending order.
- This sorting continues for every specified BY variable.

The *DESCENDING option* reverses the sort order for the variable that immediately follows in the statement so that observations are sorted from the largest value to the smallest value.

106

The BY Statement

BY statement examples:

```
by Last First;
```

```
by descending Last First;
```

```
by Last descending First;
```

```
by descending Last descending First;
```

107

Setup for the Poll

- Retrieve program **p110a01**.
- Add a BY statement to the PROC SORT step to sort the observations first by ascending **Gender** and then by descending **Employee_ID** within the values of **Gender**.
- Complete the PROC PRINT statement to reference the sorted data set.
- Submit the program and confirm the sort order in the PROC PRINT output.

109

10.09 Multiple Choice Poll

What is the **Employee_ID** value for the first observation in the sorted data set?

a. 120102
b. 120121
c. 121144
d. 121145

110

The MERGE and BY Statements

The *MERGE statement* in a DATA step joins observations from two or more SAS data sets into single observations.

```
DATA SAS-data-set ;
    MERGE SAS-data-set1 SAS-data-set2 . . . ;
    BY <DESCENDING> by-variable(s) ;
    <additional SAS statements>
RUN;
```

A *BY statement* after the MERGE statement performs a match-merge.

112

The MERGE and BY Statements

Requirements:

- Two or more data sets must be specified in the MERGE statement.
- The variables in the BY statement must be common to all data sets.
- The data sets that are listed in the MERGE statement must be sorted in order of the values of the variables that are listed in the BY statement.

113

One-to-One Merge

Merge **EmpsAU** and **PhoneH** by **EmpID** to create a new data set named **EmpsAUH**.

EmpsAU

First	Gender	EmpID
Togar	M	121150
Kylie	F	121151
Birin	M	121152

PhoneH

EmpID	Phone
121150	+61(2)5555-1793
121151	+61(2)5555-1849
121152	+61(2)5555-1665

The data sets are sorted by **EmpID**.

```
data EmpsAUH;
   merge EmpsAU PhoneH;
   by EmpID;
run;
```

114   p110d05

Final Results

EmpsAUH

First	Gender	EmpID	Phone
Togar	M	121150	+61 (2) 5555-1793
Kylie	F	121151	+61 (2) 5555-1849
Birin	M	121152	+61 (2) 5555-1665

115

Eliminating Duplicates with the SORT Procedure (Self-Study)

The SORT procedure can be used to eliminate duplicate observations.

PROC SORT Statement Options:

- The *NODUPKEY option* deletes observations with duplicate BY values.
- The *EQUALS option* maintains the relative order of the observations within the input data set in the output data set for observations with identical BY values.

117

Eliminating Duplicates with the SORT Procedure (Self-Study)

```
proc sort data=EmpsDUP
         out=EmpsDUP1 nodupkey equals;
  by EmpID;
run;
```

EmpsDUP

First	Gender	EmpID
Matt	M	121160
Julie	F	121161
Brett	M	121162
Julie	F	121161
Chris	F	121161
Julie	F	121163

EmpsDUP1

First	Gender	EmpID
Matt	M	121160
Julie	F	121161
Brett	M	121162
Julie	F	121163

118   p110d04

 **Exercises**

Level 1

7. Merging Two Data Sets One-to-One

a. Retrieve the starter program **p110e07**.

b. Add a PROC SORT step after the PROC SORT step in the starter program. The PROC SORT step needs to sort **orion.employee_addresses** by **Employee_ID** to create a new data set called **work.addresses**.

c. Add a DATA step after the two PROC SORT steps to merge the two sorted data sets by **Employee_ID** to create a new data set called **work.payadd**.

d. Submit the program and confirm that **work.payadd** was created with 424 observations and 16 variables.

Level 2

8. Merging Three Data Sets One-to-One

a. Write a PROC SORT step to sort **orion.employee_addresses** by **Employee_ID** to create a new data set called **work.addresses**.

b. Write a DATA step to merge the previous sorted data set with **orion.employee_payroll** and **orion.employee_organization** by **Employee_ID**. Create a new data set called **work.payaddorg**.

c. Write a PROC PRINT step with a VAR and add a FORMAT statement to the DATA step to create the following report:

Partial PROC PRINT Output (First 10 of 424 Observations)

Obs	Employee_ID	Employee_Name	Birth_Date	Department	Salary
1	120101	Lu, Patrick	18/08/1976	Sales Management	163040
2	120102	Zhou, Tom	11/08/1969	Sales Management	108255
3	120103	Dawes, Wilson	22/01/1949	Sales Management	87975
4	120104	Billington, Kareen	11/05/1954	Administration	46230
5	120105	Povey, Liz	21/12/1974	Administration	27110
6	120106	Hornsey, John	23/12/1944	Administration	26960
7	120107	Sheedy, Sherie	21/01/1949	Administration	30475
8	120108	Gromek, Gladys	23/02/1984	Administration	27660
9	120109	Baker, Gabriele	15/12/1986	Administration	26495
10	120110	Entwisle, Dennis	20/11/1949	Administration	28615

Level 3

9. Joining Data Sets Using the SQL Procedure

   a. Write a PROC SQL step to create a report of an inner join of **orion.employee_addresses** and **orion.employee_payroll** by **Employee_ID**. The report should include only **Employee_ID**, **Employee_Name**, **Birth_Date**, and **Salary**. **Birth_Date** should include an appropriate format.

> Documentation on the SQL procedure can be found in the SAS Help and Documentation from the Contents tab (**SAS Products** ⇨ **Base SAS** ⇨ **Base SAS 9.2 Procedures Guide** ⇨ **Procedures** ⇨ **The SQL Procedure**).

   b. Submit the program to create the following report:

Partial PROC SQL Output (First 10 of 424 Observations)

Employee_ID	Employee_Name	Birth_Date	Salary
121044	Abbott, Ray	11/12/1954	25660
120145	Aisbitt, Sandy	22/01/1964	26060
120761	Akinfolarin, Tameaka	28/12/1986	30960
120656	Amos, Salley	28/01/1974	42570
121107	Anger, Rose	24/04/1986	31380
121038	Anstey, David	13/02/1988	25285
120273	Antonini, Doris	07/06/1986	28455
120759	Apr, Nishan	04/11/1964	36230
120798	Ardskin, Elizabeth	23/06/1959	80755
121030	Areu, Jeryl	12/11/1979	26745

10.5 Merging Data Sets One-to-Many

Objectives

- Merge SAS data sets one-to-many based on a common variable by using the MERGE and BY statements in a DATA step.

121

One-to-Many Merge

Merge **EmpsAU** and **PhoneHW** by **EmpID** to create a new data set named **EmpsAUHW**.

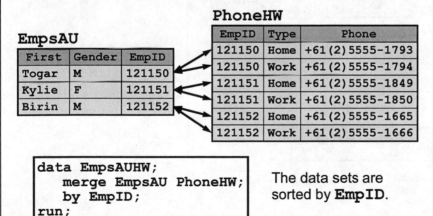

EmpsAU

First	Gender	EmpID
Togar	M	121150
Kylie	F	121151
Birin	M	121152

PhoneHW

EmpID	Type	Phone
121150	Home	+61(2)5555-1793
121150	Work	+61(2)5555-1794
121151	Home	+61(2)5555-1849
121151	Work	+61(2)5555-1850
121152	Home	+61(2)5555-1665
121152	Work	+61(2)5555-1666

```
data EmpsAUHW;
   merge EmpsAU PhoneHW;
   by EmpID;
run;
```

The data sets are sorted by **EmpID**.

122   p110d06

Execution

EmpsAU

First	Gender	EmpID
Togar	M	121150
Kylie	F	121151
Birin	M	121152

PhoneHW

EmpID	Type	Phone
121150	Home	+61 (2) 5555-1793
121150	Work	+61 (2) 5555-1794
121151	Home	+61 (2) 5555-1849
121151	Work	+61 (2) 5555-1850
121152	Home	+61 (2) 5555-1665
121152	Work	+61 (2) 5555-1666

```
data EmpsAUHW;
    merge EmpsAU
    by EmpID;
run;
```

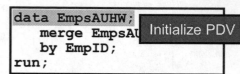

Initialize PDV

PDV

First	Gender	EmpID	Type	Phone
		.		

123

...

Execution

EmpsAU

First	Gender	EmpID
Togar	M	121150
Kylie	F	121151
Birin	M	121152

PhoneHW

EmpID	Type	Phone
121150	Home	+61 (2) 5555-1793
121150	Work	+61 (2) 5555-1794
121151	Home	+61 (2) 5555-1849
121151	Work	+61 (2) 5555-1850
121152	Home	+61 (2) 5555-1665
121152	Work	+61 (2) 5555-1666

```
data EmpsAUHW;
    merge EmpsAU PhoneHW;
    by EmpID;
run;
```

Do the **EmpID**s match?

Yes

PDV

First	Gender	EmpID	Type	Phone
		.		

124

...

Execution

EmpsAU

First	Gender	EmpID
Togar	M	121150
Kylie	F	121151
Birin	M	121152

PhoneHW

EmpID	Type	Phone
121150	Home	+61 (2) 5555-1793
121150	Work	+61 (2) 5555-1794
121151	Home	+61 (2) 5555-1849
121151	Work	+61 (2) 5555-1850
121152	Home	+61 (2) 5555-1665
121152	Work	+61 (2) 5555-1666

```
data EmpsAUHW;
    merge EmpsAU PhoneHW;
    by EmpID;
run;
```

Reads one observation
from each matching
data set.

PDV

First	Gender	EmpID	Type	Phone
Togar	M	121150	Home	+61 (2) 5555-1793

125   ...

Execution

EmpsAU

First	Gender	EmpID
Togar	M	121150
Kylie	F	121151
Birin	M	121152

PhoneHW

EmpID	Type	Phone
121150	Home	+61 (2) 5555-1793
121150	Work	+61 (2) 5555-1794
121151	Home	+61 (2) 5555-1849
121151	Work	+61 (2) 5555-1850
121152	Home	+61 (2) 5555-1665
121152	Work	+61 (2) 5555-1666

```
data EmpsAUHW;
    merge EmpsAU PhoneHW;
    by EmpID;
run;
```

Implicit OUTPUT;
Implicit RETURN;

PDV

First	Gender	EmpID	Type	Phone
Togar	M	121150	Home	+61 (2) 5555-1793

126   ...

SAS reinitializes variables in the PDV at the start of every DATA step iteration. Variables created by an assignment statement are reset to missing but variables that are read with a MERGE statement are not reset to missing.

Before reading additional observations during a match-merge, SAS first determines if there are observations remaining for the current BY group.

- If there are observations remaining for the current BY group, they are read into the PDV, processed, and written to the output data set.

- If there are no more observations for the current BY group, SAS reinitializes the remainder of the PDV, identifies the next BY group, and reads the corresponding observations.

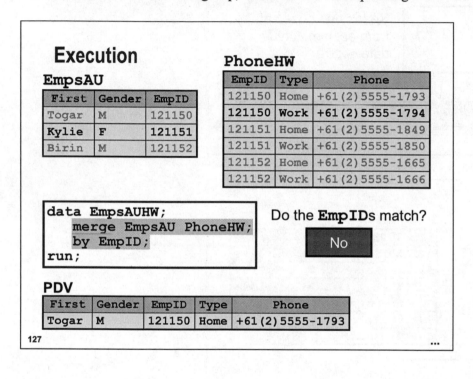

Execution

EmpsAU

First	Gender	EmpID
Togar	M	121150
Kylie	F	121151
Birin	M	121152

PhoneHW

EmpID	Type	Phone
121150	Home	+61 (2) 5555-1793
121150	Work	+61 (2) 5555-1794
121151	Home	+61 (2) 5555-1849
121151	Work	+61 (2) 5555-1850
121152	Home	+61 (2) 5555-1665
121152	Work	+61 (2) 5555-1666

```
data EmpsAUHW;
    merge EmpsAU PhoneHW;
    by EmpID;
run;
```

Do the **EmpID**s match?

No

PDV

First	Gender	EmpID	Type	Phone
Togar	M	121150	Home	+61 (2) 5555-1793

127

...

Execution

EmpsAU

First	Gender	EmpID
Togar	M	121150
Kylie	F	121151
Birin	M	121152

PhoneHW

EmpID	Type	Phone
121150	Home	+61 (2) 5555-1793
121150	Work	+61 (2) 5555-1794
121151	Home	+61 (2) 5555-1849
121151	Work	+61 (2) 5555-1850
121152	Home	+61 (2) 5555-1665
121152	Work	+61 (2) 5555-1666

```
data EmpsAUHW;
    merge EmpsAU PhoneHW;
    by EmpID;
run;
```

Is either **EmpID** the same as the **EmpID** currently in the PDV?

Yes

PDV

First	Gender	EmpID	Type	Phone
Togar	M	121150	Home	+61 (2) 5555-1793

128   ...

Execution

EmpsAU

First	Gender	EmpID
Togar	M	121150
Kylie	F	121151
Birin	M	121152

PhoneHW

EmpID	Type	Phone
121150	Home	+61 (2) 5555-1793
121150	Work	+61 (2) 5555-1794
121151	Home	+61 (2) 5555-1849
121151	Work	+61 (2) 5555-1850
121152	Home	+61 (2) 5555-1665
121152	Work	+61 (2) 5555-1666

```
data EmpsAUHW;
    merge EmpsAU PhoneHW;
    by EmpID;
run;
```

Reads the observation from the appropriate data set.

PDV

First	Gender	EmpID	Type	Phone
Togar	M	121150	Work	+61 (2) 5555-1794

129   ...

Execution

EmpsAU

First	Gender	EmpID
Togar	M	121150
Kylie	F	121151
Birin	M	121152

PhoneHW

EmpID	Type	Phone
121150	Home	+61 (2) 5555-1793
121150	Work	+61 (2) 5555-1794
121151	Home	+61 (2) 5555-1849
121151	Work	+61 (2) 5555-1850
121152	Home	+61 (2) 5555-1665
121152	Work	+61 (2) 5555-1666

```
data EmpsAUHW;
   merge EmpsAU PhoneHW;
   by EmpID;
run;
```

Implicit OUTPUT;
Implicit RETURN;

PDV

First	Gender	EmpID	Type	Phone
Togar	M	121150	Work	+61 (2) 5555-1794

130   ...

Execution

EmpsAU

First	Gender	EmpID
Togar	M	121150
Kylie	F	121151
Birin	M	121152

PhoneHW

EmpID	Type	Phone
121150	Home	+61 (2) 5555-1793
121150	Work	+61 (2) 5555-1794
121151	Home	+61 (2) 5555-1849
121151	Work	+61 (2) 5555-1850
121152	Home	+61 (2) 5555-1665
121152	Work	+61 (2) 5555-1666

```
data EmpsAUHW;
   merge EmpsAU PhoneHW;
   by EmpID;
run;
```

Do the **EmpID**s match?

Yes

PDV

First	Gender	EmpID	Type	Phone
Togar	M	121150	Work	+61 (2) 5555-1794

131   ...

Execution

EmpsAU

First	Gender	EmpID
Togar	M	121150
Kylie	F	121151
Birin	M	121152

PhoneHW

EmpID	Type	Phone
121150	Home	+61(2)5555-1793
121150	Work	+61(2)5555-1794
121151	Home	+61(2)5555-1849
121151	Work	+61(2)5555-1850
121152	Home	+61(2)5555-1665
121152	Work	+61(2)5555-1666

```
data EmpsAUHW;
    merge EmpsAU PhoneHW;
    by EmpID;
run;
```

Is the **EmpID** the same as the **EmpID** currently in the PDV?

No

PDV

First	Gender	EmpID	Type	Phone
Togar	M	121150	Work	+61(2)5555-1794

132

...

Execution

EmpsAU

First	Gender	EmpID
Togar	M	121150
Kylie	F	121151
Birin	M	121152

PhoneHW

EmpID	Type	Phone
121150	Home	+61(2)5555-1793
121150	Work	+61(2)5555-1794
121151	Home	+61(2)5555-1849
121151	Work	+61(2)5555-1850
121152	Home	+61(2)5555-1665
121152	Work	+61(2)5555-1666

```
data EmpsAUHW;
    merge EmpsAU PhoneHW;
    by EmpID;
run;
```

Reinitialize PDV

PDV

First	Gender	EmpID	Type	Phone
		.		

133

...

Execution

EmpsAU

First	Gender	EmpID
Togar	M	121150
Kylie	F	121151
Birin	M	121152

PhoneHW

EmpID	Type	Phone
121150	Home	+61 (2) 5555-1793
121150	Work	+61 (2) 5555-1794
121151	Home	+61 (2) 5555-1849
121151	Work	+61 (2) 5555-1850
121152	Home	+61 (2) 5555-1665
121152	Work	+61 (2) 5555-1666

```
data EmpsAUHW;
    merge EmpsAU PhoneHW;
    by EmpID;
run;
```

Reads one observation from each matching data set.

PDV

First	Gender	EmpID	Type	Phone
Kylie	F	121151	Home	+61 (2) 5555-1849

134   ...

Execution

EmpsAU

First	Gender	EmpID
Togar	M	121150
Kylie	F	121151
Birin	M	121152

PhoneHW

EmpID	Type	Phone
121150	Home	+61 (2) 5555-1793
121150	Work	+61 (2) 5555-1794
121151	Home	+61 (2) 5555-1849
121151	Work	+61 (2) 5555-1850
121152	Home	+61 (2) 5555-1665
121152	Work	+61 (2) 5555-1666

```
data EmpsAUHW;
    merge EmpsAU PhoneHW;
    by EmpID;
run;
```

Implicit OUTPUT;
Implicit RETURN;

PDV

First	Gender	EmpID	Type	Phone
Kylie	F	121151	Home	+61 (2) 5555-1849

135   ...

Execution

EmpsAU

First	Gender	EmpID
Togar	M	121150
Kylie	F	121151
Birin	M	121152

PhoneHW

EmpID	Type	Phone
121150	Home	+61 (2) 5555-1793
121150	Work	+61 (2) 5555-1794
121151	Home	+61 (2) 5555-1849
121151	Work	+61 (2) 5555-1850
121152	Home	+61 (2) 5555-1665
121152	Work	+61 (2) 5555-1666

```
data EmpsAUHW;
   merge EmpsAU PhoneHW;
   by EmpID;
run;
```

Do the **EmpID**s match?

No

PDV

First	Gender	EmpID	Type	Phone
Kylie	F	121151	Home	+61 (2) 5555-1849

136 ...

Execution

EmpsAU

First	Gender	EmpID
Togar	M	121150
Kylie	F	121151
Birin	M	121152

PhoneHW

EmpID	Type	Phone
121150	Home	+61 (2) 5555-1793
121150	Work	+61 (2) 5555-1794
121151	Home	+61 (2) 5555-1849
121151	Work	+61 (2) 5555-1850
121152	Home	+61 (2) 5555-1665
121152	Work	+61 (2) 5555-1666

```
data EmpsAUHW;
   merge EmpsAU PhoneHW;
   by EmpID;
run;
```

Is either **EmpID** the same as the **EmpID** currently in the PDV?

Yes

PDV

First	Gender	EmpID	Type	Phone
Kylie	F	121151	Home	+61 (2) 5555-1849

137 ...

Execution

EmpsAU

First	Gender	EmpID
Togar	M	121150
Kylie	F	121151
Birin	M	121152

PhoneHW

EmpID	Type	Phone
121150	Home	+61 (2) 5555-1793
121150	Work	+61 (2) 5555-1794
121151	Home	+61 (2) 5555-1849
121151	Work	+61 (2) 5555-1850
121152	Home	+61 (2) 5555-1665
121152	Work	+61 (2) 5555-1666

```
data EmpsAUHW;
    merge EmpsAU PhoneHW;
    by EmpID;
run;
```

Reads the observation
from the appropriate
data set.

PDV

First	Gender	EmpID	Type	Phone
Kylie	F	121151	Work	+61 (2) 5555-1850

138   ...

Execution

EmpsAU

First	Gender	EmpID
Togar	M	121150
Kylie	F	121151
Birin	M	121152

PhoneHW

EmpID	Type	Phone
121150	Home	+61 (2) 5555-1793
121150	Work	+61 (2) 5555-1794
121151	Home	+61 (2) 5555-1849
121151	Work	+61 (2) 5555-1850
121152	Home	+61 (2) 5555-1665
121152	Work	+61 (2) 5555-1666

```
data EmpsAUHW;
    merge EmpsAU PhoneHW;
    by EmpID;
run;
```

Implicit OUTPUT;
Implicit RETURN;

PDV

First	Gender	EmpID	Type	Phone
Kylie	F	121151	Work	+61 (2) 5555-1850

139   ...

Execution

EmpsAU

First	Gender	EmpID
Togar	M	121150
Kylie	F	121151
Birin	M	121152

PhoneHW

EmpID	Type	Phone
121150	Home	+61 (2) 5555-1793
121150	Work	+61 (2) 5555-1794
121151	Home	+61 (2) 5555-1849
121151	Work	+61 (2) 5555-1850
121152	Home	+61 (2) 5555-1665
121152	Work	+61 (2) 5555-1666

```
data EmpsAUHW;
   merge EmpsAU Ph
   by EmpID;
run;
```

Continue until EOF on Both Data Sets

PDV

First	Gender	EmpID	Type	Phone
Kylie	F	121151	Work	+61 (2) 5555-1850

140

Final Results

EmpsAUHW

First	Gender	EmpID	Type	Phone
Togar	M	121150	Home	+61 (2) 5555-1793
Togar	M	121150	Work	+61 (2) 5555-1794
Kylie	F	121151	Home	+61 (2) 5555-1849
Kylie	F	121151	Work	+61 (2) 5555-1850
Birin	M	121152	Home	+61 (2) 5555-1665
Birin	M	121152	Work	+61 (2) 5555-1666

141

Exercises

Level 1

10. **Merging orion.orders and orion.order_item One-to-Many**

   a. Retrieve the starter program **p110e10**.

   b. Submit the two PROC CONTENTS steps to determine the common variable among the two data sets.

   c. Add a DATA step after the two PROC CONTENTS steps to merge **orion.orders** and **orion.order_item** by the common variable to create a new data set called **work.allorders**.

   d. Submit the program and confirm that **work.allorders** was created with 732 observations and 12 variables.

Level 2

11. **Merging orion.product_level and orion.product_list One-to-Many**

   a. Write a PROC SORT step to sort **orion.product_list** by **Product_Level** to create a new data set called **work.product_list**.

   b. Write a DATA step to merge **orion.product_level** with the previous sorted data set by the appropriate common variable. Create a new data set called **work.listlevel**.

   c. Write a PROC PRINT step with a VAR statement to create the following report:

   Partial PROC PRINT Output (First 10 of 556 Observations)

Obs	Product_ID	Product_Name	Product_Level	Product_Level_Name
1	210200100009	Kids Sweat Round Neck,Large Logo	1	Product
2	210200100017	Sweatshirt Children's O-Neck	1	Product
3	210200200022	Sunfit Slow Swimming Trunks	1	Product
4	210200200023	Sunfit Stockton Swimming Trunks Jr.	1	Product
5	210200300006	Fleece Cuff Pant Kid'S	1	Product
6	210200300007	Hsc Dutch Player Shirt Junior	1	Product
7	210200300052	Tony's Cut & Sew T-Shirt	1	Product
8	210200400020	Kids Baby Edge Max Shoes	1	Product
9	210200400070	Tony's Children's Deschutz (Bg) Shoes	1	Product
10	210200500002	Children's Mitten	1	Product

Level 3

12. **Joining `orion.product_level` and `orion.product_list` One-to-Many**

    a. Write a PROC SQL step to perform an inner join of **`orion.product_level`** and
       `orion.product_list` by **`Product_Level`** to create a new data set called
       `work.listlevelsql`. The new data set should include only **`Product_ID`**,
       `Product_Name`, **`Product_Level`**, and **`Product_Level_Name`**.

       Documentation on the SQL procedure can be found in the SAS Help
       and Documentation from the Contents tab (**SAS Products** ⇨ **Base SAS** ⇨
       Base SAS 9.2 Procedures Guide ⇨ **Procedures** ⇨ **The SQL Procedure**).

    b. Write a PROC PRINT step to create the following report:

    Partial PROC PRINT Output (First 10 of 556 Observations)

Obs	Product_ID	Product_Name	Product_Level	Product_Level_Name
1	210000000000	Children	4	Product Line
2	210100000000	Children Outdoors	3	Product Category
3	210100100000	Outdoor things, Kids	2	Product Group
4	210200000000	Children Sports	3	Product Category
5	210200100000	A-Team, Kids	2	Product Group
6	210200100009	Kids Sweat Round Neck,Large Logo	1	Product
7	210200100017	Sweatshirt Children's O-Neck	1	Product
8	210200200000	Bathing Suits, Kids	2	Product Group
9	210200200022	Sunfit Slow Swimming Trunks	1	Product
10	210200200023	Sunfit Stockton Swimming Trunks Jr.	1	Product

10.6 Merging Data Sets with Non-Matches

Objectives

- Control the observations in the output data set by using the IN= option.
- Output to multiple data sets using the IN= option and the OUTPUT statement. (Self-Study)
- Compare the results of a many-to-many merge based on using the DATA step or the SQL procedure. (Self-Study)

145

Non-Matches Merge

Merge **EmpsAU** and **PhoneC** by **EmpID** to create a new data set named **EmpsAUC**.

EmpsAU

First	Gender	EmpID
Togar	M	121150
Kylie	F	121151
Birin	M	121152

PhoneC

EmpID	Phone
121150	+61 (2) 5555-1795
121152	+61 (2) 5555-1667
121153	+61 (2) 5555-1348

The data sets are sorted by **EmpID**.

```
data EmpsAUC;
   merge EmpsAU PhoneC;
   by EmpID;
run;
```

146   p110d07

Execution

EmpsAU

First	Gender	EmpID
Togar	M	121150
Kylie	F	121151
Birin	M	121152

PhoneC

EmpID	Phone
121150	+61 (2) 5555-1795
121152	+61 (2) 5555-1667
121153	+61 (2) 5555-1348

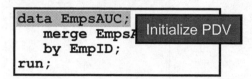

```
data EmpsAUC;
    merge EmpsA
    by EmpID;
run;
```

Initialize PDV

PDV

First	Gender	EmpID	Phone
		.	

147   ...

Execution

EmpsAU

First	Gender	EmpID
Togar	M	121150
Kylie	F	121151
Birin	M	121152

PhoneC

EmpID	Phone
121150	+61 (2) 5555-1795
121152	+61 (2) 5555-1667
121153	+61 (2) 5555-1348

```
data EmpsAUC;
    merge EmpsAU PhoneC;
    by EmpID;
run;
```

Do the **EmpID**s match?

Yes

PDV

First	Gender	EmpID	Phone
		.	

148   ...

Execution

EmpsAU

First	Gender	EmpID
Togar	M	121150
Kylie	F	121151
Birin	M	121152

PhoneC

EmpID	Phone
121150	+61(2)5555-1795
121152	+61(2)5555-1667
121153	+61(2)5555-1348

```
data EmpsAUC;
   merge EmpsAU PhoneC;
   by EmpID;
run;
```

Reads one observation from each matching data set.

PDV

First	Gender	EmpID	Phone
Togar	M	121150	+61(2)5555-1795

149   ...

Execution

EmpsAU

First	Gender	EmpID
Togar	M	121150
Kylie	F	121151
Birin	M	121152

PhoneC

EmpID	Phone
121150	+61(2)5555-1795
121152	+61(2)5555-1667
121153	+61(2)5555-1348

```
data EmpsAUC;
   merge EmpsAU PhoneC;
   by EmpID;
run;
```

Implicit OUTPUT;
Implicit RETURN;

PDV

First	Gender	EmpID	Phone
Togar	M	121150	+61(2)5555-1795

150   ...

Execution

EmpsAU

First	Gender	EmpID
Togar	M	121150
Kylie	F	121151
Birin	M	121152

PhoneC

EmpID	Phone
121150	+61 (2) 5555-1795
121152	+61 (2) 5555-1667
121153	+61 (2) 5555-1348

```
data EmpsAUC;
    merge EmpsAU PhoneC;
    by EmpID;
run;
```

Do the **EmpID**s match?

No

PDV

First	Gender	EmpID	Phone
Togar	M	121150	+61 (2) 5555-1795

151 ...

Execution

EmpsAU

First	Gender	EmpID
Togar	M	121150
Kylie	F	121151
Birin	M	121152

PhoneC

EmpID	Phone
121150	+61 (2) 5555-1795
121152	+61 (2) 5555-1667
121153	+61 (2) 5555-1348

```
data EmpsAUC;
    merge EmpsAU PhoneC;
    by EmpID;
run;
```

Is either **EmpID** the same as the **EmpID** currently in the PDV?

No

PDV

First	Gender	EmpID	Phone
Togar	M	121150	+61 (2) 5555-1795

152 ...

Execution

EmpsAU

First	Gender	EmpID
Togar	M	121150
Kylie	F	121151
Birin	M	121152

PhoneC

EmpID	Phone
121150	+61 (2) 5555-1795
121152	+61 (2) 5555-1667
121153	+61 (2) 5555-1348

```
data EmpsAUC;
   merge EmpsAU PhoneC;
   by EmpID;
run;
```

Reinitialize PDV

PDV

First	Gender	EmpID	Phone
		.	

153   ...

Execution

EmpsAU

First	Gender	EmpID
Togar	M	121150
Kylie	F	121151
Birin	M	121152

PhoneC

EmpID	Phone
121150	+61 (2) 5555-1795
121152	+61 (2) 5555-1667
121153	+61 (2) 5555-1348

```
data EmpsAUC;
   merge EmpsAU PhoneC;
   by EmpID;
run;
```

Which **EmpID**
sequentially comes first?

121151

PDV

First	Gender	EmpID	Phone
		.	

154   ...

Execution

EmpsAU

First	Gender	EmpID
Togar	M	121150
Kylie	F	121151
Birin	M	121152

PhoneC

EmpID	Phone
121150	+61(2)5555-1795
121152	+61(2)5555-1667
121153	+61(2)5555-1348

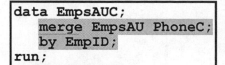

```
data EmpsAUC;
    merge EmpsAU PhoneC;
    by EmpID;
run;
```

Reads the observation from the **EmpID** that sequentially comes first.

PDV

First	Gender	EmpID	Phone
Kylie	F	121151	

155

...

Execution

EmpsAU

First	Gender	EmpID
Togar	M	121150
Kylie	F	121151
Birin	M	121152

PhoneC

EmpID	Phone
121150	+61(2)5555-1795
121152	+61(2)5555-1667
121153	+61(2)5555-1348

```
data EmpsAUC;
    merge EmpsAU PhoneC;
    by EmpID;
run;
```

Implicit OUTPUT;
Implicit RETURN;

PDV

First	Gender	EmpID	Phone
Kylie	F	121151	

156

...

Execution

EmpsAU

First	Gender	EmpID
Togar	M	121150
Kylie	F	121151
Birin	M	121152

PhoneC

EmpID	Phone
121150	+61 (2) 5555-1795
121152	+61 (2) 5555-1667
121153	+61 (2) 5555-1348

```
data EmpsAUC;
    merge EmpsAU PhoneC;
    by EmpID;
run;
```

Do the **EmpID**s match?

Yes

PDV

First	Gender	EmpID	Phone
Kylie	F	121151	

157   ...

Execution

EmpsAU

First	Gender	EmpID
Togar	M	121150
Kylie	F	121151
Birin	M	121152

PhoneC

EmpID	Phone
121150	+61 (2) 5555-1795
121152	+61 (2) 5555-1667
121153	+61 (2) 5555-1348

```
data EmpsAUC;
    merge EmpsAU PhoneC;
    by EmpID;
run;
```

Is either **EmpID** the
same as the **EmpID**
currently in the PDV?

No

PDV

First	Gender	EmpID	Phone
Kylie	F	121151	

158   ...

Execution

EmpsAU

First	Gender	EmpID
Togar	M	121150
Kylie	F	121151
Birin	M	121152

PhoneC

EmpID	Phone
121150	+61 (2) 5555-1795
121152	**+61 (2) 5555-1667**
121153	+61 (2) 5555-1348

```
data EmpsAUC;
   merge EmpsAU PhoneC;
   by EmpID;
run;
```

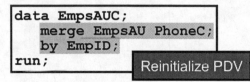
Reinitialize PDV

PDV

First	Gender	EmpID	Phone
		.	

159   ...

Execution

EmpsAU

First	Gender	EmpID
Togar	M	121150
Kylie	F	121151
Birin	M	121152

PhoneC

EmpID	Phone
121150	+61 (2) 5555-1795
121152	**+61 (2) 5555-1667**
121153	+61 (2) 5555-1348

```
data EmpsAUC;
   merge EmpsAU PhoneC;
   by EmpID;
run;
```

Reads one observation
from each matching
data set.

PDV

First	Gender	EmpID	Phone
Birin	M	121152	+61 (2) 5555-1667

160   ...

Execution

EmpsAU

First	Gender	EmpID
Togar	M	121150
Kylie	F	121151
Birin	M	121152

PhoneC

EmpID	Phone
121150	+61 (2) 5555-1795
121152	+61 (2) 5555-1667
121153	+61 (2) 5555-1348

```
data EmpsAUC;
   merge EmpsAU PhoneC;
   by EmpID;
run;
```

Implicit OUTPUT;
Implicit RETURN;

PDV

First	Gender	EmpID	Phone
Birin	M	121152	+61 (2) 5555-1667

161   ...

Execution

EmpsAU

First	Gender	EmpID
Togar	M	121150
Kylie	F	121151
EOF n	M	121152

PhoneC

EmpID	Phone
121150	+61 (2) 5555-1795
121152	+61 (2) 5555-1667
121153	+61 (2) 5555-1348

```
data EmpsAUC;
   merge EmpsAU PhoneC;
   by EmpID;
run;
```

Is the **EmpID** the same as the **EmpID** currently in the PDV?

No

PDV

First	Gender	EmpID	Phone
Birin	M	121152	+61 (2) 5555-1667

162   ...

Execution

EmpsAU

First	Gender	EmpID
Togar	M	121150
Kylie	F	121151
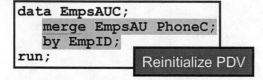 n	M	121152

PhoneC

EmpID	Phone
121150	+61 (2) 5555-1795
121152	+61 (2) 5555-1667
121153	+61 (2) 5555-1348

```
data EmpsAUC;
   merge EmpsAU PhoneC;
   by EmpID;
run;
```

Reinitialize PDV

PDV

First	Gender	EmpID	Phone
		.	

163   ...

Execution

EmpsAU

First	Gender	EmpID
Togar	M	121150
Kylie	F	121151
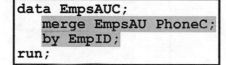 n	M	121152

PhoneC

EmpID	Phone
121150	+61 (2) 5555-1795
121152	+61 (2) 5555-1667
121153	+61 (2) 5555-1348

```
data EmpsAUC;
   merge EmpsAU PhoneC;
   by EmpID;
run;
```

Reads the observation
from the appropriate
data set.

PDV

First	Gender	EmpID	Phone
		121153	+61 (2) 5555-1348

164   ...

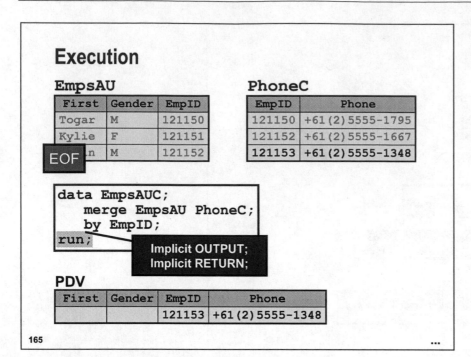

Execution

EmpsAU

First	Gender	EmpID
Togar	M	121150
Kylie	F	121151
EOF	M	121152

PhoneC

EmpID	Phone
121150	+61 (2) 5555-1795
121152	+61 (2) 5555-1667
121153	+61 (2) 5555-1348

```
data EmpsAUC;
   merge EmpsAU PhoneC;
   by EmpID;
run;
```

Implicit OUTPUT;
Implicit RETURN;

PDV

First	Gender	EmpID	Phone
		121153	+61 (2) 5555-1348

165   ...

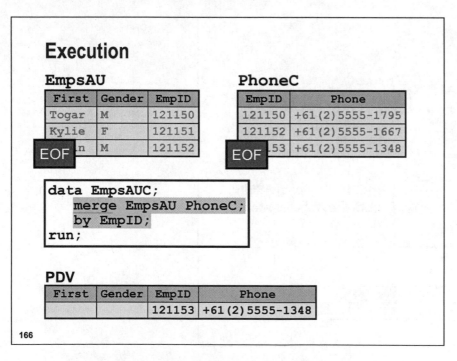

Execution

EmpsAU

First	Gender	EmpID
Togar	M	121150
Kylie	F	121151
EOF	M	121152

PhoneC

EmpID	Phone
121150	+61 (2) 5555-1795
121152	+61 (2) 5555-1667
EOF 53	+61 (2) 5555-1348

```
data EmpsAUC;
   merge EmpsAU PhoneC;
   by EmpID;
run;
```

PDV

First	Gender	EmpID	Phone
		121153	+61 (2) 5555-1348

166

Final Results

EmpsAUC

First	Gender	EmpID	Phone
Togar	M	121150	+61 (2) 5555-1795
Kylie	F	121151	
Birin	M	121152	+61 (2) 5555-1667
		121153	+61 (2) 5555-1348

The final results include matches and non-matches.

- Matches are observations that contain data from both input data sets.
- Non-matches are observations that contain data from only one input data set.

167

10.10 Quiz

How many observations in the final data set **EmpsAUC** are considered non-matches?

a. 1
b. 2
c. 3
d. 4

EmpsAUC

First	Gender	EmpID	Phone
Togar	M	121150	+61 (2) 5555-1795
Kylie	F	121151	
Birin	M	121152	+61 (2) 5555-1667
		121153	+61 (2) 5555-1348

169

The IN= Data Set Option

The *IN= data set option* creates a variable that indicates whether the data set contributed data to the current observation.

General form of the IN= data set option:

> *SAS-data-set* (IN = *variable*)

variable is a temporary numeric variable that has two possible values:

0	indicates that the data set **did not** contribute to the current observation.
1	indicates that the data set **did** contribute to the current observation.

172

The variable created with the IN= data set option is temporary. Therefore, the variable is only available during the execution phase and is not written to the SAS data set.

The IN= Data Set Option

MERGE statement examples:

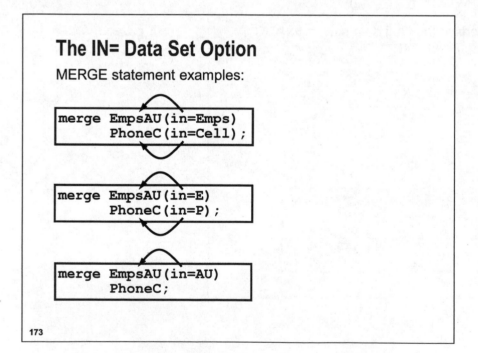

```
merge EmpsAU(in=Emps)
      PhoneC(in=Cell);
```

```
merge EmpsAU(in=E)
      PhoneC(in=P);
```

```
merge EmpsAU(in=AU)
      PhoneC;
```

173

Execution

EmpsAU

First	Gender	EmpID
Togar	M	121150
Kylie	F	121151
Birin	M	121152

PhoneC

EmpID	Phone
121150	+61 (2) 5555-1795
121152	+61 (2) 5555-1667
121153	+61 (2) 5555-1348

```
data EmpsAUC;
   merge EmpsAU(in=Emps)
         PhoneC(in=Cell);
   by EmpID;
run;
```

PDV

First	Gender	EmpID	▷ Emps	Phone	▷ Cell
Togar	M	121150	1	+61 (2) 5555-1795	1

174   p110d07
                                                              ...

Execution

EmpsAU

First	Gender	EmpID
Togar	M	121150
Kylie	F	121151
Birin	M	121152

PhoneC

EmpID	Phone
121150	+61 (2) 5555-1795
121152	+61 (2) 5555-1667
121153	+61 (2) 5555-1348

```
data EmpsAUC;
   merge EmpsAU(in=Emps)
         PhoneC(in=Cell);
   by EmpID;
run;
```

PDV

First	Gender	EmpID	▷ Emps	Phone	▷ Cell
Kylie	F	121151	1		0

175   ...

Execution

EmpsAU

First	Gender	EmpID
Togar	M	121150
Kylie	F	121151
Birin	M	121152

PhoneC

EmpID	Phone
121150	+61 (2) 5555-1795
121152	+61 (2) 5555-1667
121153	+61 (2) 5555-1348

```
data EmpsAUC;
   merge EmpsAU(in=Emps)
         PhoneC(in=Cell);
   by EmpID;
run;
```

PDV

First	Gender	EmpID	▷ Emps	Phone	▷ Cell
Birin	M	121152	1	+61 (2) 5555-1667	1

176   ...

10.11 Quiz

What are the values of **Emps** and **Cell**?

EmpsAU

First	Gender	EmpID
Togar	M	121150
Kylie	F	121151
Birin	M	121152

PhoneC

EmpID	Phone
121150	+61 (2) 5555-1795
121152	+61 (2) 5555-1667
121153	+61 (2) 5555-1348

```
data EmpsAUC;
   merge EmpsAU(in=Emps)
         PhoneC(in=Cell);
   by EmpID;
run;
```

PDV

First	Gender	EmpID	▷ Emps	Phone	▷ Cell
		121153	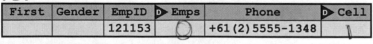	+61 (2) 5555-1348	

178

PDV Results

PDV

First	Gender	EmpID	▷ Emps	Phone	▷ Cell
Togar	M	121150	1	+61 (2) 5555-1795	1
Kylie	F	121151	1		0
Birin	M	121152	1	+61 (2) 5555-1667	1
		121153	0	+61 (2) 5555-1348	1

The variables created with the IN= data set option are only available during execution and are not written to the SAS data set.

180

10.12 Quiz

Which subsetting IF statement could be added to the DATA step to only output the matches?

a. `if Emps=1 and Cell=0;`

b. `if Emps=1 and Cell=1;`

c. `if Emps=1;`

d. `if Cell=0;`

PDV

First	Gender	EmpID	▷ Emps	Phone	▷ Cell
Togar	M	121150	1	+61 (2) 5555-1795	1
Kylie	F	121151	1		0
Birin	M	121152	1	+61 (2) 5555-1667	1
		121153	0	+61 (2) 5555-1348	1

182

Matches Only

```
data EmpsAUC;
    merge EmpsAU(in=Emps)
          PhoneC(in=Cell);
    by EmpID;
    if Emps=1 and Cell=1;
run;
```

EmpsAUC

First	Gender	EmpID	Phone
Togar	M	121150	+61(2)5555-1795
Birin	M	121152	+61(2)5555-1667

184   p110d07

The subsetting IF controls which observations are further processed by the DATA step. In this example, the only processing that remains is the implied output at the bottom of the DATA step. Therefore, if the condition evaluates to **true**, the observation is written to the SAS data set. If the condition is evaluated to **false**, the observation is not written to the SAS data set.

This subsetting IF statement can be rewritten as follows:

```
    if Emps and Cell;
```

claims.

if rxmentar = 1

Non-Matches from `EmpsAU` Only

```
data EmpsAUC;
    merge EmpsAU(in=Emps)
          PhoneC(in=Cell);
    by EmpID;
    if Emps=1 and Cell=0;
run;
```

EmpsAUC

First	Gender	EmpID	Phone
Kylie	F	121151	

185   p110d07

This subsetting IF statement can be rewritten as follows:

```
if Emps and not Cell;
```

Non-Matches from `PhoneC` Only

```
data EmpsAUC;
    merge EmpsAU(in=Emps)
          PhoneC(in=Cell);
    by EmpID;
    if Emps=0 and Cell=1;
run;
```

EmpsAUC

First	Gender	EmpID	Phone
		121153	+61(2)5555-1348

186   p110d07

The subsetting IF statement can be rewritten as follows:

```
if not Emps and Cell;
```

All Non-Matches

```
data EmpsAUC;
    merge EmpsAU(in=Emps)
          PhoneC(in=Cell);
    by EmpID;
    if Emps=0 or Cell=0;
run;
```

EmpsAUC

First	Gender	EmpID	Phone
Kylie	F	121151	
		121153	+61(2)5555-1348

187   p110d07

The subsetting IF statement can be rewritten as follows:

```
if not Emps or not Cell;
```

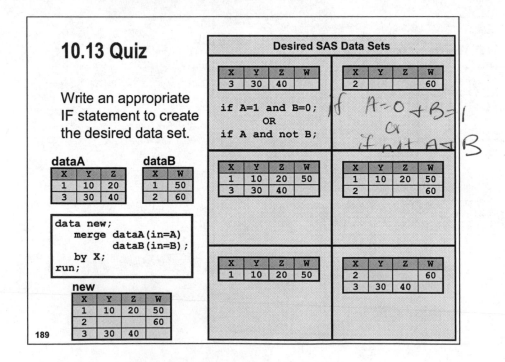

10.13 Quiz

Write an appropriate
IF statement to create
the desired data set.

dataA

X	Y	Z
1	10	20
3	30	40

dataB

X	W
1	50
2	60

```
data new;
    merge dataA(in=A)
          dataB(in=B);
    by X;
run;
```

new

X	Y	Z	W
1	10	20	50
2			60
3	30	40	

189

Desired SAS Data Sets

X	Y	Z	W
3	30	40	

```
if A=1 and B=0;
    OR
if A and not B;
```

*(handwritten: If A=0 + B=1
or
if not A + B)*

X	Y	Z	W
2			60

X	Y	Z	W
1	10	20	50
3	30	40	

X	Y	Z	W
1	10	20	50
2			60

X	Y	Z	W
1	10	20	50

X	Y	Z	W
2			60
3	30	40	

Outputting to Multiple Data Sets (Self-Study)

The DATA statement can specify multiple output data sets.

```
data EmpsAUC EmpsOnly PhoneOnly;
   merge EmpsAU(in=Emps) PhoneC(in=Cell);
   by EmpID;
   if Emps=1 and Cell=1
        then output EmpsAUC;
   else if Emps=1 and Cell=0
        then output EmpsOnly;
   else if Emps=0 and Cell=1
        then output PhoneOnly;
run;
```

192   p110d07

Outputting to Multiple Data Sets (Self-Study)

An OUTPUT statement can be used in a conditional statement to write the current observation to a specific data set that is listed in the DATA statement.

```
data EmpsAUC EmpsOnly PhoneOnly;
   merge EmpsAU(in=Emps) PhoneC(in=Cell);
   by EmpID;
   if Emps=1 and Cell=1
        then output EmpsAUC;
   else if Emps=1 and Cell=0
        then output EmpsOnly;
   else if Emps=0 and Cell=1
        then output PhoneOnly;
run;
```

193   p110d07

Outputting to Multiple Data Sets (Self-Study)

EmpsAUC

First	Gender	EmpID	Phone
Togar	M	121150	+61 (2) 5555-1795
Birin	M	121152	+61 (2) 5555-1667

EmpsOnly

First	Gender	EmpID	Phone
Kylie	F	121151	

PhoneOnly

First	Gender	EmpID	Phone
		121153	+61 (2) 5555-1348

194

Many-to-Many Merge (Self-Study)

Merge **EmpsAUUS** and **PhoneO** by **Country** to create a new data set named **EmpsOfc**.

EmpsAUUS

First	Gender	Country
Togar	M	AU
Kylie	F	AU
Stacey	F	US
Gloria	F	US
James	M	US

PhoneO

Country	Phone
AU	+61 (2) 5555-1500
AU	+61 (2) 5555-1600
AU	+61 (2) 5555-1700
US	+1 (305) 555-1500
US	+1 (305) 555-1600

```
data EmpsOfc;
   merge EmpsAUUS PhoneO;
   by Country;
run;
```

The data sets are sorted by **Country**.

195   p110d08

In a many-to-many merge, this note is issued to the log: "NOTE: MERGE statement has more than one data set with repeats of BY values." This message is meant to be informational.

A DATA step that performs a many-to-many merge does not produce a Cartesian product.

Many-to-Many Merge (Self-Study)

DATA Step Results:

EmpsOfc

First	Gender	Country	Phone
Togar	M	AU	+61 (2) 5555-1500
Kylie	F	AU	+61 (2) 5555-1600
Kylie	F	AU	+61 (2) 5555-1700
Stacey	F	US	+1 (305) 555-1500
Gloria	F	US	+1 (305) 555-1600
James	M	US	+1 (305) 555-1600

196

Many-to-Many Merge (Self-Study)

The SQL procedure creates different results than the DATA step for a many-to-many merge.

EmpsAUUS

First	Gender	Country
Togar	M	AU
Kylie	F	AU
Stacey	F	US
Gloria	F	US
James	M	US

PhoneO

Country	Phone
AU	+61 (2) 5555-1500
AU	+61 (2) 5555-1600
AU	+61 (2) 5555-1700
US	+1 (305) 555-1500
US	+1 (305) 555-1600

```
proc sql;
   create table EmpsOfc as
   select First, Gender, PhoneO.Country, Phone
   from EmpsAUUS, PhoneO
   where EmpsAUUS.Country=PhoneO.Country;
```

197   p110d08

The SQL procedure is SAS' implementation of Structured Query Language. PROC SQL is part of Base SAS software, and you can use it with any SAS data set. Often, PROC SQL can be an alternative to other SAS procedures or the DATA step.

Many-to-Many Merge (Self-Study)

PROC SQL Results:

EmpsOfc

First	Gender	Country	Phone
Togar	M	AU	+61 (2) 5555-1500
Togar	M	AU	+61 (2) 5555-1600
Togar	M	AU	+61 (2) 5555-1700
Kylie	F	AU	+61 (2) 5555-1500
Kylie	F	AU	+61 (2) 5555-1600
Kylie	F	AU	+61 (2) 5555-1700
Stacey	F	US	+1 (305) 555-1500
Stacey	F	US	+1 (305) 555-1600
Gloria	F	US	+1 (305) 555-1500
Gloria	F	US	+1 (305) 555-1600
James	M	US	+1 (305) 555-1500
James	M	US	+1 (305) 555-1600

198

 **Exercises**

Level 1

13. **Merging Using the IN= Option**

   a. Retrieve the starter program **p110e13**.

   b. Add a DATA step after the PROC SORT step to merge **work.product** and **orion.supplier** by **Supplier_ID** to create a new data set called **work.prodsup**.

   c. Submit the program and confirm that **work.prodsup** was created with 556 observations and 10 variables.

   d. Modify the DATA step to output only observations that are in **work.product** but not **orion.supplier**. A subsetting IF statement will need to be added that references IN= variables in the MERGE statement.

   e. Submit the program and confirm that **work.prodsup** was created with 75 observations and 10 variables. The supplier information will be missing in the PROC PRINT output.

Level 2

14. **Merging Using the IN= and RENAME= Options**

   a. Write a PROC SORT step to sort **orion.customer** by **Country** to create a new data set called **work.customer**.

   b. Write a DATA step to merge the previous sorted data set with **orion.lookup_country** by **Country** to create a new data set called **work.allcustomer**.

      In the **orion.lookup_country** data set, **Start** needs to be renamed to **Country** and **Label** needs to be renamed to **Country_Name**.

      The new data set should include only the following four variables: **Customer_ID**, **Country**, **Customer_Name**, and **Country_Name**.

c. Write a PROC PRINT step to create the following report:

Partial PROC PRINT Output (First 15 of 308 Observations)

```
    Obs    Customer_ID     Country    Customer_Name      Country_Name

     1          .            AD                          Andorra
     2          .            AE                          United Arab Emirates
     3          .            AF                          Afghanistan
     4          .            AG                          Antigua/Barbuda
     5          .            AI                          Anguilla
     6          .            AL                          Albania
     7          .            AM                          Armenia
     8          .            AN                          Netherlands Antilles
     9          .            AO                          Angola
    10          .            AQ                          Antarctica
    11          .            AR                          Argentina
    12          .            AS                          American Samoa
    13          .            AT                          Austria
    14         29            AU         Candy Kinsey     Australia
    15         41            AU         Wendell Summersby Australia
```

d. Modify the DATA step to store only the observations that contain both customer information and country information. A subsetting IF statement will need to be added that references IN= variables in the MERGE statement.

e. Submit the program to create the following report:

Partial PROC PRINT Output (First 7 of 77 Observations)

```
                                                          Country_
        Obs    Customer_ID     Country    Customer_Name    Name

         1          29           AU        Candy Kinsey        Australia
         2          41           AU        Wendell Summersby   Australia
         3          53           AU        Dericka Pockran     Australia
         4         111           AU        Karolina Dokter     Australia
         5         171           AU        Robert Bowerman     Australia
         6         183           AU        Duncan Robertshawe  Australia
         7         195           AU        Cosi Rimmington     Australia
```

Level 3

15. **Merging and Outputting to Multiple Data Sets**

   a. Write a PROC SORT step to sort **orion.orders** by **Employee_ID** to create a new data set called **work.orders**.

   b. Write a DATA step to merge **orion.staff** and **work.orders** by **Employee_ID**.

   The DATA step needs to create two new data sets: **work.allorders** and **work.noorders**.

   The data set **work.allorders** should include all observations from **work.orders** regardless of matches or non-matches from the **orion.staff** data set.

   The data set **work.noorders** should include the observations from **orion.staff** that do not have a match in **work.orders**.

   The new data sets should include only the following six variables: **Employee_ID**, **Job_Title**, **Gender**, **Order_ID**, **Order_Type**, and **Order_Date**.

   ✐ Outputting to multiple data sets is mentioned at the end of this section in a self-study section.

   c. Write two PROC PRINT steps to create two reports using the new data sets.

   d. Submit the program and confirm that **work.allorders** was created with 490 observations and 6 variables and **work.noorders** was created with 324 observations and 6 variables.

10.7 Solutions

Solutions to Exercises

1. **Appending Like-Structured Data Sets**

   a. Retrieve the starter program.

   b. Submit the two PROC CONTENTS steps.

```
proc contents data=orion.price_current;
run;

proc contents data=orion.price_new;
run;
```

   How many variables are in **orion.price_current**? **6**

   How many variables are in **orion.price_new**? **5**

   Does **orion.price_new** contain any variables that are not in **orion.price_current**? **No**

   c. Add a PROC APPEND step.

```
proc append base=orion.price_current
            data=orion.price_new;
run;
```

   Why is the FORCE option not needed? **The variables in the DATA= data set are all in the BASE= data set.**

   d. Submit the program.

2. **Appending Unlike-Structured Data Sets**

   a. Write and submit two PROC CONTENTS steps.

```
proc contents data=orion.qtr1_2007;
run;

proc contents data=orion.qtr2_2007;
run;
```

   How many variables are in **orion.qtr1_2007**? **6**

   How many variables are in **orion.qtr2_2007**? **5**

   Which variable is not in both data sets? **Employee_ID**

   b. Write a PROC APPEND step.

```
proc append base=work.ytd
            data=orion.qtr1_2007;
run;
```

   c. Submit the PROC APPEND step.

d. Write another PROC APPEND step.

```
proc append base=work.ytd
           data=orion.qtr2_2007 force;
run;
```

Why is the FORCE option needed? **The variable Employee_ID in the DATA= data set is not in the BASE= data set.**

e. Submit the second PROC APPEND step.

3. Using the APPEND Statement

a. Write and submit three PROC CONTENTS steps.

```
proc contents data=orion.shoes_eclipse;
run;

proc contents data=orion.shoes_tracker;
run;

proc contents data=orion.shoes;
run;
```

b. Write a PROC DATASETS step.

```
proc datasets library=orion nolist;
   append base=shoes data=shoes_eclipse;
   append base=shoes data=shoes_tracker force;
quit;
```

c. Submit the PROC DATASETS step.

4. Concatenating Like-Structured Data Sets

a. Write and submit a DATA step.

```
data work.thirdqtr;
   set orion.mnth7_2007 orion.mnth8_2007 orion.mnth9_2007;
run;
```

How many observations in **work.thirdqtr** are from **orion.mnth7_2007**? **10**

How many observations in **work.thirdqtr** are from **orion.mnth8_2007**? **12**

How many observations in **work.thirdqtr** are from **orion.mnth9_2007**? **10**

b. Write and submit a PROC PRINT step.

```
proc print data=work.thirdqtr;
run;
```

5. Concatenating Unlike-Structured Data Sets

a. Retrieve the starter program.

b. Submit the two PROC CONTENTS steps.

```
proc contents data=orion.sales;
run;

proc contents data=orion.nonsales;
run;
```

What are the names of the two variables that are different in the two data sets?

orion.sales	orion.nonsales
First_Name	First
Last_Name	Last

c. Add a DATA step.

```
data work.allemployees;
   set orion.sales
       orion.nonsales(rename=(First=First_Name Last=Last_Name));
   keep Employee_ID First_Name Last_Name Job_Title Salary;
run;
```

d. Add a PROC PRINT step.

```
proc print data=work.allemployees;
run;
```

6. Interleaving Data Sets

a. Retrieve the starter program.

b. Add a PROC SORT step after the PROC SORT step in the starter program.

```
proc sort data=orion.shoes_eclipse
          out=work.eclipsesort;
   by Product_Name;
run;

proc sort data=orion.shoes_tracker
          out=work.trackersort;
   by Product_Name;
run;
```

c. Add a DATA step.

```
data work.e_t_shoes;
   set work.eclipsesort work.trackersort;
   by Product_Name;
   keep Product_Group Product_Name Supplier_ID;
run;
```

d. Add a PROC PRINT step.

```
proc print data=work.e_t_shoes;
run;
```

7. Merging Two Data Sets One-to-One

a. Retrieve the starter program.

b. Add a PROC SORT step after the PROC SORT step in the starter program.

```
proc sort data=orion.employee_payroll
          out=work.payroll;
   by Employee_ID;
run;

proc sort data=orion.employee_addresses
          out=work.addresses;
   by Employee_ID;
run;
```

c. Add a DATA step prior to the PROC PRINT step.

```
data work.payadd;
   merge work.payroll
         work.addresses;
   by Employee_ID;
run;

proc print data=work.payadd;
   var Employee_ID Employee_Name Birth_Date Salary;
   format Birth_Date weekdate.;
run;
```

d. Submit the program.

8. Merging Three Data Sets One-to-One

a. Write a PROC SORT step.

```
proc sort data=orion.employee_addresses
          out=work.addresses;
   by Employee_ID;
run;
```

b. Write a DATA step.

```
data work.payaddorg;
   merge work.addresses
         orion.employee_payroll
         orion.employee_organization;
   by Employee_ID;
   format Birth_Date ddmmyy10.;
run;
```

c. Write a PROC PRINT step.

```
proc print data=work.payaddorg;
   var Employee_ID Employee_Name Birth_Date Department Salary;
run;
```

9. Joining Data Sets using the SQL Procedure

a. Write a PROC SQL step.

```
proc sql;
   select a.Employee_ID, Employee_Name,
          Birth_Date format=ddmmyy10., Salary
   from orion.employee_addresses as a, orion.employee_payroll as p
   where a.Employee_ID = p.Employee_ID;
quit;
```

b. Submit the program.

10. Merging orion.orders and orion.order_item One-to-Many

a. Retrieve the starter program.

b. Submit the two PROC CONTENTS steps.

```
proc contents data=orion.orders;
run;

proc contents data=orion.order_item;
run;
```

c. Add a DATA step prior to the PROC PRINT step.

```
data work.allorders;
   merge orion.orders
         orion.order_item;
   by Order_ID;
run;

proc print data=work.allorders;
   var Order_ID Order_Item_Num Order_Type
       Order_Date Quantity Total_Retail_Price;
run;
```

d. Submit the program.

11. Merging orion.product_level and orion.product_list One-to-Many

a. Write a PROC SORT step.

```
proc sort data=orion.product_list
          out=work.product_list;
   by Product_Level;
run;
```

b. Write a DATA step.

```
data work.listlevel;
   merge orion.product_level work.product_list;
   by Product_Level;
run;
```

c. Write a PROC PRINT step.

```
proc print data=work.listlevel;
   var Product_ID Product_Name Product_Level Product_Level_Name;
run;
```

12. **Joining orion.product_level and orion.product_list One-to-Many**

a. Write a PROC SQL step.

```
proc sql;
   create table work.listlevelsql as
   select Product_ID, Product_Name,
          product_level.Product_Level, Product_Level_Name
   from orion.product_level, orion.product_list
   where product_level.Product_Level = product_list.Product_Level;
quit;
```

b. Write a PROC PRINT step.

```
proc print data=work.listlevelsql;
run;
```

13. **Merging Using the IN= Option**

a. Retrieve the starter program.

b. Add a DATA step.

```
proc sort data=orion.product_list
          out=work.product;
   by Supplier_ID;
run;

data work.prodsup;
   merge work.product
         orion.supplier;
   by Supplier_ID;
run;

proc print data=work.prodsup;
   var Product_ID Product_Name Supplier_ID Supplier_Name;
run;
```

c. Submit the program.

d. Modify the DATA step.

```
data work.prodsup;
   merge work.product(in=P)
         orion.supplier(in=S);
   by Supplier_ID;
   if P=1 and S=0;
run;
```

e. Submit the program.

14. Merging Using the IN= and RENAME= Options

a. Write a PROC SORT step.

```
proc sort data=orion.customer
          out=work.customer;
   by Country;
run;
```

b. Write a DATA step.

```
data work.allcustomer;
   merge work.customer
         orion.lookup_country(rename=(Start=Country
                                      Label=Country_Name));
   by Country;
   keep Customer_ID Country Customer_Name Country_Name;
run;
```

c. Write a PROC PRINT step.

```
proc print data=work.allcustomer;
run;
```

d. Modify the DATA step.

```
data work.allcustomer;
   merge work.customer(in=Cust)
         orion.lookup_country(rename=(Start=Country
                                      Label=Country_Name)
                              in=Ctry);
   by Country;
   keep Customer_ID Country Customer_Name Country_Name;
   if Cust=1 and Ctry=1;
run;
```

e. Submit the program.

15. Merging and Outputting to Multiple Data Sets

a. Write a PROC SORT step.

```
proc sort data=orion.orders
          out=work.orders;
   by Employee_ID;
run;
```

b. Write a DATA step.

```
data work.allorders work.noorders;
   merge orion.staff(in=Staff) work.orders(in=Ord);
   by Employee_ID;
   if Ord=1 then output work.allorders;
   else if Staff=1 and Ord=0 then output work.noorders;
   keep Employee_ID Job_Title Gender Order_ID Order_Type Order_Date;
run;
```

c. Write two PROC PRINT steps.

```
proc print data=work.allorders;
run;

proc print data=work.noorders;
run;
```

d. Submit the program.

Solutions to Student Activities (Polls/Quizzes)

10.01 Quiz – Correct Answer

Which method (appending, concatenating, or merging) should be used for the given business scenario?

	Business Scenario	Method
1	The **JanSales**, **FebSales**, and **MarSales** data sets need to be combined to create the **Qtr1Sales** data set.	concatenating
2	The **Sales** data set needs to be combined with the **Target** data set by **month** to compare the sales data to the target data.	merging
3	The **OctSales** data sets need to be added to the **YTD** data set.	appending

11

10.02 Quiz – Correct Answer

How many observations will be in **Emps** after appending the three data sets?

9 observations

Emps

First	Gender	HireYear
Stacey	F	2006
Gloria	F	2007
James	M	2007

Emps2008

First	Gender	HireYear
Brett	M	2008
Renee	F	2008

Emps2009

First	HireYear
Sara	2009
Dennis	2009

Emps2010

First	HireYear	Country
Rose	2010	Spain
Eric	2010	Spain

22

10.03 Quiz – Correct Answer

How many variables will be in **Emps** after appending
the three data sets?

3 variables

Emps2008

First	Gender	HireYear
Brett	M	2008
Renee	F	2008

Emps

First	Gender	HireYear
Stacey	F	2006
Gloria	F	2007
James	M	2007

Emps2009

First	HireYear
Sara	2009
Dennis	2009

**The base data set variable
information cannot change.**

Emps2010

First	HireYear	Country
Rose	2010	Spain
Eric	2010	Spain

25

10.04 Quiz – Correct Answer

How many observations will be in **Emps** if the program
is submitted a second time?

15 observations (9 + 2 + 2 + 2)

**Be careful; observations are being added to the
BASE= data set every time you submit the program.**

38

10.05 Quiz – Correct Answer

How many variables will be in **EmpsAll2**
after concatenating **EmpsCN** and **EmpsJP**?

EmpsCN

First	Gender	Country
Chang	M	China
Li	M	China
Ming	F	China

EmpsJP

First	Gender	Region
Cho	F	Japan
Tomi	M	Japan

4 variables

First, Gender, Country, and Region

64

10.06 Quiz – Correct Answer

Which statement has correct syntax?

a.
```
set EmpsCN(rename(Country=Location))
    EmpsJP(rename(Region=Location));
```

b.
```
set EmpsCN(rename=(Country=Location))
    EmpsJP(rename=(Region=Location));
```

c.
```
set EmpsCN rename=(Country=Location)
    EmpsJP rename=(Region=Location);
```

72

10.07 Multiple Choice Poll – Correct Answer

Which method would you use if you wanted to create
a new variable at the time of concatenation?

   a. APPEND procedure

   (b.) SET statement

Example:

```
data EmpsBonus;
   set EmpsDK EmpsFR;
   if Country='Denmark'
       then Bonus=300;
   else Bonus=500;
run;
```

83

10.08 Quiz – Correct Answer

Which step is sorting the observations in a SAS data set
and overwriting the same SAS data set?

   a.
```
proc sort data=work.EmpsAU
           out=work.sorted;
   by First ;
run;
```

   b.
```
proc sort data=work.EmpsAU
           out=orion.EmpsAU;
   by First ;
run;
```

   (c.)
```
proc sort data=work.EmpsAU;
   by First ;
run;
```

105

10.09 Multiple Choice Poll – Correct Answer

What is the **Employee_ID** value for the first
observation in the sorted data set?

- a. 120102
- b. 120121
- (c.) 121144
- d. 121145

```
proc sort data=orion.sales
          out=work.sortsales;
   by Gender descending Employee_ID;
run;

proc print data=work.sortsales;
   var Gender Employee_ID First_Name
       Last_Name Salary;
run;
```

111   p110a01s

10.10 Quiz – Correct Answer

How many observations in the final data set **EmpsAUC**
are considered non-matches?

- a. 1
- (b.) 2
- c. 3
- d. 4

EmpsAUC

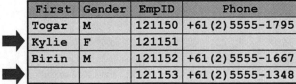

First	Gender	EmpID	Phone
Togar	M	121150	+61 (2) 5555-1795
Kylie	F	121151	
Birin	M	121152	+61 (2) 5555-1667
		121153	+61 (2) 5555-1348

170

10.11 Quiz – Correct Answer

What are the values of **Emps** and **Cell**?

EmpsAU

First	Gender	EmpID
Togar	M	121150
Kylie	F	121151
Birin	M	121152

PhoneC

EmpID	Phone
121150	+61(2)5555-1795
121152	+61(2)5555-1667
121153	+61(2)5555-1348

```
data EmpsAUC;
   merge EmpsAU(in=Emps)
         PhoneC(in=Cell);
   by EmpID;
run;
```

PDV

First	Gender	EmpID	D Emps	Phone	D Cell
		121153	0	+61(2)5555-1348	1

179

10.12 Quiz – Correct Answer

Which subsetting IF statement could be added
to the DATA step to only output the matches?

a. `if Emps=1 and Cell=0;`

(b.) `if Emps=1 and Cell=1;`

c. `if Emps=1;`

d. `if Cell=0;`

PDV

First	Gender	EmpID	D Emps	Phone	D Cell
Togar	M	121150	1	+61(2)5555-1795	1
Kylie	F	121151	1		0
Birin	M	121152	1	+61(2)5555-1667	1
		121153	0	+61(2)5555-1348	1

183

10.13 Quiz – Correct Answer

Write an appropriate IF statement to create the desired data set.

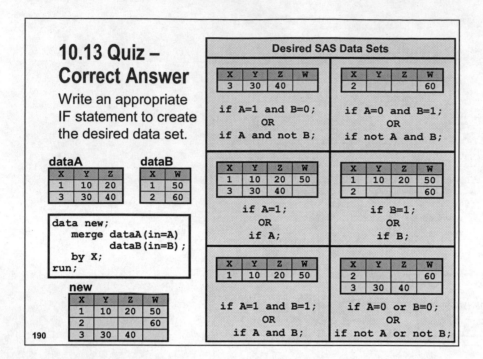

dataA

X	Y	Z
1	10	20
3	30	40

dataB

X	W
1	50
2	60

```
data new;
   merge dataA(in=A)
         dataB(in=B);
   by X;
run;
```

new

X	Y	Z	W
1	10	20	50
2			60
3	30	40	

Desired SAS Data Sets

X	Y	Z	W
3	30	40	

if A=1 and B=0;
      OR
if A and not B;

X	Y	Z	W
2			60

if A=0 and B=1;
      OR
if not A and B;

X	Y	Z	W
1	10	20	50
3	30	40	

if A=1;
   OR
if A;

X	Y	Z	W
1	10	20	50
2			60

if B=1;
   OR
if B;

X	Y	Z	W
1	10	20	50

if A=1 and B=1;
      OR
if A and B;

X	Y	Z	W
2			60
3	30	40	

if A=0 or B=0;
      OR
if not A or not B;

190

Chapter 11 Enhancing Reports

11.1 Using Global Statements

Objectives

- Identify SAS statements that are used with most reporting procedures.
- Enhance reports by using SAS system options.
- Enhance reports by adding titles and footnotes.
- Add dates and times to titles. (Self-Study)

3

Creating Reports

The PROC step is a primary method for creating reports.

SAS Procedures for Creating Reports

- PROC PRINT
- PROC FREQ
- . . .
- PROC MEANS
- PROC TABULATE

4

Example of a Basic Report

```
proc print data=orion.sales;
    var Employee_ID First_Name Last_Name Salary;
run;
```

Partial PROC PRINT Output

```
                          First_
    Obs    Employee_ID    Name        Last_Name    Salary

     1       120102       Tom         Zhou         108255
     2       120103       Wilson      Dawes         87975
     3       120121       Irenie      Elvish        26600
     4       120122       Christina   Ngan          27475
     5       120123       Kimiko      Hotstone      26190
     6       120124       Lucian      Daymond       26480
     7       120125       Fong        Hofmeister    32040
     8       120126       Satyakam    Denny         26780
     9       120127       Sharryn     Clarkson      28100
    10       120128       Monica      Kletschkus    30890
```

5   p111d01

Example of an Enhanced Report

```
options nocenter;
ods html file='enhanced.html' style=sasweb;
proc print data=orion.sales label;
    var Employee_ID First_Name Last_Name Salary;
    title1 'Orion Sales Employees';
    title2 'Males Only';
    footnote 'Confidential';
    label Employee_ID='Sales ID'
          First_Name='First Name'
          Last_Name='Last Name'
          Salary='Annual Salary';
    format Salary dollar8.;
    where Gender='M';
    by Country;
run;
ods html close;
```

6   p111d01

Example of an Enhanced Report

Partial PROC PRINT Output

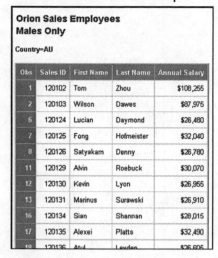

7

Statements That Enhance Reports

Many statements are used with most reporting procedures to enhance the report.

```
options nocenter;
ods html file='enhanced.html' style=sasweb;
proc print data=orion.sales label;
    var Employee_ID First_Name Last_Name Salary;
    title1 'Orion Sales Employees';
    title2 'Males Only';
    footnote 'Confidential';
    label Employee_ID='Sales ID'
          First_Name='First Name'
          Last_Name='Last Name'
          Salary='Annual Salary';
    format Salary dollar8.;
    where Gender='M';
    by Country;
run;
ods html close;
```

8

Global Statements

The following are global statements that enhance reports:

- OPTIONS
- TITLE
- FOOTNOTE
- ODS

Global statements are specified anywhere in your
SAS program and they remain in effect until cancelled,
changed, or your SAS session ends.

9

The OPTIONS Statement

The *OPTIONS statement* changes the value of one
or more SAS system options.

General form of the OPTIONS statement:

OPTIONS *option(s)* ;

- Some SAS system options change the appearance
  of a report.
- The OPTIONS statement is **not** usually included
  in a PROC or DATA step.

10

SAS System Options for Reporting

Selected SAS System Options:

DATE (default)	Displays the date and time the SAS session began at the top of each page of SAS output.
NODATE	Does not display the date and time the SAS session began at the top of each page of SAS output.
NUMBER (default)	Prints page numbers on the first line of each page of SAS output.
NONUMBER	Does not print page numbers on the first line of each page of SAS output.
PAGENO=n	Defines a beginning page number (n) for the next page of SAS output.

11

continued...

SAS System Options for Reporting

Selected SAS System Options:

CENTER (default)	Centers SAS output.
NOCENTER	Left-aligns SAS output.
PAGESIZE=n PS=n	Defines the number of lines (n) that can be printed per page of SAS output.
LINESIZE=width LS=width	Defines the line size (width) for the SAS log and SAS output.

12

SAS System Options for Reporting

```
options ls=80 date number;

proc means data=orion.sales;
   var Salary;
run;
```

```
                                  09:11 Monday, January 14, 2008    35
                       The MEANS Procedure

                     Analysis Variable : Salary

      N          Mean         Std Dev        Minimum        Maximum
    ─────────────────────────────────────────────────────────────────
    165       31160.12       20082.67       22710.00      243190.00
```

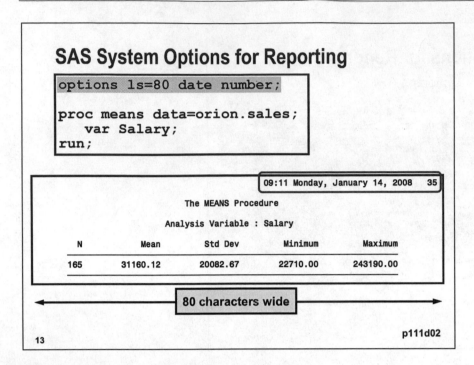

80 characters wide

13   p111d02

SAS System Options for Reporting

```
options nodate pageno=1;

proc freq data=orion.sales;
   tables Country;
run;
```

```
                                                                  1
                        The FREQ Procedure

                                   Cumulative   Cumulative
   Country   Frequency   Percent   Frequency    Percent
   ──────────────────────────────────────────────────────
   AU          63        38.18        63         38.18
   US         102        61.82       165        100.00
```

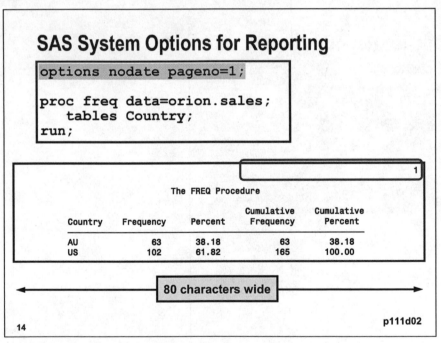

80 characters wide

14   p111d02

Setup for the Poll

- Retrieve and submit program **p111a01**.
- Review the results including the date, time, and page number in the top right corner of each page of output.
- Add the DTRESET system option to the options statement.
- Submit the program and review the results.

DTRESET	Updates date and time at the top of each page of SAS output.
NODTRESET (Default)	Does not update date and time at the top of each page of SAS output.

16

11.01 Poll

Did the date and/or time change?

- O Yes
- O No

17

The TITLE Statement

The *TITLE statement* specifies title lines for SAS output.

General form of the TITLE statement:

> **TITLE*n* '*text* ';**

- Titles appear at the top of the page.
- The default title is **The SAS System**.
- The value of **n** can be from 1 to 10.
- An unnumbered **TITLE** is equivalent to **TITLE1**.
- Titles remain in effect until they are changed, cancelled, or you end your SAS session.

19

The FOOTNOTE Statement

The *FOOTNOTE statement* specifies footnote lines for SAS output.

General form of the FOOTNOTE statement:

> **FOOTNOTE*n* '*text* ';**

- Footnotes appear at the bottom of the page.
- No footnote is printed unless one is specified.
- The value of **n** can be from 1 to 10.
- An unnumbered **FOOTNOTE** is equivalent to **FOOTNOTE1**.
- Footnotes remain in effect until they are changed, cancelled, or you end your SAS session.

20

The TITLE and FOOTNOTE Statements

```
footnote1 'By Human Resource Department';
footnote3 'Confidential';

proc means data=orion.sales;
   var Salary;
   title 'Orion Star Sales Employees';
run;
```

21   p111d03

The TITLE and FOOTNOTE Statements

```
              Orion Star Sales Employees

                 The MEANS Procedure

             Analysis Variable : Salary

  N        Mean        Std Dev       Minimum        Maximum

 165     31160.12     20082.67      22710.00      243190.00




              By Human Resource Department

                     Confidential
```

22

Changing Titles and Footnotes

TITLE*n* or **FOOTNOTE*n***

- replaces a previous title or footnote with the same number
- cancels all titles or footnotes with higher numbers.

23

Canceling All Titles and Footnotes

- The null TITLE statement cancels all titles.

```
title;
```

- The null FOOTNOTE statement cancels all footnotes.

```
footnote;
```

24

Changing and Canceling Titles and Footnotes

PROC PRINT Code	Resultant Title(s)
| ```
proc print data=orion.sales;
   title1 'The First Line';
   title2 'The Second Line';
run;
``` | |
| ```
proc print data=orion.sales;
   title2 'The Next Line';
run;
``` | |
| ```
proc print data=orion.sales;
   title 'The Top Line';
run;
``` | |
| ```
proc print data=orion.sales;
   title3 'The Third Line';
run;
``` | |
| ```
proc print data=orion.sales;
   title;
run;
``` | |

25   ...

Changing and Canceling Titles and Footnotes

PROC PRINT Code	Resultant Title(s)
| ```
proc print data=orion.sales;
   title1 'The First Line';
   title2 'The Second Line';
run;
``` | The First Line<br>The Second Line |
| ```
proc print data=orion.sales;
   title2 'The Next Line';
run;
``` | The First Line<br>The Next Line |
| ```
proc print data=orion.sales;
   title 'The Top Line';
run;
``` | The Top Line |
| ```
proc print data=orion.sales;
   title3 'The Third Line';
run;
``` | The Top Line<br><br>The Third Line |
| ```
proc print data=orion.sales;
   title;
run;
``` | |

35

11.02 Quiz

Which footnote(s) appears in the second procedure output?

a. `Non Sales Employees`

c. `Non Sales Employees`
   `Confidential`

b. `Orion Star`
   `Non Sales Employees`

d. `Orion Star`
   `Non Sales Employees`
   `Confidential`

```
footnote1 'Orion Star';
proc print data=orion.sales;
   footnote2 'Sales Employees';
   footnote3 'Confidential';
run;
proc print data=orion.nonsales;
   footnote2 'Non Sales Employees';
run;
```

37

Titles with Dates and Times (Self-Study)

Automatic macro variables &SYSDATE9 and &SYSTIME can be used to add the SAS invocation date and time to titles and footnotes.

```
title1 'Orion Star Employee Listing';
title2 "Created on &sysdate9 at &systime";
```

Double quotes must be used when referencing a macro variable.

Example Title Output:

```
        Orion Star Employee Listing
        Created on 11MAR2008 at 15:53
```

39   p111d04

Titles with Dates and Times (Self-Study)

The %LET statement can be used with %SYSFUNC and the TODAY function or the TIME function to create a macro variable with the current date or time.

> **%LET** *macro-variable* = **%SYSFUNC(today()**, *date-format***);**

> **%LET** *macro-variable* = **%SYSFUNC(time()**, *time-format***);**

- %LET is a macro statement that creates a macro variable and assigns it a value without leading or trailing blanks.
- %SYSFUNC is a macro function that executes SAS functions outside of a step.

40

Titles with Dates and Times (Self-Study)

```
%let currentdate=%sysfunc(today(),worddate.);
%let currenttime=%sysfunc(time(),timeampm.);

proc freq data=orion.sales;
   tables Gender Country;
   title1 'Orion Star Employee Listing';
   title2 "Created &currentdate";
   title3 "at &currenttime";
run;
```

Example Title Output:

```
         Orion Star Employee Listing
           Created March 11, 2008
               at 4:09:43 PM
```

41   p111d04

 **Exercises**

Level 1

1. Specifying Titles, Footnotes, and System Options

   a. Retrieve the starter program **p111e01**.

   b. Use the OPTIONS statement to establish these system options for the PROC MEANS report:

      1) Suppress the page numbers that appear at the top of each output page.

      2) Suppress the date and time that appear at the top of each output page.

      3) Limit the number of lines per page to 18 for the report. Reset the option value to 52 after the PROC MEANS step finishes.

   c. Specify the following title for the report: **Orion Star Sales Report**

   d. Specify the following footnote for the report: **Report by SAS Programming Student**

   e. After the PROC MEANS step finishes, cancel the footnote.

   f. Submit the program to create the following PROC MEANS report:

PROC MEANS Output

```
                          Orion Star Sales Report

                            The MEANS Procedure

       Analysis Variable : Total_Retail_Price Total Retail Price for This Product

          N          Mean           Std Dev          Minimum          Maximum
        ──────────────────────────────────────────────────────────────────────
         617     162.2001053     233.8530183        2.6000000         1937.20
        ──────────────────────────────────────────────────────────────────────




                        Report by SAS Programming Student
```

Level 2

2. Specifying Multiple Titles and System Options

   a. Retrieve the starter program **p111e02**.

   b. Limit the number of lines per page to 18 and then reset that option to 52 after both reports are complete.

   c. Request that each report contain page numbers starting at 1.

   d. Request that the current date and time be displayed at the top of each page, not the date and time that the SAS session began.

   e. Specify the following title to appear in both reports: `Orion Star Sales Analysis`

   f. Specify a secondary title to appear in the first report with a blank line between the titles:

                `Catalog Sales Only`

   g. Specify the following footnote for the first report:

            `Based on the previous day's posted data`

       ✎   The text specified for a title or footnote may be enclosed in single quotes or double quotes. Use double quotes when the text contains an apostrophe.

   h. Specify a secondary title to appear in the second report with a blank line between the titles:

               `Internet Sales Only`

   i. Cancel all footnotes for the second report.

j. Submit the program to create the following PROC MEANS reports:

PROC MEANS Output

```
                           Orion Star Sales Analysis                          1
                                                    16:30 Monday, January 28, 2008
                               Catalog Sales Only


                               The MEANS Procedure

         Analysis Variable : Total_Retail_Price Total Retail Price for This Product

             N          Mean         Std Dev        Minimum        Maximum
        ────────────────────────────────────────────────────────────────────
            170     199.5961765     282.9680817      2.6000000        1937.20
        ────────────────────────────────────────────────────────────────────




                        Based on the previous day's posted data
```

```
                           Orion Star Sales Analysis                          1
                                                    16:30 Monday, January 28, 2008
                               Internet Sales Only


                               The MEANS Procedure

         Analysis Variable : Total_Retail_Price Total Retail Price for This Product

             N          Mean         Std Dev        Minimum        Maximum
        ────────────────────────────────────────────────────────────────────
            123     174.7280488     214.3528338      2.7000000        1542.60
        ────────────────────────────────────────────────────────────────────
```

Level 3

3. Inserting Dates and Times into Titles

    a. Use the OPTIONS procedure to verify that the date and time will not be automatically displayed at the top of each page. If the option is not set correctly, change it.

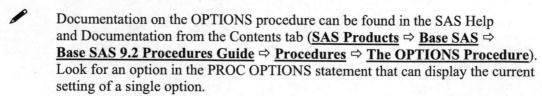

            Documentation on the OPTIONS procedure can be found in the SAS Help and Documentation from the Contents tab (**SAS Products** ⇨ **Base SAS** ⇨ **Base SAS 9.2 Procedures Guide** ⇨ **Procedures** ⇨ **The OPTIONS Procedure**). Look for an option in the PROC OPTIONS statement that can display the current setting of a single option.

    b. Retrieve the starter program **p111e03**.

c. Add a title with the following text, substituting the current date and time:

`Sales Report as of ` **`4:57 PM`** ` on ` **`Monday, January 28, 2008`**

> An example of this technique is shown in the self-study material at the end of this section.

d. Submit the program to create the following report:

PROC MEANS Output

```
              Sales Report as of 4:57 PM on Monday, January 28, 2008

                              The MEANS Procedure

      Analysis Variable : Total_Retail_Price Total Retail Price for This Product

         N            Mean          Std Dev         Minimum         Maximum
      ─────────────────────────────────────────────────────────────────────
        617      162.2001053      233.8530183       2.6000000       1937.20
```

11.2 Adding Labels and Formats

Objectives

- Display descriptive column headings using the LABEL statement.
- Display formatted values using the FORMAT statement.

45

Labels and Formats (Review)

When displaying reports,

- a *label* changes the appearance of a variable name
- a *format* changes the appearance of variable value.

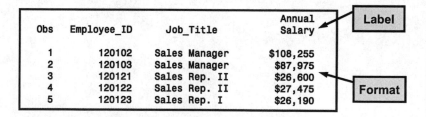

```
                                   Annual
Obs    Employee_ID    Job_Title    Salary

 1       120102    Sales Manager   $108,255
 2       120103    Sales Manager    $87,975
 3       120121    Sales Rep. II    $26,600
 4       120122    Sales Rep. II    $27,475
 5       120123    Sales Rep. I     $26,190
```

Label

Format

46

The LABEL Statement (Review)

The *LABEL statement* assigns descriptive labels to variable names.

General form of the LABEL statement:

> **LABEL** *variable* = '*label*'
>   *variable* = '*label*'
>   *variable* = '*label*' ;

- A label can be up to 256 characters.
- Labels are used automatically by many procedures.
- The PRINT procedure uses labels when the LABEL or SPLIT= option is specified in the PROC PRINT statement.

47

Assigning Temporary Labels

PROC FREQ automatically uses labels.

```
proc freq data=orion.sales;
    tables Gender;
    label Gender='Sales Employee Gender';
run;
```

```
                    The FREQ Procedure

                 ┌─────────────────────────┐
                 │  Sales Employee Gender  │
                 └─────────────────────────┘

                                Cumulative    Cumulative
Gender    Frequency    Percent   Frequency      Percent
───────────────────────────────────────────────────────
F               68      41.21          68        41.21
M               97      58.79         165       100.00
```

48   p111d05

Assigning Temporary Labels

PROC PRINT does not automatically use labels.

```
proc print data=orion.sales;
   var Employee_ID Job_Title Salary;
   label Employee_ID='Sales ID'
         Job_Title='Job Title'
         Salary='Annual Salary';
run;
```

Partial PROC PRINT Output

Obs	Employee_ID	Job_Title	Salary
1	120102	Sales Manager	108255
2	120103	Sales Manager	87975
3	120121	Sales Rep. II	26600
4	120122	Sales Rep. II	27475
5	120123	Sales Rep. I	26190

49   p111d05

Assigning Temporary Labels

The LABEL option makes PROC PRINT use labels.

```
proc print data=orion.sales label;
   var Employee_ID Job_Title Salary;
   label Employee_ID='Sales ID'
         Job_Title='Job Title'
         Salary='Annual Salary';
run;
```

Partial PROC PRINT Output

Obs	Sales ID	Job Title	Annual Salary
1	120102	Sales Manager	108255
2	120103	Sales Manager	87975
3	120121	Sales Rep. II	26600
4	120122	Sales Rep. II	27475
5	120123	Sales Rep. I	26190

50   p111d05

The FSEDIT procedure is another procedure besides the PRINT procedure
that uses the LABEL option.

Assigning Temporary Labels

Instead of the LABEL option in PROC PRINT, the SPLIT= option can be used.

The *SPLIT= option* specifies the split character, which controls line breaks in column headers.

General form of the SPLIT= option:

SPLIT='*split-character***'**

51

Without the SPLIT= option, PROC PRINT can split the headers at special characters such as the blank or underscore or in mixed-case values when going from lowercase to uppercase.

Assigning Temporary Labels

The SPLIT= option makes PROC PRINT use labels.

```
proc print data=orion.sales split='*';
   var Employee_ID Job_Title Salary;
   label Employee_ID='Sales ID'
         Job_Title='Job*Title'
         Salary='Annual*Salary';
run;
```

Partial PROC PRINT Output

Obs	Sales ID	Job Title	Annual Salary
1	120102	Sales Manager	108255
2	120103	Sales Manager	87975
3	120121	Sales Rep. II	26600
4	120122	Sales Rep. II	27475
5	120123	Sales Rep. I	26190

52   p111d05

Assigning Permanent Labels (Review)

Using a LABEL statement in a DATA step permanently associates labels with variables by storing the label in the descriptor portion of the SAS data set.

```
data orion.bonus;
   set orion.sales;
   Bonus=Salary*0.10;
   label Salary='Annual*Salary'
         Bonus='Annual*Bonus';
   keep Employee_ID First_Name
        Last_Name Salary Bonus;
run;

proc print data=orion.bonus split='*';
run;
```

53   p111d05

Assigning Permanent Labels (Review)

Partial PROC PRINT Output

Obs	Employee_ID	First_ Name	Last_Name	Annual Salary	Annual Bonus
1	120102	Tom	Zhou	108255	10825.5
2	120103	Wilson	Dawes	87975	8797.5
3	120121	Irenie	Elvish	26600	2660.0
4	120122	Christina	Ngan	27475	2747.5
5	120123	Kimiko	Hotstone	26190	2619.0
6	120124	Lucian	Daymond	26480	2648.0
7	120125	Fong	Hofmeister	32040	3204.0
8	120126	Satyakam	Denny	26780	2678.0
9	120127	Sharryn	Clarkson	28100	2810.0
10	120128	Monica	Kletschkus	30890	3089.0

54

11.03 Quiz

Which statement is true concerning the
PROC PRINT output for **Bonus**?

a. Annual Bonus will be the label.
b. Mid-Year Bonus will be the label.

```
data orion.bonus;
    set orion.sales;
    Bonus=Salary*0.10;
    label Bonus='Annual Bonus';
run;

proc print data=orion.bonus label;
    label Bonus='Mid-Year Bonus';
run;
```

56   p111d05

The FORMAT Statement (Review)

The *FORMAT statement* assigns formats to
variable values.

General form of the FORMAT statement:

FORMAT *variable(s) format* ;

- A *format* is an instruction that SAS uses to write
  data values.
- Values in the data set are not changed.

59

11.04 Quiz

Which displayed value is incorrect for the given format?

Format	Stored Value	Displayed Value
$3.	Wednesday	Wed
6.1	1234.345	1234.3
COMMAX5.	1234.345	1.234
DOLLAR9.2	1234.345	$1,234.35
DDMMYY8.	0	01/01/1960
DATE9.	0	01JAN1960
YEAR4.	0	1960

61

Assigning Temporary Formats

```
proc print data=orion.sales label;
    var Employee_ID Job_Title Salary
        Country Birth_Date Hire_Date;
    . . .
    format Salary dollar10.0
        Birth_Date Hire_Date monyy7.;
run;
```

Partial PROC PRINT Output

Obs	Sales ID	Job Title	Annual Salary	Country	Date of Birth	Date of Hire
1	120102	Sales Manager	$108,255	AU	AUG1969	JUN1989
2	120103	Sales Manager	$87,975	AU	JAN1949	JAN1974
3	120121	Sales Rep. II	$26,600	AU	AUG1944	JAN1974
4	120122	Sales Rep. II	$27,475	AU	JUL1954	JUL1978
5	120123	Sales Rep. I	$26,190	AU	SEP1964	OCT1985

63   p111d06

Assigning Temporary Formats

```
proc freq data=orion.sales;
   tables Hire_Date;
   format Hire_Date year4.;
run;
```

Partial PROC FREQ Output

```
                    The FREQ Procedure

                                     Cumulative    Cumulative
Hire_Date    Frequency    Percent    Frequency      Percent

   1974         23         13.94        23           13.94
   1975          2          1.21        25           15.15
   1976          4          2.42        29           17.58
   1977          3          1.82        32           19.39
   1978          7          4.24        39           23.64
   1979          3          1.82        42           25.45
```

64   p111d06

Assigning Permanent and Temporary Formats

Using a FORMAT statement in a DATA step permanently
associates formats with variables by storing the format in
the descriptor portion of the SAS data set.

```
data orion.bonus;
   set orion.sales;
   Bonus=Salary*0.10;
   format Salary Bonus comma8.;
   keep Employee_ID First_Name
        Last_Name Salary Bonus;
run;

proc print data=orion.bonus;
   format Bonus dollar8.;
run;
```

Temporary formats override permanent formats.

65   p111d06

Assigning Permanent and Temporary Formats

Partial PROC PRINT Output

Obs	Employee_ID	First_ Name	Last_Name	Salary	Bonus
1	120102	Tom	Zhou	108,255	$10,826
2	120103	Wilson	Dawes	87,975	$8,798
3	120121	Irenie	Elvish	26,600	$2,660
4	120122	Christina	Ngan	27,475	$2,748
5	120123	Kimiko	Hotstone	26,190	$2,619
6	120124	Lucian	Daymond	26,480	$2,648
7	120125	Fong	Hofmeister	32,040	$3,204
8	120126	Satyakam	Denny	26,780	$2,678
9	120127	Sharryn	Clarkson	28,100	$2,810
10	120128	Monica	Kletschkus	30,890	$3,089

66

 **Exercises**

Level 1

4. Applying Labels and Formats in Reports

   a. Retrieve the starter program **p111e04**.

   b. Modify the column heading for each variable as shown in the sample output that follows.

   c. Display all dates in the form ddMONyyyy. If you are running SAS 9.2, specify a width of 11 for the format to obtain the hyphens as shown in the sample output that follows. Otherwise, use a width of 9; the hyphens will not appear.

   d. Display each salary with dollar signs, commas, and two decimal places as shown in the sample output that follows. No salary in the data set exceeds $500,000.

   e. Submit the program to produce the following report:

Partial PROC PRINT Output

			Employees with 3 Dependents		
Obs	Employee Number	Annual Salary	Birth Date	Hire Date	Termination Date
9	120109	$26,495.00	15-DEC-1986	01-OCT-2006	.
11	120111	$26,895.00	23-JUL-1949	01-NOV-1974	.
12	120112	$26,550.00	17-FEB-1969	01-JUL-1990	.
14	120114	$31,285.00	08-FEB-1944	01-JAN-1974	.
18	120118	$28,090.00	03-JUN-1959	01-JUL-1984	.
20	120120	$27,645.00	05-MAY-1944	01-JAN-1974	.
23	120123	$26,190.00	28-SEP-1964	01-OCT-1985	31-JAN-2005
35	120135	$32,490.00	26-JAN-1969	01-OCT-1997	30-APR-2004
47	120147	$26,580.00	19-JAN-1988	01-OCT-2006	.
51	120151	$26,520.00	21-NOV-1944	01-JAN-1974	.

Level 2

5. Overriding Existing Labels and Formats

   a. Retrieve the starter program **p111e05**.

   b. Display only the year portion of birth dates.

   c. Display only the first initial of each customer's first name. The entire last name should be displayed.

d. Show the customer's ID with exactly six digits, including leading zeros if necessary.

> Documentation on SAS formats can be found in the SAS Help and Documentation from the Contents tab (**SAS Products** ⇨ **Base SAS** ⇨ **SAS 9.2 Language Reference: Dictionary** ⇨ **Dictionary of Language Elements** ⇨ **Formats** ⇨ **Formats by Category**). Look for a numeric format that writes standard numeric data with leading zeros.

e. Modify the column heading for each variable as shown in the sample output that follows. Be sure that the column header for the customer's last name is also split into two lines.

f. Submit the program to produce the following report:

Partial PROC PRINT Output

```
                              Customers from Turkey

                 Customer      First      Last        Birth
        Obs         ID        Initial     Name        Year

         47       000544         A        Argac       1964
         48       000908         A        Umran       1979
         49       000928         B        Urfalioglu  1969
         50       001033         S        Okay        1979
         51       001100         A        Canko       1964
         52       001684         C        Aydemir     1974
         55       002788         S        Yucel       1944
```

Level 3

6. Applying Permanent Labels and Formats

a. Retrieve the starter program **p111e06**.

b. Add permanent variable labels and formats to the **work.otherstatus** data set so that those attributes need not be repeated in subsequent steps.

1) Variable labels:
   - Employee_ID   `Employee Number`
   - Employee_Hire_Date   `Hired`

2) Format for **Employee_Hire_Date** should be displayed in the form yyyy.mm.dd.

> Documentation on SAS formats can be found in the SAS Help and Documentation from the Contents tab (**SAS Products** ⇨ **Base SAS** ⇨ **SAS 9.2 Language Reference: Dictionary** ⇨ **Dictionary of Language Elements** ⇨ **Formats** ⇨ **Formats by Category**). Look for a date format that satisfies the requirements noted above.

c. Override the permanent attributes within the PROC FREQ step so that the hire dates are grouped by calendar quarter in the form yyyyQq and the report explicitly states that the counts are by quarter as shown in the sample output that follows.

> ✎ Documentation on SAS formats can be found in the SAS Help and Documentation from the Contents tab (**SAS Products** ⇨ **Base SAS** ⇨ **SAS 9.2 Language Reference: Dictionary** ⇨ **Dictionary of Language Elements** ⇨ **Formats** ⇨ **Formats by Category**). Look for a date format that satisfies the requirements noted above.

d. Submit the program to produce the following reports. Verify that the variable attributes appear in the PROC CONENTS output.

Partial PROC PRINT Output

```
              Employees who are listed with Marital Status=0


                           Employee
              Obs           Number           Hired


               1            120102        1989.06.01
               2            120117        1986.04.01
               3            120126        2006.08.01
               4            120145        1985.06.01
               5            120149        1993.01.01
```

Partial PROC CONTENTS Output

```
              Employees who are listed with Marital Status=0

                        The CONTENTS Procedure

              Alphabetic List of Variables and Attributes


       #    Variable            Type   Len   Format      Label

       2    Employee_Hire_Date   Num    8    YYMMDDP10.  Hired
       1    Employee_ID          Num    8    12.         Employee Number
```

Partial PROC FREQ Output

```
              Employees who are listed with Marital Status=0

                        The FREQ Procedure

                          Quarter Hired


        Employee_                              Cumulative    Cumulative
        Hire_Date   Frequency    Percent       Frequency      Percent

          1974Q1        5         12.50             5          12.50
          1976Q3        1          2.50             6          15.00
          1978Q4        1          2.50             7          17.50
          1981Q1        1          2.50             8          20.00
          1981Q3        1          2.50             9          22.50
```

11.3 Creating User-Defined Formats

Objectives

- Create user-defined formats using the FORMAT procedure.
- Apply user-defined formats to variables in reports.

70

User-Defined Formats

A user-defined format needs to be created for **Country**.

Current Report (partial output)

Obs	Sales ID	Job Title	Annual Salary	Country	Date of Birth	Date of Hire
61	120179	Sales Rep. III	$28,510	AU	MAR1974	JAN2004
62	120180	Sales Rep. II	$26,970	AU	JUN1954	DEC1978
63	120198	Sales Rep. III	$28,025	AU	JAN1988	DEC2006
64	120261	Chief Sales Officer	$243,190	US	FEB1969	AUG1987
65	121018	Sales Rep. II	$27,560	US	JAN1944	JAN1974
66	121019	Sales Rep. IV	$31,320	US	JUN1986	JUN2004

Desired Report (partial output)

Obs	Sales ID	Job Title	Annual Salary	Country	Date of Birth	Date of Hire
61	120179	Sales Rep. III	$28,510	Australia	MAR1974	JAN2004
62	120180	Sales Rep. II	$26,970	Australia	JUN1954	DEC1978
63	120198	Sales Rep. III	$28,025	Australia	JAN1988	DEC2006
64	120261	Chief Sales Officer	$243,190	United States	FEB1969	AUG1987
65	121018	Sales Rep. II	$27,560	United States	JAN1944	JAN1974
66	121019	Sales Rep. IV	$31,320	United States	JUN1986	JUN2004

71

User-Defined Formats

To create and use your own formats, do the following:

 Part 1   Use the FORMAT procedure to create the user-defined format.

Part 2   Apply the format to a specific variable(s) by using a FORMAT statement in the reporting procedure.

72

The FORMAT Procedure

The *FORMAT procedure* is used to create user-defined formats.

General form of the FORMAT procedure with the VALUE statement:

```
PROC FORMAT;
     VALUE format-name range1 = 'label'
                       range2 = 'label'
                                . . .   ;
RUN;
```

73

The FORMAT Procedure

A *format-name*

- names the format that you are creating
- cannot be more than 32 characters in SAS®9
- for character values, must have a dollar sign ($) as the first character, and a letter or underscore as the second character
- for numeric values, must have a letter or underscore as the first character
- cannot end in a number
- cannot be the name of a SAS format
- does not end with a period in the VALUE statement.

74

 Format names prior to SAS®9 are limited to 8 characters.

11.05 Multiple Answer Poll

Which user-defined format names are invalid?

a. $stfmt
b. $3levels
c. _4years
d. salranges
e. dollar

76

The FORMAT Procedure

Range(s) can be
- single values
- ranges of values
- lists of values.

Labels
- can be up to 32,767 characters in length
- are typically enclosed in quotation marks, although it is not required.

78

Character User-Defined Format

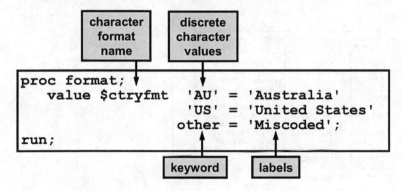

```
proc format;
    value $ctryfmt  'AU' = 'Australia'
                    'US' = 'United States'
                    other = 'Miscoded';
run;
```

The OTHER keyword matches all values that do not match any other value or range.

79   p111d07

Character User-Defined Format

```
proc format;
    value $ctryfmt   'AU' = 'Australia'
                     'US' = 'United States'
                     other = 'Miscoded';
run;

proc print data=orion.sales label;
    var Employee_ID Job_Title Salary
        Country Birth_Date Hire_Date;
    label Employee_ID='Sales ID'
          Job_Title='Job Title'
          Salary='Annual Salary'
          Birth_Date='Date of Birth'
          Hire_Date='Date of Hire';
    format Salary dollar10.0
           Birth_Date Hire_Date monyy7.
           Country $ctryfmt.;
run;
```

Part 1

Part 2

80

Character User-Defined Format

Partial PROC PRINT Output

Obs	Sales ID	Job Title	Annual Salary	Country	Date of Birth	Date of Hire
60	120178	Sales Rep. II	$26,165	Australia	NOV1954	APR1974
61	120179	Sales Rep. III	$28,510	Australia	MAR1974	JAN2004
62	120180	Sales Rep. II	$26,970	Australia	JUN1954	DEC1978
63	120198	Sales Rep. III	$28,025	Australia	JAN1988	DEC2006
64	120261	Chief Sales Officer	$243,190	United States	FEB1969	AUG1987
65	121018	Sales Rep. II	$27,560	United States	JAN1944	JAN1974
66	121019	Sales Rep. IV	$31,320	United States	JUN1986	JUN2004
67	121020	Sales Rep. IV	$31,750	United States	FEB1984	MAY2002
68	121021	Sales Rep. IV	$32,985	United States	DEC1974	MAR1994
69	121022	Sales Rep. IV	$32,210	United States	OCT1979	FEB2002
70	121023	Sales Rep. I	$26,010	United States	MAR1964	MAY1989
71	121024	Sales Rep. II	$26,600	United States	SEP1984	MAY2004
72	121025	Sales Rep. II	$28,295	United States	OCT1949	SEP1975

81

Numeric User-Defined Format

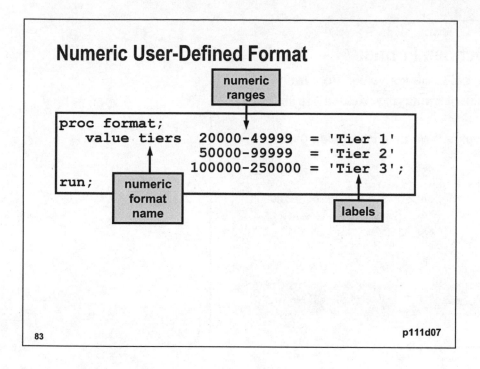

```
proc format;
   value tiers  20000-49999   = 'Tier 1'
                50000-99999   = 'Tier 2'
                100000-250000 = 'Tier 3';
run;
```

83   p111d07

11.06 Quiz

If you have a value of 99999.87, how will it be displayed
if the TIERS format is applied to the value?

a. Tier 2

b. Tier 3

c. 99999.87

d. a missing value

```
proc format;
   value tiers  20000-49999   = 'Tier 1'
                50000-99999   = 'Tier 2'
                100000-250000 = 'Tier 3';
run;
```

85

Numeric User-Defined Formats

The less than (<) symbol excludes values from ranges.

- Put < after the value if wanting to exclude the first value in a range.
- Put < before the value if wanting to exclude the last value in a range.

50000 - 100000	Includes 50000	Includes 100000
50000 - < 100000	Includes 50000	Excludes 100000
50000 < - 100000	Excludes 50000	Includes 100000
50000 < - < 100000	Excludes 50000	Excludes 100000

87

11.07 Quiz

If you have a value of 100000, how will it be displayed if the TIERS format is applied to the value?

a. Tier 2

b. Tier 3

c. 100000

d. a missing value

```
proc format;
   value tiers  20000-<50000  = 'Tier 1'
                50000- 100000 = 'Tier 2'
                100000<-250000 = 'Tier 3';
run;
```

89

Numeric User-Defined Format

keyword

```
proc format;
    value tiers      low-<50000  = 'Tier 1'
                    50000- 100000 = 'Tier 2'
                    100000<-high  = 'Tier 3';
run;
```

keyword

LOW encompasses the lowest possible value.

HIGH encompasses the highest possible value.

91   p111d07

Low does not include missing for numeric variables.

Low does include missing for character variables.

Numeric User-Defined Format

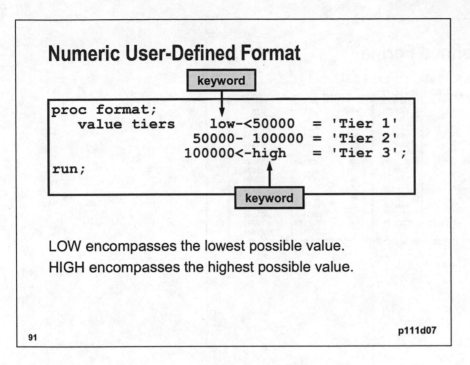

```
proc format;
    value tiers      low-<50000  = 'Tier 1'
Part 1              50000- 100000 = 'Tier 2'
                    100000<-high  = 'Tier 3';
run;

proc print data=orion.sales label;
    var Employee_ID Job_Title Salary
        Country Birth_Date Hire_Date;
    label Employee_ID='Sales ID'
          Job_Title='Job Title'
          Salary='Annual Salary'
          Birth_Date='Date of Birth'
          Hire_Date='Date of Hire';
    format Birth_Date Hire_Date monyy7.
Part 2        Salary tiers.;
run;
```

92

Numeric User-Defined Format

Partial PROC PRINT Output

Obs	Sales ID	Job Title	Annual Salary	Country	Date of Birth	Date of Hire
60	120178	Sales Rep. II	Tier 1	AU	NOV1954	APR1974
61	120179	Sales Rep. III	Tier 1	AU	MAR1974	JAN2004
62	120180	Sales Rep. II	Tier 1	AU	JUN1954	DEC1978
63	120198	Sales Rep. III	Tier 1	AU	JAN1988	DEC2006
64	120261	Chief Sales Officer	Tier 3	US	FEB1969	AUG1987
65	121018	Sales Rep. II	Tier 1	US	JAN1944	JAN1974
66	121019	Sales Rep. IV	Tier 1	US	JUN1986	JUN2004
67	121020	Sales Rep. IV	Tier 1	US	FEB1984	MAY2002
68	121021	Sales Rep. IV	Tier 1	US	DEC1974	MAR1994
69	121022	Sales Rep. IV	Tier 1	US	OCT1979	FEB2002
70	121023	Sales Rep. I	Tier 1	US	MAR1964	MAY1989
71	121024	Sales Rep. II	Tier 1	US	SEP1984	MAY2004
72	121025	Sales Rep. II	Tier 1	US	OCT1949	SEP1975

93

Other User-Defined Format Examples

```
proc format;
    value $grade      'A' = 'Good'
                'B'-'D' = 'Fair'
                    'F' = 'Poor'
            'I','U' = 'See Instructor'
                  other = 'Miscoded';
run;
```

```
proc format;
    value mnthfmt     1,2,3 = 'Qtr 1'
                    4,5,6 = 'Qtr 2'
                    7,8,9 = 'Qtr 3'
            10,11,12 = 'Qtr 4'
                      . = 'missing'
                  other = 'unknown';
run;
```

94

Multiple User-Defined Formats

Multiple VALUE statements can be in a single
PROC FORMAT step.

```
proc format;
   value $ctryfmt  'AU' = 'Australia'
                   'US' = 'United States'
                   other = 'Miscoded';
   value tiers     low-<50000  = 'Tier 1'
                  50000- 100000 = 'Tier 2'
                 100000<-high   = 'Tier 3';
run;
```

p111d07

Multiple User-Defined Formats

```
proc print data=orion.sales label;
   . . .
      format Birth_Date Hire_Date monyy7.
          Country $ctryfmt.
          Salary tiers.;
run;
```

Partial PROC PRINT Output

Obs	Sales ID	Job Title	Annual Salary	Country	Date of Birth	Date of Hire
60	120178	Sales Rep. II	Tier 1	Australia	NOV1954	APR1974
61	120179	Sales Rep. III	Tier 1	Australia	MAR1974	JAN2004
62	120180	Sales Rep. II	Tier 1	Australia	JUN1954	DEC1978
63	120198	Sales Rep. III	Tier 1	Australia	JAN1988	DEC2006
64	120261	Chief Sales Officer	Tier 3	United States	FEB1969	AUG1987
65	121018	Sales Rep. II	Tier 1	United States	JAN1944	JAN1974
66	121019	Sales Rep. IV	Tier 1	United States	JUN1986	JUN2004
67	121020	Sales Rep. IV	Tier 1	United States	FEB1984	MAY2002

p111d07

Multiple User-Defined Formats

```
proc freq data=orion.sales;
   tables Country Salary;
   format Country $ctryfmt. Salary tiers.;
run;
```

The FREQ Procedure

Country	Frequency	Percent	Cumulative Frequency	Cumulative Percent
Australia	63	38.18	63	38.18
United States	102	61.82	165	100.00

Salary	Frequency	Percent	Cumulative Frequency	Cumulative Percent
Tier 1	159	96.36	159	96.36
Tier 2	4	2.42	163	98.79
Tier 3	2	1.21	165	100.00

97

 **Exercises**

Level 1

7. Creating User-Defined Formats

a. Retrieve the starter program **p111e07**.

b. Create a character format named **$gender** that displays gender codes as follows:

F	Female
M	Male

c. Create a numeric format named **moname** that displays month numbers as follows:

1	January
2	February
3	March

d. In the PROC FREQ step, apply these two user-defined formats to the **Employee_Gender** and **BirthMonth** variables, respectively.

e. Submit the program to produce the following report:

PROC FREQ Output

```
                         Employees with Birthdays in Q1

                            The FREQ Procedure

          Birth                            Cumulative    Cumulative
          Month    Frequency    Percent    Frequency      Percent
          ─────────────────────────────────────────────────────────
          January      44        38.94        44          38.94
          February     34        30.09        78          69.03
          March        35        30.97       113         100.00


          Employee_                        Cumulative    Cumulative
          Gender   Frequency    Percent    Frequency      Percent
          ─────────────────────────────────────────────────────────
          Female       52        46.02        52          46.02
          Male         61        53.98       113         100.00
```

Level 2

8. Defining Ranges in User-defined Formats

a. Retrieve the starter program **p111e08**.

b. Create a character format named **$gender** that displays gender codes as follows:

F	Female
M	Male
Any other value	Invalid code

c. Create a numeric format named **salrange** that displays salary ranges as follows:

At least 20,000 but less than 100,000	Below $100,000
At least 100,000 and up to 500,000	$100,000 or more
missing	Missing salary
Any other value	Invalid salary

d. In the PROC PRINT step, apply these two user-defined formats to the **Gender** and **Salary** variables, respectively.

e. Submit the program to produce the following report:

Partial PROC PRINT Output

```
                   Distribution of Salary and Gender Values
                          for Non-Sales Employees

   Obs     Employee_ID   Job_Title                  Salary          Gender

    1         120101     Director               $100,000 or more    Male
    2         120104     Administration Manager  Below $100,000     Female
    3         120105     Secretary I             Below $100,000     Female
    4         120106     Office Assistant II     Missing salary     Male
    5         120107     Office Assistant III    Below $100,000     Female
    6         120108     Warehouse Assistant II  Below $100,000     Female
    7         120108     Warehouse Assistant I   Below $100,000     Female
    8         120110     Warehouse Assistant III Below $100,000     Male
    9         120111     Security Guard II       Below $100,000     Male
   10         120112                             Below $100,000     Female
   11         120113     Security Guard II       Below $100,000     Female
   12         120114     Security Manager        Below $100,000     Invalid code
   13         120115     Service Assistant I     Invalid salary     Male
```

Level 3

9. Creating a Nested Format Definition

a. Retrieve the starter program **p111e09**.

b. Create a user-defined format that displays date ranges as follows:

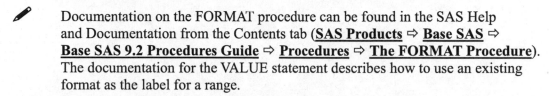

Dates through 31DEC2006	Apply the YEAR4. format
Dates starting 01JAN2007	Apply the MONYY7. format
missing	Display the text None

✎ Documentation on the FORMAT procedure can be found in the SAS Help and Documentation from the Contents tab (**SAS Products** ⇨ **Base SAS** ⇨ **Base SAS 9.2 Procedures Guide** ⇨ **Procedures** ⇨ **The FORMAT Procedure**). The documentation for the VALUE statement describes how to use an existing format as the label for a range.

c. Apply the new format to the **Employee_Term_Date** variable in the PROC FREQ step.

d. Submit the program to produce the following report:

✎ An option is required in the TABLES statement in order to display missing values as part of the main frequency report. Documentation on the FREQ procedure can be found in the SAS Help and Documentation from the Contents tab (**SAS Products** ⇨ **Base SAS** ⇨ **Base SAS Procedures Guide: Statistical Procedures** ⇨ **The FREQ Procedure**).

PROC FREQ Output

```
                          Employee Status Report

                            The FREQ Procedure

      Employee_                         Cumulative    Cumulative
      Term_Date   Frequency   Percent   Frequency      Percent
      ─────────────────────────────────────────────────────────
         None        308       72.64       308          72.64
         2002          6        1.42       314          74.06
         2003         29        6.84       343          80.90
         2004         18        4.25       361          85.14
         2005         21        4.95       382          90.09
         2006         20        4.72       402          94.81
       JAN2007         3        0.71       405          95.52
       FEB2007         3        0.71       408          96.23
       MAR2007         7        1.65       415          97.88
       APR2007         3        0.71       418          98.58
       MAY2007         4        0.94       422          99.53
       JUN2007         2        0.47       424         100.00
```

11.4 Subsetting and Grouping Observations

Objectives

- Display selected observations in reports by using the WHERE statement.
- Display groups of observations in reports by using the BY statement.

101

The WHERE Statement (Review)

For subsetting observations in a report, the WHERE statement is used to select observations that meet a certain condition.

General form of the WHERE statement:

WHERE *where-expression*;

The *where-expression* is a sequence of operands and operators that form a set of instructions that define a condition for selecting observations.

- Operands include constants and variables.
- Operators are symbols that request a comparison, arithmetic calculation, or logical operation.

102

11.08 Quiz

Which of the following WHERE statements have invalid syntax?

a.
```
where Salary ne .;
```

b.
```
where Hire_Date >= '01APR2008'd;
```

c.
```
where Country in (AU US);
```

d.
```
where Salary + Bonus <= 10000;
```

e.
```
where Gender ne 'M' Salary >= 50000;
```

f.
```
where Name like '%N';
```

104

Subsetting Observations

```
proc print data=orion.sales;
    var First_Name Last_Name
        Job_Title Country Salary;
    where Salary > 75000;
run;
```

Obs	First_Name	Last_Name	Job_Title	Country	Salary
1	Tom	Zhou	Sales Manager	AU	108255
2	Wilson	Dawes	Sales Manager	AU	87975
64	Harry	Highpoint	Chief Sales Officer	US	243190
163	Louis	Favaron	Senior Sales Manager	US	95090
164	Renee	Capachietti	Sales Manager	US	83505
165	Dennis	Lansberry	Sales Manager	US	84260

p111d08

106

Subsetting Observations

```
proc means data=orion.sales;
    var Salary;
    where Country = 'AU';
run;
```

The MEANS Procedure

Analysis Variable : Salary

N	Mean	Std Dev	Minimum	Maximum
63	30158.97	12699.14	25185.00	108255.00

107   p111d08

Setup for the Poll

- Retrieve and submit program **p111a02**.
- View the log to determine how SAS handles multiple WHERE statements.

```
proc freq data=orion.sales;
    tables Gender;
    where Salary > 75000;
    where Country = 'US';
run;
```

109

11.09 Multiple Choice Poll

Which statement is true concerning the multiple WHERE statements?

a. All the WHERE statements are used.
b. None of the WHERE statements are used.
c. The first WHERE statement is used.
d. The last WHERE statement is used.

110

The BY Statement

For grouping observations in a report, the BY statement is used to produce separate sections of the report for each BY group.

General form of the BY statement:

> **BY** <DESCENDING> *by-variable(s)*;

✐ The observations in the data set must be sorted by the variables specified in the BY statement.

112

Grouping Observations

```
proc sort data=orion.sales out=work.sort;
   by Country descending Gender Last_Name;
run;

proc print data=work.sort;
   by Country descending Gender;
run;
```

113   p111d09

Grouping Observations

Partial PROC PRINT Output

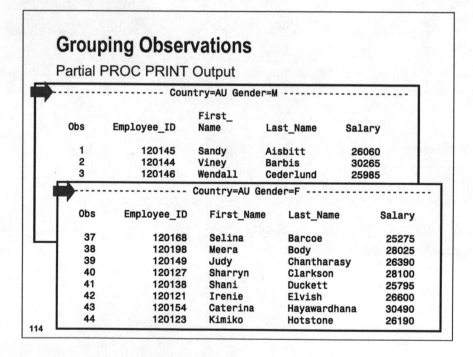

```
-------------------- Country=AU Gender=M --------------------

                       First_
Obs    Employee_ID     Name        Last_Name       Salary

 1        120145       Sandy       Aisbitt          26060
 2        120144       Viney       Barbis           30265
 3        120146       Wendall     Cederlund        25985
-------------------- Country=AU Gender=F --------------------

Obs    Employee_ID     First_Name  Last_Name       Salary

37        120168       Selina      Barcoe           25275
38        120198       Meera       Body             28025
39        120149       Judy        Chantharasy      26390
40        120127       Sharryn     Clarkson         28100
41        120138       Shani       Duckett          25795
42        120121       Irenie      Elvish           26600
43        120154       Caterina    Hayawardhana     30490
44        120123       Kimiko      Hotstone         26190
```

114

11.10 Quiz

Which is a valid BY statement for the PROC FREQ step?

a. `by Country Gender;`

b. `by Gender Last_Name;`

c. `by Country;`

d. `by Gender;`

```
proc sort data=orion.sales out=work.sort;
   by Country descending Gender Last_Name;
run;

proc freq data=work.sort;
   tables Gender;
run;
```

116

Exercises

Level 1

10. Subsetting and Grouping Observations

a. Retrieve the starter program **p111e10**.

b. Add a PROC SORT step to sort the observations in **orion.order_fact** based on the **Order_Type** variable.

> To avoid overwriting the **orion.order_fact** data set, be sure to use the OUT= option to create a new data set containing the sorted observations. Remember to use the new data set in the PROC MEANS step.

c. Restrict the PROC MEANS analysis to two **Order_Type** values: 2 and 3.

d. Modify the PROC MEANS step to generate the summary analysis separately for each selected **Order_Type** value in the sorted data set.

e. Submit the program to produce the following output:

PROC MEANS Output

```
                          Orion Star Sales Summary

-------------------------------------- Order Type=2 --------------------------------------

                            The MEANS Procedure

     Analysis Variable : Total_Retail_Price Total Retail Price for This Product

        N          Mean          Std Dev          Minimum          Maximum
     ------------------------------------------------------------------------
        170     199.5961765     282.9680817       2.6000000         1937.20



-------------------------------------- Order Type=3 --------------------------------------

     Analysis Variable : Total_Retail_Price Total Retail Price for This Product

        N          Mean          Std Dev          Minimum          Maximum
     ------------------------------------------------------------------------
        123     174.7280488     214.3528338       2.7000000         1542.60
```

Level 2

11. Subsetting and Grouping by Multiple Variables

a. Retrieve the starter program **p111c11**.

b. Sort the **orion.order_fact** data set by **Order_Type** (in ascending sequence) and **Order_Date** (in descending sequence).

> Create a new data set containing the sorted observations. Do not overwrite the **orion.order_fact** data set. Remember to use the new data set in the PROC PRINT step.

c. Divide the PROC PRINT report based on **Order_Type** using a BY statement. The orders for each order type should be displayed in reverse chronological order, that is, with more recent orders nearer the top of the report.

d. Limit the observations in the PROC PRINT report based on the following criteria:

1) Orders placed in the first four months of 2005 (January 1 to April 30).

2) Orders that were delivered exactly two days after the order was placed.

e. Add a second title to clarify that filters have been applied to the data.

f. Submit the program to produce the following report:

PROC PRINT Output

```
                        Orion Star Sales Details
                 2-Day Deliveries from January to April 2005

------------------------------------ Order Type=2 ------------------------------------

                                         Order_      Delivery_
            Obs        Order_ID           Date         Date

            409       1235611754        27APR2005    29APR2005
            410       1235611754        27APR2005    29APR2005
            411       1235591214        25APR2005    27APR2005
            412       1235591214        25APR2005    27APR2005
            413       1234972570        24FEB2005    26FEB2005
            415       1234659163        24JAN2005    26JAN2005
            417       1234588648        17JAN2005    19JAN2005
            418       1234588648        17JAN2005    19JAN2005
            419       1234538390        12JAN2005    14JAN2005


------------------------------------ Order Type=3 ------------------------------------

                                         Order_      Delivery_
            Obs        Order_ID           Date         Date

            568       1235176942        15MAR2005    17MAR2005
            569       1235176942        15MAR2005    17MAR2005
            570       1234891576        16FEB2005    18FEB2005
```

Level 3

12. Adding Subsetting Conditions

   a. Retrieve the starter program **p111e12**.

   b. Reorder the variables in the PROC PRINT step's BY statement so that the BY-line displays **Supplier_Name**, **Supplier_ID**, and **Supplier_Country**, in that order. The input data remains grouped, but not sorted, by these variables.

   ✎   An option must be added to the BY statement to support the use of grouped, unsorted data. Documentation on the BY statement can be found in the SAS Help and Documentation from the Contents tab (**SAS Products** ⇨ **Base SAS** ⇨ **Base SAS 9.2 Procedures Guide** ⇨ **Procedures** ⇨ **The PRINT Procedure**).

   c. Augment the existing WHERE criteria by further restricting the report to product names that contain either the word `Street` or the word `Running`.

   ✎   To add clauses to an existing WHERE statement without retyping or editing it, use the SAME-AND operator in a separate WHERE statement within the same step. See the documentation in the SAS Help and Documentation from the Contents tab (**SAS Products** ⇨ **Base SAS** ⇨ **SAS 9.2 Language Reference: Concepts** ⇨ **SAS System Concepts** ⇨ **WHERE-Expression Processing** ⇨ **Syntax of WHERE Expression**).

   d. Submit the program to produce the following report:

Partial PROC PRINT Output

```
                    Orion Star Products: Children Sports

---------- Supplier Name=Greenline Sports Ltd Supplier ID=14682 Country=Great Britain ----------

                 Obs      Product_ID           Product_Name

                 50     210200600015      Hardcore Kids Street Shoes


-------------- Supplier Name=3Top Sports Supplier ID=2963 Country=United States --------------

              Obs      Product_ID       Product_Name

               87     210201000169      Children's Street Shoes
               88     210201000174      Freestyle Children's Leather Street Shoes
               91     210201000179      K Street Shoes
               94     210201000187      Mona  C- Children's Street Shoes
               95     210201000189      Mona  J- Children's Street Shoes
              104     210201000205      Torino 2000 K Street Shoes
              107     210201000209      Universe 4 Children's Running Shoes
```

11.5 Directing Output to External Files

Objectives

- Direct output to ODS destinations by using ODS statements.
- Specify a style definition by using the STYLE= option.
- Create ODS files that can be opened in Microsoft Excel.

121

Output Delivery System

Output can be sent to a variety of destinations by using ODS statements.

122

Output Delivery System

Destination	Type of File	Viewed In
LISTING		SAS Output Window or SAS/GRAPH Window
HTML	Hypertext Markup Language	Web Browsers such as Internet Explorer
PDF	Portable Document Format	Adobe Products such as Acrobat Reader
RTF	Rich Text Format	Word Processors such as Microsoft Word

123

Default ODS Destination

The LISTING destination is the default ODS destination.

```
ods listing;

proc freq data=orion.sales;
   tables Country;
run;

proc gchart data=orion.sales;
   hbar Country / nostats;
run;
```

124   p111d10

Default ODS Destination

The LISTING destination directs output to the
OUTPUT window and the GRAPH window.

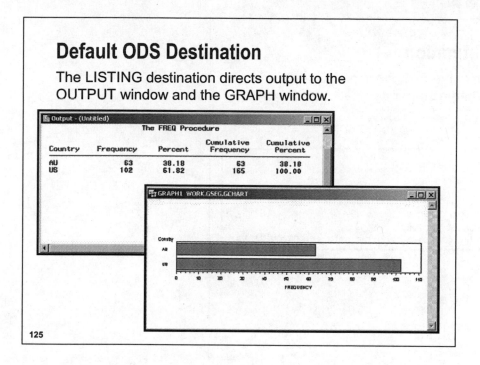

125

Default ODS Destination

The ODS LISTING CLOSE statement stops sending
output to the OUTPUT and GRAPH windows.

```
ods listing close;

proc freq data=orion.sales;
   tables Country;
run;

proc gchart data=orion.sales;
   hbar Country / nostats;
run;
```

126   p111d10

Default ODS Destination

A warning will appear in the SAS log if the LISTING
destination is closed and no other destinations are active.

Partial SAS Log

```
23    ods listing close;
24
25    proc freq data=orion.sales;
26       tables Country;
27    run;

WARNING: No output destinations active.
NOTE: There were 165 observations read from the data set ORION.SALES.
```

127

HTML, PDF, and RTF Destinations

ODS destinations such as HTML, PDF, and RTF
are opened and closed in the following manner:

> **ODS** *destination* **FILE = '** *filename.ext* **'** *<options>* **;**
>
>   *SAS code to generate a report(s)*
>
> **ODS** *destination* **CLOSE;**

128

The filename specified in the FILE= option needs to be specific to your operating environment.

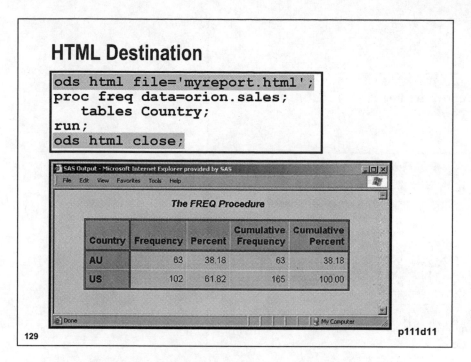

Always terminate steps with an explicit step boundary before closing the destination. Otherwise, the file is closed before the step executes.

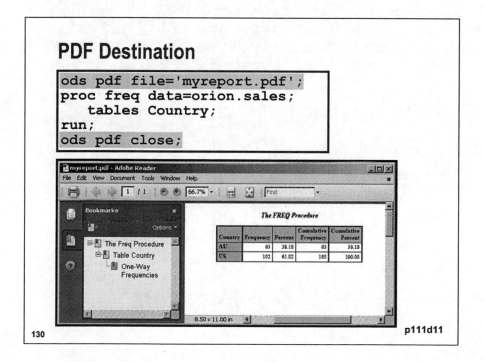

RTF Destination

```
ods rtf file='myreport.rtf';
proc freq data=orion.sales;
    tables Country;
run;
ods rtf close;
```

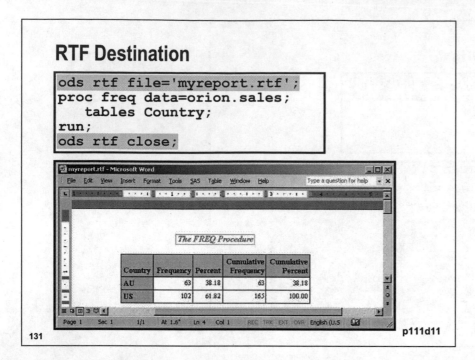

131   p111d11

The traditional RTF destination does not control vertical measurement, so page breaking is controlled by the word processor. Starting in SAS 9.2, there is a new destination, TAGSETS.RTF, which does control vertical measurement.   Documentation on the TAGSETS.RTF destination can be found in the SAS Help and Documentation from the Contents tab (**SAS Products** ⇨ **Base SAS** ⇨ **SAS 9.2 Output Delivery System User's Guide** ⇨ **ODS Language Statements** ⇨ **Dictionary of ODS Language Statements** ⇨ **ODS TAGSETS.RTF Statement**).

11.11 Quiz

What is the problem with this program?

```
ods pdf file='myreport.pdf';

proc print data=orion.sales;
run;

ods close;
```

133

Single Destination

Output can be sent to just one destination.

```
ods listing close;

ods html file='example.html';

proc freq data=orion.sales;
    tables Country;
run;

ods html close;

ods listing;
```

It is a good habit to open the LISTING destination at the end of a program to guarantee an open destination for the next submit.

135   p111d11

Multiple Destinations

Output can be sent to many destinations.

```
ods listing;
ods pdf file='example.pdf';
ods rtf file='example.rtf';

proc freq data=orion.sales;
    tables Country;
run;

ods pdf close;
ods rtf close;
```

To view the results, all destinations except the LISTING destination must be closed.

136   p111d11

Multiple Destinations

Use _ALL_ in the ODS CLOSE statement to close all open destinations including the LISTING destination.

```
ods listing;
ods pdf file='example.pdf';
ods rtf file='example.rtf';

proc freq data=orion.sales;
   tables Country;
run;

ods _all_ close;
ods listing;
```

137   p111d11

Multiple Procedures

Output from many procedures can be sent to ODS destinations.

```
ods listing;
ods pdf file='example.pdf';
ods rtf file='example.rtf';

proc freq data=orion.sales;
   tables Country;
run;

proc means data=orion.sales;
   var Salary;
run;

ods _all_ close;
ods listing;
```

138   p111d11

File Location

A path can be specified to control the location of where the file is stored.

```
ods html file='s:\workshop\example.html';

proc freq data=orion.sales;
   tables Country;
run;

proc means data=orion.sales;
   var Salary;
run;

ods html close;
```

If no path is specified, the file is saved in the current default directory.

139   p111d11

The path and file name specified in the FILE= option needs to be specific to your operating environment.

Operating Environments

The output delivery system works on all operating environments.

z/OS (OS/390) Example:

```
ods html file='.workshop.report(example)'
        rs=none;

proc freq data=orion.sales;
   tables Country;
run;

ods html close;
```

Use the RS=NONE option when creating HTML and RTF files on z/OS (OS/390).

140   p111d11

The RS= option is an alias for the RECORD_SEPARATOR= option.

RS=NONE writes one line of markup output at a time to the file. This allows the file to be read with a text editor. Without the option, the lines of markup output run together.

RS=NONE is not needed with the PDF destination. It is needed with other destinations such as CSVALL, MSOFFICE2K, and EXCELXP.

Creating HTML, PDF, and RTF Files

p111d12

Submit the following program and view the results in the appropriate application. The HTML file can be viewed in a Web browser, the PDF file can be viewed in an Adobe product, and the RTF file can be viewed in a word processor.

```
ods listing close;
ods html file='myreport.html';
ods pdf file='myreport.pdf';
ods rtf file='myreport.rtf';

proc freq data=orion.sales;
   tables Country;
   title 'Report 1';
run;

proc means data=orion.sales;
   var Salary;
   title 'Report 2';
run;

proc print data=orion.sales;
   var First_Name Last_Name
       Job_Title Country Salary;
   where Salary > 75000;
   title 'Report 3';
run;

ods _all_ close;
ods listing;
```

For z/OS (OS/390), the following ODS statements are used:

```
ods html file='.workshop.report(myhtml) rs=none';
ods pdf file='.workshop.report(mypdf)';
ods rtf file='.workshop.report(myrtf)' rs=none;
```

If you are using the SAS windowing environment on the Windows operating environment, the Results Viewer window can be used to view the HTML, PDF, and RTF files.

1. After submitting the program, go to the Results window.

2. Right-click on the word **Results** within the Results window and select **Expand All**.

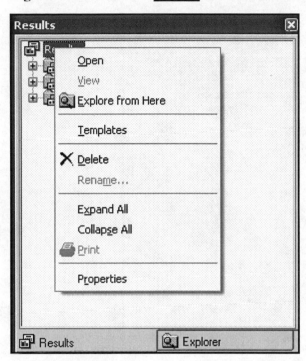

3. Double-click on the HTML file icon, the PDF file icon, or the RTF file icon.

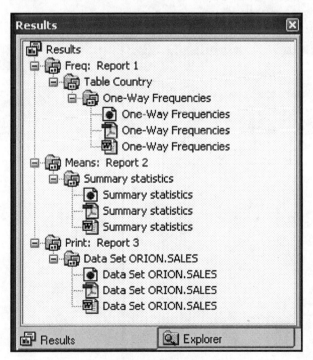

4. View the HTML, PDF, or RTF file in the Results Viewer window.

HTML File in the Results Viewer

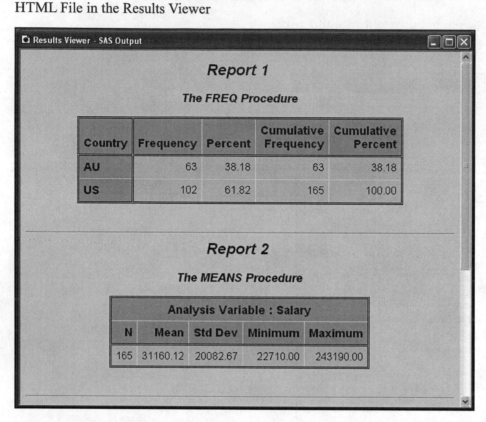

PDF File in the Results Viewer

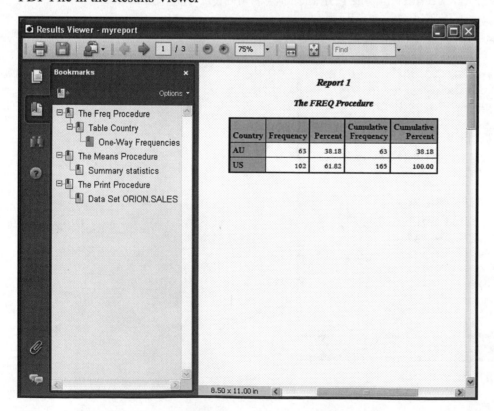

RTF File in the Results Viewer

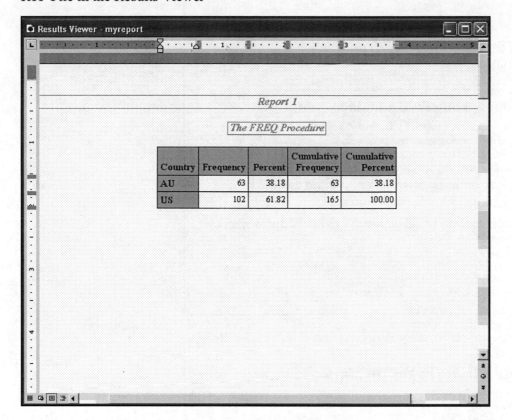

STYLE= Option

Use a STYLE= option in the ODS destination statement to specify a style definition.

> **ODS** *destination* **FILE** = ' *filename.ext* '
>   **STYLE** = *style-definition* ;

- A *style definition* describes how to display the presentation aspects such as colors and fonts of SAS output.
- STYLE= cannot be used with the LISTING destination.

143

SAS Supplied Style Definitions

Analysis	Astronomy	Banker	BarrettsBlue
Beige	blockPrint	Brick	Brown
Curve	D3d	Default	Education
EGDefault	Electronics	fancyPrinter	Festival
FestivalPrinter	Gears	Journal	Magnify
Meadow	MeadowPrinter	Minimal	Money
NoFontDefault	Normal	NormalPrinter	Printer
Rsvp	Rtf	sansPrinter	sasdocPrinter
Sasweb	Science	Seaside	SeasidePrinter
serifPrinter	Sketch	Statdoc	Statistical
Theme	Torn	Watercolor	

144

SAS Supplied Style Definitions

The following style definitions are new to SAS 9.2:

grayscalePrinter	Harvest	HighContrast
Journal2	Journal3	Listing
monochromePrinter	Ocean	Solutions

145

Some of the style definitions changed between SAS 9.1.3 and SAS 9.2.

- For example, the SAS 9.1.3 Analysis style definition produces different results than the SAS 9.2 Analysis style definition. The SAS 9.1.3 Analysis style definition is similar to the SAS 9.2 Ocean style definition.

- Another example, the SAS 9.1.3 Statistical style definition produces different results than the SAS 9.2 Statistical style definition. The SAS 9.1.3 Statistical style definition is similar to the SAS 9.2 Harvest style definition.

HTML Examples

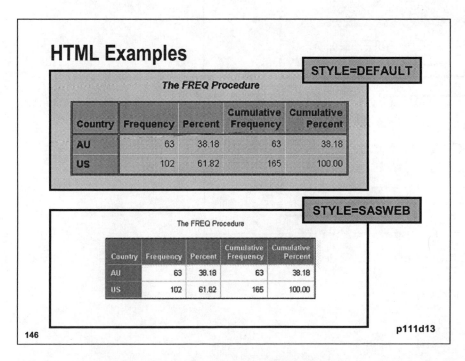

146   p111d13

By default, the HTML destination uses the DEFAULT style definition.

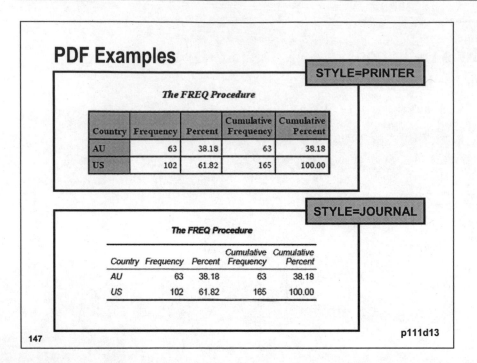

By default, the PDF destination uses the PRINTER style definition.

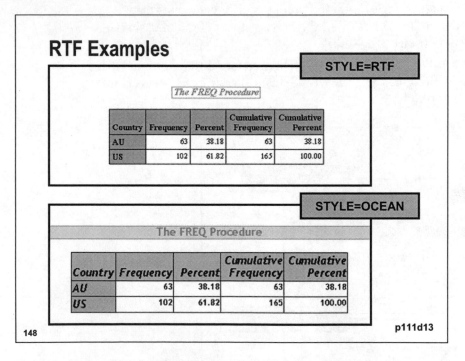

By default, the RTF destination uses the RTF style definition.

Setup for the Poll

- Retrieve **p111a03**.
- Add a STYLE= option to the first ODS statement selecting one of the following style definitions:

HighContrast	Minimal	Listing	Journal3

- Submit the program and review the results.
- Modify the STYLE= option to use one of the following style definitions:

Education	Harvest	Rsvp	Solutions

- Submit the program and review the results.

150

11.12 Poll

Did you notice a difference in the presentation aspects between the two style definitions?

O Yes

O No

151

Destinations Used with Excel

The following destinations create files that can be opened in Excel.

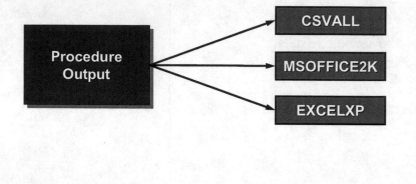

154

Destinations Used with Excel

Destination	Type of File	Viewed In
CSVALL	Comma Separated Value	Editor or Microsoft Excel
MSOFFICE2K	Hypertext Markup Language	Web Browser or Microsoft Word or Microsoft Excel
EXCELXP	Extensible Markup Language	Microsoft Excel

155

CSVALL Destination

```
ods csvall file='myexcel.csv';

proc freq data=orion.sales;
   tables Country;
run;

proc means data=orion.sales;
   var Salary;
run;

ods csvall close;
```

156   p111d14

CSVALL Destination

CSVALL does not include any style information.

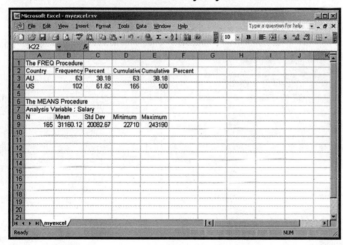

157

MSOFFICE2K Destination

```
ods msoffice2k file='myexcel.html';

proc freq data=orion.sales;
   tables Country;
run;

proc means data=orion.sales;
   var Salary;
run;

ods msoffice2k close;
```

158   p111d14

Microsoft Excel 97 or greater is needed to open a MSOFFICE2K file.

MSOFFICE2K Destination

MSOFFICE2K keeps the style information including spanning headers.

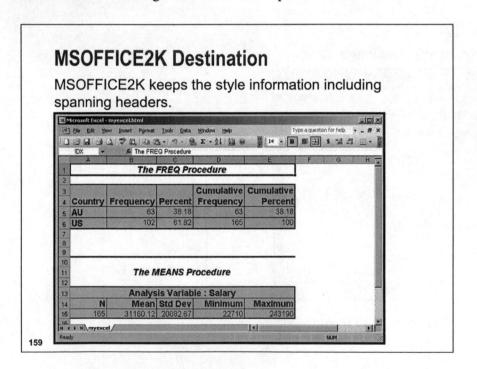

159

EXCELXP Destination

```
ods tagsets.excelxp file='myexcel.xml';

proc freq data=orion.sales;
   tables Country;
run;

proc means data=orion.sales;
   var Salary;
run;

ods tagsets.excelxp close;
```

160   p111d14

Microsoft Excel 2002 or greater is needed to open an EXCELXP file.

EXCELXP Destination

EXCELXP keeps the style information plus each procedure is a separate sheet.

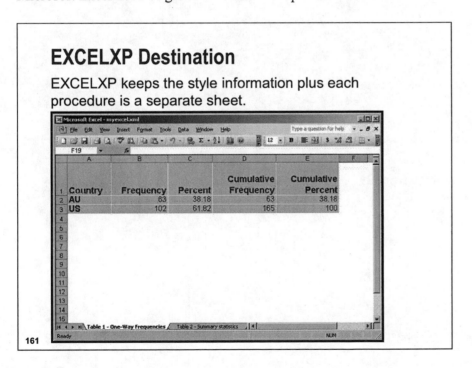

161

Keep in Mind

The file you are creating is not an Excel file.

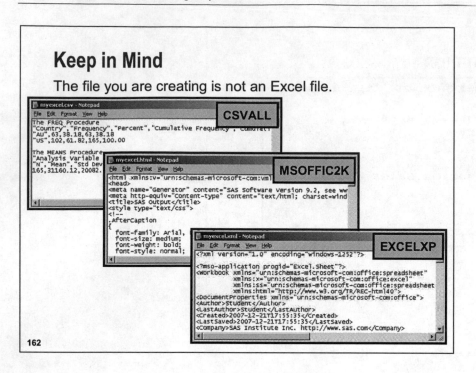

Creating Files That Open in Excel

p111d15

Submit the following program and view the results in Microsoft Excel.

```
ods listing close;
ods csvall file='myexcel.csv';
ods msoffice2k file='myexcel.html';
ods tagsets.excelxp file='myexcel.xml';

proc freq data=orion.sales;
   tables Country;
   title 'Report 1';
run;

proc means data=orion.sales;
   var Salary;
   title 'Report 2';
run;

proc print data=orion.sales;
   var First_Name Last_Name
       Job_Title Country Salary;
   where Salary > 75000;
   title 'Report 3';
run;

ods _all_ close;
ods listing;
```

For z/OS (OS/390), the following ODS statements are used:

```
ods csvall file='.workshop.report(mycsv)' rs=none;
ods msoffice2k file='.workshop.report(myhtml)' rs=none;
ods tagsets.excelxp file='.workshop.report(myxml)' rs=none;
```

CSV File in Microsoft Excel 2002

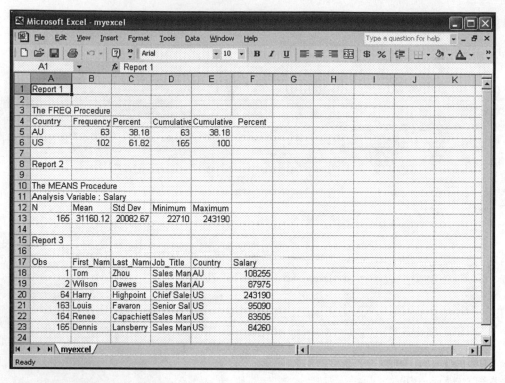

HTML File in Microsoft Excel 2002

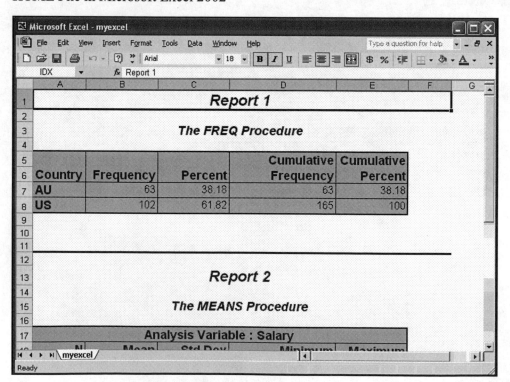

XML File in Microsoft Excel 2002

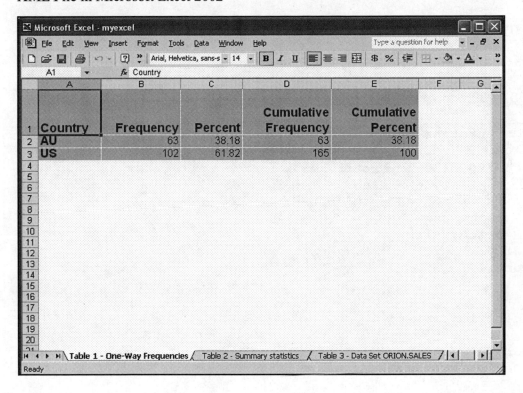

Using Options with the EXCELXP Destination (Self-Study)

p111d16

Submit the following program and view the EXCELXP documentation in the SAS log and the XML files in Microsoft Excel.

```
********** Documentation Option **********;
ods listing close;
ods tagsets.excelxp file='myexcel1.xml'
                    style=sasweb
                    options(doc='help');

proc freq data=orion.sales;
   tables Country;
   title 'Report 1';
run;

proc means data=orion.sales;
   var Salary;
   title 'Report 2';
run;

ods tagsets.excelxp close;
ods listing;

********** Other Options **********;
ods listing close;
ods tagsets.excelxp file='myexcel2.xml'
                    style=sasweb
                    options(embedded_titles='yes'
                            sheet_Name='First Report');

proc freq data=orion.sales;
   tables Country;
   title 'Report 1';
run;

ods tagsets.excelxp options(sheet_Name='Second Report');
proc means data=orion.sales;
   var Salary;
   title 'Report 2';
run;

ods tagsets.excelxp close;
ods listing;
```

For z/OS (OS/390), the following ODS statements are used:

```
ods tagsets.excelxp file='.workshop.report(myxml1)' rs=none
                    style=sasweb
                    options(doc='help');

ods tagsets.excelxp file='.workshop.report(myxml2)' rs=none
                    style=sasweb
                    options(embedded_titles='yes'
                            sheet_Name='First Report');
```

Partial SAS Log

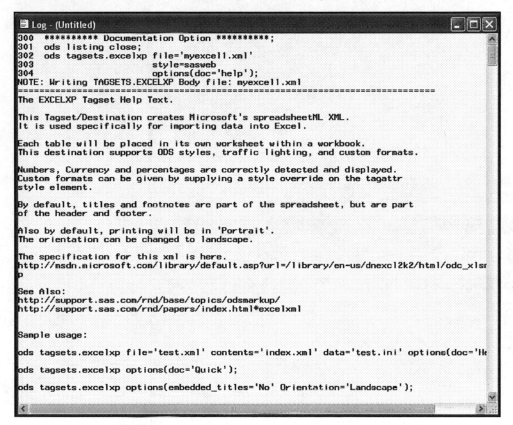

XML Files in Microsoft Excel 2002

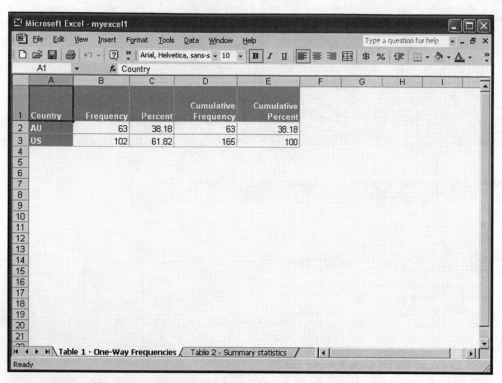

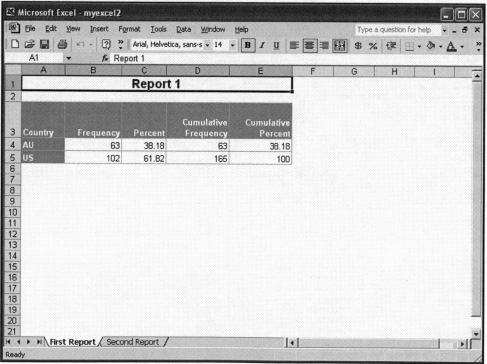

 **Exercises**

Level 1

13. Directing Output to the PDF and RTF Destinations

a. Retrieve the starter program **p111e13**.

b. Create the PDF version of the PROC PRINT report by adding ODS statements.

Use the following naming convention when creating the PDF file:

Windows or UNIX	p111s13p.pdf
z/OS (OS/390)	.workshop.report(p111s13p)

c. Submit the program to produce the following report in PDF form as displayed in Adobe Reader:

Partial PROC PRINT Output

Customer Information

Obs	Customer_ID	Country	Gender	Personal_ID	Customer_Name	Customer_FirstName
1	4	US	M		James Kvarniq	James
2	5	US	F		Sandrina Stephano	Sandrina
3	9	DE	F		Cornelia Krahl	Cornelia
4	10	US	F		Karen Ballinger	Karen
5	11	DE	F		Elke Wallstab	Elke
6	12	US	M		David Black	David
7	13	DE	M		Markus Sepke	Markus
8	16	DE	M		Ulrich Heyde	Ulrich
9	17	US	M		Jimmie Evans	Jimmie
10	18	US	M		Tonie Asmussen	Tonie
11	19	DE	M		Oliver S. Füßling	Oliver S.
12	20	US	M		Michael Dineley	Michael
13	23	US	M		Tulio Devereaux	Tulio
14	24	US	F		Robyn Klem	Robyn
15	27	US	F		Cynthia Mccluney	Cynthia
16	29	AU	F		Candy Kinsey	Candy

Obs	Customer_LastName	Birth_Date	Customer_Address	Street_ID	Street_Number	Customer_Type_ID
1	Kvarniq	27JUN1974	4382 Grahn Rd	9260106519	4382	1020
2	Stephano	09JUL1979	6468 Cog Hill Ct	9260114570	6468	2020
3	Krahl	27FEB1974	Kallstadterstr. 9	3940106659	9	2020
4	Ballinger	18OCT1984	425 Bryant Estates Dr	9260129395	425	1040
5	Wallstab	16AUG1974	Carl-Zeiss-Str. 15	3940108592	15	1040
6	Black	12APR1969	1068 Halthcock Rd	9260103713	1068	1030
7	Sepke	21JUL1988	Iese 1	3940105189	1	2010
8	Heyde	16JAN1939	Oberstr. 61	3940105865	61	3010
9	Evans	17AUG1954	391 Greywood Dr	9260123306	391	1030
10	Asmussen	02FEB1954	117 Langtree Ln	9260112361	117	1020
11	Füßling	23FEB1964	Hechtsheimerstr. 18	3940106547	18	2030
12	Dineley	17APR1959	2187 Draycroft Pl	9260118934	2187	1030
13	Devereaux	02DEC1949	1532 Ferdilah Ln	9260126679	1532	3010
14	Klem	02JUN1959	435 Cambrian Way	9260115784	435	3010
15	Mccluney	15APR1969	188 Grassy Creek Pl	9260105670	188	3010
16	Kinsey	08JUL1934	21 Hotham Parade	1600103020	21	3010

Compare this PDF output to the equivalent report that appears in the Output window.

d. Modify your ODS statements to create the RTF version of the PROC PRINT report.

Use the following naming convention when creating the PDF file:

Windows or UNIX	p111s13r.rtf
z/OS (OS/390)	.workshop.report(p111s13r)

e. Suppress the default Output window listing before generating the RTF report, then re-establish the Output window as the report destination after the RTF report is complete.

f. Submit the program to produce the following report in RTF form as displayed in Microsoft Word:

Partial PROC PRINT Output

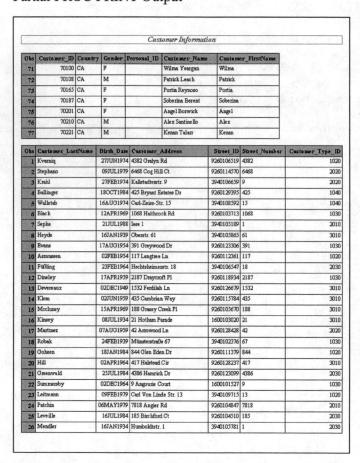

What happens if the RUN statement is moved to the end of the program?

g. Add the STYLE= option to the ODS RTF statement to use a style definitions such as Curve, Gears, Money, or Torn.

h. Submit the program and view the report in RTF form in Microsoft Word.

Level 2

14. Creating ODS Output Compatible with Microsoft Excel

a. Retrieve the starter program **p111e14**.

b. Add ODS statements to send the report to a file that can be viewed in Microsoft Excel. Choose the ODS destination (and use the associated file extension) based on whether you want

   1) style information stored in the report output

   2) the reports in a single worksheet or multiple worksheets.

   If selecting a destination that supports style information, specify the Listing style definition.

   Use the following naming convention when creating the file. For Windows or UNIX, choose an appropriate extension for the file depending on the type of file that is created.

Windows or UNIX	p111s14.xxx
z/OS (OS/390)	.workshop.report(p111s14)

c. Submit the program to produce the output file.

d. Open the file with Microsoft Excel. The report should resemble the following results. Your output will look different depending on the ODS destination you choose.

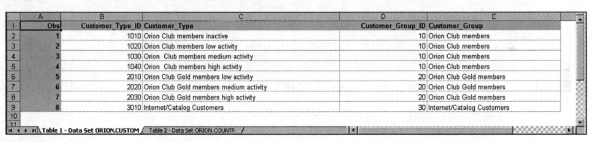

Level 3

15. Adding HTML-Specific Features to ODS Output

a. Retrieve the starter program **p111e15**.

b. Create the HTML version of the PROC PRINT report by adding ODS statements.

   Use the following naming convention when creating the HTML file:

Windows or UNIX	p111s15.html
z/OS (OS/390)	.workshop.report(p111s15)

c. Customize the title so that it becomes a clickable hyperlink when displayed in a Web browser. The hyperlink should point to the URL http://www.sas.com (the SAS home page).

 An option must be added to the TITLE statement to make it an active hyperlink. Documentation on the TITLE statement can be found in the SAS Help and Documentation from the Contents tab (**SAS Products** ⇨ **Base SAS** ⇨ **SAS 9.2 Language Reference: Dictionary** ⇨ **Dictionary of Language Elements** ⇨ **Statements** ⇨ **TITLE Statement**).

d. Submit the program to produce the following report in HTML form as displayed in Internet Explorer:

Partial PROC PRINT Output

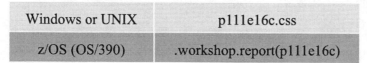

Obs	Customer_ID	Country	Gender	Personal_ID	Customer_Name	Customer_FirstName	Customer_LastN:
1	4	US	M		James Kvarniq	James	Kvarniq
2	5	US	F		Sandrina Stephano	Sandrina	Stephano
3	9	DE	F		Cornelia Krahl	Cornelia	Krahl
4	10	US	F		Karen Ballinger	Karen	Ballinger
5	11	DE	F		Elke Wallstab	Elke	Wallstab
6	12	US	M		David Black	David	Black
7	13	DE	M		Markus Sepke	Markus	Sepke
8	16	DE	M		Ulrich Heyde	Ulrich	Heyde
9	17	US	M		Jimmie Evans	Jimmie	Evans

Customer Information

16. Implementing Cascading Style Sheets with ODS Output

a. Retrieve the starter program **p111e16**.

b. Modify the ODS HTML statement so that the output generated by the program uses a cascading style sheet. The CSS definition applies a yellow background to data cells in the ODS output.

Use the following cascading style sheet:

Windows or UNIX	p111e16c.css
z/OS (OS/390)	.workshop.report(p111e16c)

 The syntax required to reference an existing CSS file can be found in the SAS Help and Documentation from the Contents tab (**SAS Products** ⇨ **Base SAS** ⇨ **SAS 9.2 Output Delivery System User's Guide** ⇨ **ODS Language Statements** ⇨ **Dictionary of ODS Language Statements** ⇨ **ODS HTML Statement**). Follow the documentation links for the STYLESHEET= option and its URL= suboption.

c. Submit the program to produce the following HTML report as displayed in Internet Explorer:

PROC PRINT Output

Customer Type Definitions

Obs	Customer_Type_ID	Customer_Type	Customer_Group_ID	Customer_Group
1	1010	Orion Club members inactive	10	Orion Club members
2	1020	Orion Club members low activity	10	Orion Club members
3	1030	Orion Club members medium activity	10	Orion Club members
4	1040	Orion Club members high activity	10	Orion Club members
5	2010	Orion Club Gold members low activity	20	Orion Club Gold members
6	2020	Orion Club Gold members medium activity	20	Orion Club Gold members
7	2030	Orion Club Gold members high activity	20	Orion Club Gold members
8	3010	Internet/Catalog Customers	30	Internet/Catalog Customers

11.6 Solutions

Solutions to Exercises

1. **Specifying Titles, Footnotes, and System Options**

   a. Retrieve the starter program.

   b. Use the OPTIONS statement.

```
options nonumber nodate pagesize=18;
proc means data=orion.order_fact;
   var Total_Retail_Price;
run;
options pagesize=52;
```

   c. Specify a title.

```
options nonumber nodate pagesize=18;
title 'Orion Star Sales Report';
proc means data=orion.order_fact;
   var Total_Retail_Price;
run;
options pagesize=52;
```

   d. Specify a footnote.

```
options nonumber nodate pagesize=18;
title 'Orion Star Sales Report';
footnote 'Report by SAS Programming Student';
proc means data=orion.order_fact;
   var Total_Retail_Price;
run;
options pagesize=52;
```

   e. Cancel the footnote.

```
options nonumber nodate pagesize=18;
title 'Orion Star Sales Report';
footnote 'Report by SAS Programming Student';
proc means data=orion.order_fact;
   var Total_Retail_Price;
run;
options pagesize=52;
footnote;
```

   f. Submit the program.

2. **Specifying Multiple Titles and System Options**

   a. Retrieve the starter program.

b. Limit the number of lines per page.

```
options pagesize=18;
proc means data=orion.order_fact;
    where Order_Type=2;
    var Total_Retail_Price;
run;

proc means data=orion.order_fact;
    where Order_Type=3;
    var Total_Retail_Price;
run;
options pagesize=52;
```

c. Request page numbers starting at 1.

```
options pagesize=18 number pageno=1;
proc means data=orion.order_fact;
    where Order_Type=2;
    var Total_Retail_Price;
run;

options pageno=1;
proc means data=orion.order_fact;
    where Order_Type=3;
    var Total_Retail_Price;
run;
options pagesize=52;
```

d. Request the current date and time.

```
options pagesize=18 number pageno=1 date dtreset;
```

e. Specify a title in both reports.

```
options pagesize=18 number pageno=1 date dtreset;
title1 'Orion Star Sales Analysis';
```

f. Specify a secondary title in the first report.

```
options pagesize=18 number pageno=1 date dtreset;
title1 'Orion Star Sales Analysis';
proc means data=orion.order_fact;
    where Order_Type=2;
    var Total_Retail_Price;
    title3 'Catalog Sales Only';
run;
```

g. Specify a footnote in the first report.

```
options pagesize=18 number pageno=1 date dtreset;
title1 'Orion Star Sales Analysis';
proc means data=orion.order_fact;
   where Order_Type=2;
   var Total_Retail_Price;
   title3 'Catalog Sales Only';
   footnote "Based on the previous day's posted data";
run;
```

h. Specify a secondary title in the second report.

```
options pagesize=18 number pageno=1 date dtreset;
title1 'Orion Star Sales Analysis';
proc means data=orion.order_fact;
   where Order_Type=2;
   var Total_Retail_Price;
   title3 'Catalog Sales Only';
   footnote "Based on the previous day's posted data";
run;

options pageno=1;
proc means data=orion.order_fact;
   where Order_Type=3;
   var Total_Retail_Price;
   title3 'Internet Sales Only';
run;
options pagesize=52;
```

i. Cancel all footnotes for the second report.

```
options pagesize=18 number pageno=1 date dtreset;
title1 'Orion Star Sales Analysis';
proc means data=orion.order_fact;
   where Order_Type=2;
   var Total_Retail_Price;
   title3 'Catalog Sales Only';
   footnote "Based on the previous day's posted data";
run;

options pageno=1;
proc means data=orion.order_fact;
   where Order_Type=3;
   var Total_Retail_Price;
   title3 'Internet Sales Only';
   footnote;
run;
options pagesize=52;
```

j. Submit the program.

3. **Inserting Dates and Times into Titles**

   a. Use the OPTIONS procedure.

```
proc options option=date;
run;
options nodate;
```

   b. Retrieve the starter program.

   c. Add a title.

```
%let currentdate=%sysfunc(today(),weekdate.);
%let currenttime=%sysfunc(time(),timeampm8.);
proc means data=orion.order_fact;
   title "Sales Report as of &currenttime on &currentdate";
   var Total_Retail_Price;
run;
```

   d. Submit the program.

4. **Applying Labels and Formats in Reports**

   a. Retrieve the starter program.

   b. Modify the column heading for each variable.

```
proc print data=orion.employee_payroll label;
   where Dependents=3;
   title 'Employees with 3 Dependents';
   var Employee_ID Salary
       Birth_Date Employee_Hire_Date Employee_Term_Date;
   label Employee_ID='Employee Number'
         Salary='Annual Salary'
         Birth_Date='Birth Date'
         Employee_Hire_Date='Hire Date'
         Employee_Term_Date='Termination Date';
run;
```

   c. Display all dates in the form ddMONyyyy.

```
proc print data=orion.employee_payroll label;
   where Dependents=3;
   title 'Employees with 3 Dependents';
   var Employee_ID Salary
       Birth_Date Employee_Hire_Date Employee_Term_Date;
   label Employee_ID='Employee Number'
         Salary='Annual Salary'
         Birth_Date='Birth Date'
         Employee_Hire_Date='Hire Date'
         Employee_Term_Date='Termination Date';
   format Birth_Date Employee_Hire_Date Employee_Term_Date date11.;
run;
```

d. Display each salary with dollar signs, commas, and two decimal places.

```
proc print data=orion.employee_payroll label;
   where Dependents=3;
   title 'Employees with 3 Dependents';
   var Employee_ID Salary
       Birth_Date Employee_Hire_Date Employee_Term_Date;
   label Employee_ID='Employee Number'
         Salary='Annual Salary'
         Birth_Date='Birth Date'
         Employee_Hire_Date='Hire Date'
         Employee_Term_Date='Termination Date';
   format Birth_Date Employee_Hire_Date Employee_Term_Date date11.
         Salary dollar11.2;
run;
```

e. Submit the program.

5. Overriding Existing Labels and Formats

a. Retrieve the starter program.

b. Display only the year portion of birth dates.

```
proc print data=orion.customer;
   where Country='TR';
   title 'Customers from Turkey';
   var Customer_ID Customer_FirstName Customer_LastName
       Birth_Date;
   format Birth_Date year4.;
run;
```

c. Display only the first initial of each customer's first name.

```
proc print data=orion.customer;
   where Country='TR';
   title 'Customers from Turkey';
   var Customer_ID Customer_FirstName Customer_LastName
       Birth_Date;
   format Birth_Date year4.
         Customer_FirstName $1.;
run;
```

d. Show the customer's ID with exactly six digits.

```
proc print data=orion.customer;
   where Country='TR';
   title 'Customers from Turkey';
   var Customer_ID Customer_FirstName Customer_LastName
       Birth_Date;
   format Birth_Date year4.
         Customer_FirstName $1.
         Customer_ID z6.;
run;
```

e. Modify the column heading for each variable.

```
proc print data=orion.customer split='/';
   where Country='TR';
   title 'Customers from Turkey';
   var Customer_ID Customer_FirstName Customer_LastName
       Birth_Date;
   label Customer_ID='Customer ID'
         Customer_FirstName='First Initial'
         Customer_LastName='Last/Name'
         Birth_Date='Birth Year';
   format Birth_Date year4.
          Customer_FirstName $1.
          Customer_ID z6.;
run;
```

f. Submit the program.

6. Applying Permanent Labels and Formats

a. Retrieve the starter program.

b. Add permanent variable labels and formats.

```
data otherstatus;
   set orion.employee_payroll;
   keep Employee_ID Employee_Hire_Date;
   if Marital_Status='O';
   label Employee_ID='Employee Number'
         Employee_Hire_Date='Hired';
   format Employee_Hire_Date yymmddp10.;
run;

title 'Employees who are listed with Marital Status=O';
proc print data=otherstatus label;
run;

proc contents data=otherstatus;
run;

proc freq data=otherstatus;
   tables Employee_Hire_Date;
run;
```

c. Override the permanent attributes within the PROC FREQ step.

```
proc freq data=otherstatus;
   tables Employee_Hire_Date;
   label Employee_Hire_Date='Quarter Hired';
   format Employee_Hire_Date yyq6.;
run;
```

d. Submit the program.

7. Creating User-Defined Formats

a. Retrieve the starter program.

b. Create a character format.

```
data Q1Birthdays;
   set orion.employee_payroll;
   BirthMonth=month(Birth_Date);
   if BirthMonth le 3;
run;

proc format;
   value $gender
      'F'='Female'
      'M'='Male';
run;
```

c. Create a numeric format.

```
data Q1Birthdays;
   set orion.employee_payroll;
   BirthMonth=month(Birth_Date);
   if BirthMonth le 3;
run;

proc format;
   value $gender
      'F'='Female'
      'M'='Male';
   value moname
      1='January'
      2='February'
      3='March';
run;
```

d. In the PROC FREQ step, apply these two user-defined formats.

```
proc freq data=Q1Birthdays;
   tables BirthMonth Employee_Gender;
   format Employee_Gender $gender.
          BirthMonth moname.;
   title 'Employees with Birthdays in Q1';
run;
```

e. Submit the program.

8. **Defining Ranges in User-Defined Formats**

   a. Retrieve the starter program.

   b. Create a character format.

```
proc format;
   value $gender
        'F'='Female'
        'M'='Male'
      other='Invalid code';
run;
```

   c. Create a numeric format.

```
proc format;
   value $gender
        'F'='Female'
        'M'='Male'
      other='Invalid code';
   value salrange
                    .='Missing salary'
        20000-<100000='Below $100,000'
        100000-500000='$100,000 or more'
               other='Invalid salary';
run;
```

   d. In the PROC PRINT step, apply these two user-defined formats.

```
proc print data=orion.nonsales;
   var Employee_ID Job_Title Salary Gender;
   format Salary salrange. Gender $gender.;
   title1 'Distribution of Salary and Gender Values';
   title2 'for Non-Sales Employees';
run;
```

   e. Submit the program.

9. **Creating a Nested Format Definition**

   a. Retrieve the starter program.

   b. Create a user-defined format.

```
proc format;
   value dategrp
                    .='None'
        low-'31dec2006'd=[year4.]
        '01jan2007'd-high=[monyy7.]
   ;
run;
```

c. Apply the new format.

```
proc freq data=orion.employee_payroll;
   tables Employee_Term_Date / missing;
   format Employee_Term_Date dategrp.;
   title 'Employee Status Report';
run;
```

d. Submit the program.

10. Subsetting and Grouping Observations

a. Retrieve the starter program.

b. Add a PROC SORT step.

```
proc sort data=orion.order_fact out=order_sorted;
   by order_type;
run;
```

c. Restrict the PROC MEANS analysis.

```
proc means data=order_sorted;
   where order_type in (2,3);
   var Total_Retail_Price;
   title 'Orion Star Sales Summary';
run;
```

d. Modify the PROC MEANS step.

```
proc means data=order_sorted;
   by order_type;
   where order_type in (2,3);
   var Total_Retail_Price;
   title 'Orion Star Sales Summary';
run;
```

e. Submit the program.

11. Subsetting and Grouping by Multiple Variables

a. Retrieve the starter program.

b. Sort the data set.

```
proc sort data=orion.order_fact out=order_sorted;
   by Order_Type descending Order_Date;
run;
```

c. Divide the PROC PRINT report.

```
proc print data=order_sorted;
   by Order_Type;
   var Order_ID Order_Date Delivery_Date;
   title1 'Orion Star Sales Details';
run;
```

d. Limit the observations in the PROC PRINT report.

```
proc print data=order_sorted;
   by Order_Type;
   var Order_ID Order_Date Delivery_Date;
   where Delivery_Date - Order_Date = 2
     and Order_Date between '01jan2005'd and '30apr2005'd;
   title1 'Orion Star Sales Details';
run;
```

e. Add a second title.

```
proc print data=order_sorted;
   by Order_Type;
   var Order_ID Order_Date Delivery_Date;
   where Delivery_Date - Order_Date = 2
     and Order_Date between '01jan2005'd and '30apr2005'd;
   title1 'Orion Star Sales Details';
   title2 '2-Day Deliveries from January to April 2005';
run;
```

f. Submit the program.

12. Adding Subsetting Conditions

a. Retrieve the starter program.

b. Reorder the variables in the PROC PRINT step.

```
proc format;
   value $country
       "CA"="Canada"
       "DK"="Denmark"
       "ES"="Spain"
       "GB"="Great Britain"
       "NL"="Netherlands"
       "SE"="Sweden"
       "US"="United States";
run;

proc sort data=orion.shoe_vendors out=vendors_by_country;
   by Supplier_Country Supplier_Name;
run;

proc print data=vendors_by_country;
   where Product_Line=21;
   by Supplier_Name Supplier_ID Supplier_Country notsorted;
   var Product_ID Product_Name;
   title1 'Orion Star Products: Children Sports';
run;
```

c. Augment the existing WHERE criteria.

```
proc format;
   value $country
       "CA"="Canada"
       "DK"="Denmark"
       "ES"="Spain"
       "GB"="Great Britain"
       "NL"="Netherlands"
       "SE"="Sweden"
       "US"="United States";
run;

proc sort data=orion.shoe_vendors out=vendors_by_country;
   by Supplier_Country Supplier_Name;
run;

proc print data=vendors_by_country;
   where Product_Line=21;
   where same
      and Product_Name ? 'Street' or Product_Name ? 'Running';
   by Supplier_Name Supplier_ID Supplier_Country notsorted;
   var Product_ID Product_Name;
   title1 'Orion Star Products: Children Sports';
run;
```

d. Submit the program.

13. Directing Output to the PDF and RTF Destinations

a. Retrieve the starter program.

b. Create the PDF version of the PROC PRINT report.

```
ods pdf file='p111s13p.pdf';
proc print data=orion.customer;
   title 'Customer Information';
run;
ods pdf close;
```

For z/OS (OS/390), the following ODS PDF statement is used:

```
ods pdf file='.workshop.report(p111s13p)';
```

c. Submit the program.

d. Modify your ODS statements to create the RTF version of the PROC PRINT report.

```
ods rtf file='p111s13r.rtf';
proc print data=orion.customer;
   title 'Customer Information';
run;
ods rtf close;
```

For z/OS (OS/390), the following ODS RTF statement is used:

```
ods rtf file='.workshop.report(p111s13r)' rs=none;
```

e. Suppress the default Output window listing.

```
ods listing close;
ods rtf file='p111s13r.rtf';
proc print data=orion.customer;
   title 'Customer Information';
run;
ods rtf close;
ods listing;
```

f. Submit the program.

What happens if the RUN statement is moved to the end of the program?

The file is empty.

g. Add the STYLE= option.

```
ods listing close;
ods rtf file='p111s13r.rtf' style=curve;
proc print data=orion.customer;
   title 'Customer Information';
run;
ods rtf close;
ods listing;
```

h. Submit the program.

14. **Creating ODS Output Compatible with Microsoft Excel**

a. Retrieve the starter program.

b. Add ODS statements to send the report to a file that can be viewed in Microsoft Excel.

```
ods csvall file='p111s14.csv';
proc print data=orion.customer_type;
   title 'Customer Type Definitions';
run;

proc print data=orion.country;
   title 'Country Definitions';
run;
ods csvall close;
```

For z/OS (OS/390), the following ODS CSVALL statement is used:

```
ods csvall file='.workshop.report(p111s14)' rs=none;
```

```
ods msoffice2k file='p111s14.html' style=Listing;
proc print data=orion.customer_type;
   title 'Customer Type Definitions';
run;

proc print data=orion.country;
   title 'Country Definitions';
run;
ods msoffice2k close;
```

For z/OS (OS/390), the following ODS MSOFFICE2K statement is used:

```
ods msoffice2k file='.workshop.report(p111s14)' rs=none;
```

```
ods tagsets.excelxp file='p111s14.xml' style=Listing;
proc print data=orion.customer_type;
   title 'Customer Type Definitions';
run;

proc print data=orion.country;
   title 'Country Definitions';
run;
ods tagsets.excelxp close;
```

For z/OS (OS/390), the following ODS TAGSETS.EXCELXP statement is used:

```
ods tagsets.excelxp file='.workshop.report(p111s14)' rs=none;
```

   c. Submit the program.

   d. Open the file with Microsoft Excel.

15. Adding HTML-Specific Features to ODS Output

   a. Retrieve the starter program.

   b. Create the HTML version of the PROC PRINT report.

```
ods html file='p111s15.html';
proc print data=orion.customer;
   title 'Customer Information';
run;
ods html close;
```

For z/OS (OS/390), the following ODS HTML statement is used:

```
ods html file='.workshop.report(p111s15)' rs=none;
```

   c. Customize the title so that it becomes a clickable hyperlink.

```
ods html file='p111s15.html';
proc print data=orion.customer;
   title link='http://www.sas.com' 'Customer Information';
run;
ods html close;
```

   d. Submit the program.

16. Implementing Cascading Style Sheets with ODS Output

   a. Retrieve the starter program.

   b. Modify the ODS HTML statement.

```
ods html file='p111s16.html' stylesheet=(url='p111e16c.css');
proc print data=orion.customer_type;
   title 'Customer Type Definitions';
run;
ods html close;
```

For z/OS (OS/390), the following ODS HTML statement is used:

```
ods html file='.workshop.report(p111s16)' rs=none
         stylesheet=(url='.workshop.report(p111e16c)');
```

   c. Submit the program.

Solutions to Student Activities (Polls/Quizzes)

11.01 Poll – Correct Answer

Did the date and/or time change?

◉ Yes

○ No

The DTRESET option uses the current date and time versus SAS invocation date and time.

```
options date number pageno=1 ls=100 dtreset;
```

18   p111a01s

11.02 Quiz – Correct Answer

Which footnote(s) appears in the second procedure output?

a. | Non Sales Employees |

c. | Non Sales Employees
Confidential |

(b.) | Orion Star
Non Sales Employees |

d. | Orion Star
Non Sales Employees
Confidential |

```
footnote1 'Orion Star';
proc print data=orion.sales;
    footnote2 'Sales Employees';
    footnote3 'Confidential';
run;
proc print data=orion.nonsales;
    footnote2 'Non Sales Employees';
run;
```

38

11.03 Quiz – Correct Answer

Which statement is true concerning the
PROC PRINT output for **Bonus**?

a. Annual Bonus will be the label.
b. Mid-Year Bonus will be the label.

Temporary labels override permanent labels.

p111d05

11.04 Quiz – Correct Answer

Which displayed value is incorrect for the given format?

Format	Stored Value	Displayed Value
$3.	Wednesday	Wed
6.1	1234.345	1234.3
COMMAX5.	1234.345	1.234
DOLLAR9.2	1234.345	$1,234.35
DDMMYY8.	0	01/01/1960
DATE9.	0	01JAN1960
YEAR4.	0	1960

DDMMYY8. produces 01/01/60.

11.05 Multiple Answer Poll – Correct Answer

Which user-defined format names are invalid?

a. $stfmt
b. ⓑ $3levels
c. _4years
d. salranges
e. ⓔ dollar

Character formats must have a dollar sign as the first character and a letter or underscore as the second character.

User-defined formats cannot be the name of a SAS supplied format.

77

11.06 Quiz – Correct Answer

If you have a value of 99999.87, how will it be displayed if the TIERS format is applied to the value?

a. Tier 2
b. Tier 3
c. ⓒ 99999.87
d. a missing value

```
proc format;
   value tiers  20000-49999  = 'Tier 1'
                50000-99999  = 'Tier 2'
                100000-250000 = 'Tier 3';
run;
```

86

11.07 Quiz – Correct Answer

If you have a value of 100000, how will it be displayed
if the TIERS format is applied to the value?

(a.) Tier 2
b. Tier 3
c. 100000
d. a missing value

```
proc format;
   value tiers  20000-<50000  = 'Tier 1'
                50000- 100000 = 'Tier 2'
                100000<-250000 = 'Tier 3';
run;
```

90

11.08 Quiz – Correct Answer

Which of the following WHERE statements have
invalid syntax?

a. `where Salary ne .;`

b. `where Hire_Date >= '01APR2008'd;`

(c.) `where Country in (AU US);`

d. `where Salary + Bonus <= 10000;`

(e.) `where Gender ne 'M' Salary >= 50000;`

f. `where Name like '%N';`

105

11.09 Multiple Choice Poll – Correct Answer

Which statement is true concerning the multiple WHERE statements?

a. All the WHERE statements are used.

b. None of the WHERE statements are used.

c. The first WHERE statement is used.

d. The last WHERE statement is used.

```
1000  proc freq data=orion.sales;
1001     tables Gender;
1002     where Salary > 75000;
1003     where Country = 'US';
NOTE: Where clause has been replaced.
1004  run;

NOTE: There were 102 observations read from the data set
      ORION.SALES.
      WHERE Country='US';
```

111

11.10 Quiz – Correct Answer

Which is a valid BY statement for the PROC FREQ step?

a. `by Country Gender;`

b. `by Gender Last_Name;`

c. `by Country;`

d. `by Gender;`

```
proc sort data=orion.sales out=work.sort;
   by Country descending Gender Last_Name;
run;

proc freq data=work.sort;
   tables Gender;
run;
```

117

11.11 Quiz – Correct Answer

What is the problem with this program?

```
ods pdf file='myreport.pdf';

proc print data=orion.sales;
run;

ods pdf close;
```

134

11.12 Poll – Correct Answer

Did you notice a difference in the presentation aspects between the two style definitions?

O Yes
O No

The first group of style definitions did not use color.

The second group of style definitions did use color.

152

Chapter 12   Producing Summary Reports

12.1 Using the FREQ Procedure

Objectives

- Produce one-way and two-way frequency tables with the FREQ procedure.
- Enhance frequency tables with options.
- Produce output data sets by using the OUT= option in the TABLES and OUTPUT statements. (Self-Study)

3

The FREQ Procedure

The FREQ procedure can do the following:

- produce one-way to *n*-way frequency and crosstabulation (contingency) tables
- compute chi-square tests for one-way to *n*-way tables and measures of association and agreement for contingency tables
- automatically display the output in a report and save the output in a SAS data set

General form of the FREQ procedure:

```
PROC FREQ DATA=SAS-data-set <option(s)>;
    TABLES variable(s) </ option(s)>;
RUN;
```

4

The FREQ Procedure

A FREQ procedure with no TABLES statement generates one-way frequency tables for all data set variables.

```
proc freq data=orion.sales;
run;
```

This PROC FREQ step creates a frequency table for the following 9 variables:

- **Employee_ID**
- **First_Name**
- **Last_Name**
- **Gender**
- **Salary**
- **Job_Title**
- **Country**
- **Birth_Date**
- **Hire_Date**

5

p112d01

By default, PROC FREQ creates a report on every variable in the data set. For example, the **Employee_ID** report displays every unique value of **Employee_ID**, counts how many observations have each value, and provides percentages and cumulative statistics. This is not a useful report because each employee has his or her own unique employee ID.

You do not typically create frequency reports for variables with a large number of distinct values, such as **Employee_ID**, or for analysis variables, such as **Salary**. You usually create frequency reports for categorical variables, such as **Job_Title**. You can group variables into categories by creating and applying formats.

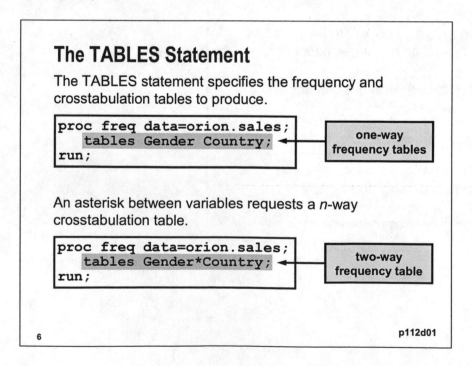

The TABLES Statement

The TABLES statement specifies the frequency and crosstabulation tables to produce.

```
proc freq data=orion.sales;
   tables Gender Country;
run;
```
one-way frequency tables

An asterisk between variables requests a *n*-way crosstabulation table.

```
proc freq data=orion.sales;
   tables Gender*Country;
run;
```
two-way frequency table

6

p112d01

The TABLES Statement

A one-way frequency table produces frequencies, cumulative frequencies, percentages, and cumulative percentages.

```
proc freq data=orion.sales;
   tables Gender Country;
run;
```

```
                        The FREQ Procedure

                                      Cumulative   Cumulative
   Gender    Frequency     Percent     Frequency      Percent

   F               68       41.21            68        41.21
   M               97       58.79           165       100.00


                                      Cumulative   Cumulative
   Country   Frequency     Percent     Frequency      Percent

   AU              63       38.18            63        38.18
   US             102       61.82           165       100.00
```

7

The TABLES Statement

An *n*-way frequency table produces cell frequencies, cell percentages, cell percentages of row frequencies, cell percentages of column frequencies, plus total frequency and percent.

```
proc freq data=orion.sales;
   tables Gender*Country;
run;
```

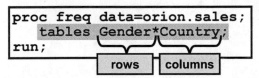

rows   columns

8

The TABLES Statement

```
                    The FREQ Procedure

                Table of Gender by Country

        Gender     Country

        Frequency|
        Percent  |
        Row Pct  |
        Col Pct  |AU      |US      |  Total

        F        |     27 |     41 |     68
                 |  16.36 |  24.85 |  41.21
                 |  39.71 |  60.29 |
                 |  42.86 |  40.20 |

        M        |     36 |     61 |     97
                 |  21.82 |  36.97 |  58.79
                 |  37.11 |  62.89 |
                 |  57.14 |  59.80 |

        Total          63      102      165
                    38.18    61.82   100.00
```

9

12.01 Multiple Choice Poll

Which of the following statements **cannot** be added
to the PROC FREQ step to enhance the report?

a. FORMAT

b. SET

c. TITLE

d. WHERE

11

Additional SAS Statements

Additional statements can be added to enhance the report.

```
proc format;
   value $ctryfmt 'AU'='Australia'
                  'US'='United States';
run;

options nodate pageno=1;

ods html file='p112d01.html';
proc freq data=orion.sales;
   tables Gender*Country;
   where Job_Title contains 'Rep';
   format Country $ctryfmt.;
   title 'Sales Rep Frequency Report';
run;
ods html close;
```

13   p112d01

Additional SAS Statements

HTML Output

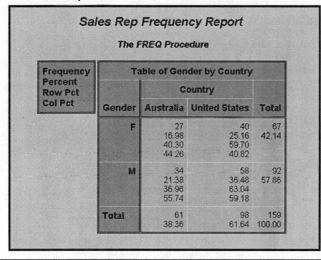

Frequency Percent Row Pct Col Pct	Table of Gender by Country		
	Country		
Gender	Australia	United States	Total
F	27 16.98 40.30 44.26	40 25.16 59.70 40.82	67 42.14
M	34 21.38 36.96 55.74	58 36.48 63.04 59.18	92 57.86
Total	61 38.36	98 61.64	159 100.00

14

Options to Suppress Display of Statistics

Options can be placed in the TABLES statement after a forward slash to suppress the display of the default statistics.

Option	Description
NOCUM	suppresses the display of cumulative frequency and cumulative percentage.
NOPERCENT	suppresses the display of percentage, cumulative percentage, and total percentage.
NOFREQ	suppresses the display of the cell frequency and total frequency.
NOROW	suppresses the display of the row percentage.
NOCOL	displays *n*-way tables in list format.

15

Options to Suppress Display of Statistics

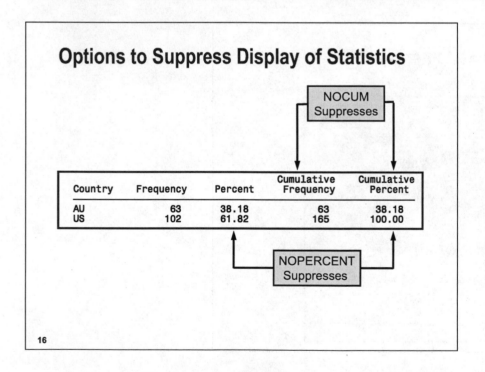

16

Options to Suppress Display of Statistics

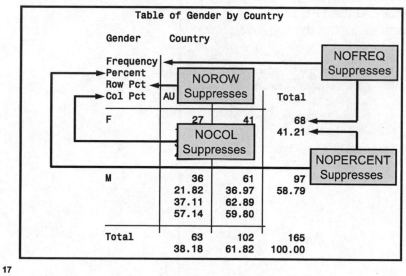

```
                    Table of Gender by Country

            Gender      Country

            Frequency ◄────────────────────  NOFREQ
            Percent                           Suppresses
            Row Pct ◄──── NOROW
            Col Pct   AU  Suppresses   Total

            F         27          41     68 ◄───
                                      41.21 ◄───
                      NOCOL
                      Suppresses           NOPERCENT
                                           Suppresses
            M         36          61     97
                   21.82       36.97  58.79
                   37.11       62.89
                   57.14       59.80

            Total     63         102    165
                   38.18       61.82 100.00
```

17

12.02 Quiz

Which TABLES statement correctly creates the report?

a. `tables Gender nocum;`

b. `tables Gender nocum nopercent;`

c. `tables Gender / nopercent;`

d. `tables Gender / nocum nopercent;`

```
            The FREQ Procedure

        Gender     Frequency

        F                 68
        M                 97
```

19   p112d01

Additional TABLES Statement Options

Additional options can be placed in the TABLES statement after a forward slash to control the displayed output.

Option	Description
LIST	displays *n*-way tables in list format.
CROSSLIST	displays *n*-way tables in column format.
FORMAT=	formats the frequencies in *n*-way tables.

21

LIST and CROSSLIST Options

```
                                         Cumulative  Cumulative
Gender  Country      Frequency   Percent  Frequency    Percent

F       Australia       27       16.36       27        16.36
F       United States   41       24.85       68        41.21
M       Australia       36
M       United States   61
```

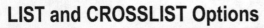

`tables Gender*Country / list;`

```
                    Table of Gender by Country

                                             Row      Column
Gender   Country     Frequency    Percent   Percent   Percent

F        Australia       27        16.36     39.71     42.86
         United States   41        24.85     60.29     40.20

         Total           68        41.21    100.00
---------------------------------------------------------------
M        Australia       36        21.82     37.11     57.14
         United States
```

`tables Gender*Country / crosslist;`

```
         Total           97
---------------------------------------------------------------
Total    Australia       63        38.18              100.00
         United States  102        61.82              100.00

         Total          165       100.00
```

p112d01

FORMAT= Option

Partial PROC FREQ Outputs

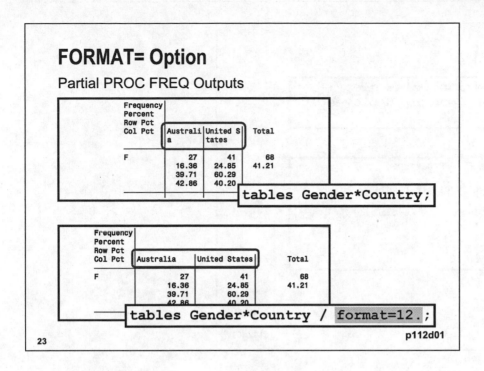

```
Frequency
Percent
Row Pct
Col Pct    Australi United S    Total
           a        tates

F                27        41        68
             16.36     24.85     41.21
             39.71     60.29
             42.86     40.20
```

tables Gender*Country;

```
Frequency
Percent
Row Pct
Col Pct    Australia    United States    Total

F                27              41        68
             16.36           24.85     41.21
             39.71           60.29
             42.86           40.20
```

tables Gender*Country / format=12.;

p112d01

23

PROC FREQ Statement Options

Options can also be placed in the PROC FREQ statement.

Option	Description
NLEVELS	displays a table that provides the number of levels for each variable named in the TABLES statement.
PAGE	displays only one table per page.
COMPRESS	begins the display of the next one-way frequency table on the same page as the preceding one-way table if there is enough space to begin the table.

24

NLEVELS Option

```
proc freq data=orion.sales nlevels;
    tables Gender Country Employee_ID;
run;
```

Partial PROC FREQ Output

```
              The FREQ Procedure

           Number of Variable Levels

           Variable         Levels

           Gender              2
           Country             2
           Employee_ID       165
```

25   p112d01

To display the number of levels without displaying the frequency counts, add the NOPRINT option to the TABLES statement.

```
proc freq data=orion.sales nlevels;
    tables Gender Country Employee_ID / noprint;
run;
```

To display the number of levels for all variables without displaying any frequency counts, use the _ALL_ keyword and the NOPRINT option in the TABLES statement.

```
proc freq data=orion.sales nlevels;
    tables _all_ / noprint;
run;
```

PAGE Option

```
proc freq data=orion.sales;
    tables Gender Country Employee_ID;
run;
```

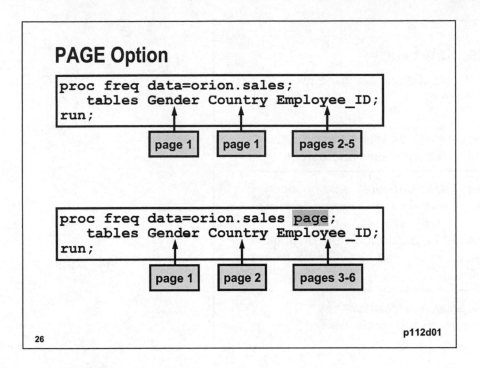

```
proc freq data=orion.sales page;
    tables Gender Country Employee_ID;
run;
```

26   p112d01

COMPRESS Option

```
proc freq data=orion.sales;
    tables Gender Country Employee_ID;
run;
```

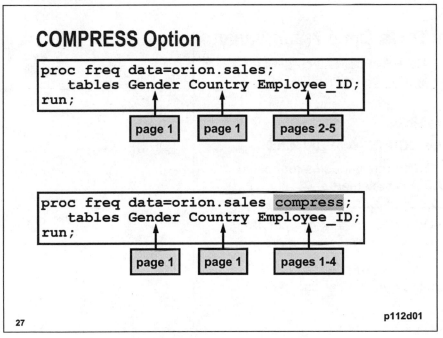

```
proc freq data=orion.sales compress;
    tables Gender Country Employee_ID;
run;
```

27   p112d01

Output Data Sets (Self-Study)

PROC FREQ produces output data sets using two
different methods.

- The TABLES statement with an OUT= option is used
  to create a data set with frequencies and percentages.

  TABLES *variables* **/ OUT=***SAS-data-set* *<options>*;

- The OUTPUT statement with an OUT= option is used
  to create a data set with specified statistics such as
  the chi-square statistic.

  OUTPUT OUT=*SAS-data-set* *<options>*;

29

TABLES Statement OUT= Option (Self-Study)

The OUT= option in the TABLES statement creates an
output data set with the following variables:

- BY variables
- TABLES statement variables
- the automatic variables **COUNT** and **PERCENT**
- other frequency and percentage variables requested
  with options in the TABLES statement

  TABLES *variables* **/ OUT=***SAS-data-set* *<options>*;

If more than one table request appears in the TABLES
statement, the contents of the data set correspond to the
last table request.

30

TABLES Statement OUT= Option (Self-Study)

```
proc freq data=orion.sales noprint;
   tables Gender Country / out=work.freq1;
run;

proc print data=work.freq1;
run;
```

PROC PRINT Output

Obs	Country	COUNT	PERCENT
1	AU	63	38.1818
2	US	102	61.8182

The NOPRINT option suppresses the display of all output.

31   p112d02

TABLES Statement OUT= Option (Self-Study)

```
proc freq data=orion.sales noprint;
   tables Gender*Country / out=work.freq2;
run;

proc print data=work.freq2;
run;
```

PROC PRINT Output

Obs	Gender	Country	COUNT	PERCENT
1	F	AU	27	16.3636
2	F	US	41	24.8485
3	M	AU	36	21.8182
4	M	US	61	36.9697

32   p112d02

TABLES Statement OUT= Option (Self-Study)

Options can be added to the TABLES statement after the forward slash to control the additional statistics added to the output data set.

Option	Description
OUTCUM	includes the cumulative frequency and cumulative percentage in the output data set for one-way frequency tables.
OUTPCT	includes the percentage of column frequency and row frequency in the output data set for *n*-way frequency tables.

33

TABLES Statement OUT= Option (Self-Study)

```
proc freq data=orion.sales noprint;
   tables Gender Country / out=work.freq3
                           outcum;
run;

proc print data=work.freq3;
run;
```

PROC PRINT Output

Obs	Country	COUNT	PERCENT	CUM_FREQ	CUM_PCT
1	AU	63	38.1818	63	38.182
2	US	102	61.8182	165	100.000

34   p112d02

TABLES Statement OUT= Option (Self-Study)

```
proc freq data=orion.sales noprint;
    tables Gender*Country / out=work.freq4
                            outpct;
run;

proc print data=work.freq4;
run;
```

PROC PRINT Output

Obs	Gender	Country	COUNT	PERCENT	PCT_ROW	PCT_COL
1	F	AU	27	16.3636	39.7059	42.8571
2	F	US	41	24.8485	60.2941	40.1961
3	M	AU	36	21.8182	37.1134	57.1429
4	M	US	61	36.9697	62.8866	59.8039

35   p112d02

OUTPUT Statement OUT= Option (Self-Study)

The OUT= option on the OUTPUT statement creates an output data set with the following variables:

- BY variables
- the variables requested in the TABLES statement
- variables that contain the specified statistics.

> **OUTPUT OUT=**SAS-data-set <options>;

If more than one table request appears in the TABLES statement, the contents of the data set correspond to the last table request.

36

If there are multiple TABLES statements, the contents of the data set corresponds to the last TABLES statement.

OUTPUT Statement OUT= Option (Self-Study)

In order to specify that the output data set contain a
particular statistic, you must have PROC FREQ compute
the statistic by using the corresponding option in the
TABLES statement.

```
proc freq data=orion.sales;
   tables Country / chisq;
   output out=work.freq5 chisq;
run;

proc print data=work.freq5;
run;
```

CHISQ requests chi-square tests and measures of
association based on chi-square.

37   p112d03

OUTPUT Statement OUT= Option (Self-Study)

PROC FREQ Output

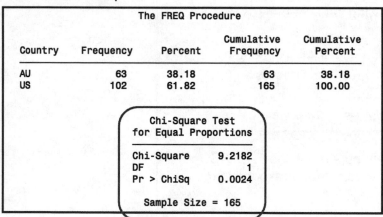

```
                    The FREQ Procedure

                                  Cumulative   Cumulative
Country   Frequency   Percent     Frequency    Percent

AU            63       38.18           63        38.18
US           102       61.82          165       100.00


                 Chi-Square Test
                for Equal Proportions

                Chi-Square     9.2182
                DF                  1
                Pr > ChiSq     0.0024

                Sample Size = 165
```

38

OUTPUT Statement OUT= Option (Self-Study)

PROC PRINT Output

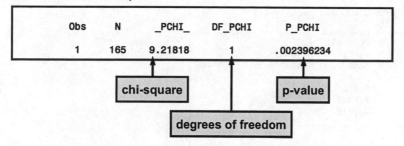

Obs	N	_PCHI_	DF_PCHI	P_PCHI
1	165	9.21818	1	.002396234

When you request a statistic, the OUTPUT data set contains that test statistic plus any associated standard error, confidence limits, p-values, and degrees of freedom.

39

12.03 Quiz

- Retrieve and submit program **p112a01**.

```
proc freq data=orion.sales;
   tables Gender / chisq out=freq6 outcum;
   output out=freq7 chisq;
run;
proc print data=freq6;
run;
proc print data=freq7;
run;
```

- Review the PROC FREQ output.
- Review the PROC PRINT output from the TABLES statement OUT= option.
- Review the PROC PRINT output from the OUTPUT statement OUT= option.

41

Output Data Sets (Self-Study)

Program **p112d04** is an example of combining multiple PROC FREQ output data sets into one data set.

Obs	Value	Frequency Count	Percent of Total Frequency	Chi-Square	P-Value
1	F	68	41.2121	.	.
2	M	97	58.7879	.	.
3	AU	63	38.1818	.	.
4	US	102	61.8182	.	.
5	Gender	.	.	5.09697	0.023968
6	Country	.	.	9.21818	0.002396

43

 **Exercises**

Level 1

1. **Counting Levels of a Variable with PROC FREQ**

   a. Retrieve the starter program **p112e01**.

   b. Modify the program to produce two separate reports:

   1) Display the number of distinct levels of **Customer_ID** and **Employee_ID** for retail orders.

      a) Use a WHERE statement to limit the report to retail sales by specifying the condition **Order_Type=1**.

      b) Display this report title: Unique Customers and Salespersons for Retail Sales.

         🖊 If you do not want to see the counts for individual levels of **Customer_ID** and **Employee_ID**, add the NOPRINT option to the TABLES statement after a forward slash.

   2) Display the number of distinct levels for **Customer_ID** for catalog and Internet orders.

      a) Use a WHERE statement to limit the report to catalog and Internet sales by specifying the condition corresponding to **Order_Type** values other than 1.

      b) Display this report title: Unique Customers for Catalog and Internet.

         🖊 If you do not want to see the counts for individual levels of **Customer_ID**, add the NOPRINT option to the TABLES statement after a forward slash.

c. Submit the program to produce the following reports:

PROC FREQ Output

```
           Unique Customers and Salespersons for Retail Sales

                            The FREQ Procedure

                        Number of Variable Levels

            Variable       Label                Levels

            Customer_ID    Customer ID             31
            Employee_ID    Employee ID            100
```

```
          Unique Customers for Catalog and Internet Sales

                           The FREQ Procedure

                       Number of Variable Levels

           Variable       Label               Levels

           Customer_ID    Customer ID            63
```

Level 2

2. Producing Frequency Reports with PROC FREQ

a. Retrieve the starter program **p112e02**.

b. Add TABLES statements to the PROC FREQ step to produce three frequency reports:

1) Number of orders in each year. Apply the YEAR4. format to the **Order_Date** variable to combine all orders within the same year.

2) Number of orders of each order type. Apply the **ordertypes.** format defined in the starter program to the **Order_Type** variable. Suppress the cumulative frequency and percentages.

3) Number of orders for each combination of year and order type. Suppress all percentages that normally appear in each cell of an *n*-way table.

c. Submit the program to produce the following output:

PROC FREQ Output

```
                        Order Summary by Year and Type

                            The FREQ Procedure

                      Date Order was placed by Customer

                                          Cumulative    Cumulative
      Order_Date    Frequency    Percent    Frequency      Percent
      ─────────────────────────────────────────────────────────────
          2003         104        21.22        104         21.22
          2004          87        17.76        191         38.98
          2005          70        14.29        261         53.27
          2006         113        23.06        374         76.33
          2007         116        23.67        490        100.00


                                Order Type

                 Order_
                  Type     Frequency      Percent
                 ─────────────────────────────────
                 Retail       260          53.06
                 Catalog      132          26.94
                 Internet      98          20.00


                    Table of Order_Date by Order_Type

          Order_Date(Date Order was placed by Customer)
                     Order_Type(Order Type)
```

Frequency	Retail	Catalog	Internet	Total
2003	45	41	18	104
2004	51	20	16	87
2005	27	23	20	70
2006	67	33	13	113
2007	70	15	31	116
Total	260	132	98	490

Level 3

3. Displaying PROC FREQ Output in Descending Frequency Order

   a. Retrieve the starter program **p112e03**.

   b. Submit the program to produce the following report:

PROC FREQ Output

```
                      Customer Demographics

                (Top two levels for each variable?)

                      The FREQ Procedure

                      Customer Country

   Customer_                          Cumulative      Cumulative
   Country     Frequency    Percent   Frequency        Percent
   ─────────────────────────────────────────────────────────────
   AU               8       10.39          8           10.39
   CA              15       19.48         23           29.87
   DE              10       12.99         33           42.86
   IL               5        6.49         38           49.35
   TR               7        9.09         45           58.44
   US              28       36.36         73           94.81
   ZA               4        5.19         77          100.00


                      Customer Type Name

                                                Cumulative      Cumulative
   Customer_Type                  Frequency    Percent  Frequency        Percent
   ─────────────────────────────────────────────────────────────────────────────
   Internet/Catalog Customers          8       10.39          8           10.39
   Orion  Club members high activity   11      14.29         19           24.68
   Orion  Club members medium activity 20      25.97         39           50.65
   Orion Club Gold members high activity 10     12.99        49           63.64
   Orion Club Gold members low activity  5       6.49        54           70.13
   Orion Club Gold members medium activity 6     7.79        60           77.92
   Orion Club members low activity      17      22.08         77          100.00


                      Customer Age Group

   Customer_                          Cumulative      Cumulative
   Age_Group   Frequency    Percent   Frequency        Percent
   ─────────────────────────────────────────────────────────────
   15-30 years     22       28.57         22           28.57
   31-45 years     27       35.06         49           63.64
   46-60 years     14       18.18         63           81.82
   61-75 years     14       18.18         77          100.00
```

   c. What are the two most common values for each variable?

      1) Country   _____   _____

      2) Customer Type   _____   _____

      3) Customer Age Group   _____   _____

   d. Modify the program to display the frequency counts in descending order.

> 🖋 Documentation on the FREQ procedure can be found in the SAS Help and Documentation from the Contents tab (**SAS Products** ⇨ **Base SAS** ⇨ **Base SAS Procedures Guide: Statistical Procedures** ⇨ **The FREQ Procedure**). Look for an option in the PROC FREQ statement that can perform the requested action.

   e. Submit the modified program.

   f. What are the two most common values for each variable?

      1) Country   _____   _____

      2) Customer Type   _____   _____

      3) Customer Age Group   _____   _____

     Do these answers match the previous set of answers?

     Which report was easier to use to answer the questions correctly?

4. Creating an Output Data Set with PROC FREQ

   a. Retrieve the starter program **p112e04**.

   b. Create an output data set containing the frequency counts based on **Product_ID**.

> 🖋 Creating an output data set from PROC FREQ results is discussed in the self-study content at the end of this section.

   c. Combine the output data set with **orion.product_list** to obtain the **Product_Name** value for each **Product_ID** code.

   d. Sort the merged data so that the most frequently ordered products appear at the top of the resulting data set. Print the first 10 observations, those that represent the ten products ordered most often.

> 🖋 To limit the number of observations displayed by PROC PRINT, apply the OBS= data set option, as in **proc print data=work.mydataset(obs=10);**.

e. Submit the program to produce the following report:

PROC PRINT Output

```
                        Top Ten Products by Number of Orders

                                Product
              Obs    Orders     Number    Product

               1       6      230100500056   Knife
               2       6      230100600030   Outback Sleeping Bag, Large,Left,Blue/Black
               3       5      230100600022   Expedition10,Medium,Right,Blue Ribbon
               4       5      240400300035   Smasher Shorts
               5       4      230100500082   Lucky Tech Intergal Wp/B Rain Pants
               6       4      230100600005   Basic 10, Left , Yellow/Black
               7       4      230100600016   Expedition Zero,Medium,Right,Charcoal
               8       4      230100600028   Expedition 20,Medium,Right,Forestgreen
               9       4      230100700008   Family Holiday 4
              10       4      230100700011   Hurricane 4
```

12.2 Using the MEANS Procedure

Objectives

- Calculate summary statistics and multilevel summaries with the MEANS procedure.
- Enhance summary tables with options.
- Produce output data sets by using the OUT= option in the OUTPUT statement. (Self-Study)
- Compare the SUMMARY procedure to the MEANS procedure. (Self-Study)

47

The MEANS Procedure

The MEANS procedure provides data summarization tools to compute descriptive statistics for variables across all observations and within groups of observations.

General form of the MEANS procedure:

```
PROC MEANS DATA=SAS-data-set <statistic(s)> <option(s)>;
    VAR analysis-variable(s);
    CLASS classification-variable(s);
RUN;
```

48

The MEANS Procedure

By default, the MEANS procedure reports the number of non-missing observations, the mean, the standard deviation, the minimum value, and the maximum value of all numeric variables.

```
proc means data=orion.sales;
run;
```

```
                         The MEANS Procedure

Variable       N         Mean       Std Dev       Minimum       Maximum
Employee_ID   165   120713.90   450.0866939    120102.00    121145.00
Salary        165    31160.12      20082.67     22710.00    243190.00
Birth_Date    165     3622.58       5456.29     -5842.00     10490.00
Hire_Date     165    12054.28       4619.94      5114.00     17167.00
```

49   p112d05

The VAR Statement

The VAR statement identifies the analysis variables and their order in the results.

```
proc means data=orion.sales;
    var Salary;
run;
```

```
                    The MEANS Procedure

                 Analysis Variable : Salary

    N        Mean       Std Dev      Minimum      Maximum
  165    31160.12      20082.67     22710.00    243190.00
```

50   p112d05

The CLASS Statement

The CLASS statement identifies variables whose values define subgroups for the analysis.

```
proc means data=orion.sales;
   var Salary;
   class Gender Country;
run;
```

```
                        The MEANS Procedure

                     Analysis Variable : Salary

                   N
Gender   Country   Obs    N     Mean      Std Dev     Minimum      Maximum

F        AU        27    27    27702.41    1728.23    25185.00     30890.00

         US        41    41    29460.98    8847.03    25390.00     83505.00

M        AU        36    36    32001.39   16592.45    25745.00    108255.00

         US        61    61    33336.15   29592.69    22710.00    243190.00
```

51   p112d05

The CLASS Statement

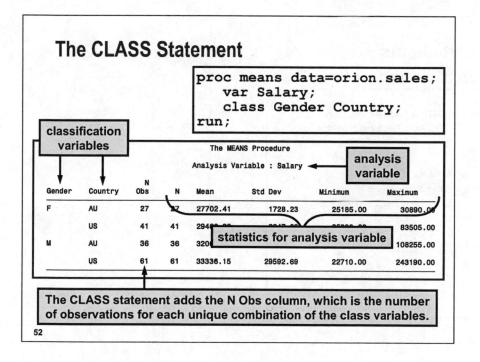

```
proc means data=orion.sales;
   var Salary;
   class Gender Country;
run;
```

classification variables

```
                        The MEANS Procedure

                     Analysis Variable : Salary
```

analysis variable

```
                   N
Gender   Country   Obs    N     Mean      Std Dev     Minimum      Maximum

F        AU        27    27    27702.41    1728.23    25185.00     30890.00

         US        41    41    294                               83505.00

M        AU        36    36    320                              108255.00

         US        61    61    33336.15   29592.69    22710.00    243190.00
```

statistics for analysis variable

The CLASS statement adds the N Obs column, which is the number of observations for each unique combination of the class variables.

52

12.04 Quiz

For a given data set, there are 63 observation with
a **Country** value of AU. Of those 63 observations,
only 61 observations have a value for **Salary**.

Which output is correct?

a.

```
Analysis Variable : Salary

                  N
Country    Obs        N

AU          63       61
```

b.

```
Analysis Variable : Salary

                  N
Country    Obs        N

AU          61       63
```

54

Additional SAS Statements

Additional statements can be added to enhance the reports.

```
proc format;
    value $ctryfmt 'AU'='Australia'
                   'US'='United States';
run;

options nodate pageno=1;
ods html file='p112d05.html';
proc means data=orion.sales;
    var Salary;
    class Gender Country;
    where Job_Title contains 'Rep';
    format Country $ctryfmt.;
    title 'Sales Rep Summary Report';
run;
ods html close;
```

56   p112d05

Additional SAS Statements

HTML Output

Sales Rep Summary Report

The MEANS Procedure

Analysis Variable : Salary							
Gender	Country	N Obs	N	Mean	Std Dev	Minimum	Maximum
F	Australia	27	27	27702.41	1728.23	25185.00	30890.00
	United States	40	40	28109.88	1874.39	25390.00	32985.00
M	Australia	34	34	28112.35	2205.81	25745.00	36605.00
	United States	58	58	27775.26	2311.91	22710.00	35990.00

57

PROC MEANS Statistics

The statistics to compute and the order to display them can be specified in the PROC MEANS statement.

```
proc means data=orion.sales sum mean range;
   var Salary;
   class Country;
run;
```

```
                    The MEANS Procedure

                 Analysis Variable : Salary

                N
   Country     Obs            Sum            Mean           Range

   AU           63      1900015.00        30158.97        83070.00

   US          102      3241405.00        31778.48       220480.00
```

p112d05

58

PROC MEANS Statistics

Descriptive Statistic Keywords				
CLM	CSS	CV	LCLM	MAX
MEAN	MIN	MODE	N	NMISS
KURTOSIS	RANGE	SKEWNESS	STDDEV	STDERR
SUM	SUMWGT	UCLM	USS	VAR

Quantile Statistic Keywords				
MEDIAN | P50	P1	P5	P10	Q1 | P25
Q3 | P75	P90	P95	P99	QRANGE

Hypothesis Testing Keywords	
PROBT	T

59

PROC MEANS Statement Options

Options can also be placed in the PROC MEANS statement.

Option	Description
MAXDEC=	specifies the number of decimal places to use in printing the statistics.
FW=	specifies the field width to use in displaying the statistics.
NONOBS	suppresses reporting the total number of observations for each unique combination of the class variables.

60

MAXDEC= Option

```
proc means data=orion.sales maxdec=0;
```

```
                      Analysis Variable : Salary

               N
Country      Obs      N       Mean     Std Dev    Minimum    Maximum

AU            63      63      30159      12699      25185     108255

US           102     102      31778      23556      22710     243190
```

```
proc means data=orion.sales maxdec=1;
```

```
                      Analysis Variable : Salary

               N
Country      Obs      N       Mean     Std Dev    Minimum    Maximum

AU            63      63     30159.0    12699.1    25185.0   108255.0

US           102     102    31778.5    23555.8    22710.0   243190.0
```

p112d05

FW= Option

```
proc means data=orion.sales;
```

```
                      Analysis Variable : Salary

               N
Country      Obs      N       Mean     Std Dev    Minimum    Maximum

AU            63      63    30158.97    12699.14   25185.00  108255.00

US           102     102   31778.48    23555.84   22710.00  243190.00
```

```
proc means data=orion.sales fw=15;
```

```
                      Analysis Variable : Salary

               N
Country      Obs      N         Mean          Std Dev          Minimum         Maximum

AU            63      63   30158.96825397   12699.13932690   25185.00000000      108255

US           102     102  31778.48039216   23555.84171928   22710.00000000      243190
```

p112d05

NONOBS Option

```
proc means data=orion.sales;
```

Analysis Variable : Salary

Country	N Obs	N	Mean	Std Dev	Minimum	Maximum
AU	63	63	30158.97	12699.14	25185.00	108255.00
US	102	102	31778.48	23555.84	22710.00	243190.00

```
proc means data=orion.sales nonobs;
```

Analysis Variable : Salary

Country	N	Mean	Std Dev	Minimum	Maximum
AU	63	30158.97	12699.14	25185.00	108255.00
US	102	31778.48	23555.84	22710.00	243190.00

63   p112d05

Output Data Sets (Self-Study)

PROC MEANS produces output data sets using the following method:

OUTPUT OUT=_SAS-data-set <options>_**;**

The output data set contains the following variables:
- BY variables
- class variables
- the automatic variables **_TYPE_** and **_FREQ_**
- the variables requested in the OUTPUT statement

65

OUTPUT Statement OUT= Option (Self-Study)

> The statistics in the PROC statement impact only the MEANS report, not the data set.

```
proc means data=orion.sales sum mean range;
   var Salary;
   class Gender Country;
   output out=work.means1;
run;

proc print data=work.means1;
run;
```

66   p112d06

OUTPUT Statement OUT= Option (Self-Study)

Partial PROC PRINT Output

Obs	Gender	Country	_TYPE_	_FREQ_	_STAT_	Salary
1			0	165	N	165.00
2			0	165	MIN	22710.00
3			0	165	MAX	243190.00
4			0	165	MEAN	31160.12
5			0	165	STD	20082.67
6		AU	1	63	N	63.00
7					MIN	25185.00
8					MAX	108255.00
9		AU	1	63	MEAN	30158.97
10		AU	1	63	STD	12699.14
11		US	1	102	N	102.00
12		US	1	102	MIN	22710.00
13		US	1	102	MAX	243190.00
14		US	1	102	MEAN	31778.48
15		US	1	102	STD	23555.84
16	F		2	68	N	68.00
17	F		2	68	MIN	25185.00
18	F		2	68	MAX	83505.00
19	F		2	68	MEAN	28762.72
20	F		2	68	STD	6974.15

default statistics

67

OUTPUT Statement OUT= Option (Self-Study)

The OUTPUT statement can also do the following:

- specify the statistics for the output data set
- select and name variables

```
proc means data=orion.sales noprint;
   var Salary;
   class Gender Country;
   output out=work.means2
          min=minSalary max=maxSalary
          sum=sumSalary mean=aveSalary;
run;

proc print data=work.means2;
run;
```

The NOPRINT option suppresses the display of all output.

68   p112d06

OUTPUT Statement OUT= Option (Self-Study)

PROC PRINT Output

Obs	Gender	Country	_TYPE_	_FREQ_	min Salary	max Salary	sum Salary	ave Salary
1			0	165	22710	243190	5141420	31160.12
2		AU	1	63	25185	108255	1900015	30158.97
3		US	1	102	22710	243190	3241405	31778.48
4	F		2	68	25185	83505	1955865	28762.72
5	M		2	97	22710	243190	3185555	32840.77
6	F	AU	3	27	25185	30890	747965	27702.41
7	F	US	3	41	25390	83505	1207900	29460.98
8	M	AU	3	36	25745	108255	1152050	32001.39
9	M	US	3	61	22710	243190	2033505	33336.15

69

OUTPUT Statement OUT= Option (Self-Study)

TYPE is a numeric variable that shows which combination of class variables produced the summary statistics in that observation.

PROC PRINT Output

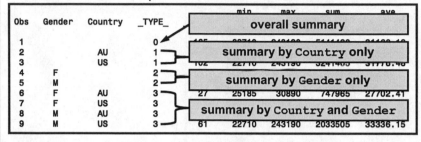

Obs	Gender	Country	_TYPE_				
				min	max	sum	ave
1			0				
2		AU	1				
3		US	1	102	22710	243190	31770.48
4	F		2				
5	M		2				
6	F	AU	3	27	25185	30890	27702.41
7	F	US	3				
8	M	AU	3				
9	M	US	3	61	22710	243190	2033505	33336.15

overall summary

summary by Country only

summary by Gender only

summary by Country and Gender

70

OUTPUT Statement OUT= Option (Self-Study)

Obs	Gender	Country	_TYPE_	_FREQ_	min Salary	max Salary	sum Salary	ave Salary
1			0	165	22710	243190	5141420	31160.12
2		AU	1	63	25185	108255	1900015	30158.97
3		US	1	102	22710	243190	3241405	31778.48
4	F		2	68	25185	83505	1955865	28762.72
5	M		2	97	22710	243190	3185555	32840.77
6	F	AU	3	27	25185	30890	747965	27702.41
7	F	US	3	41	25390	83505	1207900	29460.98
8	M	AU	3	36	25745	108255	1152050	32001.39
9	M	US	3	61	22710	243190	2033505	33336.15

TYPE	Type of Summary	_FREQ_
0	overall summary	165
1	summary by Country only	63 AU + 102 AU = 165
2	summary by Gender only	68 F + 97 M = 165
3	summary by Country and Gender	27 F AU + 41 F US + 36 M AU + 61 M US = 165

71

OUTPUT Statement OUT= Option (Self-Study)

Options can be added to the PROC MEANS statement to control the output data set.

Option	Description
NWAY	specifies that the output data set contain only statistics for the observations with the highest **_TYPE_** value.
DESCENDTYPES	orders the output data set by descending **_TYPE_** value.
CHARTYPE	specifies that the **_TYPE_** variable in the output data set is a character representation of the binary value of **_TYPE_**.

72

OUTPUT Statement OUT= Option (Self-Study)

without options

Obs	Gender	Country	_TYPE_	_FREQ_	min Salary	max Salary	sum Salary	ave Salary
1			0	165	22710	243190	5141420	31160.12
2		AU	1	63	25185	108255	1900015	30158.97
3		US	1	102	22710	243190	3241405	31778.48
4	F		2	68	25185	83505	1955865	28762.72
5	M		2	97	22710	243190	3185555	32840.77
6	F	AU	3	27	25185	30890	747965	27702.41
7	F	US	3	41	25390	83505	1207900	29460.98
8	M	AU	3	36	25745	108255	1152050	32001.39
9	M	US	3	61	22710	243190	2033505	33336.15

with NWAY

Obs	Gender	Country	_TYPE_	_FREQ_	min Salary	max Salary	sum Salary	ave Salary
1	F	AU	3	27	25185	30890	747965	27702.41
2	F	US	3	41	25390	83505	1207900	29460.98
3	M	AU	3	36	25745	108255	1152050	32001.39
4	M	US	3	61	22710	243190	2033505	33336.15

73   p112d06

OUTPUT Statement OUT= Option (Self-Study)

with DESCENDTYPES

Obs	Gender	Country	_TYPE_	_FREQ_	min Salary	max Salary	sum Salary	ave Salary
1	F	AU	3	27	25185	30890	747965	27702.41
2	F	US	3	41	25390	83505	1207900	29460.98
3	M	AU	3	36	25745	108255	1152050	32001.39
4	M	US	3	61	22710	243190	2033505	33336.15
5	F		2	68	25185	83505	1955865	28762.72
6	M		2	97	22710	243190	3185555	32840.77
7		AU	1	63	25185	108255	1900015	30158.97
8		US	1	102	22710	243190	3241405	31778.48
9			0	165	22710	243190	5141420	31160.12

74   p112d06

OUTPUT Statement OUT= Option (Self-Study)

with CHARTYPE

Obs	Gender	Country	_TYPE_	_FREQ_	min Salary	max Salary	sum Salary	ave Salary
1			00	165	22710	243190	5141420	31160.12
2		AU	01	63	25185	108255	1900015	30158.97
3		US	01	102	22710	243190	3241405	31778.48
4	F		10	68	25185	83505	1955865	28762.72
5	M		10	97	22710	243190	3185555	32840.77
6	F	AU	11	27	25185	30890	747965	27702.41
7	F	US	11	41	25390	83505	1207900	29460.98
8	M	AU	11	36	25745	108255	1152050	32001.39
9	M	US	11	61	22710	243190	2033505	33336.15

75   p112d06

12.05 Quiz

- Retrieve and submit program **p112a02**.
- Review the PROC PRINT output.
- Add a WHERE statement to the PROC PRINT step to subset **_TYPE_** for observations summarized by **Gender** only.
- Submit the program and verify the results.

77

OUTPUT Statement OUT= Option (Self-Study)

Program **p112d07** is an example of merging a PROC MEANS output data set with a detail data set to create the following partial report.

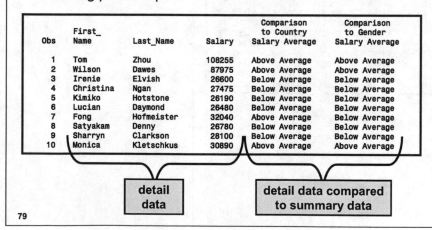

Obs	First_Name	Last_Name	Salary	Comparison to Country Salary Average	Comparison to Gender Salary Average
1	Tom	Zhou	108255	Above Average	Above Average
2	Wilson	Dawes	87975	Above Average	Above Average
3	Irenie	Elvish	26600	Below Average	Below Average
4	Christina	Ngan	27475	Below Average	Below Average
5	Kimiko	Hotstone	26190	Below Average	Below Average
6	Lucian	Daymond	26480	Below Average	Below Average
7	Fong	Hofmeister	32040	Above Average	Below Average
8	Satyakam	Denny	26780	Below Average	Below Average
9	Sharryn	Clarkson	28100	Below Average	Below Average
10	Monica	Kletschkus	30890	Above Average	Above Average

detail data

detail data compared to summary data

79

The SUMMARY Procedure (Self-Study)

The SUMMARY procedure provides data summarization tools to compute descriptive statistics for variables across all observations and within groups of observations.

General form of the SUMMARY procedure:

PROC SUMMARY DATA=_SAS-data-set_ _<statistic(s)>_
<option(s)>**;**

    VAR _analysis-variable(s)_**;**
    CLASS _classification-variable(s)_**;**
RUN;

80

The SUMMARY Procedure (Self-Study)

The SUMMARY procedure uses the same syntax as the MEANS procedure.

The only differences to the two procedures are the following:

PROC MEANS	PROC SUMMARY
The PRINT option is set by default, which displays output.	The NOPRINT option is set by default, which displays no output.
Omitting the VAR statement analyzes all the numeric variables.	Omitting the VAR statement produces a simple count of observations.

81

 **Exercises**

Level 1

5. Creating a Summary Report with PROC MEANS

   a. Retrieve the starter program **p112e05**.

   b. Display only the SUM statistic for the **Total_Retail_Price** variable.

   c. Display separate statistics for combination of **Order_Date** and **Order_Type**. Apply the **ordertypes.** format so that the order types are displayed as text descriptions, not numbers. Apply the YEAR4. format so that order dates are displayed as years, not individual dates.

   d. Submit the program to produce the following report:

Partial PROC MEANS Output

```
                 Revenue (in U.S. Dollars) Earned from All Orders

                            The MEANS Procedure

        Analysis Variable : Total_Retail_Price Total Retail Price for This Product

              Date
             Order
               was
            placed
                by    Order         N
          Customer    Type        Obs          Sum
         ─────────────────────────────────────────────
              2003    Retail       53       7938.80

                      Catalog      52      10668.08

                      Internet     23       4124.05

              2004    Retail       63       9012.22

                      Catalog      23       3494.60

                      Internet     22       3275.70

              2005    Retail       34       5651.29

                      Catalog      33       6569.98

                      Internet     23       4626.40
```

Level 2

6. Analyzing Missing Numeric Values with PROC MEANS

   a. Retrieve the starter program **p112e06**.

   b. Display the number of missing values and the number of non-missing values present in the **Birth_Date**, **Emp_Hire_Date**, and **Emp_Term_Date** variables.

   c. Suppress any decimal places in the displayed statistics.

   d. Display separate statistics for each value of **Gender**.

   e. Suppress the output column that displays the total number of observations in each classification group.

   f. Submit the program to produce the following report:

   PROC MEANS Output

```
                  Number of Missing and Non-Missing Date Values

                                The MEANS Procedure

       Employee                                                    N
       Gender     Variable       Label                          Miss     N
       ──────────────────────────────────────────────────────────────────────
       F          Birth_Date     Employee Birth Date               0    191
                  Emp_Hire_Date  Employee Hire Date                0    191
                  Emp_Term_Date  Employee Termination Date       139     52

       M          Birth_Date     Employee Birth Date               0    233
                  Emp_Hire_Date  Employee Hire Date                0    233
                  Emp_Term_Date  Employee Termination Date       169     64
       ──────────────────────────────────────────────────────────────────────
```

Level 3

7. Analyzing All Possible Classification Levels with PROC MEANS

   a. Retrieve the starter program **p112e07**.

   b. Display the following statistics in the report:

   1) Lower Confidence Limit for the Mean

   2) Mean

   3) Upper Confidence Limit for the Mean

   c. Change the α value for the confidence limits to 0.10, resulting in a 90% confidence limit.

d. All countries stored in the **work.countries** data set should be displayed in the report, even if there are no customers from that country.

> Documentation on the MEANS procedure can be found in the SAS Help and Documentation from the Contents tab (**SAS Products** ⇨ **Base SAS** ⇨ **Base SAS 9.2 Procedures Guide** ⇨ **Procedures** ⇨ **The MEANS Procedure**). Look for options in the PROC MEANS statement that can perform the requested actions.

e. Submit the program to produce the following report:

PROC MEANS Output

```
                    Average Age of Customers in Each Country

                              The MEANS Procedure

                    Analysis Variable : Customer_Age Customer Age

        Customer      N      Lower 90%                       Upper 90%
        Country      Obs     CL for Mean        Mean         CL for Mean

        AU            8      42.4983854      52.3750000      62.2516146

        BE            0           .               .               .

        CA           15      31.2270622      40.0000000      48.7729378

        DE           10      35.2564025      46.6000000      57.9435975

        DK            0           .               .               .

        ES            0           .               .               .

        FR            0           .               .               .

        GB            0           .               .               .

        IL            5      30.1150331      40.0000000      49.8849669

        NL            0           .               .               .

        NO            0           .               .               .

        PT            0           .               .               .

        SE            0           .               .               .

        TR            7      30.5050705      39.4285714      48.3520724

        US           28      35.6505942      40.4285714      45.2065486

        ZA            4      12.1696649      34.7500000      57.3303351
```

8. Creating an Output Data Set with PROC MEANS

a. Retrieve the starter program **p112e08**.

b. Create an output data set containing the sum of `Total_Retail_Price` values for each `Product_ID`.

> Creating an output data set from PROC MEANS results is discussed in the self-study content at the end of this section.

c. Combine the output data set with `orion.product_list` to obtain the `Product_Name` value for each `Product_ID` code.

d. Sort the merged data so that the products with higher revenues appear at the top of the resulting data set. Print the first 10 observations, those that represent the ten products with the most revenue.

> To limit the number of observations displayed by PROC PRINT, apply the OBS= data set option, as in **proc print data=work.mydataset(obs=10);**.

e. Display the revenue values with a leading euro symbol (€), a period that separates every three digits, and a comma that separates the decimal fraction.

f. Submit the program to produce the following report:

PROC MEANS Output

```
                          Top Ten Products by Revenue

                              Product
     Obs     Revenue          Number     Product

      1     €3.391,80      230100700009   Family Holiday 6
      2     €3.080,30      230100700008   Family Holiday 4
      3     €2.250,00      230100700011   Hurricane 4
      4     €1.937,20      240200100173   Proplay Executive Bi-Metal Graphite
      5     €1.796,00      240200100076   Expert Men's Firesole Driver
      6     €1.561,80      240300300090   Top R&D Long Jacket
      7     €1.514,40      240300300070   Top Men's R&D Ultimate Jacket
      8     €1.510,80      240100400098   Rollerskate  Roller Skates Ex9 76mm/78a Biofl
      9     €1.424,40      240100400129   Rollerskate Roller Skates Sq9 80-76mm/78a
     10     €1.343,30      240100400043   Perfect Fit Men's  Roller Skates
```

12.3 Using the TABULATE Procedure (Self-Study)

Objectives

- Create one-, two-, and three-dimensional tabular reports using the TABULATE procedure.
- Produce output data sets by using the OUT= option in the PROC statement.

85

The TABULATE Procedure

The TABULATE procedure displays descriptive statistics in tabular format.

General form of the TABULATE procedure:

```
PROC TABULATE DATA=SAS-data-set <options>;
     CLASS classification-variable(s);
     VAR analysis-variable(s);
     TABLE page-expression,
           row-expression,
           column-expression </ option(s)>;
RUN;
```

86

The TABULATE procedure computes many of the same statistics that are computed by other descriptive statistical procedures such as MEANS and FREQ.

  A CLASS statement or a VAR statement must be specified, but both statements together are not required.

Dimensional Tables

The TABULATE procedure produces one-, two-, or three-dimensional tables.

	page dimension	row dimension	column dimension
one-dimensional			✓
two-dimensional		✓	✓
three-dimensional	✓	✓	✓

87

One-Dimensional Table

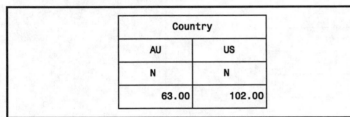

Country	
AU	US
N	N
63.00	102.00

- **Country** is in the column dimension.

88

Two-Dimensional Table

	Country	
	AU	US
	N	N
Gender		
F	27.00	41.00
M	36.00	61.00

- **Country** is in the column dimension.
- **Gender** is in the row dimension.

89

Three-Dimensional Table

Job_Title Sales Rep. I

	Country	
	AU	US
	N	N
Gender		
F	8.00	13.00
M	13.00	29.00

- **Country** is in the column dimension.
- **Gender** is in the row dimension.
- **Job_Title** is in the page dimension.

90

The TABLE Statement

The TABLE statement describes the structure of the table.

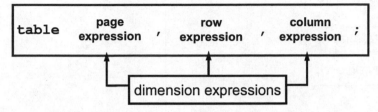

- Commas separate the dimension expressions.
- Every variable that is part of a dimension expression must be specified as a classification variable (CLASS statement) or an analysis variable (VAR statement).

91

The TABLE Statement

| table | page expression | ' | row expression | ' | column expression | ; |

Examples:

```
table Country ;
```

```
table Gender , Country ;
```

```
table Job_Title , Gender , Country ;
```

92

The CLASS Statement

The CLASS statement identifies variables to be used as classification, or grouping, variables.

General form of the CLASS statement:

CLASS *classification-variable(s)*;

- N, the number of non-missing values, is the default statistic for classification variables.
- Examples of classification variables:
  Job_Title, **Gender**, and **Country**

93

Class variables

- can be numeric or character
- identify classes or categories on which calculations are done
- represent discrete categories if they are numeric (for example, **Year**).

The VAR Statement

The VAR statement identifies the numeric variables for which statistics are calculated.

General form of the VAR statement:

VAR *analysis-variable(s)*;

- SUM is the default statistic for analysis variables.
- Examples of analysis variables:
  `Salary` and `Bonus`

94

Analysis variables

- are always numeric
- tend to be continuous
- are appropriate for calculating averages, sums, or other statistics.

One-Dimensional Table

```
proc tabulate data=orion.sales;
   class Country;
   table Country;
run;
```

Country	
AU	US
N	N
63.00	102.00

95   p112d08

If there are only class variables in the TABLE statement, the default statistic is N, or number of non-missing values.

Two-Dimensional Table

```
proc tabulate data=orion.sales;
   class Gender Country;
   table Gender, Country;
run;
```

	Country	
	AU	US
	N	N
Gender		
F	27.00	41.00
M	36.00	61.00

96   p112d08

Three-Dimensional Table

```
proc tabulate data=orion.sales;
   class Job_Title Gender Country;
   table Job_Title, Gender, Country;
run;
```

97   p112d08

Three-Dimensional Table

Partial PROC TABULATE Output

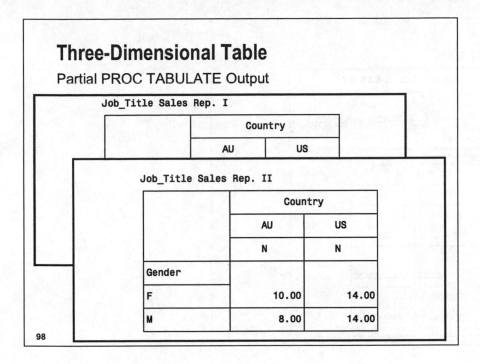

Dimension Expression

Elements that can be used in a dimension expression:

- classification variables
- analysis variables
- the universal class variable ALL
- keywords for statistics

Operators that can be used in a dimension expression:

- blank, which concatenates table information
- asterisk *, which crosses table information
- parentheses (), which group elements

Other operators include

- brackets < >, which name the denominator for row or column percentages
- equal sign =, which changes the label for a variable or a statistic.

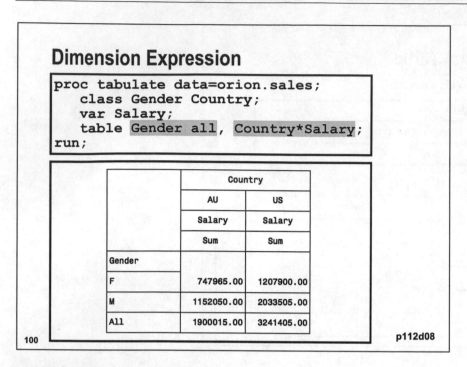

Dimension Expression

```
proc tabulate data=orion.sales;
    class Gender Country;
    var Salary;
    table Gender all, Country*Salary;
run;
```

	Country	
	AU	US
	Salary	Salary
	Sum	Sum
Gender		
F	747965.00	1207900.00
M	1152050.00	2033505.00
All	1900015.00	3241405.00

100   p112d08

If there are analysis variables in the TABLE statement, the default statistic is SUM.

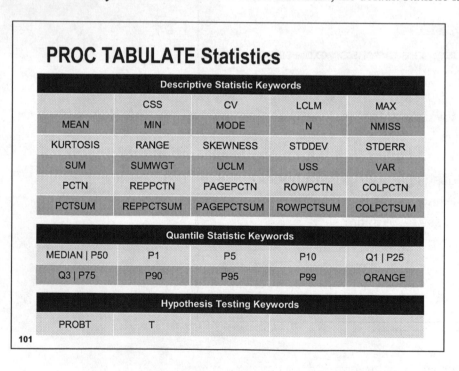

PROC TABULATE Statistics

Descriptive Statistic Keywords				
	CSS	CV	LCLM	MAX
MEAN	MIN	MODE	N	NMISS
KURTOSIS	RANGE	SKEWNESS	STDDEV	STDERR
SUM	SUMWGT	UCLM	USS	VAR
PCTN	REPPCTN	PAGEPCTN	ROWPCTN	COLPCTN
PCTSUM	REPPCTSUM	PAGEPCTSUM	ROWPCTSUM	COLPCTSUM

Quantile Statistic Keywords				
MEDIAN | P50	P1	P5	P10	Q1 | P25
Q3 | P75	P90	P95	P99	QRANGE

Hypothesis Testing Keywords				
PROBT	T			

101

PROC TABULATE Statistics

```
proc tabulate data=orion.sales;
   class Gender Country;
   var Salary;
   table Gender all, Country*Salary*(min max);
run;
```

	Country			
	AU		US	
	Salary		Salary	
	Min	Max	Min	Max
Gender				
F	25185.00	30890.00	25390.00	83505.00
M	25745.00	108255.00	22710.00	243190.00
All	25185.00	108255.00	22710.00	243190.00

Additional SAS Statements

Additional statements can be added to enhance the report.

```
proc format;
   value $ctryfmt 'AU'='Australia'
                  'US'='United States';
run;

options nodate pageno=1;

ods html file='p112d08.html';
proc tabulate data=orion.sales;
   class Gender Country;
   var Salary;
   table Gender all, Country*Salary*(min max);
   where Job_Title contains 'Rep';
   label Salary='Annual Salary';
   format Country $ctryfmt.;
   title 'Sales Rep Tabular Report';
run;
ods html close;
```

103   p112d08

Additional SAS Statements

HTML Output

	Country			
	Australia		**United States**	
	Annual Salary		**Annual Salary**	
	Min	**Max**	**Min**	**Max**
Gender				
F	25185.00	30890.00	25390.00	32985.00
M	25745.00	36605.00	22710.00	35990.00
All	25185.00	36605.00	22710.00	35990.00

Sales Rep Tabular Report

104

Output Data Sets

PROC TABULATE produces output data sets using the following method:

> **PROC TABULATE DATA=***SAS-data-set*
> **OUT=***SAS-data-set <options>*;

The output data set contains the following variables:

- BY variables
- class variables
- the automatic variables **_TYPE_**, **_PAGE_**, and **_TABLE_**
- calculated statistics

106

PROC Statement OUT= Option

```
proc tabulate data=orion.sales
              out=work.tabulate;
   where Job_Title contains 'Rep';
   class Job_Title Gender Country;
   table Country;
   table Gender, Country;
   table Job_Title, Gender, Country;
run;

proc print data=work.tabulate;
run;
```

107   p112d09

PROC Statement OUT= Option

Partial PROC PRINT Output

Obs	Job_Title	Gender	Country	_TYPE_	_PAGE_	_TABLE_	N
1			AU	001	1	1	61
2			US	001	1	1	98
3		F	AU	011	1	2	27
4		F	US	011	1	2	40
5		M	AU	011	1	2	34
6		M	US	011	1	2	58
7	Sales Rep. I	F	AU	111	1	3	8
8	Sales Rep. I	F	US	111	1	3	13
9	Sales Rep. I	M	AU	111	1	3	13
10	Sales Rep. I	M	US	111	1	3	29
11	Sales Rep. II	F	AU	111	2	3	10
12	Sales Rep. II	F	US	111	2	3	14
13	Sales Rep. II	M	AU	111	2	3	8
14	Sales Rep. II	M	US	111	2	3	14
15	Sales Rep. III	F	AU	111	3	3	7
16	Sales Rep. III	F	US	111	3	3	8
17	Sales Rep. III	M	AU	111	3	3	10
18	Sales Rep. III	M	US	111	3	3	9

108

PROC Statement OUT= Option

TYPE is a character variable that shows which combination of class variables produced the summary statistics in that observation.

Partial PROC PRINT Output

```
 Obs   Job_Title    Gender Country _TYPE_ _PAGE_  _TABLE_   N

  1                          AU     001      1       1     61
  2                          US     001      1       1     98
  3                    F      AU     011      1       2     27
  4                    F      US     011
  5                    M      AU     011
  6                    M      US     011
```

0 for **Job_Title**, 1 for **Gender**, and 1 for **Country**

109

PROC Statement OUT= Option

PAGE is a numeric variable that shows the logical page number that contains that observation.

Partial PROC PRINT Output

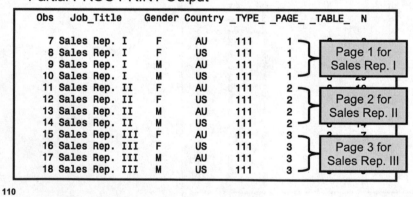

```
 Obs   Job_Title    Gender Country _TYPE_ _PAGE_  _TABLE_   N

  7 Sales Rep. I       F      AU     111      1
  8 Sales Rep. I       F      US     111      1        Page 1 for
  9 Sales Rep. I       M      AU     111      1        Sales Rep. I
 10 Sales Rep. I       M      US     111      1
 11 Sales Rep. II      F      AU     111      2
 12 Sales Rep. II      F      US     111      2        Page 2 for
 13 Sales Rep. II      M      AU     111      2        Sales Rep. II
 14 Sales Rep. II      M      US     111      2
 15 Sales Rep. III     F      AU     111      3
 16 Sales Rep. III     F      US     111      3        Page 3 for
 17 Sales Rep. III     M      AU     111      3        Sales Rep. III
 18 Sales Rep. III     M      US     111      3
```

110

PROC Statement OUT= Option

TABLE is a numeric variable that shows the number of the TABLE statement that contains that observation.

Partial PROC PRINT Output

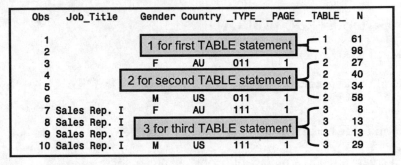

```
Obs   Job_Title    Gender Country _TYPE_ _PAGE_ _TABLE_   N

 1                                                   1     61
 2                                                   1     98
 3                    F      AU      011      1      2     27
 4                                                   2     40
 5                                                   2     34
 6                    M      US      011      1      2     58
 7   Sales Rep. I     F      AU      111      1      3      8
 8   Sales Rep. I                                    3     13
 9   Sales Rep. I                                    3     13
10   Sales Rep. I     M      US      111      1      3     29
```

111

 **Exercises**

Level 1

9. Creating a Simple Tabular Report with PROC TABULATE

   a. Retrieve the starter program **p112e09**.

   b. Add a CLASS statement to allow **Customer_Group** and **Customer_Gender** as classification variables.

   c. Add a VAR statement to permit **Customer_Age** as an analysis variable

   d. Add a TABLE statement to create a report with the following characteristics:

      1) **Customer_Group** defines the rows.

      2) An extra row that combines all groups appears at the bottom of the table.

      3) **Customer_Gender** defines the columns.

      4) The N and MEAN statistics based on **Customer_Age** are displayed for each combination of **Customer_Group** and **Customer_Gender**.

   e. Submit the program to produce the following report:

PROC TABULATE Output

Ages of Customers by Group and Gender				
	Customer Gender			
	F		M	
	Customer Age		Customer Age	
	N	Mean	N	Mean
Customer Group Name				
Internet/Catalog Customers	4.00	49.25	4.00	54.25
Orion Club Gold members	11.00	35.36	10.00	38.90
Orion Club members	15.00	32.53	33.00	47.03
All	30.00	35.80	47.00	45.91

Level 2

10. **Creating a Three-Dimensional Tabular Report with PROC TABULATE**

   a. Retrieve the starter program **p112e10**.

   b. Define a tabular report with the following characteristics:

      1) `Customer_Gender` defines the page dimension.

      2) `Customer_Group` defines the row dimension.

      3) The column dimension should display the number of customers and the percentage of customers in each category (COLPCTN).

      > Change the headers for the statistic columns with a KEYLABEL statement. Documentation on the KEYLABEL statement can be found in the SAS Help and Documentation from the Contents tab (**SAS Products** ⇨ **Base SAS** ⇨ **Base SAS 9.2 Procedures Guide** ⇨ **Procedures** ⇨ **The TABULATE Procedure**).

   c. Submit the program to produce the following two-page report:

PROC TABULATE Output

Customers by Group and Gender

Customer Gender F

	Number	Percentage
Customer Group Name		
Internet/Catalog Customers	4.00	13.33
Orion Club Gold members	11.00	36.67
Orion Club members	15.00	50.00

```
                     Customers by Group and Gender

               Customer Gender M

                                  |   Number  |  Percentage
          ------------------------+-----------+-------------
          Customer Group Name     |           |
                                  |           |
          Internet/Catalog        |           |
          Customers               |      4.00 |        8.51
          ------------------------+-----------+-------------
          Orion Club Gold         |           |
          members                 |     10.00 |       21.28
          ------------------------+-----------+-------------
          Orion Club members      |     33.00 |       70.21
```

Level 3

11. Creating a Customized Tabular Report with PROC TABULATE

   a. Retrieve the starter program **p112e11**.

   b. Modify the label for the **Total_Retail_Price** variable.

   c. Suppress the labels for the **Order_Date** and **Product_ID** variables.

   d. Suppress the label for the **Sum** keyword.

   e. Insert this text into the box above the row titles: High Cost Products (Unit Cost > $250). Suppress all titles.

   f. Display all calculated cell values with the DOLLAR12. format.

   g. Display $0 in all cells that have no calculated value.

     ✎   Documentation on the TABULATE procedure can be found in the SAS Help and Documentation from the Contents tab (**SAS Products** ⇨ **Base SAS** ⇨ **Base SAS 9.2 Procedures Guide** ⇨ **Procedures** ⇨ **The TABULATE Procedure**). Look for features of the PROC TABULATE statement, the TABLE statement, and the KEYLABEL statement that can perform the requested actions.

h. Submit the program to produce the following report:

PROC TABULATE Output

High Cost Products (Unit Cost > $250)	Revenue for Each Product			
	230100700008	230100700009	240300100028	240300100032
2003	$0	$0	$0	$1,200
2005	$2,057	$2,256	$0	$0
2006	$0	$1,136	$0	$0
2007	$519	$0	$1,066	$0

12. Creating an Output Data Set with PROC TABULATE

a. Retrieve the starter program **p112e12**.

b. Create an output data set from the PROC TABULATE results. The output data set should contain average salaries for each combination of **Company** and **Employee_Gender**, plus overall averages for each **Company**.

🖎 Creating an output data set from PROC TABULATE results is discussed in the self-study content at the end of this section.

c. Sort the data set by average salary.

d. Print the sorted data set, assigning a format and column header to the average salary column.

e. Submit the program to produce the following report:

PROC PRINT Output

```
                          Average Employee Salaries

                                      Employee       Average
              Obs    Company          Gender         Salary

               1     Orion Australia     F           $27,760
               2     Orion USA           F           $29,167
               3     Orion Australia                 $30,574
               4     Orion USA                       $31,226
               5     Orion USA           M           $32,534
               6     Orion Australia     M           $32,963
               7     Concession          F           $33,375
               8     Purchasing          M           $33,462
               9     Concession                      $33,839
              10     Concession          M           $34,650
              11     Purchasing                      $38,408
              12     Logistics           F           $39,055
              13     Purchasing          F           $41,556
              14     Marketing           M           $42,645
              15     Logistics                       $43,128
              16     Shared Functions    M           $43,428
              17     Marketing                       $44,390
              18     Shared Functions                $44,631
              19     Shared Functions    F           $46,016
              20     Marketing           F           $47,132
              21     Logistics           M           $47,630
              22     Board of Directors  F           $68,370
              23     Board of Directors              $134,034
              24     Board of Directors  M           $212,831
```

12.4 Solutions

Solutions to Exercises

1. **Counting Levels of a Variable with PROC FREQ**

   a. Retrieve the starter program.

   b. Modify the program to produce two separate reports.

```
proc freq data=orion.orders nlevels;
   where Order_Type=1;
   tables Customer_ID Employee_ID / noprint;
   title1 'Unique Customers and Salespersons for Retail Sales';
run;

proc freq data=orion.orders nlevels;
   where Order_Type ne 1;
   tables Customer_ID / noprint;
   title1 'Unique Customers for Catalog and Internet Sales';
run;
```

   c. Submit the program.

2. **Producing Frequency Reports with PROC FREQ**

   a. Retrieve the starter program.

   b. Add TABLES statements to the PROC FREQ step.

```
proc format;
   value ordertypes
         1='Retail'
         2='Catalog'
         3='Internet';
run;

proc freq data=orion.orders ;
   tables Order_Date;
   tables Order_Type / nocum;
   tables Order_Date*Order_Type / nopercent norow nocol;
   format Order_Date year4. Order_Type ordertypes.;
   title 'Order Summary by Year and Type';
run;
```

   c. Submit the program.

3. **Displaying PROC FREQ Output in Descending Frequency Order**

   a. Retrieve the starter program.

   b. Submit the program.

   c. What are the two most common values for each variable?

      The top two countries are US (United States, 28 customers) and CA (Canada, 15 customers).

      The top two customer types are Orion Club members medium activity (20) and Orion Club members low activity (17).

      The top two customer age groups are 31-45 years (27) and 15-30 years (22).

   d. Modify the program to display the frequency counts in descending order.

   ```
   proc freq data=orion.customer_dim order=freq;
      tables Customer_Country Customer_Type Customer_Age_Group;
      title1 'Customer Demographics';
      title3 '(Top two levels for each variable?)';
   run;
   ```

   e. Submit the modified program.

   f. What are the two most common values for each variable?

      The top two countries are US (United States, 28 customers) and CA (Canada, 15 customers).

      The top two customer types are Orion Club members medium activity (20) and Orion Club members low activity (17).

      The top two customer age groups are 31-45 years (27) and 15-30 years (22).

      Which report was easier to use to answer the questions correctly?

      The ORDER=FREQ option in the PROC FREQ statement sequences the frequency output in descending count order. Because the levels that occur most often appear near the top of each report, the most common data values can be identified more easily.

4. **Creating an Output Data Set with PROC FREQ**

   a. Retrieve the starter program.

   b. Create an output data set.

   ```
   proc freq data=orion.order_fact noprint;
      tables Product_ID / out=product_orders;
   run;
   ```

   c. Combine the output data set with **orion.product_list**.

   ```
   data product_names;
      merge product_orders orion.product_list;
      by Product_ID;
      keep Product_ID Product_Name Count;
   run;
   ```

d. Sort the merged data and print the first 10 observations.

```
proc sort data=product_names;
   by descending Count;
run;

proc print data=product_names(obs=10) label;
   var Count Product_ID Product_Name;
   label Product_ID='Product Number'
         Product_Name='Product'
         Count='Orders';
   title 'Top Ten Products by Number of Orders';
run;
```

e. Submit the program.

5. **Creating a Summary Report with PROC MEANS**

   a. Retrieve the starter program.

   b. Display only the SUM statistic for the **Total_Retail_Price** variable.

```
proc format;
   value ordertypes
       1='Retail'
       2='Catalog'
       3='Internet';
run;

proc means data=orion.order_fact sum;
   var Total_Retail_Price;
   title 'Revenue (in U.S. Dollars) Earned from All Orders';
run;
```

   c. Display separate statistics for combination of **Order_Date** and **Order_Type**.

```
proc means data=orion.order_fact sum;
   var Total_Retail_Price;
   class Order_Date Order_Type;
   format Order_Date year4. Order_Type ordertypes.;
   title 'Revenue (in U.S. Dollars) Earned from All Orders';
run;
```

   d. Submit the program.

6. **Analyzing Missing Numeric Values with PROC MEANS**

   a. Retrieve the starter program.

   b. Display the number of missing values and the number of non-missing values.

```
proc means data=orion.staff nmiss n;
   var Birth_Date Emp_Hire_Date Emp_Term_Date;
   title 'Number of Missing and Non-Missing Date Values';
run;
```

c. Suppress any decimal places.

```
proc means data=orion.staff nmiss n maxdec=0;
   var Birth_Date Emp_Hire_Date Emp_Term_Date;
   title 'Number of Missing and Non-Missing Date Values';
run;
```

d. Display separate statistics for each value of **Gender**.

```
proc means data=orion.staff nmiss n maxdec=0;
   var Birth_Date Emp_Hire_Date Emp_Term_Date;
   class Gender;
   title 'Number of Missing and Non-Missing Date Values';
run;
```

e. Suppress the output column that displays the total number of observations.

```
proc means data=orion.staff nmiss n maxdec=0 nonobs;
   var Birth_Date Emp_Hire_Date Emp_Term_Date;
   class Gender;
   title 'Number of Missing and Non-Missing Date Values';
run;
```

f. Submit the program.

7. Analyzing All Possible Classification Levels with PROC MEANS

a. Retrieve the starter program.

b. Display statistics in the report.

```
data work.countries(keep=Customer_Country);
   set orion.supplier;
   Customer_Country=Country;
run;

proc means data=orion.customer_dim
           lclm mean uclm;
   class Customer_Country;
   var Customer_Age;
   title 'Average Age of Customers in Each Country';
run;
```

c. Change the α value.

```
proc means data=orion.customer_dim
           lclm mean uclm alpha=0.10;
   class Customer_Country;
   var Customer_Age;
   title 'Average Age of Customers in Each Country';
run;
```

d. Display all countries.

```
proc means data=orion.customer_dim
          classdata=work.countries
          lclm mean uclm alpha=0.10;
   class Customer_Country;
   var Customer_Age;
   title 'Average Age of Customers in Each Country';
run;
```

e. Submit the program.

8. Creating an Output Data Set with PROC MEANS

a. Retrieve the starter program.

b. Create an output data set.

```
proc means data=orion.order_fact noprint nway;
   class Product_ID;
   var Total_Retail_Price;
   output out=product_orders sum=Product_Revenue;
run;
```

c. Combine the output data set with **orion.product_list**.

```
data product_names;
   merge product_orders orion.product_list;
   by Product_ID;
   keep Product_ID Product_Name Product_Revenue;
run;
```

d. Sort the merged data and print the first 10 observations.

```
proc sort data=product_names;
   by descending Product_Revenue;
run;

proc print data=product_names(obs=10) label;
   var Product_Revenue Product_ID Product_Name;
   label Product_ID='Product Number'
         Product_Name='Product'
         Product_Revenue='Revenue';
   title 'Top Ten Products by Revenue';
run;
```

e. Display the revenue values with a leading euro symbol.

```
proc print data=product_names(obs=10) label;
   var Product_Revenue Product_ID Product_Name;
   label Product_ID='Product Number'
         Product_Name='Product'
         Product_Revenue='Revenue';
   format Product_Revenue eurox12.2;
   title 'Top Ten Products by Revenue';
run;
```

f. Submit the program.

9. Creating a Simple Tabular Report with PROC TABULATE

a. Retrieve the starter program.

b. Add a CLASS statement.

```
proc tabulate data=orion.customer_dim;
   class Customer_Group Customer_Gender;
   title 'Ages of Customers by Group and Gender';
run;
```

c. Add a VAR statement.

```
proc tabulate data=orion.customer_dim;
   class Customer_Group Customer_Gender;
   var Customer_Age;
   title 'Ages of Customers by Group and Gender';
run;
```

d. Add a TABLE statement.

```
proc tabulate data=orion.customer_dim;
   class Customer_Group Customer_Gender;
   var Customer_Age;
   table Customer_Group all,
         Customer_Gender*Customer_Age*(n mean);
   title 'Ages of Customers by Group and Gender';
run;
```

e. Submit the program.

10. Creating a Three-Dimensional Tabular Report with PROC TABULATE

a. Retrieve the starter program.

b. Define a tabular report.

```
proc tabulate data=orion.customer_dim;
   class Customer_Gender Customer_Group;
   table Customer_Gender, Customer_Group, (n colpctn);
   keylabel colpctn='Percentage' N='Number';
   title 'Customers by Group and Gender';
run;
```

c. Submit the program.

11. Creating a Customized Tabular Report with PROC TABULATE

a. Retrieve the starter program.

b. Modify the label for the **Total_Retail_Price** variable.

```
proc tabulate data=orion.order_fact;
   where CostPrice_Per_Unit > 250;
   class Product_ID Order_Date;
   format Order_Date year4.;
   var Total_Retail_Price;
   table Order_Date, Total_Retail_Price*sum*Product_ID;
   label Total_Retail_Price='Revenue for Each Product';
   title;
run;
```

c. Suppress the labels for the **Order_Date** and **Product_ID** variables.

```
proc tabulate data=orion.order_fact;
   where CostPrice_Per_Unit > 250;
   class Product_ID Order_Date;
   format Order_Date year4.;
   var Total_Retail_Price;
   table Order_Date=' ', Total_Retail_Price*sum*Product_ID=' ';
   label Total_Retail_Price='Revenue for Each Product';
   title;
run;
```

d. Suppress the label for the **Sum** keyword.

```
proc tabulate data=orion.order_fact;
   where CostPrice_Per_Unit > 250;
   class Product_ID Order_Date;
   format Order_Date year4.;
   var Total_Retail_Price;
   table Order_Date=' ', Total_Retail_Price*sum*Product_ID=' ';
   label Total_Retail_Price='Revenue for Each Product';
   keylabel Sum=' ';
   title;
run;
```

e. Insert text into the box above the row titles.

```
proc tabulate data=orion.order_fact;
   where CostPrice_Per_Unit > 250;
   class Product_ID Order_Date;
   format Order_Date year4.;
   var Total_Retail_Price;
   table Order_Date=' ', Total_Retail_Price*sum*Product_ID=' '
         / box='High Cost Products (Unit Cost > $250)';
   label Total_Retail_Price='Revenue for Each Product';
   keylabel Sum=' ';
   title;
run;
```

f. Display all calculated cell values with the DOLLAR12. format.

```
proc tabulate data=orion.order_fact format=dollar12.;
   where CostPrice_Per_Unit > 250;
   class Product_ID Order_Date;
   format Order_Date year4.;
   var Total_Retail_Price;
   table Order_Date=' ', Total_Retail_Price*sum*Product_ID=' '
         / box='High Cost Products (Unit Cost > $250)';
   label Total_Retail_Price='Revenue for Each Product';
   keylabel Sum=' ';
   title;
run;
```

g. Display $0 in all cells that have no calculated value.

```
proc tabulate data=orion.order_fact format=dollar12.;
   where CostPrice_Per_Unit > 250;
   class Product_ID Order_Date;
   format Order_Date year4.;
   var Total_Retail_Price;
   table Order_Date=' ', Total_Retail_Price*sum*Product_ID=' '
         / misstext='$0'
           box='High Cost Products (Unit Cost > $250)';
   label Total_Retail_Price='Revenue for Each Product';
   keylabel Sum=' ';
   title;
run;
```

h. Submit the program.

12. Creating an Output Data Set with PROC TABULATE

a. Retrieve the starter program.

b. Create an output data set.

```
proc tabulate data=orion.Organization_Dim format=dollar12.
              out=work.Salaries;
   class Employee_Gender Company;
   var Salary;
   table Company, (Employee_Gender all)*Salary*mean;
   title 'Average Employee Salaries';
run;
```

c. Sort the data set.

```
proc sort data=work.Salaries;
   by Salary_Mean;
run;
```

d. Print the sorted data set.

```
proc print data=work.Salaries label;
   var Company Employee_Gender Salary_Mean;
   format Salary_Mean dollar12.;
   label Salary_Mean='Average Salary';
   title 'Average Employee Salaries';
run;
```

e. Submit the program.

Solutions to Student Activities (Polls/Quizzes)

12.01 Multiple Choice Poll – Correct Answer

Which of the following statements **cannot** be added
to the PROC FREQ step to enhance the report?

   a. FORMAT
   (b.) SET
   c. TITLE
   d. WHERE

12

12.02 Quiz – Correct Answer

Which TABLES statement correctly creates the report?

a. `tables Gender nocum;`

b. `tables Gender nocum nopercent;`

c. `tables Gender / nopercent;`

(d.) `tables Gender / nocum nopercent;`

```
         The FREQ Procedure

   Gender      Frequency

   F                  68
   M                  97
```

20   p112d01

12.03 Quiz – Correct Answer

The first part of the PROC FREQ output is in the SAS data set that was created with the TABLES statement.

Obs	Gender	COUNT	PERCENT	CUM_FREQ	CUM_PCT
1	F	68	41.2121	68	41.212
2	M	97	58.7879	165	100.000

The second part of the PROC FREQ output is in the SAS data set that was created with the OUTPUT statement.

Obs	N	_PCHI_	DF_PCHI	P_PCHI
1	165	5.09697	1	0.023968

42

12.04 Quiz – Correct Answer

For a given data set, there are 63 observation with a **Country** value of AU. Of those 63 observations, only 61 observations have a value for **Salary**.

Which output is correct?

a.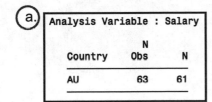

b.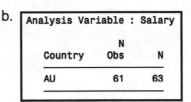

55

12.05 Quiz – Correct Answer

```
proc means data=orion.sales noprint chartype;
   var Salary;
   class Gender Country;
   output out=work.means2
          min=minSalary max=maxSalary
          sum=sumSalary mean=aveSalary;
run;
proc print data=work.means2;
   where _type_ = '10';
run;
```

Obs	Gender	Country	_TYPE_	_FREQ_	min Salary	max Salary	sum Salary	ave Salary
4	F		10	68	25185	83505	1955865	28762.72
5	M		10	97	22710	243190	3185555	32840.77

78

p112a02s

Chapter 13   Introduction to Graphics Using SAS/GRAPH (Self-Study)

13.1 Introduction

What Is SAS/GRAPH Software?

SAS/GRAPH software is a component of SAS software that enables you to create the following types of graphs:

- bar, block, and pie charts
- two-dimensional scatter plots and line plots
- three-dimensional scatter and surface plots
- contour plots
- maps
- text slides
- custom graphs

3

Bar Charts (GCHART Procedure)

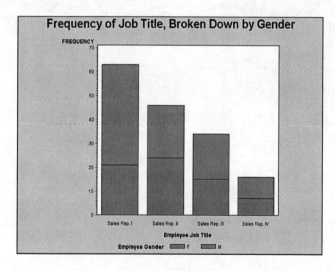

4

Pie Charts (GCHART Procedure)

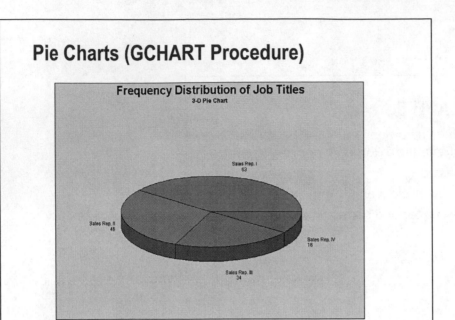

5

Scatter and Line Plots (GPLOT Procedure)

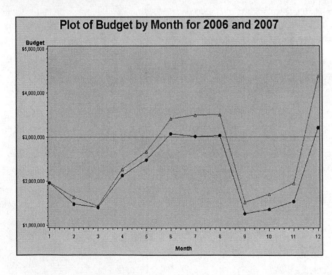

6

Bar Charts with Line Plot Overlay (GBARLINE Procedure)

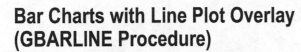

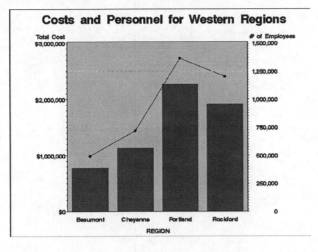

7

Three-Dimensional Surface and Scatter Plots (G3D Procedure)

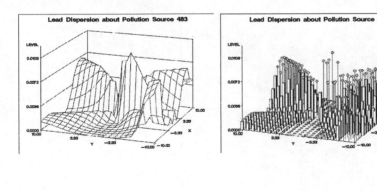

8

Three-Dimensional Contour Plots (GCONTOUR Procedure)

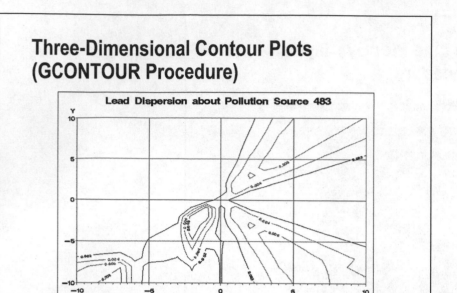

9

Maps (GMAP Procedure)

Distribution of Jobs
An Empty State Indicates No Jobs

10

Multiple Graphs on a Page (GREPLAY Procedure)

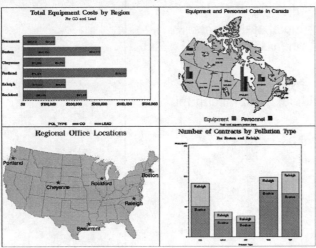

11

SAS/GRAPH Programs

General form of a SAS/GRAPH program:

> **GOPTIONS** *options*;
> *global statements*
> *graphics procedure steps*

For example:

```
goptions cback=white;
title 'Number of Employees by Job Title';
proc gchart data=orion.staff;
   vbar Job_Title;
run;
quit;
```

12

RUN-Group Processing

Many SAS/GRAPH procedures can use RUN-group processing, which means that the following are true:

- The procedure executes the group of statements following the PROC statement when a RUN statement is encountered.
- Additional statements followed by another RUN statement can be submitted without resubmitting the PROC statement.
- The procedure stays active until a PROC, DATA, or QUIT statement is encountered.

13

Example of RUN-Group Processing

```
proc gchart data=orion.staff;
   vbar Job_Title;
   title 'Bar Chart of Job Titles';
run;
   pie Job_Title;
   title 'Pie Chart of Job Titles';
run;
quit;
```

14

13.2 Creating Bar and Pie Charts

Producing Bar and Pie Charts with the GCHART Procedure

General form of the PROC GCHART statement:

PROC GCHART DATA=*SAS-data-set*;

Use one of these statements to specify the chart type:

HBAR *chart-variable . . . </ options>*;
HBAR3D *chart-variable . . . </ options>*;

VBAR *chart-variable . . . </ options>*;
VBAR3D *chart-variable . . . </ options>*;

PIE *chart-variable . . . </ options>*;
PIE3D *chart-variable . . . </ options>*;

16

The chart variable determines the number of bars or slices produced within a graph. The chart variable can be character or numeric. By default, the height, length, or slice represents a frequency count of the values of the chart variable.

Creating Bar and Pie Charts

p113d01

1. Submit the first PROC GCHART step to create a vertical bar chart representing a frequency count.

    The VBAR statement creates a vertical bar chart showing the number of sales representatives for each value of **Job_Title** in the **orion.staff** data set. **Job_Title** is referred to as the *chart variable*. Because the chart variable is a character variable, PROC GCHART displays one bar for each value of **Job_Title**.

```
goptions reset=all;
proc gchart data=orion.staff;
   vbar Job_Title;
   where Job_Title =:'Sales Rep';
   title 'Number of Employees by Job Title';
run;
quit;
```

    The RESET=ALL option resets all graphics options to their default settings and clears any titles or footnotes that are in effect.

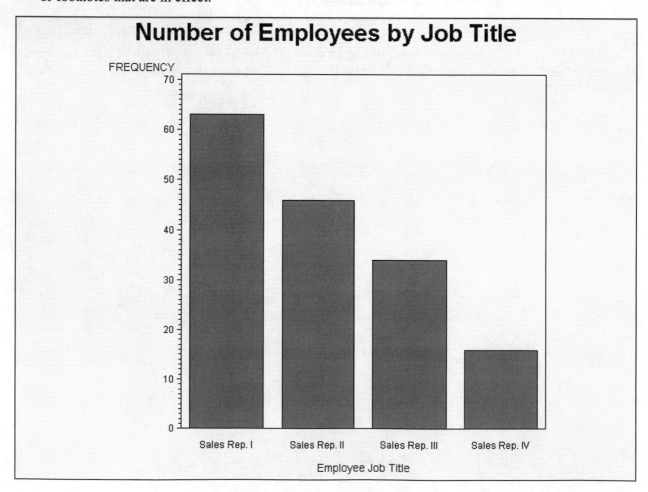

2. Submit the second PROC GCHART step to create a three-dimensional horizontal bar chart.

    The HBAR3D statement creates a three-dimensional horizontal bar chart showing the same information as the previous bar chart. Note that the HBAR and HBAR3D statements automatically display statistics to the right of the chart.

```
goptions reset=all;
proc gchart data=orion.staff;
   hbar3d Job_Title;
   title 'Number of Employees by Job Title';
   where Job_Title =:'Sales Rep';
run;
quit;
```

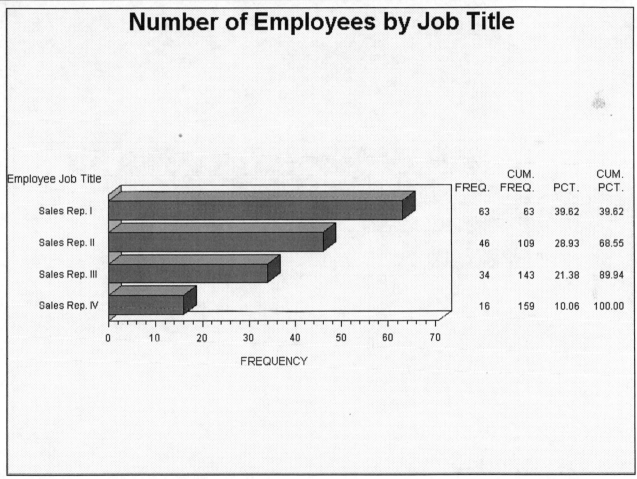

3. Submit the third PROC GCHART step to suppress the display of statistics on the horizontal bar chart.

    The NOSTATS option in the HBAR3D statement suppresses the display of statistics on the chart.

```
goptions reset=all;
proc gchart data=orion.staff;
   hbar3d Job_Title / nostats;
   title 'Number of Employees by Job Title';
   where Job_Title =:'Sales Rep';
run;
quit;
```

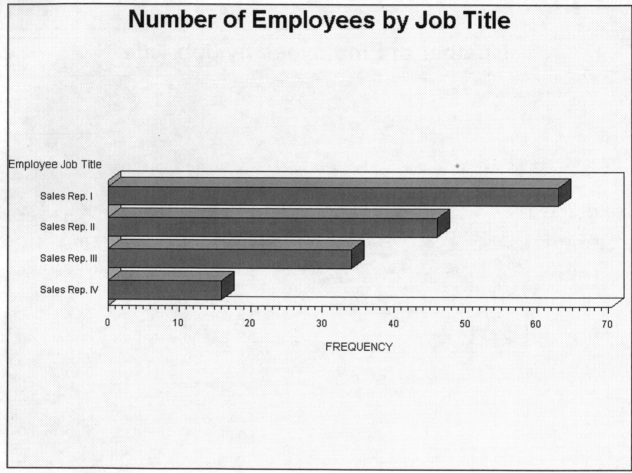

4. Submit the fourth PROC GCHART step to use a numeric chart variable.

The VBAR3D statement creates a vertical bar chart showing the distribution of values of the variable **Salary**. Because the chart variable is numeric, PROC GCHART divides the values of **Salary** into ranges and displays one bar for each range. The value under the bar represents the midpoint of the range. The FORMAT statement assigns the DOLLAR9. format to **Salary**.

```
goptions reset=all;
proc gchart data=orion.staff;
    vbar3d salary / autoref;
    where Job_Title =:'Sales Rep';
    format salary dollar9.;
    title 'Salary Distribution Midpoints for Sales Reps';
run;
quit;
```

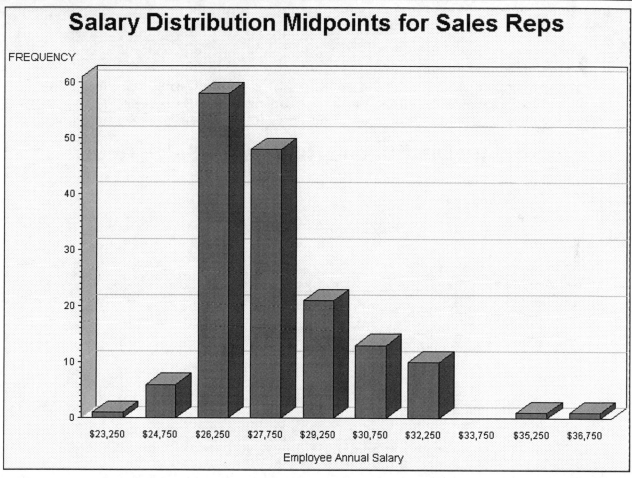

5. Submit the fifth PROC GCHART step to specify ranges for a numeric chart variable and add reference lines.

The HBAR3D statement creates a three-dimensional horizontal bar chart.

The LEVELS= option in the HBAR3D statement divides the values of **Salary** into five ranges and display a bar for each range of values.

The RANGE option in the HBAR3D statement displays the range of values, rather than the midpoint, under each bar.

The AUTOREF option displays reference lines at each major tick mark on the horizontal (response) axis.

```
goptions reset=all;
proc gchart data=orion.staff;
   hbar3d salary/levels=5 range autoref;
   where Job_Title =:'Sales Rep';
   format salary dollar9.;
   title 'Salary Distribution Ranges for Sales Reps';
run;
quit;
```

To display a bar for each unique value of the chart variable, specify the DISCRETE option instead of the LEVELS= option in the VBAR, VBAR3D, HBAR, or HBAR3D statement. The DISCRETE option should be used only when the chart variable has a relatively small number of unique values.

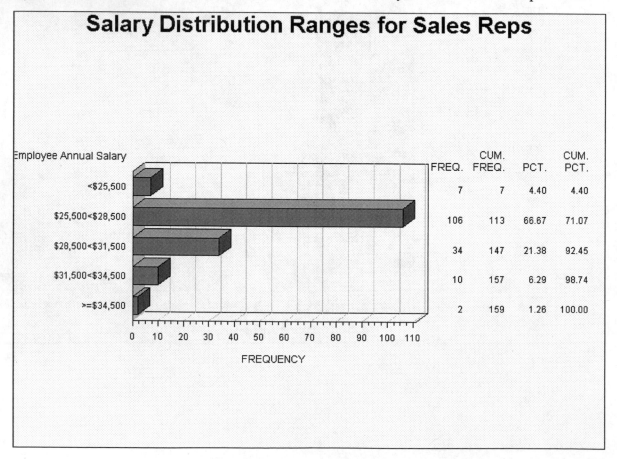

Salary Distribution Ranges for Sales Reps

Employee Annual Salary	FREQ.	CUM. FREQ.	PCT.	CUM. PCT.
<$25,500	7	7	4.40	4.40
$25,500<$28,500	106	113	66.67	71.07
$28,500<$31,500	34	147	21.38	92.45
$31,500<$34,500	10	157	6.29	98.74
>=$34,500	2	159	1.26	100.00

6. Submit the sixth PROC GCHART step to create bar charts based on statistics.

A vertical bar chart displays one bar for each value of the variable **Job_Title** by specifying **Job_Title** as the chart variable in the VBAR statement. The height of the bar should be based on the mean value of the variable **Salary** for each job title.

The SUMVAR= option in the VBAR statement specifies the variable whose values control the height or length of the bars. This variable (**Salary**, in this case) is known as the *analysis variable*.

The TYPE= option in the VBAR statement specifies the statistic for the analysis variable that dictates the height or length of the bars. Possible values for the TYPE= option are SUM and MEAN.

A LABEL statement assigns labels to the variables **Job_Title** and **Salary**.

```
goptions reset=all;
proc gchart data=orion.staff;
   vbar Job_Title / sumvar=salary type=mean;
   where Job_Title =:'Sales Rep';
   format salary dollar9.;
   label Job_Title='Job Title'
         Salary='Salary';
   title 'Average Salary by Job Title';
run;
quit;
```

If the TYPE= option is not specified, the default value of TYPE is SUM.

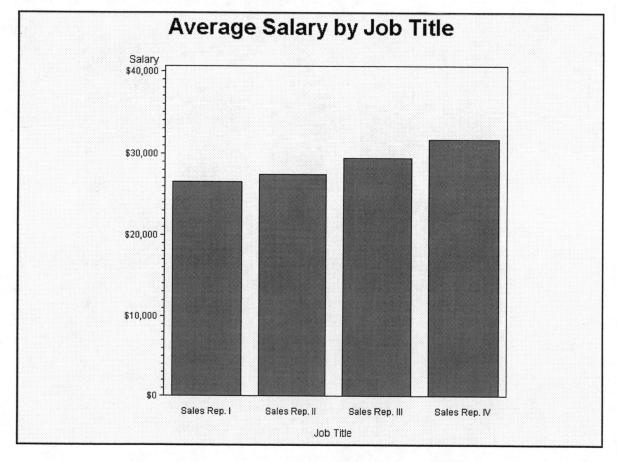

7. Submit the seventh PROC GCHART step to assign a different color to each bar and display the mean statistic on the top of each bar.

    The PATTERNID=MIDPOINT option in the VBAR statement causes PROC GCHART to assign a different pattern or color to each value of the midpoint (chart) variable.

    The MEAN option in the VBAR statement displays the mean statistic on the top of each bar. Other options such as SUM, FREQ, and PERCENT can be specified to display other statistics on the top of the bars.

```
goptions reset=all;
proc gchart data=orion.staff;
   vbar Job_Title / sumvar=salary type=mean patternid=midpoint mean;
   where Job_Title =:'Sales Rep';
   format salary dollar9.;
   title 'Average Salary by Job Title';
run;
quit;
```

Only one statistic can be displayed on top of each vertical bar. For horizontal bar charts, you can specify multiple statistics, which are displayed to the right of the bars.

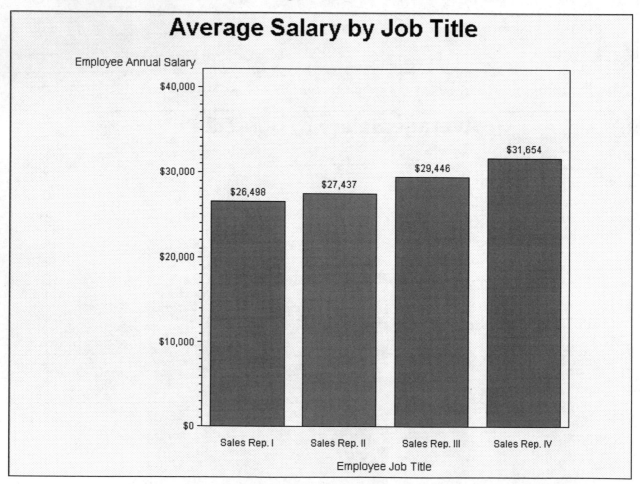

8. Submit the eighth PROC GCHART step to divide the bars into subgroups.

    A VBAR statement creates a vertical bar chart that shows the number of sales representatives for each value of **Job_Title**.

    The SUBGROUP= option in the VBAR statement divides the bar into sections, where each section represents the frequency count for each value of the variable **Gender**.

```
goptions reset=all;
proc gchart data=orion.staff;
   vbar Job_Title/subgroup=Gender;
   where Job_Title =:'Sales Rep';
   title 'Frequency of Job Title, Broken Down by Gender';
run;
quit;
```

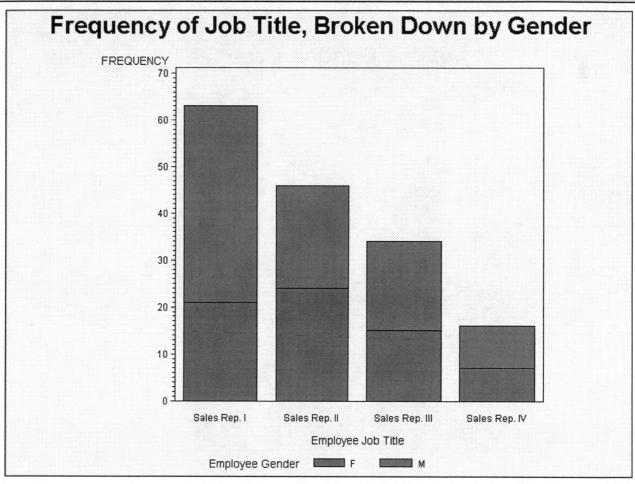

9. Submit the ninth PROC GCHART step to group the bars.

   A VBAR statement creates a vertical bar chart showing the frequency for each value of **Gender**.

   The GROUP= option in the VBAR statement displays a separate set of bars for each value of **Job_Title**.

   The PATTERNID=MIDPOINT option in the VBAR statement displays each value of **Gender** (the midpoint or chart variable) with the same pattern.

```
goptions reset=all;
proc gchart data=orion.staff;
   vbar gender/group=Job_Title patternid=midpoint;
   where Job_Title =:'Sales Rep';
   title 'Frequency of Job Gender, Grouped by Job Title';
run;
quit;
```

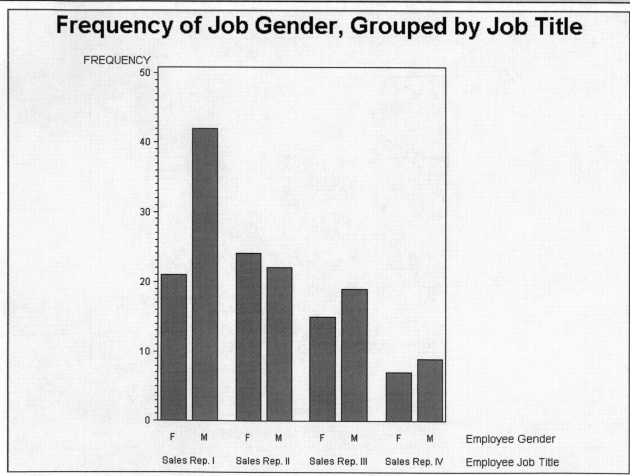

Submitting the following statements (reversing the chart and group variables) would produce a chart with two groups of four bars:

```
proc gchart data=orion.staff;
   vbar gender/group=Job_Title patternid=midpoint;
```

10. Submit the final PROC GCHART step to create multiple pie charts using RUN-group processing.

A PIE and a PIE3D statement in the same PROC GCHART step produces both a two-dimensional and three-dimensional pie chart showing the number of sales representatives for each value of **`Job_Title`**.

The TITLE2 statements specify different subtitles for each chart. The NOHEADING option on the PIE3D statement suppresses the "FREQUENCY of Job_Title" heading.

Because RUN-group processing is in effect, note the following:

- It is not necessary to submit a separate PROC GCHART statement for each graph.
- The WHERE statement is applied to both charts.
- The TITLE statement is applied to both charts.
- A separate TITLE2 statement is used for each chart.

```
goptions reset=all;
proc gchart data=orion.staff;
   pie Job_Title;
   where Job_Title =:'Sales Rep';
   title 'Frequency Distribution of Job Titles';
   title2 '2-D Pie Chart';
run;
   pie3d Job_Title / noheading;
   title2 '3-D Pie Chart';
run;
quit;
```

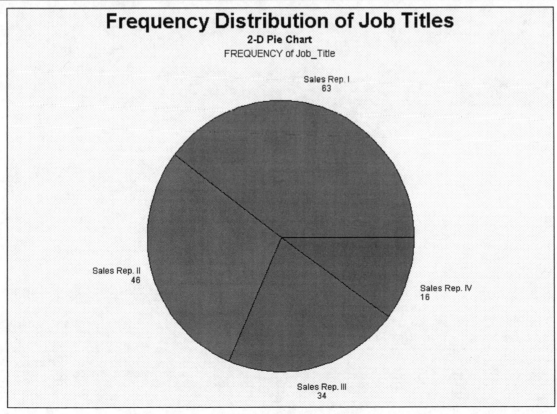

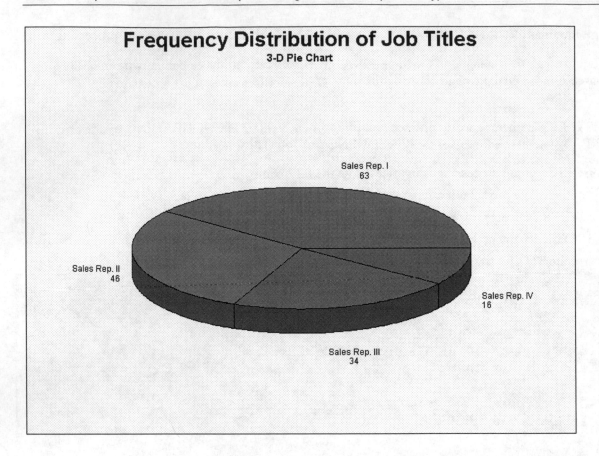

Frequency Distribution of Job Titles

3-D Pie Chart

13.3 Creating Plots

Producing Plots with the GPLOT Procedure

You can use the GPLOT procedure to plot one variable against another within a set of coordinate axes.

General form of a PROC GPLOT step:

```
PROC GPLOT DATA=SAS-data-set;
    PLOT vertical-variable*horizontal-variable </ options>;
RUN;
QUIT;
```

19

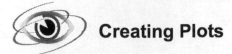

Creating Plots

p113d02

1. Submit the first PROC GPLOT step to create a simple scatter plot.

    The PROC GPLOT creates a plot displaying the values of the variable **Yr2007** on the vertical axis and **Month** on the horizontal axis. The points are displayed using the default plotting symbol (a plus).

    A FORMAT statement assigns the DOLLAR12. format to **Yr2007**.

```
goptions reset=all;
proc gplot data=orion.budget;
   plot Yr2007*Month;
   format Yr2007 dollar12.;
   title 'Plot of Budget by Month';
run;
quit;
```

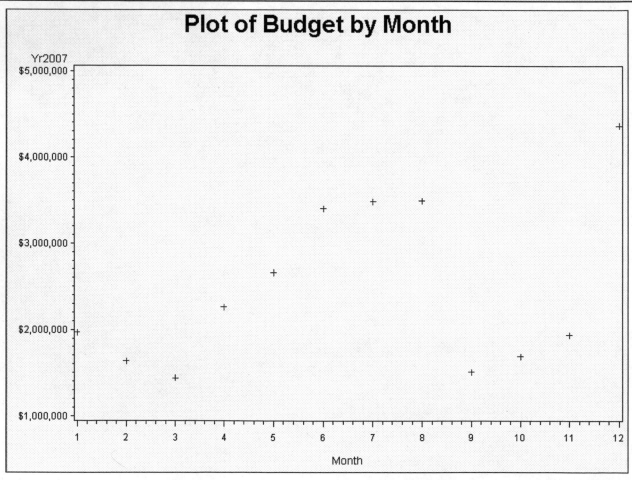

2. Submit the second PROC GPLOT step to specify plot symbols and interpolation lines.

   The SYMBOL statement specifies an alternate plotting symbol and draws an interpolation line joining the plot points. The options in the SYMBOL statement are as follows:

   - V= specifies the plotting symbol (a dot).
   - I= specifies the interpolation method to be used to connect the points (join).
   - CV= specifies the color of the plotting symbol.
   - CI= specifies the color of the interpolation line.

   The LABEL statement assigns a label to the variable **Yr2007**.

```
goptions reset=all;
proc gplot data=orion.budget;
   plot Yr2007*Month / haxis=1 to 12;
   label Yr2007='Budget';
   format Yr2007 dollar12.;
   title 'Plot of Budget by Month';
   symbol1 v=dot i=join cv=red ci=blue;
run;
quit;
```

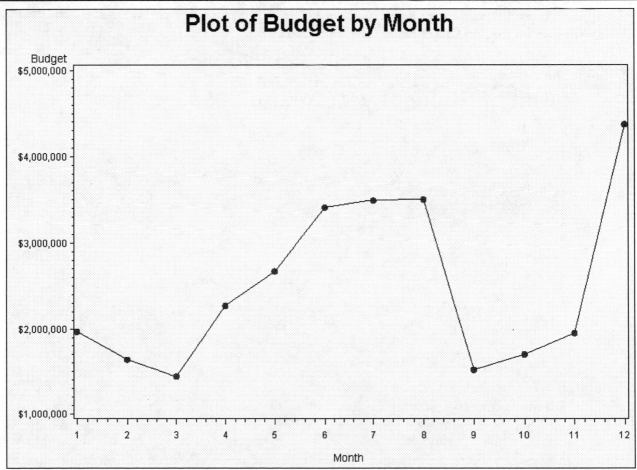

3. Submit the third PROC GPLOT step to overlaying multiple plot lines on the same set of axes.

    The PLOT statement specifies two separate plot requests (**Yr2006*Month** and **Yr2007*Month**) which results in an overlay plot with the variables **Yr2006** and **Yr2007** on the vertical axis and **Month** on the horizontal axis.

    The options on the PLOT statement are as follows:

    - The OVERLAY option causes both plot requests to be displayed on the same set of axes.

    - The HAXIS= option specifies the range of values for the horizontal axis. (The VAXIS= option can be used to specify the range for the vertical axis).

    - The VREF= option specifies a value on the vertical axis where a reference line should be drawn.

    - The CFRAME= option specifies a color to be used for the background within the plot axes.

```
goptions reset=all;
proc gplot data=orion.budget;
   plot Yr2006*Month yr2007*Month/ overlay haxis=1 to 12 vref=3000000
                                   cframe="very light gray";
   label Yr2006='Budget';
   format Yr2006 dollar12.;
   title 'Plot of Budget by Month for 2006 and 2007';
   symbol1 i=join v=dot ci=blue cv=blue;
   symbol2 i=join v=triangle ci=red cv=red;
run;
quit;
```

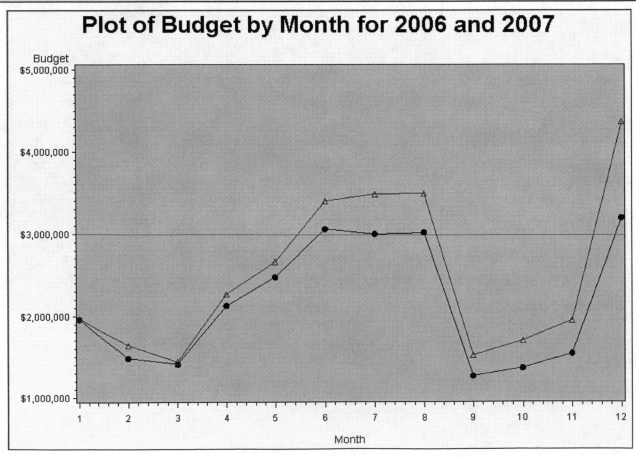

13.4 Enhancing Output

Enhancing SAS/GRAPH Output

SAS/GRAPH uses default values for colors, fonts, text size and other graph attributes. You can override these defaults using the following methods:

- Specifying an ODS style
- Specifying default attributes in a GOPTIONS statement
- Specifying attributes and options in global statements and procedure statements

22

Enhancing Output

p113d03

1. Submit the first PROC GPLOT step to use ODS styles to control the appearance of the output.

    Specify the style on the ODS LISTING statement with the STYLE= option produces a different ODS style.

```
ods listing style=gears;
goptions reset=all;
proc gplot data=orion.budget;
   plot Yr2007*Month;
   format Yr2007 dollar12.;
   label Yr2007='Budget';
   title 'Plot of Budget by Month';
run;
quit;
```

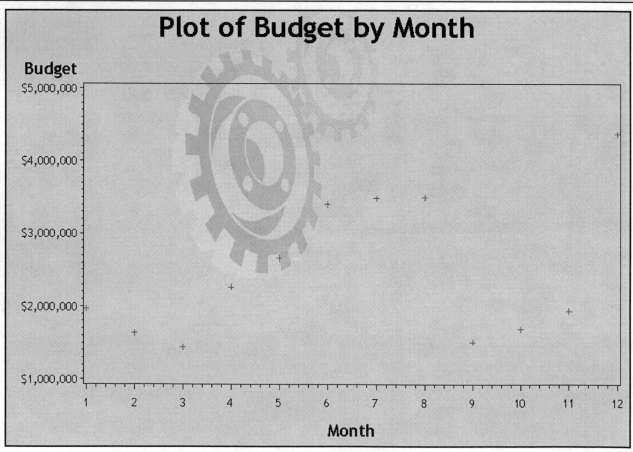

2. Submit the second PROC GPLOT step to specify the options in the TITLE and FOOTNOTE statements to control the text appearance.

    The TITLE and FOOTNOTE statements override the default fonts, colors, height, and text justification. The following options are used:

    - F= (or FONT=) specifies a font.

    - C= (or COLOR=) specifies text color.

    - H= (or HEIGHT=) specifies text height. Units of height can be specified as percent of the display (PCT), inches (IN), centimeters (CM), cells (CELLS), or points (PT).

    - J= (or JUSTIFY=) specifies text justification. Valid values are LEFT (L), CENTER (C), and RIGHT (R).

    All options apply to text following the option.

```
ods listing style=gears;
goptions reset=all;
proc gplot data=orion.budget;
   plot Yr2007*Month / vref=3000000;
   label Yr2007='Budget';
   format Yr2007 dollar12.;
   title f=centbi h=5 pct 'Budget by Month';
   footnote c=green j=left 'Data for 2007';
run;
quit;
```

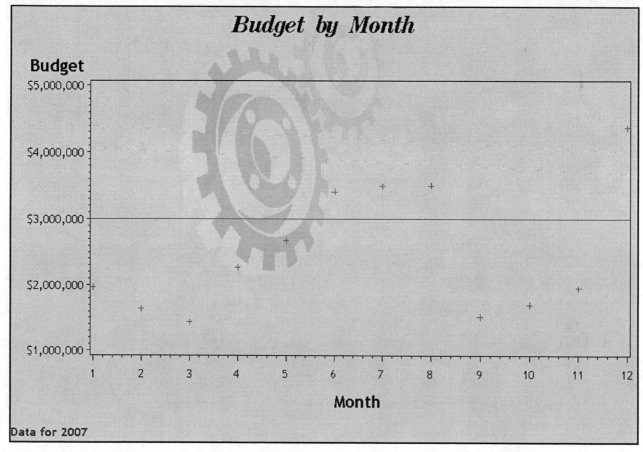

3. Submit the third PROC GPLOT step to use a GOPTIONS statement to control the appearance
    of the output.

    A GOPTIONS statement specifies options to control the appearance of all text in the graph.
    The following options are used:

    - FTEXT= specifies a font for all text.

    - CTEXT= specifies the color for all text.

    - HTEXT= specifies the height for all text.

    If a text option is specified both in a GOPTIONS statement and a TITLE or FOOTNOTE statement,
    the option specified in the TITLE or FOOTNOTE statement overrides the value in the GOPTIONS
    statement only for that title or footnote.

```
ods listing style=gears;
goptions reset=all ftext=centb htext=3 pct ctext=dark_blue;
   proc gplot data=orion.budget;
   plot Yr2007*Month / vref=3000000;
   label Yr2007='Budget';
   format Yr2007 dollar12.;
   title f=centbi 'Budget by Month';
run;
quit;
```

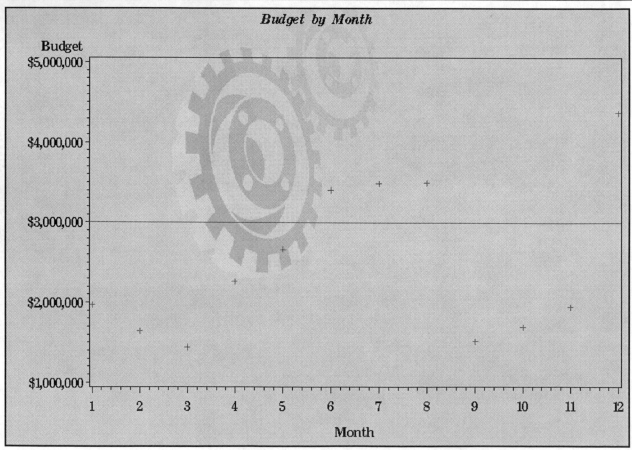

Chapter 14   Learning More

14.1 SAS Resources

Objectives

- Identify areas of support that SAS offers.

3

Education

Comprehensive training to deliver greater value to your organization

- More than 200 course offerings
- World-class instructors
- Multiple delivery methods: instructor-led and self-paced
- Training centers around the world

http://support.sas.com/training/

4

SAS Publishing

SAS offers a complete selection of publications to help customers use SAS software to its fullest potential:

- Multiple delivery methods: e-books, CD-ROM, and hard-copy books
- Wide spectrum of topics
- Partnerships with outside authors, other publishers, and distributors

http://support.sas.com/publishing/

5

SAS Global Certification Program

SAS offers several globally recognized certifications.

- Computer-based certification exams – typically 60-70 questions and 2-3 hours in length
- Preparation materials and practice exams available
- Worldwide directory of SAS Certified Professionals

http://support.sas.com/certify/

6

Support

SAS provides a variety of self-help and assisted-help resources.

- SAS Knowledge Base
- Downloads and hot fixes
- License assistance
- SAS discussion forums
- SAS Technical Support

http://support.sas.com/techsup/

7

User Groups

SAS supports many local, regional, international, and special-interest SAS user groups.

- SAS Global Forum
- Online SAS Community: www.sasCommunity.org

http://support.sas.com/usergroups/

8

14.2 Beyond This Course

Objectives

- Identify the next set of courses that follow this course.

10

Next Steps

SAS® Programming 1: Essentials is the entry point
to most areas of the SAS curriculum.

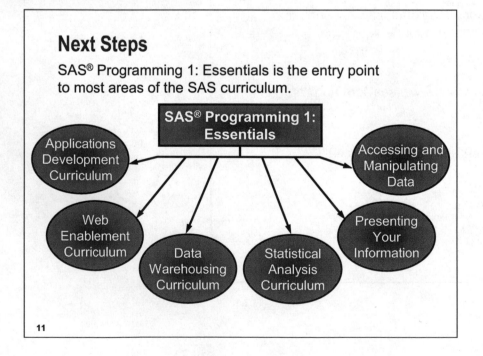

11

Next Steps

To learn more about this: Enroll in the following:

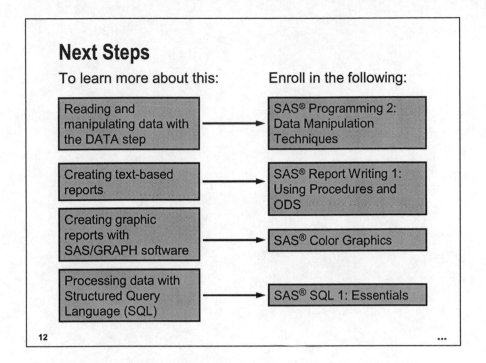

Reading and manipulating data with the DATA step	→	SAS® Programming 2: Data Manipulation Techniques
Creating text-based reports	→	SAS® Report Writing 1: Using Procedures and ODS
Creating graphic reports with SAS/GRAPH software	→	SAS® Color Graphics
Processing data with Structured Query Language (SQL)	→	SAS® SQL 1: Essentials

12   ...

Next Steps

In addition, there are prerecorded short technical discussions and demonstrations called e-lectures.

http://support.sas.com/training/

13

Appendix A Index